The Teleology of Action in Plato's *Republic*

The Teleology of Action in Plato's *Republic*

Andrew Payne

OXFORD
UNIVERSITY PRESS

UNIVERSITY PRESS

Great Clarendon Street, Oxford, OX2 6DP,
United Kingdom

Oxford University Press is a department of the University of Oxford.
It furthers the University's objective of excellence in research, scholarship,
and education by publishing worldwide. Oxford is a registered trade mark of
Oxford University Press in the UK and in certain other countries

© Andrew Payne 2017

The moral rights of the author have been asserted

First Edition published in 2017
Impression: 1

Published in the United States of America by Oxford University Press
198 Madison Avenue, New York, NY 10016, United States of America

British Library Cataloguing in Publication Data
Data available

Library of Congress Control Number: 2017941118

ISBN 978–0–19–879902–3

Printed and bound by
CPI Group (UK) Ltd, Croydon, CR0 4YY

Contents

Acknowledgments

It is right and just to give thanks for benefits received; it is also a pleasure. Here I have the pleasure of describing some of the benefits given me in the writing of this work. My chief intellectual debt is owed to David K. O'Connor, my dissertation director. It was his presentation of Plato's conception of love that brought me to think about the relation between desire, action, and human ends in the *Symposium* and the *Republic*. Over the years I have enjoyed partnership in philosophy with David Wolfsdorf and Joel Yurdin, esteemed colleagues and friends. My work on this project has benefited from their comments and from the example they provide. I have presented the ideas contained in this work in talks before audiences at Saint Joseph's University, La Salle University, Franklin and Marshall College, Dayton University, at an epistemology reading group at Swarthmore College, and at meetings of the Society for Ancient Greek Philosophy and the International Plato Society. I wish to thank members of these audiences for their comments on earlier versions of parts of this book. In particular Peter Bauman, Brad Berman, Robert Bolton, Hugh Benson, Anna Cremaldi, Lee Franklin, Christoph Horn, and Michelle Jenkins offered insightful comments. Nick Smith provided encouragement and practical guidance at a crucial stage in the preparation of the manuscript. Anthony Price helped me to sharpen my thoughts on the topic of soul-partition addressed in Chapter 6 of this work. Finally, three anonymous referees for Oxford University Press improved this project with their perceptive and detailed comments. Needless to say, none of the above are responsible for any flaws which remain.

The completion of this book was made possible by sabbatical release time granted by Saint Joseph's University, for which I am very grateful.

My family has been my greatest support. My parents, David and Corliss Payne, provided constant aid as well as impressive examples of the life of the mind. My wife, Anneliese Hoos, has offered love and encouragement in more ways than can be told. This book is dedicated to her.

1
Varieties of Teleology

1.1 Introduction

Two central passages in Plato's writings contain an unexpected and little-appreciated application of teleology. The texts in question are the ascent passage in the *Symposium* and the description of the education of the philosopher-kings or guardians in Book 7 of the *Republic*, including the famous analogy of the cave. These passages describe a step-by-step education of desire and intellect leading up to a final end. The lover of the ascent passage and the prisoner in the cave start with an awareness of bodily realities and ignorance of the higher, intelligible reality. The process of education leads them into the intelligible realm and culminates in the awareness of one central reality, the Form of Beauty in the case of the ascent passage and the Form of the Good in the *Republic*. This insight into intelligible reality allows the one who makes the ascent, the philosopher, to gain knowledge or wisdom. The result of making the ascent in the *Symposium* is the production of true virtue, which includes wisdom, while in the *Republic* Socrates links the journey upward out of the cave with the activation of dialectic, the faculty of the soul responsible for knowledge:

Then isn't this at last, Glaucon, the song that dialectic sings? It is intelligible, but it is imitated by the power of sight. We said that sight tries at last to look at the animals themselves, the stars themselves, and, in the end, at the sun itself. In the same way, whenever someone tries through argument and apart from all sense perceptions to find the being itself of each thing and doesn't give up until he grasps the good itself with understanding itself, he reaches the end [*telos*] of the intelligible, just as the other reached the end of the visible.[1]

Dialectic, the only faculty which makes the journey up to the first principle identified in the *Republic* as the Form of the Good, is thus responsible for the full attainment of knowledge (*Republic* 533c-e).

In these passages from the *Symposium* and the *Republic*, Plato develops and deepens a key theme from the Socratic dialogues, namely that humans gain happiness by the possession of good things, the chief of which is wisdom. In dialogues such as the *Euthydemus* and the *Meno*, Socrates proposes that we require wisdom in order to

---

[1] *Republic* 532a1-b2, translation by Grube as revised by Reeve. Unless otherwise specified, translations of Plato's writings are taken from Cooper (1997). Citations of the Greek text of the *Republic* are taken from S. R. Slings' 2003 edition in the Oxford Classical Texts series.

become happy, since wisdom ensures that we make correct use of any other goods that may benefit us: wealth, health, honor, and such character traits as courage. Given the centrality of wisdom for the happy life—it is either the sole good that constitutes the happy life or it is the most important good—the acquisition of wisdom through the life of philosophy is a matter of grave importance. The ascent passage in the *Symposium* and the cave analogy in the *Republic* serve to indicate, however obliquely, the nature of the process by which humans become wise.

In both of these passages, the awareness of the form which marks the achievement of wisdom is said to be the end or purpose for the sake of which the earlier stages of development and the actions they involve took place. However, this insight into the form cannot be chosen or intended as an end by the person whose actions have that insight as their end. Neither the lover of the ascent nor the prisoner in the cave knows of or believes in the form before they arrive at the peak moment of insight, and so they do not act at earlier stages of the ascent with the intention or goal of achieving this insight. In these passages, Plato suggests that our actions can be performed for the sake of an end of which we are not aware. In a special range of cases, our ends surpass our ability to intend and aim at them.

The present work contains a description and defense of the particular teleological relation in play in these and similar cases. This relation connects those actions that promote a valuable result together with that result in such a way that the actions in question are performed for the sake of that end. In the cases to be described, the agent does not intend to achieve that end and does not act with the intention of promoting that end. Central examples of this teleological relation include the lover of the ascent passage pursuing bodily beauty and beauty of the soul for the sake of insight into the Form of Beauty and the mathematical education of the philosophers for the sake of knowing the Form of the Good. In addition, the philosophers-in-training in Socrates' ideal city study music and gymnastic for the sake of attaining virtue of the soul. The parts of the soul as described by Socrates have their own proper functions or activities, and the parts of the soul carry out their functions or activities for the sake of achieving a unified soul. A further instance of this teleological relation is present in the citizens of the ideal city who perform just actions for the sake of promoting a just city.

1.2 Intentional Teleology and Natural Teleology

In order to exhibit the distinctive traits of this teleological relation, it will be helpful to place it in the broader context of teleology in general. Teleology taken as a whole is the study of the various phenomena which occur for the sake of an end or purpose. In any genuine case of teleology, where actions or events or objects are for the sake of an end, a special sort of relation holds between the end and that which is for the sake of the end. Describing this relation accurately requires the use of causal and normative or evaluative concepts. The end is something good, the actions or events or objects make a causal contribution to that end, and in some way to be explored the actions or events happen as they do because of the end to which they contribute.[2] Whether the goodness of the end plays an important explanatory role in teleology is a matter of controversy, but in all species of teleology the end must help to explain that which produces it.[3]

A diverse set of cases will fall under this very general description of teleological phenomena. To draw only upon Plato's writings, we may consider the following examples.

1)   The Demiurge or divine craftsman of the *Timaeus* made hair for the human head in order to provide a protective covering against extremes of weather which would least interfere with the sense organs located in the head (*Timaeus* 76c-d).

2)   Humans have sight for the sake of learning the patterns of the stars and planets and studying astronomy (*Timaeus* 46e-47c).

3)   The stars exhibit only two types of motion, rotation and circular revolution in the heavens, in order that they may be as perfect as possible (*Timaeus* 40a-b).

4)   A sick man is friend to a doctor for the sake of health (*Lysis* 217a, 218e).

5)   A man who loves his sick son will go to great trouble to obtain wine and a cup to hold the wine if it will cure his son (*Lysis* 219d-e).

Examples 4) and 5) are taken from the realm of particular human actions, but they suggest more general teleological relations between classes or types of objects and some higher good:

6)   Wealth and all material objects are objects of concern to us for the sake of a good (the "first friend") that we hold in higher esteem than any material object (*Lysis* 219e-220a).

In addition to describing particular actions and types of objects as being for the sake of an end, Plato envisions laws and other social institutions as being for the sake of ends. In Book 2 of the *Republic*, Glaucon describes a third class of goods consisting of activities such as physical exercise and undergoing medical treatment, activities which are not pursued for their own sake but for the sake of the rewards and results that follow from them. He goes on to describe the making of laws and their observance as belonging to this third class of goods. That is, Glaucon treats laws as exhibiting the following teleological relation:

7)   Humans make and follow laws not because it is good in itself to do so but for the sake of protection from the injustice of others (*Republic* 357b-d, 358e-359b).

Without stopping here to investigate the details of these different cases and Plato's considered view of each, we may note the diverse range of phenomena which he is

---

[2] This general account of teleological relations draws upon the account given by Woodfield (1976, 205–8). Woodfield summarizes his standard analysis of teleology as follows: "X does/has A because A → F and F is good" (208). The goodness in question need not be moral; it could be the survival of an organism or the efficiency of a motor.

[3] See Gotthelf (1988) for a defense of the claim that the goodness of the end does not play a central explanatory role in natural teleology.

willing to present as apparent cases of ordering to an end or purpose. The organs and faculties of living beings (examples 1 and 2 above), the motions of natural objects (3), the intentional actions of human beings (4 and 5), general classes of objects valued as good by human beings (6), as well as social practices, institutions, and laws (7), qualify as things which are to be explained by the purposes they serve. Thus a wide range of phenomena falls within the scope of teleology.

Historians of ancient philosophy often seek further insight into the diverse range of teleological phenomena by distinguishing between two types of teleology. The first encompasses a class of phenomena involving intentional action, as when a man cuts a board to a specified length in order to use it to replace a broken step in a flight of stairs. The second type is the sort of purposive behavior and structure seen in nature, as when a spider spins its web in such a way as to serve the purpose of catching insects. I will refer to these as intentional teleology and natural teleology or the teleology of nature.[4] The latter is typically credited to Aristotle, whose contributions to the study of nature and to biology in particular employ this sort of teleology. In the *Physics* and in his biological works, Aristotle strives to achieve systematic understanding of living organisms as beings that come to be and develop through the actualization of immanent potential for specific natures. Such processes of birth and development occur for the sake of an end without an external agent directing or fashioning the bodies of living organisms to this end. By contrast, current discussions of Plato's teleology direct our attention to his reliance on intentional teleology and in particular to his use of craft-expertise as a model for explaining the presence of purpose in the natural world.[5] The *Timaeus* bulks large in this investigation of Platonic teleology, as this dialogue features the Demiurge, the divine craftsman who fashions the natural world (*Timaeus* 27a-29a). The intelligent operations of the Demiurge involve his looking to the eternal paradigms and using these as patterns for producing the universe as a living whole (30c-31a) as well as the parts and features of the natural world: its elements, plants, animals, and heavenly bodies. The result of this divine use of craft-expertise is a world that is harmonious, beautiful, and good.

Intentional teleology is present for Plato not only in the divine use of craft-expertise but also in the human practice of crafts. While the Demiurge of the *Timaeus* uses his skill to fashion every aspect of the natural world, human craftsmen typically direct their activity to a limited area. Each craft is set apart from the other crafts by the area it takes as its subject matter, and by its ability to generate a distinctive product (*ergon*): the craft of medicine is responsible for producing human health, while carpentry is the craft we turn to when we are in need of housing. But as is the case with the Demiurge,

---

[4] The description of these two species of teleology is based on Charles (1991, 101–11); Ariew (2002, 8–10); and Johansen (2005, 69). I use the term "intentional teleology" where Ariew uses "agency-centered"; central to the present work is the thesis that agency-centered teleology includes more than intentional teleology, since one sort of agency-centered teleology is not governed by the goals intended by agents. This is the functional teleology of action.

[5] See Lennox (1985).

human practitioners of crafts act for the sake of an end by consulting a model or paradigm and taking particular steps with the goal of making their subject matter conform to the standard set by this paradigm. At *Gorgias* 503d6-504a1, Socrates speaks of the distinctive product of a craft as providing this model or paradigm:

Well then, won't the good man, the man who speaks with regard to what's best, say whatever he says not randomly but with a view to something, just like the other craftsmen, each of whom keeps his own product (*ergon*) in view and so does not select and apply randomly what he applies, but so that he may give his product some form? Take a look at painters for instance, if you would, or housebuilders or shipwrights or any of the other craftsmen you like, and see how each one places what he does into a certain organization, and compels one thing to be suited for another and to fit to it until the entire object is put together in an organized and orderly way.

The craftsmen described here exemplify intentional teleology because, like the Demiurge, they act for the sake of an end by consulting a paradigm or standard which sets for them the goal of their action. Shipwrights set out to make a product that exhibits order and goodness in virtue of its sharing in a particular form or shape derived from the paradigm set by what it is to be a ship. They shape and fit together their materials with the intention of making something that approximates to this paradigm.

   This discussion of the use of crafts to achieve a range of products allows us to speak more precisely about the role of intention within intentional teleology.[6] A doctor acts intentionally when she prescribes a regimen of drugs and physical therapy for an unhealthy patient, and when she acts as a doctor she intends to produce health. These two aspects of a doctor's actions concern the intended end or goal of her actions and her selection of means to that goal. I shall say that the doctor's actions, as instances of intentional teleology, reflect the agent's possession of a simple intention to achieve a goal as well as an intention with which a particular action is selected. All of her actions as a doctor are related to a simple intention, to produce health, and her individual medical actions are performed with the intention of producing health.[7] The presence of a simple intention and an intention with which one acts implies the presence of beliefs and desires centering on the goal of a simple intention and the suitability of particular actions to produce or promote that goal.[8] If an agent A has a simple intention

   [6] The following discussion of intentions and their relation to desires and beliefs is indebted to Audi (1973).
   [7] See Malcolm (1968) for the distinction between a simple intention and the intention with which an action is performed: "In considering intention as the cause of behavior X, it is important to distinguish between the intention to do X (let us call this *simple intention*) and…the intention to do something else Y in or by doing X (let us call this *further intention*)"; Malcolm (1968, 59).
   [8] By saying that intentions imply the presence of beliefs and desires, I wish to avoid taking sides in one contested issue in contemporary discussions of action and the role of intentions in action. On one view, having an intention is identical with having a belief-desire pair of the right sort. This view is often associated with the causal theory of action, according to which the having of belief-desire pairs is the cause of particular actions and according to which the explanation of action is a species of causal explanation achieved by pointing to those events, causes, which bring about other events, effects. See Sinhababu (2013) for a recent defense of the identification of intentions with belief-desire pairs. Opposed to this approach to intention is the family of views inspired by *Intention* by Elizabeth Anscombe (2000), according to which

to φ, this implies that A desires to φ and that A believes that she will or is at least likely to φ (or, in the case where bad luck makes φ-ing difficult or impossible, will achieve a decent approximation to φ-ing). The claim that intending to φ implies a belief about the agent's actual φ-ing reflects the intuition that intending to φ involves more than just welcoming the fact that someone does some φ-ing; it involves the agent's setting herself to φ in such a way that she believes it is at least likely that she will or does φ, as long as circumstances beyond her control do not make this impossible. Similar implications hold in the case of intentions with which one acts. When the doctor prescribes a regimen of drugs and physical therapy to an unhealthy patient with the intention of promoting health, she desires that the prescribed regimen produce health and believes (or knows) that the prescribed regimen will produce health or is at least likely to produce health.

This account of having an intention as implying desire and belief can be integrated with the examples previously given of teleological phenomena. Examples 1–3 concern the parts and natural faculties of organisms (the hair and vision of human beings) and the motions of natural bodies (the rotation and circular orbits of the stars). These are explained in terms of the actions of the Demiurge of the *Timaeus*, who acts intentionally to fashion each of these aspects of the natural world. That intentional action can be further explicated in terms of the Demiurge's wanting the world to become as good as he is, to the extent that this is possible (*Timaeus* 29d-e), and his knowledge of how to make each aspect of the created world so as to achieve this goal. That knowledge or wisdom is described as the Demiurge looking to an eternal paradigm rather than to a changing one (29a). Human actions for the sake of an end, even those that do not exemplify the use of craft, also imply the presence of intentions and hence desire for a goal or intended end and belief or knowledge about how to achieve this goal. A sick man is friend to a doctor for the sake of health (Example 4) in that the sick man intends to become healthy and befriends the doctor with the intention of becoming healthy. The father whose son is ill (Example 5) wants to cure him and so procures wine and a cup to hold the wine with the intention of promoting his son's health. This example is described in the *Lysis* as an example of a larger pattern, namely that we care for gold, and wealth, and all such commodities for the sake of a more important good, the "first friend" (Example 6). This example suggests that we provide ourselves with the material necessities of life with the intention of promoting some larger goal: a good which we desire to achieve, and which we believe we will gain by the use of these material necessities. This pattern extends to our social institutions, as when we make laws with the

---

intentions are not belief-desire pairs and are better described as an agent's attitude toward an ongoing action or nested series of actions. From the latter perspective, intentions are not the causes of actions. What is important for present purposes is that on all views mentioned here, an agent has an intention or acts with an intention only if she desires some goal or intended outcome and has some beliefs about her role in promoting that goal. For the first view mentioned, the implication follows simply from the identification of intentions with belief-desire pairs. According to the second view, an agent possesses a distinctive awareness rooted in self-knowledge of what she is doing. This awareness underwrites the agent's beliefs that, for instance, by writing a letter to a classmate from school she is maintaining a friendship.

intention of gaining protection from the injustice of our fellows (Example 7). In all these examples, an agent intends some goal and undertakes action with the intention of promoting that goal, a pattern which implies desire for the goal and belief or knowledge about the suitability of particular actions as means to promote that goal.

1.3 The Limits of Intentional Teleology: *Phaedo* 96-99

Because Plato employs a version of intentional teleology modeled on the use of crafts, he faces special difficulties in explaining action of the sort found in the ascent passage and in the analogy of the cave. Such action is carried on for the sake of understanding intelligible realities, the Form of Beauty or the Form of the Good, but the agent involved does not possess from the start the ability to inspect an intelligible paradigm and to use this model as a guide for action. As one who lacks wisdom, the agent does not possess knowledge of the form which stands at the end of the series of actions addressed in these passages. In addition, as we will see when considering these passages more closely, the agent does not have beliefs about the Form of Beauty or the Form of the Good. According to the model of intentional teleology, an agent who carries out a series of actions for the sake of understanding a form must carry out these actions with the intention of gaining this understanding of the form and so must have beliefs about how these actions are suited to promote this goal. The agents described in the ascent passage and in the image of the cave lack such beliefs. Therefore, the sense in which their actions are carried out for the sake of understanding a form will not be captured by intentional teleology.

An important passage in the *Phaedo* illustrates the difficulties that Plato will face in providing an account of human action taken for the sake of understanding the Form of Beauty or the Form of the Good. At *Phaedo* 96a5-99c8, Plato puts into Socrates' mouth an account of his intellectual autobiography. This includes his devotion to the study of nature, with only limited success; his enthusiastic reception of Anaxagoras' proposal that Mind is the cause of all things; his disillusionment with Anaxagoras' actual procedure in the study of nature; and finally his *reductio ad absurdum* of the latter's reliance on unthinking causes by applying such a causal analysis to the explanation of action. Closer attention to this passage will show how Plato's original allegiance to intentional teleology forecloses some options in the explanation of action and points him toward other explanatory strategies.

At an early stage in the intellectual development sketched at *Phaedo* 96a-99c, Socrates desired to gain the wisdom associated with inquiry into nature. He had a number of reasonable beliefs about such topics as how a person grows: by eating food, bits of matter of the required sort are added to organs and tissues already existing in the body, bone to bone and flesh to flesh (96c-d). He also believed that a tall man was taller than a smaller one by a head, and that ten was more than eight because two had been added to the eight. Later Socrates refused to recognize these beliefs as constituting knowledge of the cause of things existing or coming to be, apparently because these beliefs presupposed that the cause of a thing becoming or being large could be the movement of quantities of matter. He does not accept that the cause of twoness is the placing of one unit next to another, since a similar result of twoness can follow from a single quantity being divided into two. Socrates accepts a series of principles associated with the notion that like causes like, principles which rule out the possibility that twoness can be caused by both division and addition, two opposed and unlike processes. In particular, Socrates accepts the following principles about causation governing relations between a thing or process A and its effects of making particular things take on the property F. If the cause A is opposed by A*, and if A causes a thing to take on property F, where the property F is opposed by F*,

A causes x to be F only if

1) For all y, it is false that A causes y to be F*
2) For all y, it is false that A* causes y to be F
3) A is not F*.[9]

These principles serve to flesh out the idea that like causes like. They explain in particular why Socrates refuses to allow that the joining together of material units is a cause of a thing being two, since the same result of twoness would also result from the opposed process of division, which would go against the second principle above.

After rejecting his earlier beliefs about the growth of animals and about the cause of things coming to be two, Socrates found himself in a state of perplexity. He then welcomed the teaching of Anaxagoras that Mind arranges all things and is responsible for all (97c1-4), a doctrine which he took to mean that a cosmic intelligence is at work in the arrangement of all features of the natural world. Such an intelligence would make all things to exist in the way that is best for them. Given this much, the problem of finding a causal explanation for any existing state of affairs, such as the shape and position of the earth, is resolved into the problem of discovering how it is best for that state of affairs to be as it is. Once this problem is solved, the operations of Mind suffice to explain how that state of affairs came to be and why it is as it is. Mind will understand what is best for each thing to be, in the manner of a wise craftsman who understands how high and deep each step should be in a flight of stairs and cuts the treads and risers accordingly. In a similar way, Mind fashions each thing in the universe to fit the standard set by what is best for it. On this account, Socrates apparently does not distinguish between different senses of Mind providing what is best for a thing. Mind could provide what is best for a thing by promoting its interest (humans have hair on their heads because this is best for them, as it protects the head from temperature extremes), or Mind could provide what is best for a thing by making a thing so that it will best serve some purpose, either carrying out its own function (the step should be deeper than the

---

[9] This presentation of the principles to which Socrates' discussion of causes commits him is derived from Matthews and Blackson (1989) and Burge (1971).

average person's foot) or promoting the good of some other being (the step should allow humans to walk easily up and down the flight of stairs). Without distinguishing these implications of Mind making each thing for the best, Socrates welcomed gladly the possibility of explaining the being and becoming of each thing by relating it to what is best.

Of course, Socrates was then disappointed by the contrast he found between this ambitious program of teleological explanation and the explanations actually offered by Anaxagoras. The latter appealed to precisely the sort of unthinking and undirected causes that had caused him such perplexity when reflecting on the cause of human growth and of twoness. Such things as air, ether, or water do not suffice to explain the shape and position of the earth, since the same factors could equally well have been responsible for bringing about a quite different shape and position for the earth.

In order to spell out what he found lacking in the use of such unthinking causes, Socrates at *Phaedo* 98c2-99b2 compares Anaxagoras' procedure to an obviously unsatisfactory explanation of his sitting in prison and awaiting death:

That [appeal to air and water and ether to explain the earth's position] seemed to me much like saying that Socrates' actions are all due to his mind, and then in trying to tell the causes of everything I do, to say that the reason that I am sitting here is because my body consists of bones and sinews, because the bones are hard and are separated by joints, that the sinews are such as to contract and relax, that they surround the bones along with flesh and skin which hold them together, then as the bones are hanging in their sockets, the relaxation and contraction of the sinews enable me to bend my limbs, and that is the cause of my sitting here. Again, he would mention other such causes for my talking to you: sounds and air and hearing, and a thousand other such things, but he would neglect to mention the true causes, that, after the Athenians decided it was better to condemn me, for this reason it seemed best to me to sit here and more right to remain and to endure whatever penalty they ordered. For by the dog, I think these sinews and bones could long ago have been in Megara or among the Boeotians, taken there by my belief as to the best course, if I had not thought it more right and honorable to endure whatever penalty the city ordered rather than escape and run away. To call those things causes is too absurd. If someone said that without bones and sinews and all such things, I should not be able to do what I decided, he would be right, but surely to say that they are the cause of what I do, and not that I have chosen the best course, even though I act with my mind, is to speak very lazily and carelessly.

The approach to explaining action that Socrates finds obviously unsatisfactory will accept the role of Mind as a cause: he does whatever he does by intelligence or mind (98c4). But the rest of this defective explanation employs only unthinking causes which have no special connection to the effect they are supposed to explain. Socrates' bones, sinews, joints, etc. could perform their distinctive functions either in the course of an escape to Megara or while sitting in prison in Athens. To follow through on the original stipulation that Socrates does what he does by Mind, it is necessary that we supply as part of the explanation of the action his selection of what is best. This selection or choice of what is best results in sitting in prison and not escaping to Megara because it seems fitting and more just to Socrates to accept the punishment handed down by the Athenians rather than escape. Spelling out the causal role of Mind in generating action, then, requires specification of the agent's selection of what is best. The agent's selection of the best contains a representation of the effect promoted by the action (doing what is just by accepting punishment), so that the agent's mind will be similar or at least not opposed to that effect. This avoids the unwanted scenario of unthinking causes being equally able to bring about a range of different effects in addition to the particular effect they are supposed to explain.

These reflections on Plato's use of intentional teleology in the *Phaedo* point to a particular difficulty he faces in the ascent passage and in the image of the cave. In both texts, Plato has Socrates describe the understanding of a form as the end for the sake of which all the actions of the series took place. Yet the nature of intentional teleology does not license this last assertion. According to *Phaedo* 96-99, it is in virtue of an agent's selection of what is best that his actions can be explained by Mind as a cause. The ascent passage and the image of the cave present an agent who lacks wisdom, since he begins with a concern for sensible things. The agent carries out a series of actions all of which are for the sake of achieving wisdom, the understanding of intelligible reality. Because such an agent lacks wisdom and is not aware of the existence of the forms, he will not be able to intend gaining knowledge of the forms as a goal. His selection of the best will direct him to a goal that falls short of this result. His selection of the best, as this appears to him, might lead to wisdom, but it equally might also lead to a range of different effects other than understanding of a form. As a result, the model of intentional teleology employed in the *Phaedo* will not support the claim that the actions mentioned in the ascent passage and in the image of the cave are carried out for the sake of understanding the forms.

As the discussion of *Phaedo* 96-99 shows, intentional teleology is not well suited to provide a full explication of the ascent passage and the image of the cave. In order to capture the sense in which these texts describe actions for the sake of an end, I will argue, Plato introduces a new variant of teleology, one that employs a different sense of the term *ergon*. This term was previously used to refer to the distinctive product of a craft, as at *Gorgias* 503d-504a. In place of this sense of the term, Plato draws upon a related use of *ergon* to refer to the characteristic activity of an artifact or organ or living thing. In this sense of the term, the *ergon* of a knife is cutting while that of the eye is seeing. The performance of an *ergon* brings about certain characteristic results or secures certain benefits for the agent. If one of the characteristic results of an *ergon* is insight into intelligible reality, such as the understanding of a form that is achieved in the ascent passage and in the image of the cave, then this will allow Plato to explain the sense in which actions are carried out for the sake of this understanding. Because the performance of an *ergon* brings about certain characteristic results including understanding of intelligible reality, a reply is available to the objection that these actions could just as well have brought about a range of different effects other than the understanding of the form they are supposed to explain. As long as we are talking about the genuine performance of a function, it is no accident that these and no other results were brought about. In this way, the performance of an *ergon* in the sense of character-istic activity plays a role similar to the mind's selection of the best in the *Phaedo* pas-sage: it ensures that a particular set of results qualify as being appropriately caused by a series of actions. However, the performance of an *ergon* here does not presuppose wis-dom or the insight into the forms characteristic of the full possession of mind. Thus, an agent who lacks wisdom but carries out a function that promotes understanding of intelligible reality can still act for the sake of understanding forms. I will refer to this version of teleology as the functional teleology of action.

The functional teleology of action, thus understood, provides an underutilized way to describe the orientation of a human life toward a single end. In many discussions of ancient ethics, the proposal that a good human life is one that is oriented toward a sin-gle highest end is often paired with a commitment to intentional teleology. To live rationally in pursuit of a single end in one's life is understood as a matter of coming to understand one's highest end and then selecting the correct means to achieve that goal. Julia Annas claims, "Ancient ethics takes its start from what is taken to be the fact that people have, implicitly, a notion of a final end, an overall goal which enables them to unify and clarify their immediate goals. Ethical theory is designed to enable us to reflect on this implicit overall goal and to make it determinate."[10] Ancient ethical thought is here characterized as performing two related tasks: making explicit and determinate the content of our highest end, happiness, and modifying and adjusting our smaller-scale goals so that they effectively serve this overall goal. Actions that fit into a good human life are those that have been selected with the intention of serving our medium-range goals and ultimately our single long-range goal, happiness. Terry Penner begins his summary of the psychology of action he finds in Socrates, Plato, and Aristotle as follows: "In deciding what to do, people often work with a distinction between what is good as a means (to something else) and what is good as an end. If one does x for the sake of y, then one is taking x to be good as a means and y to be good as an end."[11] Despite their many differences, Annas and Penner share the conception that acting for the sake of a single highest end is a matter of forming a conception of the ultimate end of action and selecting the actions deemed good as means to the end.

Without denying that Annas and Penner's picture of ancient ethics applies to many ancient thinkers, we should beware of applying it indiscriminately to every ancient ethical system. As we will see, the development of erotic desire by pursuing bodily beauty for the sake of the Form of Beauty is not well described à la Penner as taking the love of bodily beauty to be good as a means to the Form of Beauty. Nor is Annas' pic-ture of ancient ethics as clarification of an implicit end a simple consequence of the claim that a good human life is oriented toward a single highest end. Plato's account of the education of the philosopher-rulers for insight into the Form of the Good depicts lives whose actions are oriented toward a single highest end, the attainment of

---

[10] Annas (1993, 11–12).   [11] Penner (2011, 260).

wisdom. However, performing these actions for the sake of that highest end does not require acting with the intention of promoting that end as a goal. As long as the actions in question perform human functions in the proper way and thereby contribute to the final end of attaining wisdom, they do not need to be performed with the intention of attaining wisdom.

1.4   The Functional Teleology of Action: An Overview

This general and abstract description of Plato's use of the functional teleology of action will be set out in more detail, first with regard to the *Symposium* and then in dealing with the *Republic*. In these texts he indicates that when humans act in pursuit of goods and in doing so perform functions characteristic of human beings, their actions can promote a further and unintended end. Chapter 2 of the present work is devoted to locating the functional teleology of action in the ascent passage of the *Symposium*. The lover described in the ascent passage pursues particular human beings and fields of knowledge which he desires as beautiful and as a result arrives at an awareness of the Form of Beauty. Although this end is not a conscious goal of these actions and in many cases cannot be intended as a goal by the lover, the actions in question are for the sake of that end. Beginning in Chapter 3, an effort will be made to describe the functional teleology of action in the *Republic*. The notion of acting for the sake of an unintended end will be used to address several contested issues in the interpretation of this inexhaustible dialogue. Chapters 3 and 4 take up the enigmatic first book of the dialogue. *Republic* 1 poses vexing puzzles both in the interpretation of the particular arguments it contains and in understanding the relation of this book to the rest of the *Republic*. Much of the controversy over this book has stemmed from Socrates' apparent use of the craft analogy, or the comparison he frequently draws between a virtue such as justice and crafts such as medicine or navigation. I argue that Socrates in Book 1 employs the craft analogy in some respects, but also begins to revise it. He describes justice as being similar to a craft in having a definite context of action, a type of action in which we can expect the just man to be especially valuable in the way that a doctor is especially valuable when it comes to promoting human health. This context of action is the practice of forming and maintaining partnerships and associations, in particular the political partnership of ruling and being ruled. This practice of engaging in partnerships is the function which the virtue of justice perfects. Despite this similarity between crafts and justice, Socrates describes justice not as a craft but as a self-transmitting power, a power which operates by making the people and objects around it similar to itself. Justice, understood as a self-transmitting power, works according to the functional teleology of action, as its final effects of making other people and communities just is an end that need not be intended. Thus, Book 1 puts in play many of the concepts which will be crucial for describing this teleology of action in the rest of the *Republic*. In particular, the concept of the function or characteristic activity of the just man, namely forming and maintaining partnerships, will appear in later chapters.

Chapter 5 takes up the division of goods introduced by Glaucon at the start of Book 2 of the *Republic* as he requests that Socrates praise justice for itself and not for its rewards. The chapter is devoted to two interpretive goals: to clarify the task assigned to Socrates of praising justice for itself; and to expound the motives for his recourse to the city as the site of justice. With regard to the first goal, Glaucon divides goods into three classes: things welcomed merely for their own sake; things welcomed for their own sake and for the sake of their results; and things welcomed merely for their results. Close analysis of this structure and of the examples used sheds light on the particular task assigned to Socrates: he should praise justice for itself, which amounts to explaining how justice is an activity which perfects important functions of the human soul. Some of the results of being just may be mentioned in the course of this praise of justice, namely those beneficial results which indicate the good condition of the soul that is just. The second goal of this chapter is achieved by drawing out the implications of the notion that justice perfects or completes functions of the human soul. One of these functions is that of forming and maintaining partnerships. The city is itself an example of a partnership, an association of citizens each of whom places his or her work at the disposal of the other citizens. Attention to this particular function helps to explain Socrates' turn to the city and to political affairs in the investigation of justice.

Much of the discussion in the third, fourth, and fifth chapters is devoted to spelling out the concepts that provide the basis for the teleology of action in the *Republic*. These sections prepare the way for the examination of particular cases of the functional teleology of action. But the fifth chapter also indicates a set of examples of the Platonic teleology of action that is our focus. Books 2 and 3 of the *Republic* contain extended discussion of the examples given of the first and third classes of goods: harmless pleasures for the first class, and exercise, undergoing medical treatment, and the use of various crafts for the third. Socrates comments on many of these examples in the course of the *Republic*, and these discussions allow us to map out more precisely the teleological relationship between goods of the third class and goods of the second class. When goods of the third class are pursued in the best way, as happens in Socrates' ideal city, they are pursued for the sake of an unintended end, namely the psychic goods of justice and temperance, which belong to the second class. Education in music and gymnastic involves acting for the sake of virtue in this way.

Socrates' use of the best city to investigate the nature of justice relies on the city-soul analogy. Success in understanding the nature of justice in the city will shed light on the nature of justice in the soul only if the city and the soul are similar in structure. The structure of the soul, then, is the theme of Chapter 6. To vindicate the claim that the soul possesses roughly the same structure as the city, it is necessary to characterize Socrates' conception of a part of the soul in Book 4 and to identify the sort of conflict between desires that will lead to partition of the soul. Chapter 6 sets forth an account of the three parts of the soul, namely reason, spirit, and desire. Each part is characterized as involving a particular kind of activity, an object that is required to complete this activity, and an end achieved by that activity. With this account of the parts of the soul, it is possible to explain how a soul with parts may still form a complex unity. The three parts of the soul support each other by performing their own activities and, in the right circumstances, generate a unified soul. In such circumstances, we can say that the parts of the soul carry out their own activities for the sake of a unified soul.

Chapter 7 uses the concepts introduced in the previous three chapters to provide an account of Socrates' defense of justice in Book 4. In the special sense of actions that carry out the function of forming and maintaining partnerships, just actions are performed for the sake of a state of character that expresses itself in proper self-rule and the ability to act in society. This state of character, the virtue of justice, is a crucial element in a happy life. In the right circumstances, such as those of Socrates' best city, the virtue of justice transmits itself from the soul of the just person through just actions into the partnerships to which the just person belongs. One instance of such a just partnership is the city. Establishing a just city is one of the ends for the sake of which the just person acts via Plato's functional teleology of action. This account of the relationship between psychic justice, just acts, and the just city allows for a strong response to David Sachs' charge that Plato has committed a fallacy of equivocation by setting out to praise justice, construed as actions conventionally recognized as just, but providing instead a praise of justice as a psychic state of harmony. In this way, an awareness of Plato's use of teleology allows us to restate his defense of justice in a more compelling form.

The focus shifts in the final chapters from the proper interpretation of the ethical argument of the *Republic* to the education of the guardians. The education that Socrates prescribes for the guardians in Books 6 and 7 requires them to make an intellectual ascent from a view of the world shaped by the senses to knowledge of the forms. This ascent culminates in an understanding of the Form of the Good. This most important form is described indirectly by Socrates through three images, the Sun, the Divided Line, and the Cave. The education of the guardians, which is figured in the image of the Cave, is set forth in more literal terms in Book 7 with the description of the five propaedeutic studies (arithmetic, plane geometry, solid geometry, astronomy, and harmonics). Thus, the education of potential guardians includes as a central feature intense study of higher mathematics. Potential guardians will be prepared by this mathematical study for understanding the Form of the Good.

Chapter 8 begins the discussion of the intellectual ascent to the Form of the Good by providing an overview of the three images of Sun, Divided Line, and Cave. Each image uses vision as an analogue to or comparison term for knowledge. In order to grasp the significance of this use of vision, Chapter 8 includes an account of a Platonic theory of vision present in the *Timaeus*. Acquaintance with this theory of vision will allow us to appreciate the significance of vision in the three images. In particular, the Divided Line features a comparison between the states of imagination and belief in the visible section of the line. Familiarity with the Platonic theory of vision from the *Timaeus* will allow us to specify the way in which imagination provides images of the external objects which belief allows us to perceive. Imagination and belief provide an instance of a pervasive pattern in the Divided Line: a lower section of the line contains images that are used for the sake of gaining insight into the entities contained in a higher section.

The intelligible section of the Divided Line, and in particular the cognitive state of dianoia, provide the main focus of Chapter 9. Dianoia is characterized as employing hypotheses and using visible objects as images of intelligible objects. These procedures of dianoia are illustrated by Socrates through reference to the practices of his contemporaries in the field of geometry. I argue that the use of dianoia involves reliance on hypotheses where these hypotheses include definitions of numbers and geometrical figures. Geometers use these definitions and visible diagrams to prove conclusions that hold true of intelligible realities. The entire practice of positing definitions and other hypotheses, drawing visible diagrams, and proving particular conclusions is a case of devising images in words, or intelligible images of intelligible realities. The use of dianoia by mathematicians and others is thus another instance of using images for the sake of gaining insight into the originals of those images.

Chapter 10 examines Socrates' claim that mathematical study, in the best case, is carried out for the sake of understanding the Form of the Good. This chapter proceeds by a close analysis of several of the propaedeutic studies. Mathematical inquiry into the propaedeutic studies generates definitions of mathematical objects: definitions that use the notions of ratio and proportion. Although this is not the intention of the mathematicians who respond to the demands internal to their discipline, the formulation of these definitions leads the mind to become acquainted with intelligible realities and ultimately with the Form of the Good. This process of education through mathematics illustrates the functional teleology of action, since it produces a result that is not foreseen or intended (insight into the Form of the Good), but which is nevertheless the purpose of this process.

2

The Teleology of Action in the Ascent Passage of the *Symposium*

2.1 Introduction

The previous chapter provided an introduction to three different varieties of teleology: intentional teleology, natural teleology, and Plato's functional teleology of action. The third variety of teleology is distinguished from the first by the particular way in which actions are oriented toward their end or purpose. While intentional teleology points to the content of an agent's intentions and associated beliefs about the object of her desires in order to explain how her actions are performed for the sake of an end, this third variety of teleology relies on functions to orient actions to ends. The agent need not be able to identify the purpose or end promoted by her actions according to this Platonic version of teleology, while the ability to do this is a necessary condition of intentional teleology. The functional teleology of action is similar to natural teleology in its reliance on functions, but it sets out to explain the purpose of human actions. In contrast, natural teleology focuses on the structure of living things and their non-intentional behavior. In order to spell out these general and impressionistic claims about Plato's use of functions in the explanation of action, I provide here a more detailed discussion of the ascent passage in the *Symposium* (210a-212a).[1]

The ascent passage presents a series of actions motivated by erotic desire such that all the actions in the series are performed for the sake of a single end, the vision of the Form of Beauty. In order to gain insight into the sense in which all of these actions are oriented toward the vision as their purpose or end, an analysis of the for-the-sake-of relation as it appears in the ascent passage is presented. This analysis features prominently the notion of function, which appears at *Symposium* 206b-207c in Diotima's discussion of the function (*ergon*) of eros, namely giving birth in the beautiful. Close examination of the ascent passage thus provides insight into the contours of the relation that holds between actions and ends in the functional teleology of action. It also points to the central role of the concept of function in this way of understanding purposive action. Both the relation of action to end and the concept of function will appear again when our attention turns to the *Republic* in succeeding chapters.

---

[1] See Payne (2008) for a more thorough discussion of the issues raised in this chapter.

2.2   The Form of Beauty as Unintended End of the Ascent

In the ascent passage, Plato puts in Diotima's mouth a striking account of the progressive stages of love for beauty. A lover who proceeds correctly through the different stages of love will desire one beautiful body, then many beautiful bodies; he will come to desire and love the beauty of the soul, then the beauty of laws and customs, and finally the beauty of the sciences. As the final stage of this development he will become aware of the Form of Beauty, a reality which stands apart from all other beautiful things. Diotima chooses to emphasize the teleological ordering of this sequence of loves, as she speaks of the vision of the Form of Beauty as the purpose or end [*telos*] of this progression:

For whoever has been led correctly up to this point in matters of love, by beholding beautiful things in order and correctly, is coming now to the final end of loving, and suddenly he will catch sight of something amazingly beautiful in its nature; it is for the sake of this, Socrates, that all his earlier labors took place.... (*Symposium* 210e2-6)[2]

A few lines later Diotima provides a review of the entire ascent. She makes the proper development of love turn on the teleological structure of the ascent:

When someone rises up from these earlier loves, through loving boys correctly, and begins to see that beauty, then he has almost reached the end. For this is what it is to proceed correctly in love, or be led by another: starting from those beautiful things one goes always upwards for the sake of that beauty.... (211b5-c2)

The Form of Beauty is the most prominent beauty in the experience of the lover; it is that in virtue of which all other beautiful things are beautiful. This is reflected in its place within the series of actions which make up the ascent. The vision of the form is that for the sake of which all other actions in the ascent are performed.

   That the ascent exhibits a teleological structure of actions performed for the sake of a final end is clear, but we should look closer at how exactly the earlier actions of the ascent are for the sake of the final vision. It is tempting to turn to intentional teleology for an account of the orientation of these actions toward their end. Such an explanation of the teleological structure of the ascent is provided by Martha Nussbaum in *The Fragility of Goodness*. According to Nussbaum, Diotima encourages us to build a life around the contemplation of the Form of Beauty. Such a life is preferable to one devoted to loving contingent human beings. Like the lover of the ascent, we are expected to opt to pursue the vision of the Form of Beauty in light of the risks inherent in loving frail human beings:

---

   [2] All translations from the *Symposium* are by the author and are based on Burnet's text in the Oxford Classical Texts series. Here and elsewhere, *telos* is translated as "end" rather than "goal," since the latter introduces unwanted suggestions of conscious intentions or plans to achieve an end.

Such a life [one dominated by erotic love for persons] is not 'livable'; we must find another way. Instead of flesh and all that mortal rubbish, an immortal object must, and therefore can, be found. Instead of painful yearning for a single body and spirit, a blissful contemplative completeness. It is, we see, the old familiar *erōs*, that longing for an end to longing, that motivates us here to ascend to a world in which erotic activity, as we know it, will not exist.[3]

Nussbaum explains the status of the form as the purpose of the ascent by directing our attention to the content of the lover's motivations. The lover seeks an escape from the distress of love for contingent humans. He hopes to achieve a blessed and complete life through contemplation of the Form. Thus, the lover ascends with the goal of achieving this vision of the Form of Beauty.

This recourse to intentional teleology cannot provide a satisfactory explanation of the fact that the lover acts in the ascent for the sake of the vision of the Form of Beauty. The Form does not appear in the lover's beliefs or knowledge at any stage prior to the vision. As a result, he cannot act at previous stages of the ascent with the intention of achieving the vision. The first move of the ascent occurs when the lover becomes aware that all bodily beauty is akin, so that it is senseless to esteem one case of bodily beauty over another. Another early step in the ascent involves desire for beauty of the soul, which makes possible the lover's devotion to a single beloved. These transitions involve the human capacity to redirect the desire for beauty in light of what seems most fitting and in response to a new type of beauty, the beauty of the soul. But the Form of Beauty does not here operate as an aspect of what the lover is attempting to achieve. Even so, Diotima will assert that these actions are carried out for the sake of the vision of the Form of Beauty. Until the final state of the ascent, the lover is devoted to beauty in its varied instances: beautiful bodies, souls, customs, laws, and sciences. Only after the lover has arrived at the beauty of the sciences (210c6) does he become aware of the Form of Beauty. Diotima speaks of this event as the lover suddenly catching sight of something "amazingly beautiful in its nature," something different from all other particular instances of beauty. It is not beautiful in the way that shapes and colors are beautiful, and it is not beautiful in the way that a human being is beautiful, in his face and hands. In the vision of the Form of Beauty the lover finds something unexpected, something set apart from his previous experiences of beauty. This indicates that the Form of Beauty does not progress through the ascent with the intention of achieving the vision of the Form of Beauty. As a result, intentional teleology will not succeed in explaining the sense in which the vision of the form is that for the sake of which all the stages of the ascent take place. Any interpretation such as Nussbaum's which employs intentional teleology will experience similar difficulties in articulating the relation between the actions of the ascent and their end.[4]

---

[3] Nussbaum (1986, 183).

[4] Frisbee Sheffield ascribes the lover's orientation toward the vision of the form as due to the influence of a more experienced guide or mentor, apparently the person mentioned at *Symposium* 210a6. This approach to the teleology of the ascent does not do justice to the contributions made by the lover in the step-by-step development of erotic desire. See Sheffield (2006, 101–10, 113–20). Kurt Sier discusses

2.3 The Function of Eros

Our task is to understand what Diotima means when she asserts that all stages of the ascent are for the sake of the vision of the Form of Beauty. An earlier instance of teleology in Diotima's speech can shed light on this aspect of the ascent passage. At 206e2 she informs Socrates that eros is not, as he previously thought, eros of the beautiful. In fact it is eros of generation and giving birth in the beautiful. Both men and women are pregnant in body and in soul, and the presence of beauty triggers the desire which leads us to bring forth offspring of different types, a process which Diotima refers to as giving birth in the beautiful. When humans and other animals are in the presence of beauty, they are stimulated to produce offspring after their own kind. They thus provide replacements for their mortal nature and achieve a qualified version of immortality (208a7-b4). As Diotima describes the extremes to which erotic love drives mortal creatures—they pursue intercourse with each other, nurture their offspring, even die in defense of their offspring—she provides an explanation for this: the cause of this behavior is the fact that "mortal nature seeks as far as possible to exist forever and to be immortal" (207d1-2). Eros carries out its daemonic role of connecting mortals and gods by driving mortal creatures to act for the sake of immortality (208b5-6).

Diotima introduces the function of eros as the activity through which erotic desire pursues its end of gaining immortality. The immortality in question is not simply mere uninterrupted existence; eros seeks the eternal possession of good and beautiful things or eternal happiness, as Diotima instructs Socrates at 205a-206a. Once Socrates accepts this characterization of the end pursued by eros, Diotima turns to specifying the activity connected with erotic desire that allows lovers to pursue this end: " 'Since this is what love always is,' she said, 'in what way and in what action would the drive and striving of those who follow it be called love? What is this function (*ergon*)?' " (206b1-3).[5] Socrates is not able to answer this question, and so Diotima introduces one of the characteristic elements of her teaching on eros. Giving birth in the beautiful is the function or characteristic activity by which eros pursues its end, namely possessing the good forever. Human beings and other mortal creatures can draw closer to this end only by generating new offspring under the influence of beauty: "For by the same argument as the one earlier, mortal nature seeks as far as possible to exist always and to be

---

teleology in depth in his book on Diotima's speech but gives preference to intentional teleology. In the ascent passage humans are encouraged to form reliable judgments about their goals based on self-knowledge. "Mit der Selbstreflexion verknüpft ist ein richtiges Urteil über die intendierten Objekte und ein Vorbegriff von den antizipierten Zielen"; Sier (1997, 293).

  [5] The translation of 206b1-3 follows Christopher Gill in Plato, *Symposium* (Penguin Putnam: New York, 1999). Gill translates the two questions at 206b1-3 as follows: ' "In what way and in what type of action must people pursue this goal, if the enthusiasm and intensity they show in this pursuit is to be called love? What function does love really have: can you tell me?" ' The second question apparently restates the first, and so in asking for a specification of an *ergon* Diotima is asking about the distinctive way of acting that pursues eternal happiness and is also rightly termed eros. In the lines following 206b1-3 she describes giving birth in the beautiful as the activity which is proper to erotic desire and allows it to seek its end of gaining immortality. I owe thanks to David Sedley for comments on the translation of this passage.

immortal. It is capable of this only by coming to be, which always leaves behind another new being in place of the old ..." (207c9-d3). To spell out Diotima's answer to her question at 206b1-3, giving birth in the beautiful is the function or typical activity which eros carries out and thus pursues its end of gaining immortality.

A further source for understanding this activity of giving birth in the beautiful is the account of functions offered by Socrates in Book 1 of the *Republic*. As he attempts to justify to Thrasymachus his claim that justice is a virtue, Socrates defines a function as follows: the function of a thing x is that task or activity that only x can do or which x does especially well. For instance, the function of the eye in humans is to see because it is only with the eyes that we can see. If more than one thing can perform a given task or produce a certain result, the function of performing that task or securing that result belongs to the one thing that performs that task best or best secures that result. The function of a pruning-knife is to cut slips from a vine, not because it is the only thing that can perform this task, but because it does the job better than a dagger or a scythe (*Republic* 352d-353a). Based on this passage and on Diotima's speech, the sorts of things that have functions are organisms such as horses, organs or parts of organisms such as eyes and ears, desires such as erotic and sexual desire, and tools or artifacts such as knives or hammers. For all such things, animals, or organs, or desires, or tools, a thing has a function just in case there is some activity that only it performs or that it performs better than other things capable of carrying out that activity.

In order to gain clarity on the concept of function that is presently in play, it will be helpful to add several comments on what functions are and how they operate. First, there is a conceptual connection between a thing's characteristic activity and its function. In speaking of a thing's characteristic activity, I have in mind the fact that, although a given thing can perform or can be used to perform a myriad of activities or tasks, just one is elevated to the status of what the thing typically does. A pruning-knife can perform a potentially infinite number of tasks, from cutting slips from a vine to cutting bread to opening letters. But only one of these activities is the characteristic activity we identify as the function of a pruning-knife: cutting slips from a vine, that activity for which the pruning-knife is the best implement. Contemporary discussions of the function of biological traits have made this point from a different angle. The function of the heart in vertebrates is to beat and thereby to circulate blood. The heart produces a large range of effects by virtue of doing what hearts naturally do, such as producing the thudding sound of a beating heart. But only the activity of beating to circulate blood is central to the heart's performance of its function.[6] So the function of a thing and the characteristic activity that thing typically performs must be understood together; we learn what the function of a thing is in part by learning to discern the characteristic activity of that thing. When Diotima sets forth the function of eros as giving birth in the beautiful, she has already identified the object of love, namely having

---

[6] On this point see Hardcastle (2002).

the good forever, and she then goes on to describe what lovers do to pursue this lofty object. It is this activity, as opposed to other activities put forward by speakers in the *Symposium*—searching for one's other half or possessing beauty and goodness or feeling a moralized sense of shame before the beloved, to mention a few—that is characteristic of love.

Second, the characteristic activity that is connected with a function typically produces an effect that is beneficial to some organism, usually the organism some part or aspect of which performs the function (the function's owner, as it were) or the being that uses a tool that has the function.[7] The effect of blood circulation produced by the heart's characteristic activity of pumping blood is good for the heart's owner in most cases. When the eye performs its characteristic activity of seeing, this performance is something welcomed for itself and also for its consequences, according to the classification of goods introduced at *Republic* 357b-d. Diotima spells out the beneficial effects of giving birth in the beautiful at *Symposium* 207d-208b: mortals can draw closer to their desired end of immortality only if they reproduce themselves by leaving behind a replacement that shares as much as possible of the same nature. This can occur in the sort of reproduction that comes to mind most readily for us, by human beings producing another human being, but it also occurs when a person studies to replace lost opinions and knowledge with new opinions and knowledge. In all cases, a mortal creature achieves the closest to immortality that is possible for it, namely a qualified immortality that consists in the survival of a replacement offspring similar in nature to the parent.

Third, we must bear in mind here and elsewhere that functions are carried out in paradigmatic conditions. A pruning-knife carries out its function not when it is applied to concrete or to vines that have been turned to jelly by a special chemical infusion, but by being used on vines that have grown normally. If the heart has the function in vertebrates to circulate blood by beating, this presupposes that the heart is joined to a system of veins and arteries that is in good condition. If such paradigmatic conditions are not present, it is still true that the function of a pruning-knife is to cut slips from vines and that the function of the heart is to circulate blood by beating, but all claims about the typical results of performances of functions will be qualified accordingly.

With these remarks in place concerning the notion of a function, we may proceed to Diotima's description of the function of eros. We read in her speech that giving birth in the beautiful is the function of eros. In light of the account of functions offered in *Republic* 1, this claim should be spelled out as the claim that giving birth in connection with beauty is that activity or process which eros alone carries out, or which it carries out better than other desires. Apparently, Diotima will affirm the former option; although every desire is a desire for something good, eros differs from other desires by its focus on beauty and by its capacity for reproduction and giving birth. This

---

[7] This point about functions is made effectively in Sorabji (1964).

reproduction takes place either at the level of the body, by creating new organisms, or at the level of the soul. Humans are capable of desire for beauty of the soul, and this shows itself in psychic pregnancy and the subsequent "birth" of virtue, wisdom, and political and artistic innovations (209a-e). Diotima connects this psychic pregnancy and creativity with the relationship of an older male lover and a younger male beloved, thus reworking the sort of erotic relationship that Phaedrus and Pausanias took as a starting point in their speeches on eros. Diotima praises the lover-beloved relationship by pointing to the beauty of the offspring produced by the relationship: "As a result such men share much more in common than those who have children with each other, and they have a firmer friendship, because they have a share in more beautiful and immortal offspring" (209c5-7). Giving birth in the beautiful has its point in the production of beautiful offspring that allow the "parents," the lover and beloved, to gain some measure of immortality. Eros has this activity of giving birth in the beautiful as its function because no other desire carries out this activity.

With the notion that the function of eros is giving birth in the beautiful, it is possible to provide a first sketch of Plato's functional teleology of action. Diotima claims that eros operates for the sake of immortality. This is not to be understood by way of intentional teleology as the claim that humans experience eros or fall in love with the intention of producing offspring or extending their existence indefinitely into the future. This would be to attribute to Diotima an overly intellectualistic conception of eros. Instead of this implausible reading of her claim that eros is for the sake of immortality, we may articulate a different conception of the workings of erotic desire. The lover desires his beloved as beautiful, and the influence of beauty on the soul of the lover shows itself in his readiness to create poetry, speeches, works of art, and acts of virtue. The lover's erotic desire thus helps to cause the creation of new "offspring" of various kinds, which bring about a human version of immortality. The creation of these offspring counts for Diotima as the performance of the function of eros, giving birth in the beautiful. She praises as better performances of this function the creation of offspring which lead to a greater share of immortality, such as the creation of famous works of poetry and lasting political innovations. By praising these performances of the function of eros over those expressions of bodily desire which we more readily associate with eros, she shows that she understands the point of eros as the attainment of immortality. The full benefit of giving birth in the beautiful is seen when a lover creates the most beautiful and most lasting children. Full success in performing the function of eros is achieved when the fullest version of immortality is achieved. If this is the case, then eros operates for the sake of gaining immortality. In making this claim, Diotima need not describe the lover as acting with the intention to become immortal. In the normal case, the lover falls in love with a beautiful person, a process that typically happens best with a minimum of planning, gives birth to new offspring, and thus achieves some measure of immortality. The lover would then act for the sake of an end without ever acting with the intention to promote this end.

2.4 Teleology in the Ascent Passage

Having gained insight into Diotima's understanding of how eros operates for the sake of an end, we may return to the ascent passage. Within the compass of roughly two Stephanus pages we find a series of episodes of desire for beauty which, like steps on a ladder, lead the lover up to the experience of the Form of Beauty. Important stages in the progressive development of love are marked by performance of the function of eros, giving birth in the beautiful. At the start of the ascent the lover is focused on one beautiful body and creates beautiful speeches or *logoi*. These are presumably speeches or poems offered in praise of the beloved, perhaps of the sort which Hippothales creates in service to his beloved Lysis (*Lysis* 204c-e). The first step in the development of love comes when the lover directs his eros to all beautiful bodies. With the help of an unnamed guide or mentor, he realizes that all bodily beauty is akin, so that it is foolish to single out one instance of bodily beauty for special attention (210a8-b5). Love for particular persons reappears at the next stage, when the lover desires the beauty of the soul: "After this he must think that the beauty found in souls is more to be honored than that in bodies, so that if there is someone decent in soul, even if he has only a little bodily beauty, that is enough to love and care for him and to seek to give birth to such ideas as will make young men better . . ." (210 b6-c3). The second round of giving birth in the beautiful, namely creating ideas and discourses on moral topics which are intended to improve the youth, will likely cause the lover to consider one of the crucial factors in moral education, the role of customs and laws in shaping character. This brings the lover to the next stage in the ascent, which is an awareness of the beauty of customs and laws. Perhaps to put this appreciation of laws and customs on a broader and firmer epistemic footing, the lover turns next to the beauty of the different kinds of knowledge (210c3-7). Here the lover is able to find beauty in the widest possible range of objects, and thus "turned toward the great sea of beauty," he performs the function of eros for a third time by producing beautiful ideas and theories (*logous kai . . . dianoēmata*, 210d4-6). These productions of wide-ranging scientific inquiry prepare the way for the final insight into beauty, the vision of the Form of Beauty. This is a divine beauty, one that stands above all the instances of beauty previously experienced. Unlike all sensible instances of beauty, it is not beautiful in one way or aspect and ugly in another. Unlike the sort of beauty which Socrates finds most accessible, it does not appear in the manner of a face or hands or anything associated with the human body (211a5-7). It is not beautiful as a particular science or account is beautiful, as one thing that is beautiful within a larger whole. Even when we achieve a scientific awareness of the beauty of the natural world, we tend to see the beautiful object as beautiful in virtue of its fitting aptly into a surrounding context, as when we see as beautiful the wing of a flying bird or the slope of a hill within a landscape or the stars in the heavens (211a7-b1). The Form of Beauty is set apart from all such beautiful things, since its beauty is single in form and stems solely from itself. The distinctive nature of the Form of Beauty is shown also in the fact that it makes possible the most successful performance of the function of eros. Diotima tells us at 212a3-7 that the lover must achieve the vision of the Form of Beauty in order to carry out this function in the best way:

> …only then will it become possible for him to give birth not to images of virtue (because he's in touch with no images), but to true virtue (because he is in touch with the true Beauty). The love of the gods belongs to anyone who has given birth to true virtue and nourished it and if any human being could become immortal, it would be he.

The completion of the function of eros by giving birth to true virtue allows the lover of the ascent to draw as close as humanly possible to the purpose of eros, gaining immortality and the eternal possession of the good.

One important feature of the ascent passage is the distinction that Diotima forcefully draws between the many beautiful things that the lover experiences before the vision of the form and the nature of the form itself. These are all beautiful, but Diotima associates the many beautiful things with a particular nature or type of thing and denies such association to the form. The lover begins with desire for beautiful bodies (210a4-8) and progresses when he comes to realize that the beauty of bodies is one and the same (210a8-b3). He moves upwards when he becomes aware that the beauty of souls is more honorable than the beauty of bodies (210b6-c3). Then comes the move to beauty in laws and practices (210c3-6), followed by the beauty of sciences (210c6-7). As a philosopher he beholds the great sea of beauty while contemplating many and beautiful theories or speeches (210d3-5). The association of beauty with a determinate type of thing is broken decisively when the lover arrives at the Form of Beauty. This is not the beauty associated with bodies or anything human, it is not a particular type of science or theory, it is not "in" anything. Diotima describes it as being beautiful "itself by itself with itself," the insistent use of the reflexive pronoun "itself" marking its independence from and distinction from the other instances of beauty and from the particular types of beauty which the lover previously experienced.

One result of the strict separation that Diotima enforces between the many beautiful things and the Form of Beauty is that the lover does not have experience of or beliefs about the Form prior to the vision. The lover's orientation toward beauty in the earlier stages of the ascent is exclusively a concern for bodily beauty, or beauty of the soul, the beauty found in laws and customs, or the beauty of the sciences. The lover will conceive of such things on the model of a beautiful such-and-such—a beautiful body or law or soul. Nothing in the description of the lower stages of the ascent indicates that the lover is capable of conceiving of something that is simply beautiful: beautiful in a way that is independent of its being a body or law or soul. Becoming aware of the Form of Beauty is a further step, one that alters the lover's ability to carry out the function of eros. His awareness of these particular forms of beauty allows him to give birth in the beautiful along the way, but these instances of carrying out the function of eros amount only to giving birth to images of virtue, because the lover is in touch only with images of beauty. Giving birth to true virtue follows only upon contact with true or real beauty

(212a2-5). The lover gives birth to true virtue only upon achieving the vision of the Form of Beauty, which indicates that he does not have contact with the Form prior to the vision. Humans have contact with forms through the mind, either through knowledge or through belief. Given that the lover does not have contact with the Form of Beauty prior to the vision, it follows that he has neither knowledge nor belief about the Form. This confirms our claim that the sense in which the earlier stages of the ascent take place for the sake of the vision of the Form of Beauty cannot be spelled out using intentional teleology.

The lover's ascent can be grasped not simply through a listing of the items desired as beautiful—bodies, souls, laws and customs, sciences, the Form of Beauty—but through a consideration of the changes it brings within the lover. The ascent works within the lover a progressive development of his moral character. The first stage of giving birth in the beautiful involves poetic compositions praising the beauty of the beloved. This is an important step in turning the lover toward an external source of beauty, but as the case of Hippothales in the *Lysis* indicates, it is also compatible with neglect of the lover's own capacities for living a well-ordered life. Love for beauty of the soul inspires poetry or speeches that have the capacity to improve the character of the young, a form of giving birth in the beautiful that presupposes the achievement by the lover of a well-formed character. The development of the lover's moral capacities is matched by his attainment of a broader scientific culture, as seen in his creation of theories in the sciences and in his awareness of the broad sea of beauty in the universe as a whole. Finally, the vision of the Form of Beauty results in the lover creating true virtue, presumably in the lover and in those humans he loves, in contrast to the images of virtue accessible to those who have seen only images of beauty. The creation of true virtue elevates the lover to the status of one who is worthy of friendship with the divine (212a5-6). To explicate the contrast between the true virtue of one who has seen the Form of Beauty and the images of virtue available to those who have seen only bodily instances of beauty, we may refer to Socrates' distinction at *Phaedo* 68d-69b between the simulated virtue of those who serve the body and the true virtue of the philosopher. A man who faces danger in battle out of fear of some more pressing danger cannot claim to be courageous; a man who restrains some of his bodily desires and thus sacrifices the enjoyment of particular pleasures in order to enjoy some greater bodily pleasure is no model of temperance. The philosopher or lover of wisdom will exhibit true courage and true temperance by treating bodily desires and physical dangers with the proper sense of their triviality. Out of love of wisdom the philosopher will, in a sense, neglect and treat with contempt the bodily things whose use constitutes courage and temperance. With an appreciation of wisdom, one of the most beautiful among beautiful things, the philosopher will perform the virtuous action gladly in the knowledge that her actions stem from wisdom and align themselves with wisdom. One who has achieved only the image of virtue will see virtuous actions as necessary but unwelcome means to achieve the end of bodily well-being. The philosopher will rejoice in the virtuous actions, since she will see them as noble or beautiful instantiations of wisdom.

As Aristotle puts it in the *Nicomachean Ethics*, the virtuous person acts for the sake of what is noble or beautiful (*tou kalou heneka*, *Nicomachean Ethics* 1115b12-3, 23-4). The lover who acts for the sake of the vision of the Form of Beauty and gives birth to true virtue has achieved the full development of moral character.

This account of the changes worked within the lover in the course of the ascent allows for another perspective on the claim that the earlier stages of the ascent have the final stage as their end. The lover of wisdom who gives birth to true virtue has made his way through earlier stages of moral development, in which virtuous actions are seen as necessary but unwelcome, and has won through to a state in which he sees virtuous actions as worth pursuing for themselves. The earlier stages are described as steps that the lover uses to move up to the final stage. That is, the earlier stages in which only the images of virtue were available to the lover were necessary for arriving at the final stage of full virtue; we typically acquire virtue by first doing the actions of a virtuous person in an imperfect and incomplete way. Producing images of virtue in this way is necessary for the full possession of virtue and makes a genuine contribution to that achievement; from the standpoint of one who has attained the vision of the Form of Beauty, part of the value of these images of virtue consists in the aid they provide to the lover's attempts to give birth to true virtue. Thus, the production of images of virtue in the early stages of the ascent was carried out for the sake of the later creation of true virtue. The truth of this assessment of the images of virtue, namely that they have as their end the creation of true virtue, does not depend on the lover's ability to act at an early stage of the ascent with the intention of achieving true virtue.

2.5   Objections to the Functional Teleology of the Ascent

So far I have argued that the ascent passage provides an example of an agent who acts for the sake of an unintended end. This claim, if true, forms an essential part of the functional teleology of action: but what exactly is this teleological explanation by reference to an unintended end? Here it will be helpful to confront several objections to this type of teleology. A first objection draws upon an alleged confusion about the very notion of intentional action and its ends. The objection may arise that the notion of an unintended end of action reveals a basic misapprehension of action. All action, strictly speaking, is intentional action. If we are concerned with purposeful human action as opposed to mere animal behavior, as for instance when I raise my arm to hail a taxi as opposed to when my arm jerks spasmodically due an involuntary reflex, then we must explain this action by reference to some intention to promote an end seen as choiceworthy. If action as understood in this more precise sense is inherently action undertaken with the intention to promote an end or goal, then the notion of an unintended end of action can only be evidence of confusion. An intentional action may of course have many unintended results. If I raise my arm with the intention of hailing a taxi, this may cause the man across the street to mistake my raising my arm for a greeting. But such unintended results are not the ends or purposes of intentional action. The ends of intentional action are expressed, strictly speaking, only by the intentions of the actions in question.

In reply, I accept that all properly human action is intentional, and that all the actions addressed by Plato's functional teleology of action are intentional in the sense that they are performed with an intention to promote a goal in the manner suggested by the objector. But this does not show that the actions in question are performed for the sake *only* of those goals that are intended by the agents. The present work considers the possibility that an intentional action can be performed for the sake of an intended end and also for the sake of a further, unintended end. When we consider actions that engage our fundamental human capacities to love and value beauty and to know fundamental truths about the world, as opposed to trivial actions such as raising an arm to hail a taxi, we will find that our intentions do not encompass the whole purpose of our actions. Intentions play a necessary role in initiating and guiding action, but if they also cause further unintended results in virtue of carrying out functions, then these results can qualify as unintended ends of action. Intentions are a necessary feature of the actions that are featured in the ascent passage, but the contents of these intentions do not exhaust the purposes of those actions.

A second possible objection attempts to dispute the claim that the ascent passage contains a genuine version of teleology distinct from intentional and natural teleology. According to this objection, we should not accept the claim that the earlier stages of the ascent are for the sake of the final vision in any real sense apart from the familiar varieties of teleology. To show that the earlier stages of the ascent have the vision of the Form of Beauty as their end or purpose, it does not suffice to show that the actions at the earlier stage produce or cause the vision of the Form of Beauty. To adapt one of Aristotle's examples, suppose that a man comes to town in order to collect a debt from one of his acquaintances. After collecting the debt, he chances to visit a museum exhibition featuring beautiful works of art. The man is carried away by the experience of beauty accessible to him in the exhibition and decides to devote his life to the pursuit of beauty in art. Here the man's action of coming to town to collect a debt helped to bring about his experience of beauty and the change it worked in his life. However, he did not come to town for the sake of the experience of beauty, since his intentions were fixed on the goal of collecting the debt. He did not come to town with the intention of experiencing beauty; this was only a happy accident and not the purpose of his coming to town. This second objection will claim that the same reasoning applies to the lover's vision of the Form of Beauty. To the extent that this result was not a goal or intended end for the lover in the course of the ascent, it is not one of the purposes or ends of those actions.

To meet this second objection, I propose to formulate general characteristics of the functional teleology of action. The result will be a set of conditions which are necessary and jointly sufficient for an action or set of actions $A_1, A_2, \ldots, A_N$ to be for the sake of an end E in the particular way found in the ascent passage. The actions in question are typically performed for the sake of a particular end without the actions being performed with the intention of achieving that end. The actions described in the ascent passage will be central cases of this teleological relation, but the relation is not limited to these actions; looking ahead to the *Republic*, the attempt will be made to formulate the conditions at a general level that does not require that the actions arise out of specifically erotic desire.

The lover's actions in the ascent are compared to steps on a ladder leading up to the vision of the Form of Beauty (211c3). At the metaphorical level, the actions at the earlier stages of the ascent are lower than the final vision, which implies that they are of lesser value than the final vision. The steps on the ladder allow the lover to move up to the higher level; or, to put the matter less poetically, the actions taken at the earlier stages help to bring about the final vision. They make a causal contribution to the achievement of the ascent. Finally, the metaphor of the ladder suggests that these earlier actions have value partly in virtue of their contributions to the final vision. The value of a ladder consists, completely or in part, in its ability to help us climb up to a higher level. As a first approximation to these three aspects of the actions taken in the earlier stages of the ascent, consider the following three conditions:

C'   Actions $A_1, A_2, \ldots, A_N$ are of lesser value than E.

C''   Actions $A_1, A_2, \ldots, A_N$ causally contribute to the obtaining of E.

C''' The value of actions $A_1, A_2, \ldots, A_N$ derives in part from their making a causal contribution to the obtaining of E.

The lover's actions of loving bodily beauty; then choosing to love one person for the beauty of his soul; giving birth to speeches that make the young better; and finally devoting himself to the beauty of the sciences would satisfy these three conditions. These actions are of lesser value than the vision of the Form of Beauty, in part because of the surpassing beauty of the Form and in part because of the true virtue which results from the vision. At the same time these actions in the earlier stages of the ascent prepare the way for the final vision; they form the steps on the ladder without which the lover could not reach the heights of the vision. This is part of their value, as the third condition suggests; in the wake of the final vision the lover will assess these earlier actions positively in light of the contribution they made to that ultimate result.[8]

These three conditions still allow any sequence of actions that by chance produce an event of greater value than those actions to be done for the sake of that chance event. This is seen in the case of the debt collector who experiences beauty as an unintended result of coming to town to collect money owed to him. To rule out this sort of chance production of a valuable result, I turn to the notion of a function. A central feature of

---

[8] These first three conditions on the relation between the earlier stages of the ascent and the final vision echo the conditions laid down by Richard Kraut in his description of the for-the-sake-of relation in Aristotle's *Nicomachean Ethics*. He speaks of an activity A being for the sake of an end B just in case A produces or causes B, B is more valuable than A, and B provides a norm for evaluating performances of A; see Kraut (1989, 200–1). I avoid speaking of norms in relation to the ascent passage, since this would support the dubious idea that what is presented in the ascent passage is a general model for rational or ethical behavior.

this notion in Plato's writings is the linkage between the thing's function and the thing's ability to accomplish a particular valuable result. As discussed earlier, the function of a thing is the characteristic activity that only that thing performs or which it performs better than any other thing. Performing a function typically produces some valuable effect, an effect that is either constituted by the performance of the function or is produced as a separate result. There is an intimate connection between a thing with a function and the limited range of effects it brings about in virtue of performing that function, between eyes and seeing or between pruning-knives and cutting slips from a vine. We evaluate good and bad performances of this function by their relative efficacy in bringing about this result. Contemporary discussions of the function of biological traits have made this point from a different angle. The function of the heart in organisms is to pump blood, an activity that causes circulation of the blood. The heart can have any number of effects on the world as it performs its function, such as the effect of producing the sounds of a beating heart, or even in exceptional circumstances the effect of causing blood to spurt from a severed artery. The fact that the heart's beating can at times bring about such undesirable results is not relevant to an evaluation of the heart's performance of its function; only the heart's ability to circulate blood is relevant to such an evaluation.

These remarks on the notion of a function suggest a revision of the second condition above and the addition of a fourth condition. The resulting set of conditions is as follows:

C_1 Actions $A_1, A_2, \ldots, A_N$ are of lesser value than E.

C_2 Actions $A_1, A_2, \ldots, A_N$ causally contribute to the obtaining of E in virtue of their performing the function F.

C_3 The value of actions $A_1, A_2, \ldots, A_N$ derives wholly or in part from their making a causal contribution to the obtaining of E.

C_4 Actions $A_1, A_2, \ldots, A_N$ perform the function F in the best way only if they causally contribute to the obtaining of E.

The revised second condition requires that actions not only produce the end in question but do so by performing a function belonging to the agent of those actions. In the case of the ascent passage, this will be the function of eros, giving birth in the beautiful. Actions which perform a function have characteristic or typical results; in the case of actions in the ascent, the final vision is one of those results. The fourth condition draws upon the fact that we can evaluate performances of a function by their efficacy in producing a particular result. For Diotima the best way to perform the function of eros is the life of philosophic activity that culminates in the vision of the Form of Beauty. No other way of life mentioned—pursuing eros in the fashion of a poet or a politician, for example—achieves this awareness of the highest beauty. Apparently she gives preference to the philosophic life over these other modes of living because it offers the most intense experience of beauty in the vision of the Form of Beauty and because it results in the creation of the most beautiful and most lasting offspring, true virtue. Because the vision of the Form of Beauty stands at the center of the philosophic life, we can say that for Diotima the best way of performing the function of eros requires achieving the vision of the Form. The fourth condition above puts this thought in a more general form: actions which carry out some function in the best way may be expected to achieve a particular result. In combination with the other three conditions, the actions in question are performed for the sake of that result when they help to bring it about.

Diotima utilizes this version of teleology as part of a larger project of praising the philosophic life as the best possible human life. My goal here is not to evaluate this comparison of the philosophic life to other possible ways of life; for present purposes, the main point is the idea that achieving a certain result provides a criterion for evaluating different ways of performing a function. At different parts of her speech, Diotima speaks of different ways of giving birth in the beautiful: the bodily reproduction that all animals pursue (206c-208b), the lives of poetry and politics (209a-e), the life of philosophy depicted in the ascent. She measures these ways of living against the standard provided by the function of eros: the greater the success one gains in carrying out this function, the better the life one leads in pursuit of the common purpose of all lovers: the eternal possession of the good. All instances of giving birth in the beautiful are valuable, Diotima says, but this does not prevent her from asserting that the life of philosophy is the most rewarding for a human being because its performance of the function of eros brings us closest to the creation of true virtue and the eternal possession of the good.

Taken together, these four conditions provide a framework for understanding why actions at the earlier stage of the ascent are performed for the sake of the final vision. Those actions are oriented toward the final vision of the Form of Beauty in a way that combines causal and normative elements. The lover's actions bring about the final vision not by chance but in virtue of their being performances of the function of eros, giving birth in the beautiful. By creating poems, speeches, and theories concerned with beauty, the lover is prepared to engage in the vision of the Form of Beauty. Achieving this vision is a necessary aspect of the best performances of the function of eros, according to Diotima; any performance of the function of eros that does not lead to the vision will be second best. The fact that the best performances of a certain type of activity must feature the production of some result is an indication that producing this result is one purpose of that activity. Performances of that activity are incomplete or could be improved if they fail to produce that result. Achieving this result gives to those actions their full value and worth. These observations can be illustrated by considering the actions of the ascent in relation to the final vision. Because the penultimate stages of the ascent count as fully successful performances of the function of eros only if they result in the vision of the Form of Beauty, we can say that achieving this result is part of the point of going through those early stages and performing that function.

If the actions of the ascent passage are performed for the sake of the final vision of the Form of Beauty, then we have the resources needed to answer the second objection.

That objection asserted that any unintended result of an action could not be the pur-pose or end of that action; at best, the unintended result would be like the debt collector arriving at a better way of life centered on the experience of beauty. This outcome is a welcome result of the debt collector's actions but not the goal or end of those actions. In reply to this objection, we should note that the lover's achieving the vision of the Form of Beauty is different from the debt collector arriving by chance at a new devotion to beauty. The vision of the form flows out of a series of performances of the function of eros, and it is required for the best performance of that function. The debt collector arrives at a new way of living, but this is only a happy accident arising from setting out to recover money owed to him. We do not evaluate acts of debt collection by asking whether such actions have led to moral improvement; that is not what we can legitimately expect from such actions. It is not required for the best performance of a debt collector's function that he come to see the relative unimportance of wealth; indeed, people who perform this function well are probably less likely to arrive at that result than one who does not perform that function or performs it badly. To spell out the contrast, in the ascent passage the lover's actions perform a function which is expressed fully only by bringing about an unintended result, the vision of the Form of Beauty; in the debt collector case, the function of the actions involved, if there is one, has no particular tie to the valuable result produced. In light of this difference between the two cases, we can agree that the debt collector's actions were not carried out for the sake of the end of experiencing beauty but still assert that the lover's actions were performed for the sake of the vision of the form.

A third possible objection to this account of the teleology of the ascent will dispute the claim that the ascent is a genuine case of acting for an end that is unintended. According to this objection, we should accept that the lover's actions occur for the sake of the final vision of the form, but this fact is due to the influence of a guide who intends to lead the lover toward that vision. Socrates mentions such a guide at 210a6-7: "For it is necessary, [Diotima] said, for one who takes up this matter correctly to make a start while still young by loving beautiful bodies, and first, if the leader leads correctly, to love one beautiful body.…"[9] Under the guidance of an experienced teacher, the lover moves through the stages of the ascent for the sake of the final vision, but this is still a case of intentional teleology. The intentions in question belong to the teacher, and not the pupil. This objection can be raised with regard not only to the lover of the ascent passage but for any supposed case of an agent acting for the sake of an unintended end. We may suppose that a primary agent acts for the sake of an end that is not intended by that primary agent. But why not suppose that the action in question is carried out for the sake of an end in virtue of the intentions of a guiding agent who leads the primary agent through the steps of a process whose final stage is foreseen and intended by the guiding agent? An experienced cook may teach a child or novice to make cookies by instructing them first to mix butter, sugar, and eggs, then to combine flour, salt,

---

[9] 210a4-7. The leader or educator in matters of eros is mentioned also at 210e2-3 and 211c1.

and baking powder, to combine the dry and wet ingredients, to arrange spoonfuls of the mixture on a flat sheet, and finally to place the sheet in a heated oven. At the end the novice may say, "Ah, now I understand that what I was doing was for the sake of these cookies!" In such a case, we may allow that someone can act for the sake of an unintended end, but we still should say that it is intentional teleology that is at the bottom of the novice's actions being for the sake of their end.[10] Call this the guiding agent objection to the notion of the functional teleology of action.

The force of this objection depends on the sort of guidance involved in the relation between the novice and the expert. In the imagined case of the cook and the novice, the latter's role in making the cookies is largely a matter of implementing the intentions of the expert. How well or badly the novice performs as a cook is simply a matter of how well or badly the expert knows his field and uses clear instructions to put the novice through the required steps: and how closely the novice follows these instructions. Here the expert is the one whose performance determines success in producing the right sort of object, and therefore we are right to attribute success in achieving the end to the expert's knowledge. This will be a clear case of intentional teleology. However, the objection is considerably weaker if the instruction involved requires more from the learner than executing the instructions of the expert. In cases where success in producing the goal intended by the instructor depends on how well the learner forms and acts on his own beliefs and desires, the learner makes his own contribution to success in achieving the end even as he benefits from the influence of a guide. In such cases, the learner's actions are not given simply by the instructions of an expert. Their success in promoting the end depends in part on the novice's excellent performance of some function. This suggests that the sense in which the novice's actions are for the sake of the end is not based simply on the intentions of the guiding agent, but involves the quality of his own actions.

The ascent passage presents such a case of a novice who acts for the sake of an unintended end even while he acts under the influence of a guide. The lover of the ascent is guided in erotic matters by an unnamed leader, presumably someone who helps to reshape and redirect the lover's erotic interest. The opening of the ascent passage at 210a6-b6 indicates some of the results of the interaction between the lover and the guide:

First, if the leader leads correctly, he will love one body and give birth to beautiful speeches there; then he will realize that the beauty of any one body is related to the beauty of any other body, and that as long as it is necessary to follow the beauty of form it would be most unreasonable not to suppose that the beauty of bodies is one and the same. After realizing this he will take a stand as a lover of all bodies, relenting from the excessive desire for one body because he looks down on this desire and considers it something small.

The progression of the lover's beliefs and desires shows the effect of Socratic questioning: the lover should come to identify a single trait, beauty, found in all beautiful bodies,

---

[10] I owe thanks to an anonymous referee for presenting this objection.

and should realize that all bodily instances of this trait are of equal value and hence equally worthy of love. We may suppose that the lover here has gone through a series of elenctic refutations similar to the one that Agathon undergoes at 199c-201c, where as a result of Socrates' questions he becomes aware that love is not a great and beautiful god and that to be a lover is to lack and need what is beautiful and good. The lover's response to this guidance at 210a-b is not simply a matter of giving correct answers to leading questions. He first creates beautiful speeches in response to the beauty of one body, he becomes a lover of all bodies, and he comes to look down upon excessive attachment to any one body. These steps of generalizing and redirecting love occur again when the lover comes to value beauty of the soul over beauty of the body (210b6-7) and expresses his love of beauty in philosophic theories (210d3-6). Such a development of eros may require the guidance of an expert, but it also calls for the active participation of the lover. It is possible to react to the questions of Socrates in a number of ways, not all of which lead to the heights of the ascent and the vision of the Form of Beauty. When the lover does achieve this result it is due in part to his success in carrying out the function of giving birth in the beautiful. This will not be simply a matter of carrying out the instructions of an expert, but will require the commitment of the lover's own beliefs and desires. The resulting vision of the Form of Beauty will be an unintended result, but still a result which flows from the lover's own commitments. Hence it is a purpose for the sake of which the lover acts.

2.6 Functional Teleology, Natural Teleology, Intentional Teleology

After this review of the functional teleology of action in the ascent passage, we can substantiate the claim put forward in the first chapter that this teleology of action is distinct from both natural teleology and intentional teleology. First, natural teleology typically shows itself in non-intentional behavior or structure exhibited both by human and non-human animals. The teleological explanation of animal behavior or structure often involves reference to the functions performed or accomplished by this behavior or structure, as when we say that birds have wings for the sake of flying. The functional teleology of action shares with the teleology of nature this reliance on the notion of function; in both sorts of teleology, the behavior or action to be explained produces certain beneficial results by virtue of performing some function. However, the ascent passage concerns itself with explaining a particular subset of those human actions motivated by eros, the desire for beauty, namely those actions which carry out the function of eros in an especially valuable way. In this passage, Plato takes up the human propensity to choose and prefer objects of love as beautiful, not only in the selection and pursuit of sexual partners but also in attraction to and love for moral character, social norms and customs, and bodies of knowledge. The functional teleology of action asserts that the actions inspired by such love and attraction work toward an unintended end. Only those humans who can engage in the philosophic life will achieve this end, the vision of the Form of Beauty. Achieving this end will come as the unforeseen climax of a series of choices to pursue a particular way of life: to prefer psychic beauty to bodily, to value the beauty of norms and customs, to devote oneself to the beauty of knowledge. In addition, natural teleology typically appeals to structural or behavioral properties which all (or all typical) members of a species share: humans have eyelashes for the sake of providing protection to the eyes. By contrast, the functional teleology of action explains not just any human action but those human actions which carry out functions in an excellent way. Since the teleology of action concerns itself with the purpose of the properly human exercise of capacities for choice and action, and since it seeks to explain some of these actions but not all, it is not simply another variety of the teleology of nature.

Although the functional teleology of action deals with the purpose of intentional actions, it is also distinct from intentional teleology. Plato's intentional teleology relies on the model of expertise in a craft, according to which the end or purpose of an action is the making of a product that conforms to the agent's knowledge of a paradigm. A doctor employs the medical craft for the sake of producing health in a patient and a carpenter organizes bricks, stones, wood, and mortar into the form of a house. The best practitioner of the craft is the one who knows the paradigm thoroughly and succeeds in bringing the subject of the craft to an organized state as similar as possible to the paradigm. Here the end or purpose of the craft-practitioner's actions is identical with her intended end or goal. Acting for the sake of an unintended end is not explicable on this model; it would be analogous to Socrates' bones and sinews causing him to stay in prison in Athens when the same causes could just as well bring him to Megara or Boeotia. Even if some unintended but beneficial result should follow from the use of craft-expertise, it would be related only accidentally to the wisdom instantiated in the craft. The doctor does not qualify as a more skillful doctor if her patient, once healed, is able to return to his job and become wealthy. Similarly, she does not count as less skillful if her patient, once healed, is drafted for service in the military, and then injured in battle. Thus, there is no analogue within intentional teleology to the role of functions in the functional teleology of action, namely functions that produce further results that qualify as the ends of action. The best performances of a function are signaled not by the agent's knowledge of the end and of the means to produce this end but by the production of a result that fulfills or completes the earlier tendencies of the function. When Diotima asserts that the vision of the Form of Beauty is the end of the ascent, this signals that Plato no longer relies only on intentional teleology.

3

Justice, Function, and Partnerships in *Republic* 1

3.1   Introduction: A Positive Account of *Republic* 1

The previous chapter examined a model case of Plato's functional teleology of action in the ascent passage of the *Symposium*. An important task in this discussion of the *Symposium* was the description of the function of eros, giving birth in the beautiful. Only with this function set forth was it possible to analyze the functional teleology of action. Turning to the *Republic*, our goal is to examine similar patterns of actions carried out for the sake of ends. In order to describe this pattern in the *Republic*, it is necessary to identify the concepts basic to the functional teleology of action as they appear in this dialogue's discussion of justice. The starting point for our treatment of the *Republic* is Book 1. As I will argue in this and in the next chapter, Plato introduces the concepts of justice, function, craft, and power in this first book. An important feature of Book 1 is the identification of a function or characteristic activity connected to justice. Engaging in partnerships or associations is the function which the virtue of justice makes good. This function will appear again in later chapters in our discussion of the functional teleology of just actions.

To state the obvious, Book 1 of the *Republic* is a puzzling work. This first book is clearly meant to introduce the theme of the entire work, the nature and value of justice, but the quality of argumentation seems to be mixed at best. The arguments employed by Socrates in his refutation of Polemarchus (331d-336a), in his refutation of Thrasymachus (338c-347d), and in his positive arguments for the value of justice (347d-354a) fail to clarify the nature of justice, as Socrates himself admits at 354b-c. The positive arguments for the value of justice in particular are frequently described as so obviously weak that we may wonder why they are employed at all. H. W. B. Joseph reports his first impression of Book 1 of the *Republic* as follows:

> I remember being much puzzled and dissatisfied with the first book of Plato's *Republic*, when I first read it; and I do not suppose the experience to be uncommon. The writing is brilliant, the dramatic interest greater than anywhere later in the book. But the argument is elusive, and in places has an appearance of being scarcely serious, or even unfair.[1]

---

[1]   Joseph (1935, 1).

Joseph's initial puzzlement and dissatisfaction were later replaced by an appreciation of what he took to be the main result of the refutation of Polemarchus: Plato wishes to show that Socrates' inquiry into the nature of justice cannot be satisfied by any specification of duties. Socrates asks Cephalus whether justice is really the same as telling the truth and returning what one has borrowed, and an investigation of the relation between justice and particular duties structures the ensuing conversation with Polemarchus:

This question, or rather the wider question it implies, viz. whether any list of duties can tell us what justice is, whether justice can be defined by specifying the *erga dikaiosunēs* [functions of justice], is handed over by Cephalus to Polemarchus, and I have suggested that it is Plato's main purpose, in the discussion which follows between him and Socrates, to show that the answer is No.[2]

Joseph's reaction to the refutation of Polemarchus has become part of one common interpretive strategy for making sense of the confusing arguments of Book 1. This strategy, which we may term the anti-functional reading of Book 1, focuses on the negative results of this first book. Justice cannot be identified with any specific duty or list of duties or indeed with any set of actions.[3] While Socrates succeeds in refuting Thrasymachus' definition of justice as the interest of the stronger, his own positive arguments for the benefits of justice are of little value.

This chapter and the next contain a more positive construal of Book 1, one that traces the concepts fundamental to Plato's functional teleology of action as this will appear in the later books of the *Republic*. Although Socrates by his own admission does not arrive at a satisfactory account of what justice is, he does clarify the function or characteristic activity which is the context for being just and which justice by its operation makes good. Whereas for Joseph the main result of Book 1 is the negative claim that justice cannot be understood through its *ergon*, its distinctive product or characteristic activity, the present claim is that Book 1 begins the work of the *Republic* precisely by investigating the *ergon*, the function or characteristic activity, typical of the just person. At 332e3-4, Socrates asks Polemarchus, "What about the just man? In what action and in what work [*ergon*] is he most capable of benefiting friends and harming enemies?" I take it that this question sets the agenda for Book 1, even if Socrates will go on to deny that the just person will ever harm anyone. The development of Book 1 and the refutation of Polemarchus in particular point to a particular

---

[2] Joseph (1935, 4). A similar estimation of Book 1 appears in White (1979, 8): "I urge readers of all kinds not to dwell too much on Book I of the *Republic*. It is an introduction and is not intended by Plato to be a complete, or even a fully cogent, treatment of the issues which it broaches...."

[3] Julia Annas provides a succinct statement of this strategy: "Socrates brings four objections to [Polemarchus' proposal that justice is giving to each what is owed]. They are commonly taken to be feeble if not sophistical; but in fact they are quite effective. For they show up the inadequacy of the notion that one can say what justice is by specifying kinds of action at all" (1981, 23). Nickolas Pappas also supports this reading of *Republic* 1: "The conversations of Book 1 constitute a progression away from conceptions of justice that look for that trait in some feature of the actions one performs, toward a view of justice as a characteristic of the person performing them" (1995, 29).

answer to Socrates' question: the just person is most capable of benefiting others in the activity of engaging in partnerships or associations, a key instance of which is the political association of ruler and ruled. All of Socrates' arguments in Book 1 can be criticized as begging important questions or failing to spell out crucial concepts, but they bring to light a compelling conception of the particular sphere of life in which the just man operates, namely the task of maintaining partnerships. To answer Socrates' question, this is the action or work in which the just person benefits others.

This account of the positive results achieved in Book 1 will provide the basis for treatment of two disputed topics, namely the role of the craft analogy in Book 1 and the relation of this book to the rest of the *Republic*. Socrates' use of comparisons between justice and crafts such as medicine, music, and horsemanship suggests to some commentators that he conceives of justice on the model of a craft.[4] Others have observed that Socrates and Polemarchus encounter difficulties in defining justice soon after they agree that justice is a craft that helps friends and harms enemies. They take this as evidence that justice is something quite different from a craft.[5] Related to this dispute over the role of the craft analogy is disagreement over the relation of Book 1 to the rest of the *Republic*. Terence Irwin, C. D. C. Reeve, and Nickolas Pappas claim that Socrates uses the craft analogy in *Republic* 1 and then sets it aside beginning in Book 2. They see *Republic* 1 as part of Plato's critical examination of Socrates' legacy. Characteristically Socratic ideas, including the craft analogy, are developed in Book 1 and then rejected in the rest of the *Republic*.[6] Others locate the craft analogy in Book 1 but deny that it is abandoned later in the *Republic*, making for a closer fit between Book 1 and the rest of the work.[7]

The important result of Book 1 is the insight that justice operates in and through the activity of partaking in partnerships. The later books of the *Republic* continue to unfold this insight, which indicates that this first book is closely integrated into the whole to which it belongs. The continuity between Book 1 and the rest of the *Republic* reveals itself in Socrates' treatment of justice as a power of a particular sort. Justice is a power that is lodged primarily in individual human beings, but it transmits its characteristic marks of friendship and concord to the associations and groups that constitute political communities. In doing this, justice is the sort of power that makes people and their associations just. To coin a term of art, justice is a self-transmitting power. This conception of justice emerges from examination of the arguments Socrates uses in his conversations with Polemarchus and Thrasymachus. In these discussions, Socrates adopts a nuanced approach to the so-called craft analogy. Justice is like a craft in having

---

[4] Julia Annas characterizes Socrates as using the craft analogy in Book 1 while allowing for the possibility that Plato wishes to treat justice in ways that go beyond the craft analogy; see Annas (1981, 24–8). Kimon Lycos (1987, 159–64) gives a careful account of Socrates' effort to affirm and deny different parts of the conventional understanding of craft as it applies to justice, but still supports the claim that Socrates in *Republic* 1 seeks to uphold a suitably nuanced version of the craft analogy.

[5] See Schiller (1968, 3–4) and White (1979, 63–4).

[6] See Irwin (1977, 178–9); Irwin (1995, 169–71, 180); Reeve (1988, 4–5); and Pappas (1995, 29–30).

[7] See Penner (1988); Hemmenway (1999); and Parry (1996, 11).

a defined context of operation and a characteristic activity and in using reason to deliberate in pursuing its ends. But unlike most crafts, justice operates not by generating a separate product but by making harmonious the associations to which the just person belongs. In this first book of the *Republic* Socrates has already embarked on a train of thought typical of the work as a whole: he has begun to modify the craft analogy in order to emphasize the model of justice as self-transmitting power. As we will see in a later chapter, this is the model of justice employed in the defense of justice completed in Book 4.[8]

3.2 Crafts and Powers

Several terms in the previous paragraphs require explication before turning to closer examination of *Republic* 1. A craft is a body of practical knowledge which allows its practitioner to generate a distinctive product (*ergon*) which is proper to that craft (*Charmides* 165c8-d6). For instance, the product proper to the craft of medicine is health, and the product proper to navigation is safety in sailing. The link between a craft and its product enters into the identity of the craft, so that two crafts differ if they have different products. Coordinate with each craft and its distinctive product is an object, a particular context of operation relative to which the craft operates and relative to which a craft practitioner is an expert (*Ion* 537c5-d4). The doctor uses her craft relative to the domain of our bodies and their good or bad health, and the navigator operates in the area of sea-voyages. Finally, crafts for Plato and his audience signal instances of rationality in action. Craft practitioners can give an account of their procedures in pursuing the results distinctive of their crafts; a craft is a rational faculty as opposed to an intuitive knack for guessing successfully how to succeed in producing a desired result (*Gorgias* 465a2-6). Allied to this condition of rationality in a craft is a distinctive way of acquiring a craft. Crafts are taught by their practitioners to students who learn them, so that a man who claims to be a sculptor might support this claim by naming the expert sculptor under whose tutelage he acquired the craft of sculpting statues (*Protagoras* 319b3-d7).

The craft analogy is the claim that virtue is either itself a craft or similar enough to a craft that we can profitably understand what virtue is on the model of a craft. This short description of the craft analogy covers only the core elements of the comparison between virtue and craft. Scholars differ over a range of issues related to the craft analogy, such as whether a craft's product must be a result separate from and external to the

---

[8] Because Book 1 anticipates characteristic claims about justice made in Book 4, I find implausible the hypothesis that *Republic* 1 was composed as an aporetic Socratic dialogue prior to the composition of the later books. This hypothesis is defended by Friedländer (1964, 50–1) and Vlastos (1991, 248–51). Kahn (1993) opposes this hypothesis while Tarán (1985) argues that Book 1 of the *Republic* was written both to anticipate themes characteristic of the *Republic* as a whole and to indicate the insufficiency of Socratic elenchus with its reliance on conventional moral opinion to refute decisively the immoralist position of Thrasymachus.

craft itself, whether virtue construed as a craft has only instrumental value, whether the force of the analogy is that virtue is simply one craft among others, and whether Plato introduces the analogy in order to develop a theoretical account of virtue.[9] Here I wish to remain neutral on these issues, touching as they do on the proper interpretation of dialogues other than the *Republic*. Whatever is the case there, I claim that Plato in *Republic* 1 has Socrates employ the craft analogy in the refutation of Polemarchus but quickly modifies it by introducing the notion of a self-transmitting power.

In this exposition of the notion of a craft, mention is made of the *ergon* or distinctive product of a craft. In order for a craft to be the particular thing it is, it must produce some definite beneficial effect: health for medicine, safety in sailing for navigation, a house for carpentry, and so on. But the term *ergon* may be translated in a variety of ways depending on the context of its use: it may be rendered also as "work," "function," or "task." For instance, at 335c Socrates tells us that it is not the *ergon* of heat but of its opposite to cool. As David Wolfsdorf notes, the term *ergon* is like the English "work" in being ambiguous between a process and an object, between an ongoing activity and the result produced by that activity.[10] Both senses of the term are present in Book 1, and one of Socrates' achievements is his describing both senses of the term in their respective contexts and connecting justice with the activity-sense of the term *ergon*. In this chapter, I will attempt to translate *ergon* either as "distinctive product" or as "characteristic activity" to signal which sense of the term I take to be in play.

Allied to the notion of craft is the broader and more inclusive notion of power. A craft is itself a power, in that it gives its owner the capacity to generate its distinctive product by the operation of knowledge. Thus, a craft such as navigation fits the brief account of powers found at *Republic* 478c1-d5:

Powers are a class of the things that are that enable us – or anything for that matter – to do whatever we are capable of doing. Sight, for example, and hearing are among the powers… Here's what I think about them. A power has neither color nor shape nor any feature of the sort that many other things have and that I use in my own case to distinguish those things from one another. In the case of a power, I use only what it is set over and what it does, and by reference to these I call each the power it is: What is set over the same things and does the same I call the same power; what is set over something different and does something different I call a different one.

This passage is the most informative general account of powers in the *Republic*. Each power will have an object, a property or being to which it is linked by its nature. The craft of medicine as a power is set over our bodies, sight is set over color, and the double is set over the half. In addition, each power has something that it does or produces (*ho ti apergazesthai*). A power is associated with an activity or a result which

[9] Discussion of the craft analogy was stimulated by Irwin (1977, 71–101). See also Irwin (1995, 68–77). Critical discussion of Irwin's account is provided by Roochnik (1986) and Klosko (1981). A helpful account of the strengths of the craft analogy can be found in Tiles (1984).
[10] Wolfsdorf (2008b, 103).

the power enables its possessor to carry out or achieve in relation to its object. The senses of "activity" and "result" must be construed broadly here to cover such diverse things as medicine healing the body, sight seeing color, and the double being twice the half. Taken thus broadly, a power has an object and a way of acting in relation to that object. For the powers that are crafts, this way of acting reveals itself in a distinctive product (*ergon*).[11]

One type of power will be of special significance for our discussion of *Republic* 1. A craft typically generates a product distinct from it in quality and in ontological category: medicine generates health, farming generates food. Some powers, though, generate products that are themselves powers, tokens of the same type. The operation of such a power involves making its object such as to possess the same power. This type of power is illustrated by a famous passage from the *Ion* that comes after Socrates has ascertained that the rhapsode Ion is able to speak well about Homer but not about any other poet. If Ion possessed a craft he would be able to speak authoritatively about all poets, but since this is not the case it is something else that manifests itself in his rhapsodic exertions. Socrates tells Ion at 533d1-e5 that he is inspired by a power that allows him similarly to inspire others:

[I]t's a divine power that moves you, as a "Magnetic" stone moves iron rings…. This stone not only pulls those rings, if they're iron, it also puts power in the rings, so that they in turn can do just what the stone does – pull other rings – so that there's sometimes a very long chain of iron pieces and rings hanging from one another. And the power in all of them depends on this stone. In the same way, the Muse makes some people inspired herself, and then through those who are inspired a chain of other enthusiasts is suspended.

Socrates' larger goal in this context is to distinguish clearly between a craft and what rhapsodes and poets draw upon, namely a divine power quite different from the calm self-possession of the craft practitioner. While the craft-practitioner possesses and can teach her own variety of knowledge, as shown by the ability to explain and justify her work, the poet is inspired by an external power. Socrates' metaphor for the operation of this divine power suggests that some powers are like the magnet which, as it operates, endows its objects with a power of like type: just as the iron rings affected by the stone become magnets themselves, the poets inspired by the divine power of the Muse acquire the power to inspire others. Powers which thus make their objects like themselves I shall refer to as self-transmitting powers. In general, crafts are not self-transmitting powers. They are teachable and thus are transmitted from teacher to student, but this aspect of crafts is distinct from their securing their distinctive product. The doctor's distinctive product is health, and she can produce health without teaching the craft of medicine. The doctor uses her craft in the central case to generate health in her patients; she need not make them doctors in the process. In most cases a

---

[11] This discussion of powers draws heavily upon Benson (1997).

craft can operate and produce its distinctive product without transmitting its own rational knowledge to anyone else.

Examination of an important exception to the generalization that crafts are not self-transmitting powers will prepare our transition to the *Republic*. This is the royal craft discussed in the *Euthydemus* in the second protreptic discourse (*Euthydemus* 288d-292e). Socrates proposes that it is the political or royal craft which is capable of using well all the products of other, subordinate crafts. The craft of military strategy produces victory in battle but then turns this product over to the royal craft to be used beneficially. The royal craft which uses all other crafts and their products must itself be beneficial to us, and it turns out that this knowledge benefits us by making the citizens whom it affects wise and able to partake of knowledge (*Euthydemus* 282b4-c1). The conversation soon runs aground as Socrates and Cleinias are unable to find a product proper to the royal craft by which it benefits us. Apparently, it is not sufficient to cite the royal craft itself as the benefit generated by the royal craft; this does not move us any closer to understanding the benefit provided by the royal craft. All other benefits, though, have been agreed earlier to be neither good nor bad and are therefore not such as to secure happiness. Despite the difficulties in which Socrates finds himself here, this passage directs our attention to the idea of a political craft, one distinct from all other subordinate crafts, which in some way uses the products of the other, subordinate crafts. Socrates attempts to spell out the nature of this political craft by speaking of it as a knowledge that works by making other people knowledgeable and wise. In other words, the royal craft operates as a self-transmitting power. It benefits us by transmitting itself from the one who has it, the ruler, to those ruled in a political community. Further progress in investigation of this self-transmitting power will require specification of its object and its characteristic manner of acting in relation to this object. For this, we turn to Book 1 of the *Republic*.[12]

3.3 The Refutation of Polemarchus

I propose that justice is described as a self-transmitting power in Book 1.[13] As a power, it has as its object the field of associations and partnerships and it acts upon its object by producing friendship and concord. Three different sections of Book I are relevant for these claims: the refutation of Polemarchus' proposal that justice is giving to each what is appropriate (331d-336a), the refutation of Thrasymachus' claim that justice is the advantage of the stronger (338c-347d), and the positive arguments Socrates offers

---

[12] For discussion of the relation between this passage and the *Republic*, see Sprague (1975, 48–56).

[13] The claim that justice in *Republic* 1 is treated as a self-transmitting power rather than a craft is also found in Lycos (1987, 103–5). Lycos observes that "Socrates ... wants to convince his interlocutors that there must be an 'internal' relation between justice and power if the ordinary belief that justice is part of human excellence is to be *rationally* grounded" (1987, 74). Waterlow (1972, 29–30) points out that justice in Book 4 of the *Republic* is a self-propagating trait. Kamtekar (2008, 127–50) characterizes virtues in Book 4 as powers that allow the three parts of the soul to attain their best condition.

for the superiority of the life of the just person over that of the unjust (347d-354a). In the present chapter the refutation of Polemarchus will be the focus of our inquiry, as this section introduces many of the key concepts to be developed further in Book 1, namely the concepts of function, of partnership, and of self-transmitting power. The refutation of Thrasymachus and the positive arguments used by Socrates to respond to the sophist will be examined in the following chapter.

The conception of justice as a self-transmitting power, one that acts through the formation of partnerships and associations, emerges first in Socrates' refutation of Polemarchus' proposal that it is just to give to each person what is owed. The discussion with Polemarchus falls naturally into four sections: first, 331d-332d, in which Polemarchus states his conception of justice as giving to each person what is owed or appropriate, leading to a candidate definition of justice as a craft of helping friends and harming enemies; second, 332d-334b, in which Socrates uses the comparison between justice and various crafts to seek unsuccessfully for a clearer specification of justice's characteristic activity; third, 334b-335b, in which Polemarchus qualifies his understanding of friends and enemies; and fourth, 335b-336a, in which Socrates brings Polemarchus to agree that it is not just to harm anyone.

Polemarchus enters the discussion of justice at 331d4 in an attempt to defend his father's claim that justice is a matter of paying one's debts and telling the truth. He rephrases this basic intuition in terms of Simonides' claim that it is just to give what is owed to each person. In a passage reminiscent of the opening stages of elenchus in other dialogues, Socrates probes this intuition with a series of questions aimed at spelling out what conception of justice it entails. Giving to each what is owed does not require returning a borrowed weapon to a friend who has taken leave of his senses, because one owes it to a friend to do something good and nothing bad (332a9-10). Polemarchus' recourse to Simonides thus allows him to handle Socrates' example and to reconcile justice with friendship. If the return of a loaned object would do harm to its owner, a friend is just by not returning the object. Socrates then raises the issue of what is owed to enemies, and Polemarchus declares that what is appropriate to enemies is owed to them, namely something bad. After recasting Simonides' saying in the form of the judgment that giving to each what is appropriate is just, Socrates then introduces the topic of crafts. Medicine is the craft that gives certain owed and appropriate things to bodies, namely drugs, food, and drink, while cookery gives the owed and appropriate seasonings to meats. "Now, what does the craft give and to whom does it give it, if it should be called justice?"[14] Polemarchus answers, "If we must follow the earlier

---

[14]   Translation by author. The Grube-Reeve translation of 332d2-3 ("What does the craft we call justice give, and to whom or what does it give it?") renders *an* and the optative *kaloito* as if it were the indicative *kaleitai* found in previous lines ("the craft we call medicine…the craft we call cooking," 432c7, 10–11). This makes Socrates' question sound as if it contains an assertion that justice is a craft directly comparable to medicine and cooking. The preferred translation follows that of Reeve in *Republic* (Indianapolis, IN: Hackett Publishing, 2004): "Now what does the craft we would call justice give, and to whom or what does it give it?" and that of Allan Bloom in *The Republic of Plato*, 2nd edition (New York: Basic Books, 1991): "Now then, the art that gives what to which things would be called justice?" The use of *an* with the optative in contrast to the

answers, the craft that gives benefits to friends and harm to enemies." This exploration of Polemarchus' conception of justice ends with a question at 332d7-9 that puts Simonides' claim about justice into the form of a definition: "Simonides means, then, that to treat friends well and enemies badly is justice? – I believe so."

The sequence of question and answer at 332d7-9 which concludes the first section of the refutation of Polemarchus indicates two important points. First, as is often remarked, the view that Polemarchus attributes to Simonides has deep roots in traditional Greek morality. The notion that the good and admirable man will show his strength in helping his associates and doing down his enemies can be illustrated in a wide range of texts from ancient Greek poetry and rhetoric.[15] We do not know precisely what Simonides said to suggest that giving what is owed to each person is just; the surviving fragments of Simonides do not contain this thought. In any case, Polemarchus interprets Simonides' sentiment about giving to each what is owed in accordance with this conventional intuition about justice. This fits the customary view of Simonides as a traditionalist who expresses the moral views that structure the life of the Greek city-state. As Ruby Blondell notes, the *Clouds* presents Simonides as one of the three old-fashioned poets whose work Strepsiades refuses to sing for his father after his new-fangled sophistic education.[16] Second, the candidate definition of justice as helping friends and harming enemies allows justice to appear as both a self-transmitting power and a power that undermines justice in others. Andrew Jeffrey remarks that helping one's friends here involves at least giving aid to them, furthering their plans and projects, and making them stronger. A friend who has been treated well will be in a better position to treat his friends well and to do the opposite to his enemies. At the same time, treating one's enemies badly involves harming their interests, thwarting their plans, and putting them in a weaker position. An enemy who has been thus treated will be less able to help his friends and less able to harm his enemies and thus will be less just.[17] If justice amounts to helping friends and harming enemies, then acting justly will enable one's friends to be more just and will weaken the ability of one's enemies to be just. Justice will transfer itself to one's friends and allies, but it may also remove justice from one's enemies.

---

earlier use of indicatives signals that Socrates is asking what justice will give and to whom on the condition that it is a craft; the condition is one that Socrates may later deny. Polemarchus' reply at 332d4-6 is put in terms of this condition: "If we are to follow the previous answers [by treating justice as a craft comparable to medicine and cooking], Socrates, it gives benefits to friends and does harm to enemies."

[15] Theognis writes in 337-40, "Zeus grant I may repay my friends, who are so kind,/ Cyrnus, and even more my enemies./ I'd feel then like a god on earth, could I but get/ revenge before my appointed death-day comes." Solon begins his fragment 13 with the following prayer: "Bright daughters of Olympian Zeus and Memory,/ Pierian Muses, hearken to my prayer./ Grant me that I have fortune from the blessed gods,/ and good repute from all men all the time;/ may I be honey to my friend, gall to my foes, honoured on sight or feared respectively"; translation by West (1993, 69). Blundell (1989, 26–59) provides an overview of this theme in ancient Greek culture. Adam (1963, Vol. 1, 12) *ad* 331e-332b gives a list of references to passages in ancient Greek literature that illustrate the pervasive influence of helping friends and harming enemies as crucial illustrations of human virtue.

[16] Blondell (2002, 175, n. 41).   [17] Jeffrey (1979, 56–8).

In the second section, Socrates and Polemarchus examine justice on the model of a craft. Working with the supposition that justice is a craft, Socrates asks Polemarchus to identify the action (*praxis*) and the function or work (*ergon*) with regard to which the just man is most powerful and capable of helping friends and harming enemies (332e3-4). Polemarchus is unable to do so; for whatever field of action or product supplied, Socrates is able to mention a craft other than justice which, in relation to that field of action, will be more capable of generating a valuable product and so has a better claim to the description of being the craft that is most capable of helping friends and harming enemies (farming, shoemaking, carpentry, horsemanship, music, etc.). When Polemarchus eventually settles on a rather trivial field of action and product by which the just man provides benefit, guarding money deposited with him, Socrates suggests that the practitioner of a craft is most skillful in performing opposed actions within his area of expertise. The boxer is best at striking a blow and defending against it, and a skillful doctor is best at poisoning as well as healing. Similarly, Socrates suggests, a just man would then be best able to steal money as well as to guard it. When Socrates points out that thus justice turns out to involve stealing for the benefit of one's friends and to the harm of one's enemies, Polemarchus at 334b7-9 refuses to accept the consequence: "By God, no, but I no longer know what I was saying; but this still seems so to me at least, that justice is to benefit one's friends and harm one's enemies." Polemarchus thus rejects the consequences that Socrates derived from the hypothesis that justice is a craft that allows one to help friends and harm enemies, namely that justice has to do with stealing money or property. These consequences are derived partly from the conditional assumption that justice is a craft, but also from the characteristic activity or distinctive product that Socrates began to investigate at 332e, i.e. the specification of the *ergon* of justice. In whatever manner it operates, though, Polemarchus reaffirms the claim that justice benefits friends and harms enemies.

The manner in which Polemarchus denies part of Socrates' proposed description of justice encourages us to consider more closely what went wrong in the application of the parallel between justice and crafts such as medicine. The assumption that justice is a craft is one that Socrates could deny; he does not himself assert that justice is a craft but only asks what the craft of justice would give and to whom, while Polemarchus goes along with the assumption that justice is a craft in order to follow the path laid down by his previous answers. However, the heart of the problem lies in the investigation of the object and the method of acting to be ascribed to justice. Justice cannot be confined to the trivial matter of guarding money or deposited property, and the ability to steal cannot be one of the characteristic marks of the just. To retrace our steps, it seems that the train of thought leading to these specious results depends on assertions about who is most capable and useful in acting within a given context. Socrates and Polemarchus agree that a doctor is the most capable person when it comes to producing sickness and health, that a musician is the most useful partner to have when it comes to playing a lyre, and that farming is most useful when it comes to producing food.

A principle asserting the supremacy of a craft relative to its context of action seems to be presupposed:

SC   For any craft C with object O and product P, the practitioner of C is the person who is best able to benefit us in dealing with O and producing P.

Socrates appeals implicitly to this principle or a close relative of it in order to refute Polemarchus' various attempts to specify an action or product typical of justice. For whatever object or product Polemarchus specifies, if we can find some craft other than justice that deals with that object and generates that product, then this craft and not justice has a better claim to benefit us as we deal with that object. When it comes to building a house, the carpenter will be the most beneficial person because the carpenter has a special connection to building houses and producing shelters. The most striking example of this use of SC comes when Polemarchus puts forward the idea that justice is concerned especially with partnerships and associations (*koinōnēmata*, 333a14). Socrates then proposes that the most useful partner (*koinōnos*, 333b1) for playing checkers or building a house or playing music will be the expert checkers player or housebuilder or musician: that is, the practitioners of the respective crafts. The just person is thus deprived of a promising avenue for exercising justice.

Polemarchus' suggestion that justice is useful in partnerships and other associations reflects a valuable intuition: justice is the virtue that allows us to be good partners in a common undertaking, whether it be a private financial contract, playing music together in a band or orchestra, or working together to build a house. A single trait or set of traits shows up in the good partner in all these endeavors: responsiveness to the needs of other partners, the ability to coordinate individual desires with the desires of the group, and the ability to think in terms of goods which are achieved by the group and which cannot be achieved by individuals acting alone. Justice, thus construed as the virtue of partnerships, is the social virtue, the one that is exercised in relation to others by displaying the traits of a good partner.[18] These are traits that interact with but cannot be reduced to the traits of knowing how to profit from financial contracts, play music, or build a house.

---

[18] If these reflections on the connection between justice and the traits of a good partner are on target, then Plato is here taking the first steps in a journey that will end in Aristotle's discussion of justice in Book 5 of the *Nicomachean Ethics*. There Aristotle introduces general justice as "complete excellence – not absolutely, but in relation to others.... It is complete because he who possesses it can exercise his excellence towards others too and not merely by himself; for many men can exercise excellence in their own affairs, but not in their relations to another. This is why the saying of Bias is thought to be true, that 'rule will show the man'; for a ruler is necessarily in relation to other men and in partnership. For this same reason justice, alone of the excellences is thought to be another's good, because it is related to others; for it does what is advantageous to another, either a ruler or a partner" (*Nicomachean Ethics* V.1 1129b26-1130a5). Aristotle discusses specific justice as the virtue exhibited in praiseworthy distribution and exchange of goods in the context of various partnerships and associations. Thus, Aristotle shares with Plato the conception of justice as the virtue that allows us to be good partners in our shared endeavors. I owe this understanding of Aristotle's conception of justice to David K. O'Connor; see O'Connor (1988). A similar account of justice is provided in Woodruff (2012).

Polemarchus is not able to defend his proposal that partnerships represent the context of action for justice, but we may be confident that Plato at least is aware of the strengths of this view. It will resurface again in a different form when Thrasymachus suggests at 343d2-e7 that the unjust man always gets the better of the just man in their partnerships. Although the sophist praises the unjust man as wise and derides the just as a useful idiot, he shares the conviction that justice is especially useful (for someone other than the just person, that is) in the context of partnerships. And later in Socrates' second positive argument for the benefits of justice, it is justice that is responsible for whatever groups achieve in their common action (352c).

It seems that the principle SC stands in the way of exploring an attractive conception of justice. But this principle cannot be questioned lightly. It seems to reflect an important aspect of Socrates' understanding of crafts and indeed of wisdom in general in the *Republic*. Each craft is complete and without deficiency in its relation to its object, so that the craft prescribes what is advantageous to the thing over which it is set (342b-c). Each craft has its own power by which it produces its distinctive product and thus benefits that over which it is set, so that even if a navigator becomes healthy while sailing, it is still the craft of navigation that he practices as he produces safety for the crew of his ship. Presumably this is because the doctor is a more useful craftsman of health in a variety of contexts than is the navigator; the latter's production of health is an accidental result of his sailing. This connection between a craft, the product associated with the craft, and the usefulness of the craftsman is borne out finally by Socrates' description of a thing's function (*ergon*) at 353a as that which can be produced only by that thing or which is best produced by that thing. If some distinctive product or characteristic activity can be associated with a craft, then the practitioner of that craft will be either the only one who can produce it or the one who can produce it best.

If the principle SC is one that Socrates ought to and does take seriously, we should ask whether it has been applied well in the case of justice. Polemarchus proposes at 333a13 that justice is useful for dealing with contracts, a proposal that Socrates treats as the claim that justice is useful for partnerships in general. He then gains Polemarchus' agreement with the claims that the most useful partner in playing checkers is the expert checkers player, the most useful partner for building a house is the expert carpenter, and so on. It is worth taking the time to disentangle the misunderstanding of partnerships concealed in this line of argument. Socrates effectively treats being a good and useful partner in the performance of a given action as defined solely by the contours of excellence in that action and not by any traits distinctive of partnership as such. The distinctive product secured by the good partner in that action is identified with the product secured by the craftsman acting alone: victory in playing checkers, or building a house. As a result, the distinctive habits of being a partner disappear from view. In answer to Socrates' questions, Polemarchus agrees that the most useful partner in playing music is the musician, the most useful partner in building a house is a housebuilder, and so on. This ignores the fact that such activities as playing music, building a house, and practicing medicine can be carried on by single individuals outside any partnership. Such activities do not have any essential connection to part-nerships and so cannot be expected to reveal the virtue that is typically employed in partnerships of various kinds. These activities do not provide a suitable test for the claim that the just person and not the musician or doctor is the most beneficial partner.

According to this analysis of 332d-334b, Socrates and Polemarchus are engaged in an unsuccessful search for the characteristic activity in which the just man shows him-self to be especially beneficial. The search has thrown up a promising candidate for this activity, namely the activity of forming and maintaining partnerships, but the strengths of this view remain undeveloped for now. This approach should be contrasted with Joseph's anti-functional interpretation. The fact that the search for the characteristic activity of the just person is so far unsuccessful leads Joseph and others to affirm that no action or set of actions can provide a satisfactory definition of justice. Such an inter-pretation may be based upon the perception of similarity between this passage and many others in the Socratic dialogues which feature destructive criticism of candidate definitions of a virtue, as for example *Charmides* 159b-160d. Here Charmides pro-poses as a candidate definition that temperance is doing things in a quiet and slow manner. He also agrees that temperance is something fine. Socrates then details a range of actions, such as writing, playing music, learning, and remembering, in which acting vigorously and quickly is more admirable than acting quietly and slowly. Socrates then draws a conclusion at *Charmides* 160b7-9, directly contradicting the original candidate definition: "We conclude then that temperance would not be a kind of quietness, nor would the temperate life be quiet, as far as this argument is concerned at any rate, since the temperate life is necessarily an admirable thing." In this familiar pattern, a candidate definition is offered which identifies a virtue with a particular type of action. Socrates observes that the virtue in question is always valuable and then points out that actions which do not satisfy the definition are just as or even more valu-able than those that do satisfy the definition. Alternatively, he may bring his interlocu-tor to agree that actions which satisfy the definition are not valuable and do not count as virtuous, as in his conversation with Cephalus at *Republic* 331c1-d3. In either case, the virtue cannot be identified with the proposed action, a conclusion that contradicts the original candidate definition.

The second section of the refutation of Polemarchus does not fit this familiar pat-tern. Socrates' ability to lead his interlocutor into *aporia* does not lead to the rejection of the proposed definition of virtue. The proposed definition put forward at 332d7-8, namely that justice is benefiting friends and harming enemies, is reaffirmed by Polemarchus at 334b7-9 after he gives up the attempt to spell out the characteristic activity in which the just man shows himself to be beneficial. This is because the activ-ity in question, which Polemarchus surmises to be a matter of forming associations and partnerships, is not claimed to be identical to justice. Socrates proposes and Polemarchus agrees that an expert checkers player is a better partner than the just man when it comes to playing checkers and that the housebuilder is a better partner when it comes to laying bricks for a house. These examples of craft-practitioners making better partners than the just suffice to show that it is possible to engage in partnerships without exercising justice. If this discussion were predicated on the assumption that the action of engaging in partnerships is identical to being just, then these observations would suffice to defeat the proposed identification. Instead, we find Polemarchus and Socrates continuing to cast about for a particular sort of partnership in which the just person will be more useful than the housebuilder or expert at checkers. Polemarchus finally gives up the search for the characteristic activity in which the just man is useful because his best guess leads to conclusions which he finds unacceptable, though they are logically compatible with his original definition (justice is useful as long as the objects it guards are not in use; justice is a craft of stealing used to benefit friends and harm enemies). The logical relation between the activity sought and the virtue of justice to be defined is not that of identity; rather, the activity is a necessary but not sufficient condition for the virtue of justice, since it is the sort of action which is the context for the exercise of the virtue. The presence of the virtue presumably will make a person useful and beneficial in carrying out that action.

To recap the results of the analysis thus far of the second stage of the refutation of Polemarchus, we find that discussion has centered on the puzzle of specifying how and in what activity the just person is beneficial. "In what action and in what work is he most capable of benefiting friends and harming enemies?" (332e3-4). As is often the case in Plato's writings, Socrates shows greater skill in posing suggestive questions than in answering them; his investigation of this question about the context of action and the product of justice is hamstrung by a failure to recognize partnerships as an object of a power and a way of acting with others that is distinct from the objects of other crafts and distinct from any activity that can be carried out singly. If we notice the blockage that results from making this mistake, though, we will better appreciate those arguments later in Book 1 in which Socrates and his interlocutors recognize partnerships as the object or context of action in relation to which justice operates.

Because the theme of partnership will be crucial for the present reading of *Republic* 1, it will be helpful to sketch here a general account of what partnership is. A partnership or association (*koinōnia*) arises when two or more parties undertake common action aimed at achieving some goal. Socrates mentions as cases of partnership two people playing checkers as a team or two people laying bricks and stones together to build a house (333b1-5). The two parties take as their goal winning a game of checkers or building a house and act together to achieve such a goal. A further variation of the general description of common action aimed at achieving a goal appears in the type of partnership that features an exchange of goods or services. This exchange variation is present in Polemarchus' original proposal at 333a13 that contracts (*sumbolaia*) constitute something in the use of which justice is beneficial in times of peace. Socrates asks whether by contracts Polemarchus means partnerships, and Polemarchus agrees. Contracts establishing an exchange of goods or services can be considered partnerships, in the sense that both parties to a contract provide some benefit to the other party on the condition that the other party reciprocates. The exchange itself is the goal aimed at by the two parties, as each party believes that he or she benefits by making the exchange.

Beyond these simple examples of partnership mentioned in the refutation of Polemarchus, a variety of more complicated types of partnerships can be distinguished under the general heading of different parties acting together to achieve a common goal. At 341c10-d4, Socrates brings up the case of a group of sailors sailing a ship under the direction or rule of a navigator or ship's captain. The sailors and the captain work together to achieve the goal of crossing the ocean and arriving safely at their destination. This case is complicated by the fact that the sailors accept directions or orders from the navigator, who takes this role because he is assumed to know best how the different tasks involved in sailing a ship are to be accomplished. Finally, the most complex form of partnership for our purposes is a city or political community. A city is a partnership that comes to be in its simplest form when practitioners of different crafts (at least three or four, says Socrates) make available to the entire group their distinctive products and engage in exchange of these products (369c1-4; 369e3-370a6). A political community often features a differentiation of roles under some ruler or rulers. The healthy city or city of pigs, which is discussed first in Book 2, does not feature rulers, but most political communities or associations involve partnerships under the direction of rulers. In this sense, most political associations are similar to the ship example, in which the sailors cooperate under the direction of a captain or navigator. The minimal condition for the formation of a city or political community, if we are to take the healthy city as the simplest case of a political community, is an exchange of goods similar to a contract.

A special feature of partnerships is the way in which the members of the partnership pursue their common goal. To constitute a partnership, it is not enough that multiple parties pursue independently the same goal. This can lead to conflict rather than cooperation, as when two opposing players in a game of checkers pursue the same goal of victory knowing that at most one can achieve that goal. Nor does partnership arise merely from two individuals each independently pursuing a single goal that both can achieve. If Marissa makes a monetary donation to the local animal shelter and Robert makes a similar donation to the same shelter, they are both acting with the same intention of supporting the welfare of abandoned animals, but they are not thereby acting as partners with each other. Even if each is aware that the other makes a donation, this does not suffice to establish a partnership. Partnership arises only when the two parties choose to act by pooling their efforts, as when Robert and Marissa combine their funds to make a joint donation in both their names. How best to describe such shared action is a subject of controversy in contemporary debates.[19] However, one reliable signal of partnership is an agreement voiced by two or more agents that they will together

---

[19] According to Margaret Gilbert, the pervasive and defining feature of properly social phenomena is the presence of a plural subject, a 'we', that undertakes action; see Gilbert (1989) and Gilbert (1990). Michael Bratman argues that such shared action is best explained in a reductive fashion by assigning to each individual that shares action an individual intention to engage in action with another agent; see Bratman (1993) and Bratman (1999). Plato's use of partnership in the *Republic* does not address this debate,

pursue some goal. Socrates and Polemarchus at 335e8-11 express such an agreement to defend Simonides and other wise men against the charge of saying what is false, namely that a just man will harm his enemies: "You and I shall fight as partners, then, against anyone who tells us that Simonides, Bias, Pittacus, or any of our other wise and blessedly happy men said this. – I, at any rate, am willing to be your partner in the battle."

Explicit agreement to act as partners as voiced here by Socrates and Polemarchus is typically not necessary for partnership to exist. However, a partnership typically features some more or less explicit agreement on the terms of the partnership. A contract exists only when both parties agree to the terms of the contract, though the terms may be left imprecise or subject to amendment over time. Two people playing checkers as a team will form a partnership only if they share the same understanding of the rules of checkers and agree that their goal is to win the game. In more complex forms of partnership the agreement involved may be tacit and presumed rather than expressed and affirmed by declaration. For instance, Socrates in the *Crito* gives a plausible account of the sort of agreement involved in political partnerships such as a city. Speaking in the voice of the laws of Athens, he tells us that by choosing to live in Athens as an adult he has agreed to obey its laws. Given that Socrates had the option to live elsewhere but chose to live in Athens, this amounts to an agreement to the terms of the partnership that is the city of Athens (*Crito* 51d-e).

Our analysis of the second stage of the refutation of Polemarchus had led us to see that Socrates and Polemarchus attempted to specify the activity or function connected with justice, the context of action or object in relation to which the just person will be beneficial. The activity of engaging in partnerships was suggested by Polemarchus, but he was unable to defend this proposal. As a result, our two interlocutors were unable to identify the function of justice. To continue with the discussion of the second stage of the refutation of Polemarchus, we find a further consequence of the failure to identify the function of justice. Between 333e and 334b, Socrates and Polemarchus rely on a variant of SC to arrive at the absurd conclusion that justice is a craft of stealing. The previous application of SC restricted justice to the task of keeping money and deposited property safe. Following on this conclusion, which has the unwelcome feature of showing justice to be useful only when dealing with objects that are not in use, Socrates proposes that justice is like other crafts in being most capable of producing both benefit and harm by generating its own distinctive product and by producing an opposed, harmful effect. The doctor who is best able to prevent disease is also best able to produce disease, and similarly the just man is not only most skilled at protecting money and property but also best at stealing it. These examples presuppose a principle related to SC, but one that stresses the harmful abilities of a craft:

HC   For any craft C with product P, the practitioner of C is the person most capable of destroying P.

though it supports Gilbert's conclusions about the importance of shared action for ethics and political philosophy.

This principle seems acceptable to Polemarchus because he believes that justice is a craft that both benefits friends and harms enemies. Such a craft will not only benefit friends by producing its distinctive product, as SC tells us, but can also do harm by destroying that product. The second section of the refutation of Polemarchus ends when he rejects the result that the just man is a kind of thief, one who is especially good at stealing money as a way of helping his friends and harming his enemies. Polemarchus has good reason to reject this result because it shows the just man as precisely the sort of person who would not make a good partner. The just man cannot be the sort of person who is good at destroying partnerships by theft or fraud.

The fourth section of the refutation of Polemarchus will see Socrates revisiting HC and the question of whether the just person will do harm. Before this, though, the third section of the refutation intervenes. Here Socrates queries Polemarchus' understanding of friends and enemies. The latter first identifies a friend as one who seems useful while an enemy is one who seems harmful (*poneros*). When Socrates points out that humans are capable of misidentifying the useful and harmful, the good and the bad, Polemarchus revises his account of friend and enemy: the friend is the one who both seems and is useful and good, and the enemy both seems and is harmful and bad. With this revision in place, Socrates summarizes the current version of Polemarchus' position: "So you want us to add something to what we said before about justice, when we said that it is just to treat friends well and enemies badly. You want us to add to this that it is just to treat well a friend who is good and to harm an enemy who is bad?" (335a6-9). The third section of the refutation thus draws our attention to the distinction between being and seeming good and identifies friend and foe with good and bad respectively.

After clarifying Polemarchus' understanding of friends and enemies, Socrates completes the refutation of the proposal that justice is giving to each what is owed by helping friends and harming enemies. This fourth section of the refutation of Polemarchus falls into four subsections. First, Socrates gains assent to the idea that harming humans always involves making them worse in terms of virtue. Whenever humans are harmed, they become less virtuous. Second, Socrates conducts a brisk induction on crafts and natural powers. The use of a craft such as music or horsemanship will not make people worse at the craft, and it is not the characteristic activity of heat but of cold to cool. Similarly, justice in its use will not make people worse at virtue, and the *ergon* of justice will not involve harming people. Third, Socrates concludes that since the *ergon* of justice does not include harming people, it is not just to harm anyone. Finally, Socrates recruits Polemarchus to fight with him in defense of Simonides and other wise men against anyone who should assert that Simonides believes it is just to harm enemies. Our attention will focus on the second and third subsections since these are relevant to the relation of justice to craft and the characteristic activity of the just person.[20]

---

[20] The first section has drawn criticism from those who see an equivocation in the use of the concept of harm. Socrates and Polemarchus agree that when horses and dogs are harmed, they are also made worse

The second sub-section compares justice to crafts and natural powers in order to characterize the *ergon* of justice. The order of presentation of the items compared should be observed. First, Socrates and Polemarchus agree that musicians are not able to make others unmusical by use of the craft of music, and horsemen do not make others less skillful with horses by using their craft. A similar claim is presented about justice: just men cannot make others unjust by the use of justice. Following the agreement about justice comes two observations about natural powers and their *erga* or characteristic activities: it is not the *ergon* of heat but of cold to cool things, and it is not the *ergon* of dryness to make things wet. The presence of the final set of observations about natural powers requires explanation. Up to now, Socrates has employed comparisons between justice and crafts. Why should he now place justice in relation to heat and dryness? Justice would seem to have even less to do with such natural powers than with human practices such as music and horsemanship.

I propose that Socrates deploys the examples of heat and dryness because these natural powers, unlike crafts, are self-transmitting powers and thus answer better to his sense of how justice affects others. The assertion that a craft will not make people less proficient at the craft apparently depends on a particular conception of how crafts are passed on through instruction from teacher to student. An expert musician uses her craft not simply in playing difficult pieces of music but also in providing instruction in the elements of musical practice: given the goal of producing harmonious sound, how much should one tighten the strings, and what is the best approach to striking the strings? To the extent that a good musician possesses not simply divine inspiration but a craft, we expect that such a musician will be able to transmit her craft to students through the process of instruction. This seems to be the background to Socrates and Polemarchus' agreement at 335c that the musician and horseman using their crafts as teachers will not make their students worse musicians or horsemen. Such instruction is not, however, a necessary part of the craft securing its distinctive product.[21] Music's

with respect to their virtues, but a different sense of harm is used when Socrates speaks of harm to human beings, who can be harmed by being unjustly deprived of their wealth or reputation. See Allan (1940, 25) and Cross and Woozley (1966, 20–2). This objection is not convincing because it does not allow for the possibility that Socrates is already working with an unconventional sense of what harm is for a human being. Later in the *Republic* Socrates will defend the paradoxical position that a just man deprived of his reputation, money, and health is better off than an unjust man who enjoys all external and bodily goods. For Socrates, a person's standing with respect to virtue is the single most important element in a person's well-being or lack thereof. The importance of virtue over other goods as elements in well-being explains why Socrates believes that a person is harmed only if that person is changed for the worse with respect to virtue. This is a controversial position, to be sure, and the passage 335b-c does next to nothing to motivate it. But when Socrates suggests that humans are harmed only if they are made worse with respect to virtue, we should take this not as an equivocation on the meaning of harm but as a compressed and suggestive indication of a position to be explored later.

[21] Young (1974) argues that at 335c Socrates is asking whether a given craft produces in its objects the distinctive product of that craft. However, this is based on a strained reading of *aphippous* at 335c11. Young takes *aphippous* to refer to horses who are affected by the craft of horsemanship. But as *Protagoras* 350a5-6, Xenophon *Hellenica* 3.4.12, and Plutarch *Aristides* 11.7 indicate, the adjective *aphippos* refers to persons unskilled in dealing with horses or terrain unsuited for the use of cavalry, not to horses who are deficient

distinctive product is musical sound, and horsemanship operates primarily in training and working with horses. These distinctive products can be secured without transmitting the craft to anyone else through instruction. The case is different with heat and dryness, which are such as to make the things they affect hot and dry. In carrying out their characteristic activities, they pass on to their objects the relevant powers of heating and drying other objects. These natural powers are like that of the Magnesian stone mentioned in the *Ion* in that the exercise of their function involves making their objects share in the same power, as a stone exposed to heat becomes hot and thus capable of heating other stones. These self-transmitting powers are brought in not simply as random examples of the sort of thing that happens with crafts and justice; Socrates mentions them at 335d3-9 as helping to explain why justice will not make others unjust: "For [*gar*] it is not the function of heat to cool things, but rather of its opposite?" "Yes." "Nor is it the function of dryness to wet things, but rather of its opposite?" "Indeed." "Nor the function of the good to harm but of the opposite." If Socrates mentions these self-transmitting natural powers as part of an explanation for the fact that justice in operation will not make others unjust, he must understand justice to work like a self-transmitting power. Presumably, these natural powers are brought in at 335d as an explanation of the fact that just people do not make others unjust because they provide a better explication of the way that justice does not harm others than do the crafts of music and horse training. Just human beings, by using justice, make others just as a necessary part of their carrying out the *ergon* of justice, however that is conceived.

The description of justice operating on the model of a self-transmitting power rather than on the model of a craft allows us to answer two objections to Socrates' argument. First, Andrew Jeffrey claims that Socrates improperly assumes that the just person will take on the role of an instructor in some craft. This assumption is not one that Polemarchus must accept; justice as Polemarchus originally conceives it is not the sort of thing one uses to teach one's enemies how to be more just. For Polemarchus it is part of being just to defeat one's enemies and thus make them less able to help friends and harm enemies; on this view, the point of justice is certainly not to make enemies more skillful by instruction.[22] But Socrates is not committed to describing justice as a craft that one teaches to others; the comparison to heat and dryness suggests an alternate model of how justice affects others. Clearly, Socrates has not said enough yet to convince Polemarchus or anyone else that justice should be conceived as a self-transmitting power. He has yet to describe any model, besides teaching, which would allow justice to be transmitted to others. Even so, he is not confined to describing justice as the sort of thing that affects others only by teaching them to be just. Second, both Jeffrey and Charles Young present a counter-example to the claim that a craft in use never makes others less skillful, a case that we can refer to as that of the Overly Skillful

---

in their specific excellence. Accordingly, the adjective at 335c11 refers to men who are made worse at dealing with horses.

[22] Jeffrey (1979, 66).

Instructor. A virtuoso musician plays difficult pieces of music with such precision that an aspiring student is discouraged from attempting to make progress in the craft, seeing the great distance from the valley of his own incompetence to the mountaintop of the virtuoso's accomplishments; or the virtuoso's bravura execution of showy passages encourages a student to attempt similar displays, with untoward effect on the student's playing. In either case, the musician's use of his craft has the effect, unintentional perhaps but real, of making the student less musical.[23] This objection presupposes, though, that the only way for the just person to affect others is by instruction in justice. The comparison of justice to heat and dryness suggests that when the just person acts, making others just rather than unjust is a necessary part of carrying out the *ergon* of justice. Again, the central ideas behind Socrates' conception of justice are merely indicated and not explicated; the argument loses force due to the compression of these ideas. But this is to be expected in the first book of ten devoted to an exploration of justice.

This construal of justice as a self-transmitting power allows us to find a more charitable reading of Socrates' argument that the just person will do no harm. In the third subsection of the examination of justice and harm, Socrates wishes to draw the consequences secured by the preceding discussion. If harming humans entails making them worse in virtue and if justice in use does not make others unjust, then justice will never be used to harm others. To describe the line of thought followed by Socrates more precisely, it is not the function of the just man to harm anyone, friend or otherwise (335d12-13). Socrates then rephrases this conclusion a few lines later: "For it has become clear to us that it is never just to harm anyone" (335e5-6). Socrates here treats a statement about the *ergon* of the just man as implying the general claim that doing harm is unjust. He takes the statement

(I) It is no part of the *ergon* of the just man to harm anyone

to imply the following statement:

(II) It is unjust to harm anyone.

The transition from (I) to (II) deserves closer attention, since on some plausible interpretations of (I) it is not possible to infer from it (II). The function of the doctor does not include breaking bones; it is to heal the sick. In most cases breaking a person's

---

[23] "I know a person, for example, who stopped playing the piano when she first heard Rubinstein play, thinking that, since she would never be able to play that well, there was no point in playing at all. She stopped practicing, with the result that today she is a poor pianist. This is a case about which we could say that a musician, however inadvertently, unintentionally, and blamelessly, has, by practicing music, made someone unskilled in music"; Young (1974, 101). Jeffrey relates the second sort of case of the Overly Skilled Instructor: "A story about the cellist Piatigorsky illustrates the point. Noting that a talented student's playing deteriorated the more virtuosic his own playing of passages for demonstration, he resorted to deliberate mistakes. The student improved greatly and observed on graduating with distinction: 'Piatigorsky is certainly a fine teacher. But what a lousy cellist!' Would it not be correct to say that before Piatigorsky became 'a lousy cellist' his expertise *qua* performer made the student worse, that he made him worse *tēi mousikēi* [by the craft of music]?"; Jeffrey (1979, 69, n. 26).

bones will be a way of impairing his health, and in such cases a doctor will not break the patient's bones. But in some cases healing the sick may involve breaking or cutting bones, as in an amputation or other surgery. The function of the doctor does not include breaking bones, but it does not exclude it either; in cases where breaking bones is a necessary means to the end set by the doctor's *ergon*, the doctor may and indeed must break bones. Similarly, on some conceptions of justice, doing harm is not part of the nature of justice but is not excluded by it. If the nature of justice is to give to each person what is owed or appropriate, just punishment may involve inflicting evils on a wrongdoer. A criminal serving a life sentence in prison has lost the good of freedom and thus is harmed: yet on this conception of justice that is simply an aspect of receiving what is owed or appropriate.

Despite the prevalence of this conception of justice, Socrates thinks that establishing (I) allows him to infer (II); because doing harm is not part of the function of the just person, justice always excludes doing harm to anyone. Within the context of the refutation of Polemarchus, his confidence in this inference must rest on the belief that justice is related to harm in the way that the craft of medicine is related to disease. Doing justice to another person always benefits that person or at least does not do harm, just as the doctor's treatment of a patient produces health or at least does not create more disease in the patient. The comparison of justice to heat and dryness suggests that justice affects its objects by driving out its opposite, injustice, and making them just, a process which excludes harm. To specify the general idea that justice operates by making its objects just, we may recall that Socrates typically describes just punishment as benefiting the person punished by removing injustice from the soul.[24] Although we do not find an explicit discussion of why it is never just to do harm, the comparison of justice at 335d to heat and dryness suggests that he would explain the injustice of doing harm by asserting that justice in action will affect others by making them just, a result that is never harmful.

Having attended carefully to the arguments that make up the refutation of Polemarchus, we can sum up the important results of this section of Book 1. Socrates at 332e introduces what I take to be the leading question of Book 1, namely "What is the function or characteristic activity through which justice operates?" We do not find a definitive answer to this question, but an important candidate-answer has been brought to our attention: justice operates in the activity of forming and maintaining partnerships and associations. This answer has not found approval from Socrates because, given his present understanding of partnerships as reducible to activities which can be carried out alone, it seems to conflict with the principle SC. Any activity for which we form partnerships seems to be carried out better by some craft-practitioner

---

[24] At *Republic* 445a, Socrates poses the question of whether being unjust is profitable as long as one escapes punishment, and thus is not made better by chastisement. The link between punishment and being made better is present as well at 591b and in Socrates' exchange with Polus at *Gorgias* 472e–481a. Socrates' argument in the *Gorgias* that the unjust man is benefited by being punished relies on the claim at 478d that just punishment frees the soul from the greatest evil, vice, and makes it more just.

acting alone. Due to this apparent conflict with SC, the proposal that the activity of justice is found in partnerships is rejected. However, Socrates and Polemarchus do agree that justice can be characterized as a trait that does no harm. The argument for this conclusion is interpreted most charitably if we assume that Socrates thinks of justice as a self-transmitting power, one that carries out its characteristic activity by making those exposed to it just. As we will see, these concepts of the function of justice and of justice as a self-transmitting power will find further application in the course of the *Republic* and in the discussion of the teleology of just actions.

If Socrates believes that justice is a self-transmitting power, it would explain why he objected to Cephalus' and Polemarchus' descriptions of justice. Both father and son focus on justice's provision of the wrong sort of benefits in social interactions: speaking the truth, or returning deposited property, or giving material aid to allies. The just man will perform these actions in (almost) all cases, but this is by way of carrying out his characteristic activity as a just person, namely partaking in partnerships and thus aiding others in becoming just. If justice operates to make others just through the medium of partnerships and associations, then Polemarchus is right to assert that justice benefits friends, those with whom we form useful partnerships and associations. But justice affects us in a way that is more profound than he suspected. In achieving a just partnership with others, we do not merely gain a safe place to deposit money and reliable partners for exchange of services. We gain companions in the lifelong task of becoming just and virtuous ourselves.

4

The Defense of Justice in *Republic* 1

4.1 Introduction

Our larger concern in this book is Plato's functional teleology of action: the understanding of human action as oriented toward ends or purposes which, in some cases, are not intended as goals. In considering the ascent passage in the *Symposium* we observed a particular case of this understanding of action. By giving birth in the beautiful and thus exercising the function of eros at different stages of his development, the philosopher-lover acts for the sake of gaining insight into the Form of Beauty. In order to apply the same understanding of action to the *Republic*, it is necessary to identify a function or characteristic activity linked with justice. Our analysis of the refutation of Polemarchus has brought to our attention several concepts which will play a role in the teleological understanding of action in the *Republic*. Socrates asks Polemarchus to specify the function or characteristic activity which allows the just person to be especially beneficial. Although the two are not able to agree on the nature of this function, they consider a promising candidate, namely the activity of engaging in partnerships. In the refutation of Polemarchus we also find Socrates introducing the notion that justice is a craft or comparable to a craft, although his arguments are most charitably treated by assuming that he does not conceive of justice strictly on the lines of such crafts as medicine or music but as a self-transmitting power.

The refutation of Polemarchus, of course, occupies only four Stephanus pages; even if the results of the previous chapter are accepted, this is slender support on which to build a larger interpretation of the *Republic*. In order to develop further the basis for a teleological understanding of action in the dialogue, we turn first to the further course of Book 1. Following the refutation of Polemarchus we find Thrasymachus' entry into the dialogue and his iconoclastic account of justice as the interest of the stronger. Socrates then refutes Thrasymachus and provides his own positive arguments for the value of justice; he wishes to show that justice and not injustice benefits a human being and thus that the life of a just person is better and more choiceworthy than the life of an unjust. The present chapter will consider these aspects of Socrates' defense of justice in *Republic* 1: Thrasymachus' conception of justice; Socrates' refutation of Thrasymachus; and the positive arguments for justice. In these later sections of Book 1, the concepts developed in the refutation of Polemarchus reappear. As we will see, the concepts of function, of partnership as the special activity associated with justice, and of self-transmitting power play a crucial role in the arguments developed by Thrasymachus and Socrates in Book 1.

If Book 1 of the *Republic* provides us with insight into the function associated with just actions, then it puts us in a position to sketch a further application of the for-the-sake-of relation discussed in Chapter 2. That relation holds between actions that carry out a given function and certain valuable results of those actions, which, even if they are not intended as such, qualify as ends for the sake of which those actions are performed. By drawing upon the positive arguments which Socrates employs near the end of Book 1, the for-the-sake-of relation can be specified provisionally as holding between just actions which carry out the function of forming partnerships and associations and the positive results of promoting friendship and concord within the associations to which the just agent belongs. This account of the functional teleology of just actions appears in Book 1 only as a rough sketch; the arguments of Book 1 are pronounced at 354b-c to be insufficient since they are not based on insight into what justice is. Even so, this provisional account of the ends of just action will orient our account of the defense of justice in Book 4.

4.2 Thrasymachus on Justice

At the end of the refutation of Polemarchus, Socrates and Polemarchus agree that the just man will not do harm to anyone. This agreement is based implicitly on the conception of justice as a self-transmitting power. Like dryness and heat, justice acts by making its object like itself. This description of justice as a self-transmitting power leaves unexplained why it is that the just man is good, as Socrates and Polemarchus agree at 335d10, and why it is that the just man benefits others rather than harms them when he makes them just. If the just man is foolish and weak rather than wise and strong, so that making others just is a way of harming them, then Socrates' entire position will be undermined. These are precisely the issues that take center stage in the rest of *Republic* 1 in the wake of Thrasymachus' forceful intervention and his account of justice as the interest of the stronger and the good of another.[1] As we will see, Socrates refutes Thrasymachus by pointing out that he cannot affirm that justice is the advantage of the stronger or ruler, that ruling is a craft, and also that crafts work to the advantage not of the craft-practitioner or ruler but of the object of the craft or the ruled. Before considering this refutation in more detail, it is necessary to examine Thrasymachus' conception of justice and his arguments for it. Thrasymachus' account of justice contains the

---

[1] Whether Thrasymachus can consistently describe justice both as the interest of the stronger and as the good of another has been much debated. For reasons of space I will assume without argument that Thrasymachus speaks most accurately when he describes justice as the interest of the stronger, namely the ruler. Justice is the good of another not in every case but from the perspective of non-ruling citizens. See Kerferd (1947) and Nicholson (1974). This issue is not central to the claims of this chapter, though. What is important here is that Socrates refutes the claim that justice is the interest of the stronger by using the assertion that ruling is a craft and by providing an account of how crafts operate, not by setting forth any detailed account of justice.

insight that justice operates in the realm of partnerships, especially the partnership of ruler and ruled.

The important advance in understanding justice within the discussion between Thrasymachus and Socrates is made by Thrasymachus himself. When he first bursts into the conversation like a beast falling upon its prey, he tells Socrates to give his own answer to the question of what justice is and instructs him not to give such answers as "the necessary" or "the useful" or "the advantageous" (336c-d). Commentators frequently remark upon Thrasymachus' choleric and arrogant temper; less often do they consider the thought lying behind his instructions. Such phrases as "the necessary" or "the useful" are so general as to apply to almost any right action carried out in any context. Thrasymachus expects that a satisfactory account of justice will be more specific than these laudatory phrases. After the sophist announces proudly that justice is the advantage of the stronger, Socrates asks a series of questions designed to encourage Thrasymachus to unfold the meaning of his formula. Socrates asks whether this formula implies that a champion wrestler eating meat is just, under the assumption that the stronger in question is someone who is strong in body. To fend off this ridiculous interpretation of his idea, Thrasymachus tells us that the stronger whose advantage is just are those who rule political communities, be they democrats or tyrants or oligarchs. All these rulers make laws that work to their own advantage, and the ruled benefit their rulers by doing what is just as this is defined by law. For Thrasymachus, then, justice as the advantage of the stronger shows itself in a very particular context, namely in political associations and partnerships where the relations between ruler and ruled are mediated by law. We may ascribe to Thrasymachus the idea that the object of justice, in the sense of the area of life it governs, is the field of political associations. The distinctive product of justice is the advantage of the stronger party to such associations. He will also claim that a proper account of justice, even if his own proposal is found wanting, must be more specific than the qualities he forbade Socrates to use. A proper account will gain this specificity by relating justice to political associations and partnerships.

Socrates replies to Thrasymachus' initial statement of his position by asking whether rulers ever make mistakes (339b-c). As they make laws and issue edicts aiming at their own advantage, do they ever mistakenly command actions that in fact work against their advantage? Once he understands the question fully, Thrasymachus replies that rulers will not make such mistakes. The true ruler, or the ruler in the precise sense, is the one who exercises a craft in ruling. Just as the true doctor, the doctor who acts in accordance with the craft of medicine, will not make mistakes, so the true ruler always commands what is to his advantage. As we will see in the following section, this set of statements allows Socrates to catch Thrasymachus in a contradiction. He points out that crafts work to the advantage not of the craft-practitioner but to the advantage of the person or object ruled by the craft. Thrasymachus' true ruler, the one who exercises a craft of ruling, will not work for his own advantage. According to this train of thought, the laws and other institutions defining justice that flow from this true ruler will not produce the advantage of the stronger and of the ruler but of the weaker and the ruled. In setting out Thrasymachus' position, though, we should note that the question of crafts and their necessary features comes into play because he believes that a strong ruler will not weaken himself by making mistakes in the pursuit of his own advantage. Such a ruler will possess a craft of ruling.

Because Thrasymachus believes that the true ruler is one who possesses a craft of ruling, I take it that Thrasymachus is not a legalist or conventionalist, one who believes that justice is defined strictly by the laws and other conventions of a given society.[2] The option of legalism is presented to Thrasymachus at 340c, when Socrates asks him whether he wishes to say that justice is what the stronger believes to be to his advantage, whether or not it is in fact so. Thrasymachus refuses this option at 340c6-7, apparently because on this account the ruler is not stronger: "Do you think I would call someone who is in error stronger at the very moment he errs?" This indicates that for Thrasymachus it is possible to be in error about justice even as one sets up the conventions that define justice; hence, he is no conventionalist. Also, Thrasymachus believes that the laws made by some actual rulers in actual cities may differ from what is just, the advantage of the stronger; hence, he is no legalist. Of course, this does not lessen the distance between Thrasymachus' conception of justice as a tool for the exploitation of the weak by the strong and the ordinary understanding of justice as morally binding rules that promote the good of all in society. For Thrasymachus, justice is an objective matter about which it is possible to go wrong and also possible to have knowledge. However, the point of justice in his view is to serve the interests of the strong, not to protect the interests of all.

As noted, Socrates attempts to refute Thrasymachus by pointing to an inconsistency in his position: the true ruler pursues his own interest using a craft, but crafts do not promote the interest of those who exercise them. This is a genuine problem for Thrasymachus' position as he has stated it, but it is not one that he sees as fatal to his basic conception of justice. He replies to Socrates' questions by setting forth in his second speech (343b1-344c9) a more detailed account of justice as a trait which, along with its opposite injustice, can only be defined in relation to the context of partnerships and associations, especially the political association of rule. He rebuts Socrates' claim that every craft examines and aims at the good of the ruled by proposing the craft of shepherding. Thrasymachus points out that shepherds fatten their sheep not with the goal of benefiting them but of serving their own and their masters' interests, thus reminding us of the place of the Greek shepherd within a larger household; the shepherd may well have been a slave who cared for the sheep as part of his service to the master of the household. In order to understand the conduct of the shepherd toward his sheep, it is necessary to consider the shepherd first as pursuing his own interests, as being the ruler of the sheep, and second as pursuing the interest of his master, in

---

[2] For discussion of this point, see Hourani (1962, 110–20), Kerferd (1964), and Hadgopoulos (1973).

the shepherd's capacity as one ruled (343b1-4). In both cases, it is the interest of the stronger, or ruler, that explains the shepherd's conduct. The same pattern is asserted to hold when we consider rulers in cities, those who truly rule (343b5); they consider their subjects in the same light as do shepherds their sheep. Seen in this way, justice and just actions serve the interests of the stronger, those who rule, and work against the interests of the weaker, those who obey. The important relationship is not the simple one of craft-practitioner to object of craft, the shepherd in relation to the sheep, but the network of associations contained within a political community (shepherd and master, citizens and rulers).

This strategy of examining mundane associations and extrapolating from them to political life is present also in Thrasymachus' argument to the effect that injustice is more beneficial than justice. The just man has less than the unjust in a range of every-day associations: in contracts and other partnerships (343d4-5) the unjust man profits while the just comes away having less. In bearing the burdens of public life through taxes and holding office the just man allows his affairs to suffer. In contrast, the unjust man uses his injustice in the context of public life to benefit himself and his friends. And finally, perfect or complete injustice is found in the one man who achieves despotic rule over the city by enslaving his fellow citizens (344b5-c3). This description of justice and injustice suggests that Thrasymachus sees both as arising whenever two or more people form an unequal association structured by some formal or informal agreements, conventions, or laws. Such an association that gives rise to justice will be unequal and will be an association between one who has more and one who has less, because in a fully equal association there would be no stronger party. Justice would not appear in such an association since it would not contain the advantage of the stronger. Given such an unequal association, though, one in which one party benefits unfairly, we have the context or framework within human life of justice. Justice is seen in actions taken by the weaker party which are faithful to the terms of the association and which therefore benefit the stronger party. Injustice is seen in actions by the stronger party which establish and exploit the terms of the association and which therefore benefit the stronger party. Tyranny or despotic rule is the height of injustice and the association that affords the greatest benefit to the stronger, unjust party. By providing this account of the framework for justice and injustice, Thrasymachus has provided an answer to Socrates' question at 332e3-4. The action or work in which the just man is most beneficial is the action of ruling and being ruled. Thrasymachus' answer contains a disconcerting twist, of course; the just man is most beneficial to someone else, namely the unjust man.

4.3 The Refutation of Thrasymachus

As mentioned already, Socrates attempts to refute Thrasymachus. He asks a series of questions which lead the sophist to fill out his conception of justice. In the process of doing so, Thrasymachus commits himself to an inconsistent set of beliefs about just-ice. He accepts the following four beliefs about justice:

TJ1   Justice is the advantage of the stronger (338c1-2, 338e6-339a3).

TJ2   The stronger are the rulers in a given society (338e1-6).

TJ3   Rulers exercise a craft of ruling when they set up laws that establish what is best for the rulers (340e8-341a2).

TJ4   No craft of ruling produces the advantage of the practitioner of the craft, the ruler (346d9-e2).

The first two beliefs are asserted by Thrasymachus himself in his initial account of just-ice and the third in reply to Socrates' first round of questioning, when he asserts that the ruler in the precise sense possesses a craft of ruling analogous to the doctor's craft. The final belief is one that Thrasymachus assents to reluctantly at 346d9-e2 as Socrates argues that every craft, with the exception of the wage-earner's craft, benefits the ruled, the weaker party and the object of the craft, and not the ruler, the stronger party who exercises the craft.

Like the refutation of Polemarchus, the refutation of Thrasymachus is notable more for the way in which significant concepts are brought on stage than for the substantive results it secures. Socrates succeeds in refuting Thrasymachus in the sense that he shows that Thrasymachus lacks knowledge on the subject of justice. He does not suc-ceed in showing that Thrasymachus' proposed definition of justice as the advantage of the stronger is false. The refutation would demonstrate this only if rulers always or typically employ a craft of ruling that meets Socrates' criteria: a body of practical knowledge that benefits only the object of the craft or person ruled and not the craft-practitioner and ruler. Thrasymachus could have maintained his position to greater effect if he had expanded on his example of the shepherd who feeds and waters his sheep but does so for the ultimate benefit of his master. As we will see in the next chap-ter, Glaucon and Adeimantus perceive that the full resources of a Thrasymachean account of justice have not yet been exhausted.

Although the refutation of Thrasymachus does not settle the issue of whether justice is the advantage of the stronger, it shows that Socrates shares Thrasymachus' interest in a particular sort of partnership, the sort that involves rule by one party over another. As indicated in the previous section, Thrasymachus understands justice as arising when partnerships and associations are formed, especially in the partnership that is a political community whose laws are set by the rulers. He introduces the parallel between craft-practitioners and rulers at 340d1-341a4 to emphasize that the true ruler will not make mistakes in crafting laws for his own benefit. Socrates accepts the paral-lel; in the following pages he treats crafts in general as examples of a stronger party exercising rule over a weaker, as at 342c8-9: "Now, surely, Thrasymachus, the crafts rule over and are stronger than the things of which they are the crafts?" Examples of this pattern include navigation, medicine, horsebreeding, and shepherding.

To illustrate Socrates' acceptance of the parallel between ruling and use of a craft, we may examine his use of the example of the navigator. He focuses on this example in order to provide a counter-example to Thrasymachus' description of the ruler as one who uses his craft to benefit himself. The navigator described by Socrates at 341c10-d4 sails on a boat and is a partner with a group of sailors, but he is not for that reason engaging in the same action as they are. "What about a navigator? Is a navigator in the precise sense a ruler of sailors or a sailor?" "A ruler of sailors." "We shouldn't, I think, take into account the fact that he sails in a ship, and he shouldn't be called a sailor for that reason, for it isn't because of his sailing that he is called a navigator, but because of his craft and his rule over sailors?" "That's true." This short exchange is used by Socrates to undermine Thrasymachus' claim that justice is the advantage of the stronger; he makes the point that a craftsman in the strict sense is what he is not because he is paid for his efforts but because of his knowledge and the benefit he provides for those who stand in need of his craft. But the passage also makes the point that a navigator in the strict sense is not simply one sailor among others but is engaged in a different activity, namely ruling over sailors. To expand on this point, the navigator and the sailors are engaged in a type of partnership which requires that one or more partners carry out a range of first-order activities involved in sailing (rowing, looking for rocks in the water, setting sails) while another partner carries out the distinct action of ruling over the sailors. This action of ruling over sailors is not simply sharing in the actions of rowing, looking for danger, and setting sails; it involves possessing knowledge about the proper route to sail, how to hold a boat to that route safely, and imparting directions to the sailors as they carry out their first-order activities in order to achieve this.

This action of a navigator ruling over sailors is of course pressed into service frequently by Plato and others to serve as an image of wider forms of rule, and in particular as an image of political rule.[3] The ruler in such a political partnership will co-operate with his fellow citizens in the life of the city, but the ruler and the ruled will each carry out their distinct actions in somewhat the way that a navigator, a lookout on the prow of a ship, and a group of rowers will coordinate their actions. But just as the navigator, the lookout, and the rowers are not simply engaged in the actions of steering a ship, scanning the waves for obstacles, and rowing but are also coordinating their actions together as partners in the activity of sailing a ship, so the various citizens in their

[3] Pindar ends Pythian 10, offered in praise of the ruling family of Thessaly, with the following words celebrating his patron Thorax: "But, even as gold showeth its nature, when tried by the touchstone, so it is with an upright mind. We shall further praise his [Thorax's] noble brethren, in that they increase and exalt the State of Thessaly; and it is in the hands of high-born men that there resteth the good piloting [*kubernasies*] of cities, while they pass from sire to son"; translation by John Sandys, *Pindar* (Cambridge, Massachusetts: Harvard University Press, 1915), 295. Aristotle in chapter 2 of Book 1 of the *Politics* illustrates the notion of a master's rule over his slave by describing the slave as a living tool for the master, just as a lookout is a living tool for the navigator of a ship; see *Politics* 1253b23-33. Xenophon presents the young Cyrus agreeing in conversation with his father that a man should make himself worthy of rule before attempting to arrange the affairs of his household or of a state. As one of several instances offered in support of this claim, Cyrus agrees that a man should not expect to lead ships to safety by taking the helm before he learns navigation; see *Cyropaedia* I.6.6-7.

distinct offices are not simply paying taxes, serving on juries, and enacting laws but also are coordinating their actions as partners in political life. This coordination of activity when achieved both by ruler and ruled as partners in political life counts as one specific way of carrying out the characteristic activities of the human soul, namely deliberating, caring for one's body and external affairs, and ruling (353d3-10).

Socrates does not spell out these features of the craft of navigation, nor does he assert any parallels between navigation and justice. He introduces the example of navigation in order to claim that crafts, as bodies of practical knowledge, do not seek the advantage of the stronger, the ruler, but that of the weaker, the ruled (342e). However, Socrates' reliance on this example shows that he is able to adjust his favored conceptual model, the concept of a craft, to the field of partnerships and to the particular partnership of political rule. And as we will see in the next section, the use of the concept of partnership is not limited to the refutation of Thrasymachus. Socrates takes a page out of Thrasymachus' book by treating partnerships as the context for just and unjust actions in his positive arguments for the value of justice in the final pages of Book 1.

4.4 Socrates' Positive Arguments for Justice

At 348b Socrates shifts from refutation of the claim that justice is the advantage of the stronger to arguing for the positive claim that the life of the just is more profitable and choiceworthy than the life of the unjust. It is noteworthy that from this point on Socrates speaks of justice as related to the context of associations and rule. His first positive argument for the value of justice speaks of two just people taking part in a just action on equal terms, with neither party having more or less. A just person will expect to have more than an unjust person when they associate in some action. This argument accepts the basic framework for justice set up by Thrasymachus, namely action carried out in some association, but attempts to dispute the latter's claim that the just person will always get the short end of the stick in such an association. His second argument places justice firmly in the context of associations and partnerships: justice is the trait that is responsible for friendship and concord in groups and in the relations between the different parts of an individual's soul. His third argument describes justice as the virtue that perfects the soul's characteristic activities of deliberating, caring for the body or for external affairs, and ruling. Here again justice is found in the soul's associations, either with the body or with other human beings in the activity of ruling. Although Socrates draws conclusions about the value of justice that are directly opposed to Thrasymachus', he does so by accepting the sophist's insight concerning the particular activity and context in which justice is located.

The first of Socrates' positive arguments relies on a comparison of doubtful worth between justice and crafts such as medicine and music to conclude that justice is similar to wisdom (349b-351a). The just man wishes to outdo or have more than (*pleonek-tein*) the unjust but is content to accept equal shares in a just action with another just man. The unjust man tries to outdo both the just and the unjust. A similar pattern holds for the musician and the doctor; they try to outdo the person who lacks craft-expertise and is unlike them while accepting equal shares of performances of craft-activities with the person who is similarly wise and is like them. The unjust person is compared to the person who lacks craft-expertise because he or she wants to outdo and have more than everyone else, both just and unjust. Therefore, the unjust person is likened to the ignorant and bad while the just is likened to the wise and good.

This argument—for convenience it will be referred to as the non-pleonectic argument—is of little value because it is unclear what to make of the notion of "having more than" or outdoing another when it comes to two musicians tuning their lyres or two doctors prescribing food for a patient. It is not clear whether two doctors who prescribe the same diet for a patient are accepting equal shares in an action in a sense that is importantly similar to a just person who is happy to take equal shares with another just person in a common project.[4] Doctors and other craft-practitioners can be expected to agree with each other on how best to promote the good of the subject matter on which their craft operates; so much is required by the objective nature of a craft as a body of practical knowledge. They may even share with each other a common devotion to the good of the subject matter of their craft.[5] But this does not amount to doctors and other craft-practitioners refusing to compete with other doctors or accepting the ties of mutual support that we expect will unite just persons engaged in political community, the sort of reciprocal support that leads Thrasymachus to speak of justice as another person's good. The sort of agreement and unity of expert opinion to be expected from doctors devoted to the care of their patients need not extend to the sort of agreement and unity to be found in just people who recognize each other as fitting partners in a common project. Thus, the traits typical of crafts, namely commitment to objectivity and devotion to the good of a defined subject matter, do not capture what is distinctive of justice. As is said in a different context while commenting on military crafts, the Spartans take it upon themselves to outdo everyone else in matters relating to war (*Laches* 183a1). If a non-Spartan is an expert in military strategy, this will not keep the Spartan expert from seeking to outdo him in this craft, for instance by

---

[4] See Gutglueck (1988) for a careful discussion of the semantics of the Greek verb *pleonektein*, commonly translated as "to outdo" or "to have more than." As Gutglueck shows, Socrates equivocates by moving from the standard sense of *pleonektein*, having or taking more than one's share of material resources, to a non-standard sense of acting in a way that goes beyond proper measure in such contexts as choosing the right amount of tension in tuning a lyre or choosing the right amount of medicine to prescribe a patient.

[5] Salkever (1993) brings out this aspect of crafts; in commenting on the non-pleonectic argument he notes that craft-practitioners must commit themselves to pursuing certain goods internal to the practice of their crafts. Here Salkever appeals to the notion of goods internal to a practice set forth by Alasdair MacIntyre (1981). Such craft-practitioners will accept an ethical horizon foreign to Thrasymachus' unjust man, who is motivated by pleonectic desire to pursue political power, honor, and money. Even if we allow that doctors and musicians will share this ethical horizon defined by their allegiance to the goods internal to their respective crafts, this ethical outlook will center on healing the sick and playing music, not on promoting the good of other craft-practitioners as partners in a common endeavor.

conquering him and his city on the field of battle.[6] Justice differs from crafts by express-ing itself in an association of mutual support, as Socrates himself will suggest in his second argument.

Socrates' second argument proposes that just people are more powerful and capable of acting than the unjust (351b-352d). This argument, for convenience the band of thieves argument, builds upon one assumption of the non-pleonectic argument, namely that justice makes possible a form of noncompetitive cooperation between just persons. At 351b, he asks Thrasymachus whether an unjust city will attempt to enslave other cities. The latter affirms that this is so; given his praise of the tyrant as living the best and most unjust life, he conceives of the unjust city as dominating all other cities and holding them in slavery. Socrates' next question asks whether there is a connec-tion between the political supremacy Thrasymachus admires and justice: "Will a city that becomes stronger than another have this power without justice, or is justice neces-sary for it to have this power?" (351b7-9). The following considerations are marshaled to support the latter alternative: a group of people acting for a common goal, whether as a military formation or even a band of thieves, will not be able to accomplish their end if they are riven by injustice, the characteristic activity of which (*ergon*, 351d8) is to produce hatred and conflicts in groups. Justice, on the other hand, produces concord and friendship. Since the characteristic activity of injustice is to produce conflict, its presence in a single person will result in that person losing control over himself (351d-e). The opposite occurs in the case of the just, who are more capable or powerful in acting. In this argument-sketch Socrates articulates the results of being just in terms of being powerful and increased ability to act effectively. Justice is valuable because it promotes harmony within individuals and groups and thereby allows us to act more capably. Justice is connected in this second argument to a particular object or context of action, namely the association of different individuals working for a common goal or the interaction of different parts of an individual. The capacity for cooperative action

---

[6] Rachel Barney performs the valuable service of taking the argument at 349b-351a seriously and exam-ining its structure carefully; see Barney (2006, 52-4). She claims that Socrates thinks of outdoing another (*pleonektein*) as a matter of "maximizing one's possession of some good in a zero-sum context," where one person having more of that good is the same as others having less of that good. Socrates then wants to make the point that practicing a craft is not pleonectic in this sense. One musician playing in tune does not pre-vent a second from doing so as well. This interpretation does not save Socrates' argument, though, because some important crafts are pleonectic in the defined sense of seeking to maximize some good in a zero-sum context. The military craft (*stratēgikē*) attempts to secure victory, which is certainly an attempt to maximize a good in a zero-sum context; in a war between Athens and Sparta, Sparta's victory is Athens' defeat. The craft of ruling is one that, on Thrasymachus' account, is pleonectic; if Thrasymachus succeeds fully as an unjust ruler, no one else in his city can partake in the good of rule. Although this conception of rule is disputed by Socrates, the argument at 349b-351a cannot presume that Thrasymachus is wrong in his con-ception of the ruling craft; this is to be established by the argument, not to be assumed. Finally, it is not clear on Barney's interpretation why Socrates says that the musician and doctor want to outdo the non-musician and the non-doctor. These statements suggest either that crafts are compatible with trying to outdo others in the sense Barney specifies or that Socrates equivocates by employing a different sense of outdoing others.

which justice makes possible, as is implied in the first argument, is here linked with greater power for action.

Although the band of thieves argument is fairly brief, we may draw upon it to sketch Socrates' conception of justice. First, justice produces concord and friendship, effects opposed to the conflict and hatred produced by injustice. Second, justice produces friendship and concord both in an individual and in a group such as a city. This second claim is based on the fact that Socrates treats injustice as present with its own power in a city or clan or army or single individual (351d-352a). Because justice is described at 351d4-5 as producing effects opposed to the effects of injustice in the same subjects, we may ascribe to Socrates the claim that justice is like injustice in being a single trait found in cities, clans, armies, and individual humans. Third, Socrates ascribes to justice in individuals the responsibility for the capacity of groups to act together to achieve their ends. A group of agents will not be capable of accomplishing anything if they wrong each other, and will achieve more if they do not commit injustice against each other (351c8-d2). Even the misguided deeds of a group of criminals must be traced back to the limited presence of justice in the individual criminals (351c1-6).

To trace the workings of justice, the following genetic account seems appropriate. It is present at the basic level in just individuals in the form of internal harmony and agreement. In these individuals, justice produces concord and friendship. Presumably, this is a matter of achieving harmony between the beliefs and desires of individuals, allowing these individuals to be single-minded in pursuit of their goals and able to affirm the value of their own characters and actions. This internal state of harmony also allows individuals to honor the commitments they make to each other, which in turn encourages other individuals to act as reliable partners. Justice thus present in individuals promotes trust and harmony between individuals and counteracts the hatred and conflict between individuals that is produced by whatever injustice infects their association. Thus, justice produces concord and friendship at the group level. At each step in the process, justice makes just individuals or groups more capable of acting.

Within the ensemble of concepts developed in *Republic* 1, justice appears at 351b-352d as a self-transmitting power rather than as a craft. The just person is characterized by particular valuable traits, concord and friendship, which she transmits to the larger groups to which she belongs and which are then characterized as just. As justice operates, it directly benefits the just person by making her more capable of acting and gives the same benefit to those groups to which she belongs. In this respect, justice operates like heat, a power that gives the same trait to its immediate object and to those entities affected by this object. It differs from a craft, which according to Socrates is a form of knowledge that does not benefit the craft-practitioner. The benefit derived from a craft is directed to the object on which the craft operates and which is typically distinct from the practitioner. By contrast, the just person is more capable of acting by virtue of her own justice considered as an internal state and by virtue of the harmony and concord that her justice fosters in the associations to which she belongs. By describing justice as a self-transmitting power, Socrates addresses one of the main

points of contention between him and Thrasymachus, namely whether and how justice benefits the just person.

The sequence of these two positive arguments, the non-pleonectic argument and
the band of thieves argument, follows a pattern noted previously in the refutation of
Polemarchus. At 335b, Socrates asserts a genuine similarity between crafts and justice:
the use of the craft of music does not make others less musical, and similarly the use of
justice will not make others unjust. He attempts to explain this similarity between
crafts and justice by reference to the natural powers of heat and dryness. The explanation
at 335 does not run very deep; it seems to consist mainly in the assertion that the just
man makes others just in the manner of a self-transmitting power like heat. The non-
pleonectic argument also asserts a genuine similarity between crafts like music and
medicine and justice; those who possess these crafts can be expected to agree with each
other in contexts relevant to the exercise of the crafts, and similarly just people can be
expected to agree with each other in their shared endeavors. But this similarity is only
superficial, as noted above in evaluating the non-pleonectic argument. In order to
explain better why just people agree, what sort of agreement is in question, and how
this agreement stems from the function of justice, Socrates moves on to the band of
thieves argument. This argument provides the material for a more explicit description
of how justice generates agreement and harmony between individuals. The agreement
that holds between just people is not simply the sort of agreement on how best to heal a
patient that is compatible with competitive and unjust relations between doctors. Just
people enjoy relations characterized by concord and friendship, terms that imply
mutual support and involvement in reciprocally beneficial associations.[7] These relations arise due to the concord and friendship within just individuals. Thus, the transition from the non-pleonectic argument to the band of thieves argument amounts to
the transition from an observation on the character of justice (just people accept equal
shares in their association) to an explanation of this fact about justice (harmonious
relations between just people arise out of harmonious relations within the soul of the
just person). The craft analogy is helpful insofar as it points to an important characteristic of justice and just people, as in the non-pleonectic argument, but it must be set
aside in favor of the model of self-transmitting powers in order to understand how this
characteristic arises.

The third of Socrates' positive arguments is notable for the way it explicitly defines
the concepts of characteristic activity or *ergon* and of virtue. The *ergon* or characteristic
activity of a thing, be it a pruning knife, an eye, or a horse, is that activity which only
that thing can perform or which the thing in question performs better than anything
else. The eye has the characteristic activity of seeing because no other part of living
things performs the activity of seeing. A pruning knife has the function of cutting slips

---

[7] Kamtekar (2004) notes that in fourth-century Greek discussions of politics concord (*homonoia*) was
seen as a central virtue of cities in their internal relations and in their relations to each other. It was praised
as the opposite of *stasis*, faction, or conflict within a city.

from vines because, although other tools could be used to perform the same activity, it does a better job of cutting slips from vines than a sword or a letter-opener. Given this understanding of what characteristic activities are and the possibility of performing them well or badly, the virtues can be defined directly. For a thing that has a characteristic activity, a virtue is that trait or property of the thing, which by its presence, allows the thing to perform its characteristic activity well. The characteristic activity of the human soul involves caring for and ruling over some subject (perhaps the body or other persons), deliberating, and living. Carrying out this characteristic activity, we may expect, will involve forming and maintaining partnerships, including political associations. Justice, one of the human virtues, will allow the soul to deliberate and rule well in managing the body and participating in political life and so will contribute to living well. Socrates takes this to establish that injustice is never more profitable than justice (354a8-9).

When Socrates sets forth this notion of the *ergon* of a thing as the thing's characteristic activity, we should take this as the exposition of one sense of the term "*ergon*" and not a definition meant to govern every use of the term. Up to this point, the most common use of the term in Book 1 was to refer to the distinctive product of a craft. A crucial step in the refutation of Thrasymachus is the stipulation that every craft has its own distinctive product, health for medicine, a house for carpentry, a wage for the wage-earning art, and so on. If 352d-353a is taken as governing every use of the term "*ergon*," this would require Socrates to revise most of his preceding arguments. In addition, we may observe that *ergon* as distinctive product and *ergon* as characteristic activity are had by different sorts of things. It is crafts or bodies of knowledge that have distinctive products, while it is artifacts or living creatures and their organs that have characteristic activities. A craft such as medicine can employ an indefinitely wide range of doctrines and procedures in pursuit of its end, health. There is no set repertoire of activities that constitute medical knowledge; in a sense, medicine is simply whatever body of expertise and procedures that promotes health. On the other hand, the substances or substance-like objects that have characteristic activities do not exhibit the same variability in repertoire. A horse is a creature with a particular organization of parts and internal systems that allows it to perform particular activities well (galloping, carrying a rider, pulling heavy loads). Similarly, there is very little that an eye or an ear can be said to do besides seeing or hearing, and this because of their peculiar structures and compositions. As a result, we can say that bodies of knowledge are oriented toward their distinctive products by producing them as distinct results, while substances such as horses or eyes or knives show themselves to be the sort of things they are in their own characteristic activities.

4.5   The Significance of Book 1 for the *Republic*

Following Joseph's anti-functional interpretation, many scholars hold that the moral of Book 1 is that justice cannot be understood by finding an action or set of actions that

defines justice; any action will be at times just and at times unjust. But the correct conclusion to be drawn from the refutation of Polemarchus and from Book 1 as a whole is
rather different. When Socrates asks Polemarchus to identify the action or product
through which the just man benefits his friends, he is not asking him to specify an
action-type that is identical with being just. Rather, he wants to learn the action whose
internal requirements suit it for justice in somewhat the way that the internal structure
of the eye suits it for seeing. If Polemarchus and Socrates are not able to specify such an
action, this is not because no particular action could ever be the context of justice but
because the two friends fumble the examination of partnerships and associations. This
is a mistake which Plato sets right in the course of Book 1. Starting with Thrasymachus'
entry into the conversation and continuing through the positive arguments for justice,
Plato asks us to consider partnerships in general, and ruling in particular, as the special
province of the just. The opportunities in partnerships for coordination of action, consideration of the needs of the other party, and identification with the common good
make the activity of forming and maintaining partnerships especially well suited for
justice, even if some partnerships are unjust.

Allied to the claim that justice can be linked to a particular activity or function is the
identification of certain distinctive products of justice. Socrates' positive arguments
for the value of justice reveal that he sees friendship and concord as the distinctive
products of justice. When justice is present in a partnership the parties involved benefit
each other and become more closely united with each other. These traits of friendship
and concord can be passed on to the larger groups within which the original partnership is located. As an example of this pattern, Socrates apparently conceives of the
human being as an association of different elements, including the body and the soul.
The friendship and concord between these elements of a just human being will also
show up in the groups to which the human being belongs, such as a city.

Socrates does not, in Book 1, unfold this functional teleology of just actions. He
does not there defend claims of a teleological nature about the purpose or end of just
actions. His main concern is to refute Thrasymachus' claim that justice is the advantage of the stronger and to assert that justice pays by making the life of the just better
and happier. However, the discussions with Polemarchus and with Thrasymachus have
led to the development of the concepts necessary to specify the for-the-sake-of relation
set out previously in Chapter 1 in relation to Diotima's speech in the *Symposium*, and
we may use these concepts to fill out one possible realization of this for-the-sake-of
relation. Suppose that a ruler in a Greek city state carries out his office in accordance
with social and legal conventions by using public funds to strengthen the city's outer
walls instead of converting the funds to his own private use. In the imagined case, his
actions promote friendship and concord in the city. Regardless of whether the ruler
intended to bring about these valuable results, he acted for the sake of promoting
friendship and concord in the city. This is because the ruler's actions are not simply
cases of force exerted in a beneficial manner; they are better described as particular
steps in an ongoing process of give and take between the ruler and his fellow citizens, a

process which requires that the ruler and the ruled at least in some minimal way trust each other, affirm the interests and priorities of both parties, and find ways of acting that are beneficial for all parties. When the ruler's actions carry out this function of forming and maintaining partnerships in the best way, this is signaled by the production of friendship and concord in the city, which are necessary features of performing this function in the best way. These are among the ends or purposes of the ruler's actions, whether or not the ruler intends to bring them about.[8] This account of the ends of just action is not present in *Republic* 1, but its constituent elements (the function carried out by just actions, the results which follow upon the best performance of this function) are present in the arguments Socrates uses. As we will see in later chapters, the basic model of performing just actions for the sake of instilling positive features in a city will appear again in the course of Socrates' defense of justice.

A further issue in the interpretation of Book 1 is the role of the craft-analogy. At times the anti-functional, aporetic reading of Book 1 takes the form of opposition to the craft analogy. Nickolas Pappas writes as follows:

This argument [for the conclusion at 334a-b that the just man will be the best thief] seems so misguided that we are tempted to throw out any comparison between virtue and an occupational skill, or at least to reconsider the subject matter of which justice may be called a skill.... *Technē*'s built-in assumption that human activities progress toward specific goals will keep it from illuminating the nature of justice, of which we might say that it is its own goal, or that it has for a goal not some distinct product, but a human life.[9]

Indeed, Plato moves away from the craft analogy in Book 1. Self-transmitting power begins to replace craft as the preferred model for justice. However, the deficiencies of the craft analogy must be stated more precisely. Crafts are not disanalogous to justice because they have a limited context of action and pursue specific goals; justice also operates in the limited context of partnerships and produces the goods of concord and friendship within groups. The dissimilarity between crafts and justice lies in the variability of means open to crafts in pursuit of their ends, such that a doctor will be the most skillful poisoner as well as being the one most capable of prescribing healthful

---

[8]   To give a more fine-grained interpretation of the claim that the just ruler acts for the sake of promoting friendship and concord in the city, we may provide the following specification of the for-the-sake-of relation first described in Chapter 1:

1) A ruler performs actions of using his office to expend public funds on strengthening the outer walls of his city, actions which are of lesser value than friendship and concord in the city
2) The ruler's actions of using his office to expend public funds on strengthening the outer walls of his city causally contribute to friendship and concord in the city in virtue of performing the function of forming and maintaining partnerships with his fellow citizens
3) The value of the actions of using one's office to expend public funds on strengthening the outer walls of one's city derives in part from their producing friendship and concord in the city
4) The actions of using one's office to expend public funds on strengthening the outer walls of a city perform the function of forming and maintaining partnerships in the best way only if they causally contribute to friendship and concord in the city.

[9]   Pappas (1995, 35–6).

medicines. As a self-transmitting power, justice never produces its opposite and never does harm in the pursuit of its ends.

A final issue is the relation of Book 1 to the rest of the *Republic*. Many commentators see an important break between the Socratic and aporetic discussion of Book 1 and the Platonic theories developed later in the *Republic*. By contrast, this chapter presents the case for a strong continuity of concepts and positive results between Book 1 and the rest of the *Republic*. Book 1 should be read as a preliminary and exploratory statement of the main theses about justice developed in the *Republic*. The arguments of *Republic* 1 fall well short of giving sufficient grounds for believing that justice is better than injustice when it comes to living a happy life. They assert rather than establish a connection between justice and wisdom on the basis of the non-pleonectic argument's shaky analogy between justice and craft. Thrasymachus' claim at 348c12 that justice is only high-minded simplicity remains a live option to be confronted in later books. Full understanding of the way in which justice operates within just people to benefit them must await the more complex psychology developed in Book 4. Yet even though these arguments are incomplete, they indicate that Socrates' conception of justice in Book 1 is an earlier version of the definition of justice achieved later in the *Republic*. Just actions carry out the function of engaging in partnerships, either when the different parts within a person achieve harmony or when the different persons within a group act together for a common goal. Rather than using the craft analogy in Book 1 as the best tool for investigating virtue, Socrates introduces a different model, that of self-transmitting power. This model anticipates the fuller account of justice in Book 4 as a power that causes humans to avoid pleonectic behavior and renders humans and cities just (443b1-5).

5

The Division of Goods and the Completion of Justice

5.1 Introduction

The previous two chapters described Book 1 of the *Republic* as setting the stage for an account of the ends of just action by linking justice to the function or characteristic activity of engaging in associations and partnerships. This reading of Book 1 emerges from the attempt to provide a charitable reading of the often perplexing arguments about justice that appear in this book. Even on this charitable reading, though, it is clear that Socrates cannot be satisfied with the investigation of justice. We have not asked and answered the question of what justice is, Socrates tells us at 354b, and so we cannot claim to know whether it is more beneficial than injustice. Plato renews the investigation of justice in Book 2 by placing in Glaucon's mouth a serious challenge to Socrates' claim that justice is preferable to injustice. This challenge begins with a division of goods into three classes: those goods we choose for their own sake and not for their results; those we choose both for their own sake and for their results; and those we choose only for their results. Glaucon then requests a fuller defense of justice, one that will clarify why justice is worth choosing for its own sake. He and his brother Adeimantus provide a demonstration of the desired defense by praising injustice. Socrates responds to the request for an account of justice by introducing a new topic for investigation: the nature of the best city. We will be better able to examine justice if we find it present on a larger scale in a city. After seeing justice writ large in this way we will be better able to identify it in the human soul. This leads into Socrates' audacious program for the best city: the use of a principle of specialization to assign each member of the city to that occupation or task for which he or she is best suited, the class structure of guardians, auxiliaries, and wage earners, and the program of education through music and gymnastic.

A number of issues remain up for interpretation after this summary of important elements of Books 2 and 3. First, we would like to know exactly what Socrates is expected to do when Glaucon and Adeimantus ask him to praise justice for itself. Different options for understanding Socrates' task exist in the scholarly literature, and the choice between these options will influence our judgment as to whether the task has been successfully completed. Second, we may question the strategy that

Socrates adopts in response to this request. Why should he take on the investigation of the best city and the myriad complications it brings as part of the search for justice in the soul? Is this strategy simply a device for Plato to lead the conversation in a new direction? Third, Socrates devotes much attention to the description of the different groups within his best city. What should we learn from this account of the inner workings of the best city, and how does this contribute to our understanding of the soul of the just person?

A key text from Book 2 draws these questions together and connects them to our theme of teleology. At 360d8-e5, Glaucon is midway through his praise of injustice. After explaining the nature and origin of justice and injustice respectively, he makes the following point about the correct way to judge between the lives of justice and injustice:

> As for the choice between the lives we're discussing, we'll be able to make a correct judgment about that only if we separate the most just and the most unjust. Otherwise we won't be able to do it. Here's the separation I have in mind. We'll subtract nothing from the injustice of an unjust person and nothing from the justice of a just one, but we'll take each to be complete in his own way of life (*teleon eis to heautou epitēdeuma*).

Glaucon goes on to fill out the notion of finding the completion of the just and the unjust man by placing both in a social context. To be completely unjust, the unjust man must be skillfully unjust and must gain the rewards of good reputation, wealth, and friends. To be completely just, the just man must stand in a quite different relation to his community. He must take care to be just and not to seem to be just. He will therefore gain the reputation for injustice, even to the point of being unfairly punished by the authorities in his city.

This passage at 360d-e brings to the fore several issues that will take center stage in this chapter. First, Glaucon offers the recommendation to consider the just and the unjust man as complete in their respective ways of life as part of his request that Socrates praise justice for itself. Consideration of what is meant by praising justice for itself will occupy the first section of the chapter. Second, Glaucon's request that Socrates present the just man as complete in his way of life is the source of the turn to political affairs. The recommendation to separate the just man from the unjust man will require Socrates to specify the just man's own way of life and to present the just man as living this life to the full. This recommendation can with good reason be taken by Socrates as a request to explicate the characteristic activity or function of the just man. As we have seen in the previous chapter, a strong candidate for the function of the just man is already in play, the activity of forming partnerships and associations. As a result, Socrates will reply to Glaucon's recommendation by describing a particular style of forming partnerships, namely the best city. Thus, Socrates' turn to political affairs is his way of complying with the request to take the just man as complete in his particular way of life. And third, the completion of the just man's life as found in the best city will require a particular sort of integration of different tasks and activities. In this best city, various crafts are pursued for the sake of unintended ends such as virtue in the soul. This teleological structure of activities within the best city is an indication of how the soul of the just person will be unified.

5.2 Praising Justice for Itself and the Division of Goods

When Glaucon recommends at 360d-e that Socrates present the just man as complete in his own way of life, he does so in the course of setting a particular task for the older man. This task is a matter of praising justice for itself (358d2-3). Carrying out this task involves giving justice the praise it deserves as a member of the second of three classes of goods, the class of things we welcome for their own sake and for the sake of their results. Obviously our interpretation of this first part of Book 2 will be of great import for our understanding of the rest of the *Republic*, since our conception of the task set for Socrates will affect our judgment of whether he succeeds in defending justice. Before examining in Chapter 7 the positive arguments that Socrates offers in support of his conviction that justice benefits the just man more than injustice can, it is necessary to spell out what it means to praise justice for itself.

Glaucon begins Book 2 with a division of goods into three classes (357b4-d2):

Tell me, do you think there is a kind of good we welcome, not because we desire what comes from it, but because we welcome it for its own sake – joy, for example, and all the harmless pleasures that have no results beyond the joy of having them?

Certainly, I think there are such things.

And is there a kind of good we like for its own sake and also for the sake of what comes from it – knowing, for example, and seeing and being healthy? We welcome such things, I suppose, on both counts.

Yes.

And do you also see a third kind of good, such as physical training, medical treatment when sick, medicine itself, and the other ways of making money? We'd say that these are onerous but beneficial to us, and we wouldn't choose them for their own sakes, but for the sake of the rewards and other things that come from them.

We find three sorts of goods: those welcomed only for their own sake (here referred to for convenience as Class 1 goods), those welcomed both for their own sake and for their consequences (Class 2 goods), and those welcomed only for their consequences (Class 3 goods). The division of goods exhibits a fairly simple formal structure: there are two ways of welcoming or valuing goods, for themselves and for their consequences; and the first and third types of good each exhibit the sort of good for which the one or the other way of valuing goods is appropriate, but not both. Class 2 goods are those for which both ways of valuing are appropriate.

After Socrates claims at 358a that justice belongs in the second class of goods, his young interlocutor requests that he praise justice in a way that accords with its standing in this class. Doing so will require showing that we ought to value justice for itself, leaving out of the account the rewards and reputation commonly attached to justice in society. Glaucon then praises injustice to provide a model for the praise of justice he wishes to hear. Unfortunately, the exact nature of the task set for Socrates is not easy to grasp. Two different interpretations of what it means to praise justice for itself and thus of the task set for Socrates have been offered. The first, represented by Christopher Kirwan and Terence Irwin, takes Glaucon to be demanding from Socrates a defense of justice that does not rely on any of the beneficial consequences of justice. The only benefits of justice allowed to count in its defense are those constituted by the state of being just.[1] I refer to this as the inner-nature interpretation of Socrates' task. The second interpretation, defended by Robert Heinaman and Nicholas White among others, is less restrictive in that it allows Socrates to bring in a subset of the beneficial consequences of justice.[2] I refer to this as the extended-nature reading of the required defense of justice. The most permissive variant of this reading is Heinaman's; he holds that Socrates is allowed to utilize all beneficial causal consequences of justice other than the rewards of justice dependent on a reputation for being just. A new version of the extended-nature interpretation of Socrates' task will be presented and defended here. He is allowed to defend justice both by explaining the nature of justice itself and by mentioning a particular sort of beneficial consequence of justice, the sort of consequence that testifies to the good working order of the soul that is just. To introduce a term that will be explained later, these consequences are criterial benefits of justice. Other beneficial consequences of justice, those we may describe as fringe benefits of being just, are not allowed to count in the praise of justice.[3]

Both the inner-nature and the extended-nature readings of Socrates' task labor under their own difficulties. According to Irwin and Kirwan, Glaucon wishes to hear from Socrates a defense of justice that forswears all use of the consequences of justice. This aspect of the inner-nature interpretation is difficult to square with Glaucon's own praise of injustice in a speech offered expressly as a model for Socrates to follow. Glaucon and Adeimantus attempt to show in their speeches that injustice is something good in itself, and both seem to appeal to the causal consequences of injustice in order to establish that injustice is good in itself. An apparent case of this comes at 362b2-c6, where Glaucon retails the goods enjoyed by the unjust man:

---

[1] Kirwan (1965); Irwin (1995, 181–93). Foster (1937) also interprets the task presented to Socrates at 357a–358a as that of showing that justice is a good independent of any of its consequences, though he also holds that Socrates proceeds to carry out a quite different task, that of establishing that happiness is a natural consequence of justice. Reeve (1988, 28–33) presents a similar reading with the claim that Glaucon wants to be shown that justice is a homoiomerous essential component of happiness, i.e., that justice is necessary for happiness and justice is a part of like nature with the whole it helps to constitute, happiness.

[2] White (1984); Heinaman (2003). See also Annas (1981, 59–63), who claims that Plato has Socrates praise justice both for its intrinsic nature and for its consequences as separate tasks. Mabbott (1937) anticipates Annas' emphasis on the dual nature of Socrates' task, that of showing both that justice is valuable apart from its consequences and showing that it brings with it valuable consequences. Sachs (1963, 148–51) proposes that to value justice for itself is to value it for the effects it brings about on its own, a reading similar to White's.

[3] A fuller statement of this interpretation of praising justice for itself is contained in Payne (2011).

In any contest, public or private, he's the winner and outdoes his enemies. And by outdoing them, he becomes wealthy, benefiting his friends and harming his enemies. He makes adequate sacrifices to the gods and sets up magnificent offerings to them. He takes better care of the gods, therefore, (and, indeed, of the human beings he's fond of) than a just person does. Hence it's likely that the gods, in turn, will take better care of him than of a just person.

If this description of beneficial consequences of injustice is meant to establish that injustice is good in itself, then the implication is that Socrates may bring in at least some of the consequences of justice in the course of arguing that the just man is happier than the unjust. At the same time, the extended-nature interpretation defended by White and Heinaman allows that praising justice for itself can involve appeal to the consequences of justice. In this case, the value of justice will depend on a feature it shares with goods of the third class: having beneficial consequences. Here we face the danger of losing our grasp on the key distinction between goods of the second class and goods of the third class. Any extended-nature interpretation of praising justice for itself must preserve the difference between Class 2 and Class 3 goods.

I begin the investigation of praising justice for itself with two preliminary remarks about the division of goods based on a brief survey of the examples given of the three classes. First, the goods mentioned are all human activities, things that people do. Pleasure, a Class 1 good, is not a uniform quantity that the hedonist mines from various sources; it is the act of enjoyment (*to chairein*). The harmless pleasures that Glaucon mentions appear again in Book 9 as the pleasures of the rational part of the soul. They are the pleasures that the philosopher associates with and derives from learning. These are not to be assimilated to the pleasures of the lover of gain but are processes of "filling" the soul with truth and reality. In other words, these goods of the first class are perhaps better described as enjoyments, to catch the sense that they are processes connected to activities that people carry on. Similarly, Glaucon does not speak of health but of being healthy (*to hugiainein*) along with seeing (*to horan*) and understanding (*to phronein*) as examples of Class 2 goods. His examples of Class 3 goods follow the pattern of being activities which humans carry on, activities which are referred to either by infinitives (*to gumnazesthai, to kamnonta iatreuesthai*) or substantives standing in for activities. Second, the division of goods is not intended as an exhaustive division of all goods. The Form of Justice and the Form of Beauty are not human activities, though they are surely good. Nor is it an exhaustive division of all human activities, since activities such as walking and sitting are neither good nor bad, as Socrates mentions at *Gorgias* 467-468a. The division of goods focuses instead on those human activities that are such as to make an important contribution to human happiness by making a person's life pleasant, healthy, intelligent, and equipped with necessary goods such as money. There are of course other ways to divide the field of goods, but Glaucon's approach is well suited to his purpose, namely to put in play again the question raised by Thrasymachus in Book 1: is justice or injustice the better option to choose if one is concerned to live a happy life? Socrates provides at 358a1-3 his preliminary assessment of justice in precisely these terms: it belongs to the finest class, the class of things to be welcomed both for themselves and for their consequences "by anyone who is going to be blessed with happiness."

How exactly do Class 3 goods differ from the more valuable Class 2 goods? A first step toward answering this question is Heinaman's observation that Class 3 goods are onerous (357c, 358a) or difficult (358a, 364a). By contrast, Class 2 goods are welcomed for themselves. To describe this difference more precisely, Class 2 goods are activities that constitute the good condition of the agent in some respect. We learn from Book 1 that the excellence of the eyes is sight, by which the characteristic activity or function of the eyes is carried out or completed. Seeing is the activity in which a person carries out the function of the eyes and can attain their excellence (352e-353c). Similarly, the function of the soul is found in caring for and ruling over a subject, presumably the body and external goods, and in deliberation (353d). It is by the active use of understanding that the human soul carries out these functions and can achieve excellence therein. We do not find a function in Book 1 corresponding so closely to being healthy, the third example given of a Class 2 good. But in Book 4 Socrates tells us that health is produced by establishing the different parts of the body in a natural order of ruling and being ruled (444d3-4). Being healthy would accordingly be the condition of having and maintaining the different parts of the body in such an order. This condition ensures that the body and its various parts perform their functions well.

As illustrated by Glaucon's examples, on the other hand, Class 3 goods are activities that remedy deficiencies or needs of the agent. They produce good results for their agents as external results and are therefore beneficial, but the benefit comes from alleviating some present lack or distress in the agent. Onerous or difficult exercise is not an expression of the strength or health of the body in the way that joggers or bicyclists today experience their hobbies as enjoyable; it is a laborious process of building up bodily strength and health that is absent. Undergoing medical treatment while sick is a process that is intended to address some disease; as the example of open-heart surgery suggests, it is a response to ill condition of the body. The practice of medicine does not, simply by its production of health in the patient, benefit the practitioner (342d3-5). As a form of moneymaking, it is practiced in order to supply its practitioner with the wealth that he lacks. The practice of medicine and the other forms of moneymaking mentioned in the third division of goods thus are cases in which a Class 3 good remedies a defect or lack in the agent, as in the examples of exercise and undergoing medical treatment. The defect in question is the lack of wealth on the part of the doctor or housebuilder.

Present in *Republic* 1 is the term *ergon*, as we have seen in the two previous chapters. The term *ergon* is there employed in a way which allows us to draw a further contrast between Class 2 and Class 3 goods. As mentioned earlier, a Class 2 good such as seeing carries out and perfects the characteristic activity or function (*ergon*) of some agent, such as the eye's function of sight; as activities, Class 2 goods constitute such functions. Class 3 goods also are activities that are responsible for states that Plato will describe with the term *ergon*, but these states are results separate from the activities. This contrast corresponds to the two different senses of the term *ergon* observed in Chapter 3: an *ergon* can be a characteristic activity or function or it can be the distinctive product of a craft. When Glaucon presents the division of goods, this apparently represents a conscious decision on Plato's part to distinguish between goods that are activities constituting their *erga* and goods that are activities generating *erga* as distinctive products. This does not imply that the term *ergon* is merely equivocal; for both Class 2 and Class 3 goods, the *ergon* of an activity represents the distinctive benefit or contribution to a happy life generated by that activity.

The contrasts set forth thus far between Class 2 and Class 3 goods concern the ways in which the two classes may be identified: as activities perfecting the good condition of an agent and as activities which remedy a lack or deficiency in an agent. In addition, we may distinguish between different ways in which the two sorts of good are responsible for valuable results. Both sorts of goods consist of activities or processes that have valuable results distinct from and not constituted by those activities or processes. Being healthy, a Class 2 good, allows people to pursue and obtain more readily ends such as honor and wealth, a fact that provides sufficient reason for recognizing health as valuable. Undergoing medical treatment while sick, a Class 3 good, produces health. In these two cases, there is a conceptual distinction to be drawn between the ways in which Class 2 and Class 3 goods relate to their products. In order to set forth this distinction I here introduce the semi-technical notion of a fringe benefit. If x brings with it y as a fringe benefit, then x and y are goods of different types, x produces y as a separate result, and the standards for evaluating x as a good of its type do not include the production of y. As an example of this notion of a fringe benefit, consider the case of an electrician who takes a job at a factory located within walking distance of his home. Employment at this factory affords the electrician a suitable wage in return for the use of his creative abilities and technical skill; in this sense, the job fulfills the criteria for being a good job. The job also brings with it the fringe benefit of a short commute to work, a genuine benefit that is produced by taking the job but a benefit the production of which is not part of the criteria for judging jobs as good. In this example, the fringe benefit is of lesser value than the good that produces it, but this is no part of the notion of a fringe benefit as I wish to define it; in some cases the fringe benefit produced may be more valuable than the good that produces it.

With this semi-technical notion in hand, we can distinguish between the ways in which being healthy, a Class 2 good, and undergoing medical treatment, a Class 3 good, relate to the valuable results which they produce. Being healthy has a number of valuable results, in the sense that being healthy makes a positive contribution to the healthy person's pursuit of these goods: honor and wealth, to name only two. A healthy person is typically better able than a sickly person to gain honor and wealth, especially if he happens to live in a society in which status, reputation, and wealth are highly prized and the object of fierce competition. But valuing health does not require that one use one's health to gain honor and wealth; a person who prizes health above all else might choose not to use health to pursue these particular goods. In this case, the healthy but unambitious and financially unmotivated person is no less healthy, his bodily condition is no less good, and it is no less true that he welcomes being healthy for its own sake. In this sense, honor and wealth are fringe benefits of health. Health is welcomed by many in part because health allows them to gain honor and wealth, but the criteria for judging a person's bodily condition to be a case of good health do not include the production of honor and wealth.

On the other hand, there is a closer relation between Class 3 goods and their valuable consequences. Success in medical treatment brings health and success in money-making brings wealth, but not as fringe benefits. The standards for evaluating medical treatment as good do include the production of health. Success in medical treatment is *measured by* the production of health. Health is not a consequence that we can choose not to pursue even as we commit ourselves to success in medical treatment; it is the result aimed at in medical treatment and which gives purpose to that activity. While Class 2 goods relate to at least some of their valuable results in the manner of a valuable activity to its fringe benefits, Class 3 goods relate to their valuable results as activities to the criterial benefits of those activities, those valuable results that signal success in the activity.[4] I say that Class 2 goods relate to *some* of their valuable results in the manner of an activity to its fringe benefits because it may be the case that Class 2 goods as well as Class 3 goods will have valuable results that are not fringe benefits but are criterial benefits; this will become important when we consider Socrates' task of praising justice for itself.

One aspect of the notion of fringe benefits is that what counts as a fringe benefit is topic-sensitive. Wealth is a fringe benefit of health but not a fringe benefit of money-making. Under some broad notion of causal consequence, wealth is a causal consequence both of health and of moneymaking. But being a fringe benefit is a more fine-grained relation than that of causal consequence; the assertion that wealth is a fringe benefit of health but not of moneymaking requires for its truth not only causal relations but also normative facts about what is required for success in moneymaking and what is required for good health. To identify the fringe benefits of an activity *A*, it is necessary to know not only its valuable consequences but also which of those consequences are relevant to evaluating specimens of *A* as good or bad instances of their type.

---

[4] The distinction drawn here between the fringe benefits and the criterial benefits of an activity is similar to the distinction drawn by Cross and Woozley (1966, 66–8) between the consequences and the results of an activity. For Cross and Woozley the consequences of an activity are the broad range of unintended and often random effects produced by an activity, while the results of an activity are those intended effects which signal success in the performance of an activity, as the production of health indicates success in medical practice. Consequences in this sense are similar to fringe benefits and results are similar to criterial benefits, although on my account criterial benefits need not be intended. Cross and Woozley see results as produced by Class 3 goods only, whereas I argue that Class 2 goods also bear criterial benefits or, in their terminology, results. Accordingly, they treat Socrates' task in praising justice for itself to be that of showing that it is good apart from both consequences and results. On my reading, Socrates can appeal to the benefit that justice brings apart from anything else it produces, and he can also appeal to its criterial benefits.

Opposed to the fringe benefits of an activity are what I refer to as its criterial bene-fits. Where fringe benefits are valuable results that follow from some activity but do not serve to measure the success of that activity as an instance of its type, criterial benefits are those valuable results of an activity whose presence or absence provides evidence of success or failure in carrying out that activity. As an example of the diffe-rence between criterial and fringe benefits, consider the case of seeing, a Class 2 good, and two results that we are able to accomplish by the use of this activity: identifying a line of printed letters and producing visual memories. Both results are goods, but the first is commonly used in the context of a visit to the ophthalmologist as a test to evaluate the strength of a person's eyesight. The second may be a more valuable good, but the storing of visual perception as memory depends on the proper functioning of a distinct set of psychic processes that can malfunction without any defect in seeing. So a perfectly sighted person can lack visual memories if the process of storing visual perception as memories has gone wrong. In this case, we cannot use the absence of visual memories as a means to evaluate the person's sight. In contrast to the criterial benefit of identifying a line of printed letters, producing visual memory is a fringe benefit of seeing. As noted previously in setting forth the notion of a fringe benefit, what counts as a criterial benefit will depend on the activity that generates it; a single good can be a criterial benefit of one activity and a fringe benefit of a different activity. Also, the example of seeing shows that a Class 2 good can have both criterial and fringe benefits, a point which will take on importance when we turn to the speeches of Glaucon and Adeimantus.

After this extended series of observations on Class 2 and Class 3 goods and their results, we are ready to return to the question of what it means to praise justice or any other Class 2 good for itself. I propose that to praise a Class 2 good for itself is to praise it as a valuable activity and to praise it for its criterial benefits while excluding all of its fringe benefits. This description of what it means to praise justice for itself is preferable to the other interpretations on offer because it accords better with the procedures fol-lowed by Glaucon and Adeimantus as they instruct Socrates on the sort of defense of justice they wish to hear.

Glaucon begins his speech with an account of the essences of justice and injustice. This account draws upon a view of human nature as characterized by excessive, pleo-nectic desire. Injustice, as symbolized by the use of the ring of Gyges, provides the ful-fillment of our natural desires because it is the path that all or almost all of us will follow when given the chance. Glaucon connects successful injustice and the fulfill-ment of human nature as he introduces the story of the ancestor of Gyges. If the power to do injustice with complete impunity were given to the unjust man and to the just man, the same unjust actions would result: "The reason for this is the desire to outdo others and get more and more [*dia tēn pleonekian*]. This is what anyone's nature pursues as good, but nature is forced by law into the perversion of treating fairness with respect (359c4-6)." These considerations lead Glaucon at 360c5-d2 to assign justice to the class of necessary, instrumental goods and injustice to the class of intrinsic goods: "This, some would say, is a great proof that one is never just willingly but only when compelled to be.... Indeed, every man believes that injustice is far more beneficial to himself than justice." Doing injustice is naturally good and suffering injustice is bad, a fact that leads to the origin of justice in the attempt to evade the badness of suffering injustice by devising laws and conventions that prescribe just conduct. This origin of justice tells us the essence of justice, according to Glaucon.

The fact that Glaucon spends a large part of his speech describing the essences of justice and injustice and connecting the latter to allegedly fundamental human drives is well explained by the current account of praising justice for itself. In order to praise justice or any Class 2 good for itself, it is necessary to determine the valuable activity constituting that good. On this basis, we may identify the criterial benefits and the fringe benefits of that activity. The sequence of Glaucon's thought at 359-60 shows that he treats injustice as a Class 2 good on the basis of its completing and perfecting human nature as this expresses itself in pleonectic desire. The workings of this desire are the valuable activity at the heart of injustice, and its typical results of gaining wealth, power, prestige, and pleasure are the criterial benefits that indicate success in acting upon human nature. Justice is defined as a prudential strategy of settling for the second-best outcome of following laws that demand equal treatment for all, an outcome that leads the just person to refrain from harming others in return for not being harmed. It lacks an intrinsically valuable activity, and so Glaucon treats it as a Class 3 good. Like painful medical treatment in relation to health, justice has a criterial benefit: not being harmed by the injustice of others. The description of the essence of injustice affords Glaucon a rationale for including some of the valuable results of injustice in its praise: honor in society, good reputation, wealth, the aid of many powerful friends, family connections, and success in competitive endeavors (362b). These are the valuable results that testify to the good operation of the activity that is central to injustice.

The distinction between the central activities linked to justice and injustice and their criterial benefits also allows us to understand what Glaucon has in mind at 360d-361d. As we noticed at the start of this chapter, he recommends that we judge between justice and injustice by examining the just man and the unjust, taking each as complete in his way of life. He follows this recommendation in his own speech by comparing the lives of the just man and the unjust using a procedure of praising each life for its central activity and for its criterial benefits. He tells us first at 360e1 that we must compare the lives of the most just man and the most unjust man. This is not a matter of imagining justice and injustice in the superlative degree, as if we are to compare the lives of Gandhi and Hitler in terms of their respective happiness. Instead, Glaucon tells us to provide the just man and the unjust with what is needed for the distinctive practice of each to be complete. The distinctive activity of justice and injustice must be given to the just man and the unjust man respectively, but also the criterial benefits of these activities, those benefits that signal success in or completion of the relevant activity. For the unjust man this means allowing him to operate as a skillful craftsman of unjust gain while avoiding the reputation of injustice. The reputation for justice is one of the criterial benefits of injustice, since it is necessary for the unjust man to be completely unjust that he deceive everyone in society and not pay the penalty for his injustice. By contrast, the just man is concerned not to seem just but to be just (361b7-8). Accordingly, the reputation for justice is a fringe benefit of justice, not a criterial benefit. Glaucon says at 361c3-4 of the just man, "We must strip him of everything except justice and make his situation the opposite of an unjust person's." I take this to mean that just action and its criterial benefits should be awarded to the just man, in light of the injunction at 360e to provide the just man with what is needed for his justice to be complete. What is stripped away is the reputation for justice, one of the fringe benefits of justice, and the benefits it produces. The just man's situation is opposite to that of the unjust in the sense that in Glaucon's thought experiment he lacks the external rewards usually awarded to the just, while the unjust man is awarded these. However, Glaucon uses a single procedure to "polish up the statues" of the just and the unjust: give to each man his characteristic activity and its criterial benefits while leaving out the fringe benefits. Socrates is expected to follow the same procedure, though it is open to him to provide his own specification of the function or characteristic activity of the just man and its criterial benefits.

This reading of Socrates' task presented possesses an important advantage over the extant versions of the inner-nature and extended-nature readings presented earlier: it makes better sense of the fact that Glaucon both asks Socrates to focus on what justice does in the soul of the just person and mentions the results of injustice in his own praise of injustice. Kirwan and Irwin's inner-nature reading draws our attention to Glaucon's first presentation of Socrates' task at 358b4-6: "I want to know what justice and injustice are and what power each itself has when it's by itself in the soul." This focus leads them to deny that Socrates' task will involve any mention of the valuable consequences of being just. As mentioned earlier, this is hard to square with Glaucon's procedure at 362b-c, where he assigns to the unjust person wealth, good reputation, social connections, success in various competitive endeavors, and friendship with the gods. On the reading presented here, the central part of Glaucon's praise of injustice is his account of the essence of injustice, the valuable activity of acting upon pleonectic desire. But success in acting on pleonectic desire is signaled by winning wealth, honor, prestige in society, and the various goods Glaucon mentions. The successfully unjust person will gain these goods, and Glaucon mentions them as criterial benefits of being unjust. Therefore, Socrates' praise of justice should similarly start with the description of the psychic activity that is justice. To this extent, Kirwan and Irwin are correct. However, their inner-nature reading of Socrates' task fails to make sense of the evident fact that Glaucon mentions many of the beneficial results of injustice. In the terms of the present interpretation, he mentions the criterial benefits of injustice. Socrates will then be allowed to mention criterial benefits of justice, following Glaucon's lead. What those benefits are will depend on the nature of justice, an account of which Socrates is expected to provide. He is expected to exclude the fringe benefits of justice, which include the reputation for justice and the success in society dependent on this reputation.

This reading of Socrates' task is superior to the extended-nature reading provided by Heinaman, according to which Socrates is allowed to mention all the valuable consequences of justice except for those that depend on good reputation. As already mentioned, this reading of Socrates' task threatens to erase the distinction between praising justice as a Class 2 good and praising it as a Class 3 good. At 362b-c, Glaucon assigns to the unjust person various valuable consequences of his injustice and apparently takes these valuable consequences of injustice to be relevant to the praise of injustice for itself. The heart of Heinaman's argument is that since wealth, success, etc., are relevant to praising injustice for itself, they are also relevant to praising justice for itself. But this last inference should be resisted. What is a criterial benefit of injustice (wealth, success in competitive endeavors, pleasure) may be only a fringe benefit of justice. The just and the unjust person will employ different measures of human flourishing. The unjust man who takes as his model the ancestor of Gyges will identify the successful human life with the life of the tyrant, a life which is alleged to be worth having apart from all consequences but also has criterial benefits of wealth, political office, honor, and social connections. The just man need not dismiss these benefits as lacking all value, but he will evaluate a human life as successful using criteria other than the possession of these goods. In other words, he treats them as at best fringe benefits of his central concern, justice. From this perspective, to praise justice for itself is compatible with using those valuable consequences of justice which attest to a person's success in being just, an activity that is valuable in itself. By incorporating mention of this activity as valuable apart from all consequences and using it to determine the criterial benefits of justice, the present reading of Socrates' task maintains the necessary distinction between praising justice as a Class 2 good and praising it as a Class 3 good.

Another advantage of the notion of a fringe benefit is that it allows us to explain the treatment in Glaucon's speech of the benefits that follow from the reputation for justice. Glaucon tells Socrates that he cannot appeal to these benefits when he takes up the defense of justice, but at the same time, he appeals to these benefits in his own praise of injustice, as at 362b2-4. It may seem at first that Glaucon either is confused or is stacking the deck in favor of injustice, but the explanation for his procedure is straightforward using the notion of a fringe benefit. A reputation for justice and the benefits that follow from it are fringe benefits of being just. Hence, such consequences of being just are to be excluded from the praise of justice. But a reputation for justice is not a fringe benefit of being unjust: it is a criterial benefit of being unjust. Success in being unjust often consists in being one thing and seeming to be the opposite. As long as society punishes open injustice, successful injustice must gain at least the reputation of justice. Glaucon's differential treatment of justice and injustice, awarding the latter and not the former the benefits connected with a reputation for justice, is motivated by a single rule: when we praise an activity for itself, we must focus on the valuable activity and its criterial benefits. The activity's fringe benefits cannot count. This explains Glaucon's treatment of the benefits following from a reputation for justice without appealing, as do Annas and Foster, to a distinction between natural and artificial production of benefits which is absent from the text.[5]

The result of these reflections on goods and their results is a new version of the extended-nature interpretation of Socrates' task. When he is told to praise justice for itself, he is allowed to appeal to the activity itself of being just and also to a restricted subset of the results of justice, namely the criterial benefits of justice. I have argued that this interpretation of Socrates' task makes good sense in light of the three classes of goods set forth at 357b-d and in light of the instructions given to Socrates by Glaucon and Adeimantus in their speeches. Whether it conforms to Socrates' actual procedure in praising justice in the middle books of the *Republic* is a question to be addressed in Chapter 7.

5.3 Justice Completed: The Turn to the Best City

After Glaucon and Adeimantus complete the praise of injustice, they request that Socrates give a similar praise of justice. The latter agrees to come to the defense of justice and begins this task by describing the origins and structure of the best city. It might be thought that Socrates has made a difficult task even harder by turning from the investigation of justice as a trait of human beings to the problem of designing an ideal political community. He supports his procedure at 368d-369b with a particular methodological claim, namely that understanding what justice is in a city will help us to understand what justice is in an individual soul. This methodological claim is illustrated with a comparison of understanding what justice is to the task of reading letters: if a piece of text is hard to read because it is far away from us, written in small letters, and our eyesight is not the best, then we will be better able to read the text if we first view the same letters written larger and on a larger surface and then turn back to the first piece of text (368d). When Glaucon asks how the case of smaller and bigger letters is similar to the case of justice, Socrates replies that there is justice both in an individual human being and in an entire city. A city is clearly larger than a single person, and so perhaps there is more justice in a city. Therefore, Socrates suggests, it will be easier to understand what justice is at the level of a city (368e).

Socrates' procedure in this section of Book 2 has drawn its share of unfavorable comment. To many commentators, the transition to political matters is based on questionable assumptions. Socrates' justification for this method of investigating the nature of justice is puzzling at best and specious at worst. Julia Annas has this to say about the move to political affairs:

...[T]he idea that justice in the city can illuminate justice in the individual only gets off the ground if 'justice' has the same sense as applied to both.... We may be surprised that Plato does

---

[5] See Annas (1981, 66-8) and Foster (1937, 387-8).

not even consider the possibility at the outset that justice in the case of cities, and collections of individuals, might be a very different matter from justice in the case of an individual. His failure to do so has implications which become obvious later.[6]

While Annas asks us to look critically at the assumption that apparently motivates the inquiry into justice in the city, Jonathan Barnes takes Plato to task for doing a sloppy job of justifying the turn to political affairs.[7] The metaphor of looking at letters of different size does not help at all to justify Socrates' procedure, says Barnes, since a series of large letters written on a large surface can be harder to read than the same letters printed smaller on a smaller surface. What is essential for easy legibility is not looking at larger letters but getting the relation right between the viewer, the distance to the printed letters, and their size relative to the previous two items.[8] The apparently sensible strategy of trying to understand justice in a human being by looking at a larger sample of the same thing cannot succeed, because justice does not come in larger or smaller sizes and because the truism that a city is larger than a man only spreads further confusion. "But Athens isn't larger than Aristides: the State and the individual are – so far as size goes – incommensurable; that is to say, there is no measure of size common to States and individuals, to Athens and to Aristides, by reference to which one might be larger than the other."[9] Two grounds of opposition to Socrates' procedure emerge from these passages: first, that his turn to political affairs is based on the unsupported assumption that cities and souls are just in the same fashion, and second, that the justification for the inquiry into justice in the city that is offered by Socrates in terms of seeing justice writ large is unconvincing.

As I will argue shortly, Socrates possesses the resources to mount a strong reply to this opposition; his conception of the function of justice as forming associations and partnerships provides sufficient reason for introducing the topic of the best city. Before spelling out this reply, though, it will be helpful to place our discussion of 368d–369b in relation to the general topic of the city-soul analogy in the *Republic*. Clearly the passage implies a strong similarity between justice in the city and justice in the soul, but saying this much leaves open the precise nature of the analogy between city and soul. This analogy is one of the leitmotifs of the dialogue, extending as it does from the present passage in Book 2 through the comparison in Book 4 of the three classes within the best city (wage earners, auxiliaries, guardians) to the three parts of the soul (appetite, spirit, reason) to the comparison in Books 8 and 9 of defective cities and corresponding souls (timocratic, oligarchic, democratic, and tyrannical). Because the analogy appears in different places within the dialogue and can serve a variety of purposes, each passage featuring the analogy must be examined carefully to discern the degree of similarity implied between city and soul. Implausibly strong versions of the analogy are at times ascribed to Socrates on the basis of passages in Book 4 and 5; for example, Bernard Williams interprets the passage 435e from Book 4 as implying that a city

---

⁶ Annas (1981, 72–3).   ⁷ Barnes (2012).   ⁸ Barnes (2012, 32).   ⁹ Barnes (2012, 34).

exhibits a property F if and only if its citizens exhibit F.[10] Nothing so strong is to be found in the present passage 368d-369b. The passage implies a similarity between justice in the city and justice in the soul and does not support a general claim for the similarity of any property of cities and humans. Socrates imagines that people who lack sharp eyesight and are expected to read a series of letters from far off will benefit from being able to read the same letters elsewhere written larger, but he does not claim here that justice in a city is identical to justice in a human being. When Glaucon asks how the case of the letters writ small and large has a bearing on the investigation of justice, Socrates says only that a city is larger than a man and that there is more justice in a city. He proposes that they first investigate what justice is in cities and then examine the likeness of the greater thing in the form of the smaller. Exactly what the similarity between justice in the city and justice in the soul is remains to be determined. The more substantive implications of the city-soul analogy arrive only in Book 4, namely that the city and the soul have roughly the same three elements and that the cardinal virtues of wisdom, courage, temperance, and justice arise in city and in soul out of similar interactions between the elements. Relative to 368d-369b, the city-soul analogy consists only of the claim that justice in the city and justice in the soul are similar enough that understanding justice in the larger entity will aid Socrates and Glaucon in completing the task of understanding justice in the smaller.

The previous discussion of Book 1 and the function associated with justice allows us to see that Socrates is not merely making an unmotivated assumption when he treats justice in the city as being similar to justice in the soul. The function of justice is forming and maintaining partnerships and associations. That is, the person who is just demonstrates this virtue in the particular way that she carries on partnerships, and the virtue of justice ensures that this activity of carrying on partnerships is done in the best way. On the basis of Book 1 it is not clear whether justice is a trait that is lodged primarily in the soul or in a political community; Socrates follows Thrasymachus' lead in speaking of justice as a trait that shows itself in the relations between ruler and ruled within a political community and in dealings between individuals who form associations in which they share activity. He also suggests that justice shows up in the harmonious relations between a person's internal parts or aspects. With this conception of the function of justice as a jumping-off point, a sensible first step would be to examine this function to see how it can be done well. Cities provide a clear case of this function, since a city is at the most basic level a partnership, an association of those who are unable to live or to live well on their own. Socrates speaks of cities in these terms at 369c1-4: "And because people need many things, and because one person calls on a

---

[10] Williams (1973, 197). Lear (1992) and Ferrari (2005) resist in different ways the main theme of Williams' paper, namely that the city-soul analogy is the source of much confusion and obscurity in the *Republic*. Lear emphasizes the reciprocal causal influence between cities and the souls of the individuals who make them up, while Ferrari claims that Plato intends to use the analogy as a useful heuristic to gain insight into the structure of justice and other virtues, not as a device to peer into the souls of the inhabitants of different cities.

second out of one need and on a third out of a different need, many people gather in a single place to live together as partners and helpers. And such a settlement is called a city." The inquiry into justice turns to politics not because Plato makes an unexamined assumption about the similarity between civic and psychic justice or because he seizes upon a pretext for bringing in extraneous political considerations, but because cities are signal examples of the activity of partnership that is at the heart of justice. The *Republic*'s ethical inquiry into justice generates the political inquiry into the best city because justice is the virtue of partnerships and associations and because a city is a clear example of a partnership.

Socrates' justification of the turn to justice in the city also makes better sense once we consider justice as a trait that we evince in the process of forming associations and partnerships. He claims that justice is easier to understand in the city than in the soul (368e7-369a1). Some straightforward explications of this claim can be rejected immediately. Socrates cannot expect that his contemporaries will share an untroubled consensus on the nature of the just city; disagreements over this topic would later tear Athens apart and lead to the death of Polemarchus.[11] A better explication of Socrates' claim that it is easier to understand justice in the city will assert that the characteristic activity of justice, forming partnerships and associations, is more evident to us as it happens in cities. The thesis that the soul is an association of parts is a controversial claim yet to be established by the arguments of Book 4. But we all can appreciate already that cities involve citizens making agreements with each other, addressing potential conflicts between parts, cooperating with others, adjusting their pursuit of their ends in light of the fact that others are pursuing the same or conflicting ends, and ruling and being ruled. Given our familiarity with the idea that a city is constituted by a web of associations, we can more easily observe the activity of forming partnerships and associations in a city.

In addition, the thesis that justice is exhibited in forming associations helps to provide a context for Socrates' comparison between reading letters that spell out the word justice and understanding justice in the city and in the soul. This comparison may seem forced, but it is likely that the comparison is based in a Platonic conception of what is involved in reading words. In the *Sophist* and *Philebus*, Plato articulates the view that the letters of the alphabet form distinct classes (voiced letters, mutes, and an intermediate class) which combine in regular patterns to form syllables.[12] It requires a skilled grammarian to know which sounds and letters will associate (*koinōnein*) with each other to form syllables and which will not.[13] Learning to read requires more than simply memorizing the individual units of the alphabet and sounding out words; it

---

[11] Gifford (2001) describes the tragic fate of Cephalus' family against the backdrop of Athenian history in the late fifth century BCE.

[12] *Philebus* 18b6–d2. See Menn (1998) for an illuminating exposition of Plato's conception of the letters and their significance for philosophical method.

[13] *Sophist* 252e9–a12.

requires the ability to perceive and recognize regular patterns of association between letters and syllables. Making out the word "justice" written first in large and then in small letters involves recognizing recurring patterns of associations of letters and syllables. The comparison of reading a word and understanding justice is well founded if being just involves entering into some associations and avoiding others. Socrates' comparison of reading the word "justice" and understanding justice is intelligible, provided that justice is a trait evinced in human associations.

In supporting his decision to investigate justice in the city, Socrates also says that there is perhaps more justice in a city than in a man. Barnes dismisses this claim as well as the allied claim that a city is larger than a man: he claims that justice does not come in different sizes and that it is not strictly true that a city like Athens is larger than a man like Aristides. Using the notion of the activity of forming associations, though, we can provide a satisfying account of what Socrates has in mind here. A city is larger than a man, considered as a setting for justice, because a city encompasses many more partnerships than a single man does. A city as a whole contains a greater number of partnerships and a greater range of types of partnerships than one human being can ever hope to become a party to. If justice is present in a city as the trait that ensures that these partnerships go well, then it will be present more widely than it can be in one just man. This is true whether we consider a man as being himself an association of parts or simply as one party to a set of partnerships with other citizens.

Based on these points, we can understand the rationale for Socrates' recourse to the city and to political affairs as the jumping-off point for understanding justice. He has been operating since Book 1 with the intuition that the characteristic activity of the just person is forming and maintaining partnerships and associations. A city serves as a comparatively clear and evident example of this activity. It is reasonable to work from the more evident case of this activity, the city, toward an understanding of the less evident case, the soul. Accordingly, until Socrates and Glaucon learn from the arguments of Book 4 in what sense the soul is an association of parts, the easier way for them to study justice is to examine cities.

In addition, Socrates' turn to the city allows him to fulfill Glaucon's request that he portray the just man as complete in his own way of life. As we have seen, this can be rephrased as the request that Socrates present the just man as one who has the benefits which are constituted by the activity of being just as well as the criterial benefits of justice which follow upon that activity. Socrates will fulfill this request by describing the just city and using this as a model to determine the nature of the just man. The just man carries out his characteristic activity by forming partnerships with his fellow citizens. As long as he is lodged within the just city, he will gain the criterial benefits of concord and friendship with the other members of the city, benefits that result from his excellent performance of his characteristic activity. Gaining the benefits of concord and friendship will be one of the ends for the sake of which the just man performs just actions, and gaining these benefits is the completion of justice in the soul. A further sense in which there is more justice in the city than in the individual soul is that the justice of the soul is fulfilled and completed by enjoying concord and friendship with the other members of the just city.

5.4 The Teleological Structure of Activities and Goods in the Best City

Socrates turns to the investigation of the best city at 369b. As described in the previous section, his procedure is a matter of reading the letters of justice writ large in the city in order to gain insight into justice writ small in the human soul. That is, he will take up the activity of forming and carrying on partnerships in the more familiar realm of political life in hopes of learning how something similar goes on in the soul. Socrates' ambitious, at times outrageous program for the best city contains a host of noteworthy measures: the principle of specialization, the censorship of music and poetry, the community of women and children among the guardian class. Within this remarkable range of political designs, one pattern will be the focus of consideration in the final section of this chapter. In Socrates' best city a range of activities are presented which are related to each other as ends and means to ends. Crafts as practiced in the best city are activities which are Class 3 goods and which are performed for the sake of Class 2 goods. These crafts are for the sake of Class 2 goods but they are not carried out with the intention of achieving Class 2 goods. One lesson to draw from Books 2–4 is that in the best city the parts cooperate and support each other in a teleological structure: medicine and other crafts are practiced for the sake of such goods as justice and virtue. This pattern within the best city is one that is relevant to Socrates' ultimate goal of understanding justice in the soul. The teleological structure of activities within the best city suggests that the soul also exhibits a similar structure.

Books 2 and 3 are replete with discussions of Class 3 goods. As Socrates, Glaucon, and Adeimantus set the outlines of the city in speech and lay down guidelines for the education of the city's guardians, they treat Class 3 goods as activities that are productive, when performed rightly, of Class 2 goods. Such activities as physical training, medicine, and various forms of moneymaking take shape in their best form in the kallipolis. These best forms of Class 3 goods not only contribute to bodily goods and external goods such as health and wealth, as we would expect, but they also contribute to psychic goods by making the residents of the kallipolis more receptive to justice and temperance. In this light, these Class 3 goods provide instances of the functional teleology of action: they are activities carried out for the sake of ends that are not intended.

A first instance of this pattern can be found in Socrates' discussion of medical treatment in Book 3. Undergoing medical treatment and the practice of medicine promote bodily health, but Socrates at 404-7 qualifies this natural train of thought. The doctor whom Socrates approves for the practice of medicine in the kallipolis is not concerned to produce health at any cost or by any means. A patient who is forced by doctor's orders to live out his life in a time-consuming round of treatments is unable to perform his own function and has no profit in living, either for himself or for his city (407a1-2, e1-2). The proper use of medicine is to heal serious illness and wounds by administering purges and performing surgeries that quickly restore the patient to health. Failing this, the "political Asclepius," to use Glaucon's words, allows the patient to die (406d7-e3, 409e4-410a3). Leaving aside our qualms about the political Asclepius' disregard for codes of medical ethics, we may characterize Socrates' conception of best medical practices as follows. The practice of medicine is expected to produce health, but to do so under the condition that those being healed should be returned to the performance of their own tasks or functions as quickly as possible. This is a result that promotes not only health but also justice in the city, where justice is understood as each citizen performing his own task.

The other forms of moneymaking are similar to medicine in producing their own distinctive products but also serving justice when they are practiced in the best way. The practice of farming, weaving, carpentry, sailing, and other crafts is described in the context of the healthy city whose genesis is complete at 372b-c. As Class 3 goods, these crafts are present in the city to meet the deficiencies and needs that humans share (369b-c). When such a craftsman puts his distinctive product at the city's disposal to meet the needs of all, the result is a healthy city. Glaucon identifies as the closest thing to justice in it the fact that the city is based on the need that each member of the city has for all the others (371e12-372a2). Of course, it is possible to practice these forms of moneymaking in a bad way, as when the healthy city is sickened by the production of excessive ornamentation, painting, luxurious food, and other such frippery (373a). But in the best city, Socrates suggests, the crafts will produce their objects in a quite different, more healthful way:

Or must we rather seek out craftsmen who are by nature able to follow the tracks of the nature of the beautiful and graceful in their work, so that our young people will live, as it were, in a healthy place and be benefited on all sides, so that whenever something of those beautiful works strikes their eyes and ears it will be like a breeze that brings health from a good place, leading them unwittingly, from childhood on, to resemblance, friendship, and harmony with the beauty of reason?[14]

The best way of practicing the crafts is one which produces health in a metaphorical sense, but more importantly literally produces in the youth of the city a psychic state of harmony and friendship with reason. This state of psychic harmony bears an obvious kinship with justice, as Socrates will later describe it in Book 4; we could think of this

---

[14] 401c4–d3. I alter the Grube-Reeve translation, rendering *ichneuein tēn tou kalou te kai euschēmonos phusin* literally; Grube-Reeve have "to pursue what is fine and graceful in their work." Plato's metaphor of following the tracks of the beautiful is carefully chosen; it suggests that the craftsmen are at a cognitive distance from the reality of beauty, since they are looking only at traces left by their quarry rather than at the beast itself. At 432b-d, Socrates employs a similar metaphor of hunting and following tracks (*kindeuneuomen ti echein ichnos*, 432d2–3) to describe his search for the nature of justice. Other uses of the metaphor appear at 410a and 462a.

state of psychic harmony as a young person's possession of well-formed desires and moral sentiments, a state which disposes the young to attaining justice once the reasoning part of the soul gains its full authority.

This passage at 401c4-d3 suggests a link between the division of goods and the teleology of action. The functional teleology of action observed in the *Symposium* proposes that, within a well-defined range of cases, actions carried out with the intention of promoting one goal can be explained as being done for the sake of some further, unintended end. Crucial for defining this range of cases are the conditions that such an action must perform a function and that this function is performed best only if a particular result is achieved. Such a result, for instance gaining the vision of the Form of Beauty, need not be intended but is nevertheless an end for the sake of which the action is performed. This pattern of acting for the sake of an unintended end describes the relation between the productive work of the craftsmen mentioned at 401c-d and the psychic state of harmony it produces in the youth of the best city. Socrates surely does not wish to stipulate that craftsmen in the best city must understand the importance of psychic harmony for the young and intend to produce this psychic state as they weave cloth, throw pots, and build houses. This would require the craftsmen to attain a degree of knowledge of the soul that would make them more than craftsmen of the money-making class and would go against the Socratic injunction to practice justice by "doing one's own thing." But if the craftsmen produce items that are beautiful and thus carry out their functions in the best way, then the beauty, grace, and harmony of their products may be taken up into the souls of the young and thus promote both psychic harmony and justice. As long as the craftsmen are "following the tracks of the nature of the beautiful and graceful" in their work, they will produce not just beautiful cloth, pots, and buildings but also beautiful souls. This last result is an unintended end for the sake of which they perform their activities as craftsmen.[15]

Another case of a Class 3 good exhibiting the functional teleology of action in its production of a Class 2 good arrives at 410a-412a as Socrates explains the real purpose for physical training. The person who is well educated in music[16] will also take

---

[15] A more precise account of the sense in which the craftsmen produce their wares for the sake of an unintended end, psychic harmony in the young, is furnished by filling out the formal account of the for-the-sake-of relation provided in Chapter 1:

1) The craftsmen perform actions of weaving cloth, throwing pots, building houses, etc., which are of lesser value than psychic harmony in the young
2) The actions of weaving cloth, throwing pots, building houses, etc., causally contribute to psychic harmony in the young in virtue of performing the functions of various crafts
3) The value of the actions of weaving cloth, throwing pots, building houses, etc., derives in part from their producing psychic harmony in the young
4) The actions of weaving cloth, throwing pots, building houses, etc., perform the functions of the crafts of weaving, pottery, and carpentry in the best way only if they causally contribute to psychic harmony.

[16] "Music" is a conventional translation for Plato's *mousikē*, with the proviso that Platonic music includes exposure to poems and stories with moral import as well as training in the use of musical harmonies or scales to which these poems and stories are set. Platonic music includes much of what we think of as the fine arts.

up physical training, but the real benefit from this discipline is not bodily health and strength but harmony in the soul. The spirited part of the soul needs to be tamed and softened by exposure to music and hardened by physical training. The purpose of applying both physical training and music to the souls of the young is to harmonize the philosophic and spirited parts of the soul so as to produce temperance and courage (410d-411a). In light of this aptitude of music and gymnastic to produce harmony in the soul, Socrates declares that those who established the practice of education through music and gymnastic did not do so in the way that is commonly assumed, assigning to gymnastic the care of the body and to music the care of the soul. Rather, Socrates asserts that these founders of education established both music and education for the sake of the soul (410b10-c6). This claim about the purpose of the founding of Athenian and Greek educational practices amounts to an attribution of a novel purpose for institutions and practices already long established. When education in music and gymnastic is first introduced at 376e, Socrates says it would be hard to find a better schooling for the guardians than that "which has already been found over a long period of time"; this is gymnastic for the body and music for the soul.[17] Socrates' revision of the purpose of gymnastic, then, is not a case of allowing that while the traditional mode of education may take bodily health as its goal in employing gymnastic, he proposes a new goal, psychic harmony. Rather, Socrates makes the historical claim at 410b-c that the real purpose of gymnastic education since its inception was and is psychic harmony.

Socrates' argument for this historical claim about the purpose of gymnastic proceeds in a fashion we would expect from a proponent of the functional teleology of action. He does not consider the intentions or goals of the founders of gymnastic education; these intentions or goals are likely now lost in the mist of time and may, for all Socrates knows, in fact accord with the view of the many that gymnastic is mainly useful for fostering bodily health and strength. Instead of appealing to the goals and intentions connected with the inception of gymnastic education, Socrates sets out what he takes to be evident facts about the effects of gymnastic and musical education on the souls of students and makes several claims about how best to pursue this education. Used together and in the right amounts, gymnastic and music nurture a soul that

[17] This claim that gymnastic has as its purpose bodily strength and not psychic well-being fits the conventional understanding of physical training in Plato's day. Xenophon has Socrates in *Memorabilia* 3.12 rely on the conventional understanding of physical training to convince an out-of-shape youth to engage in physical and military training; training the body leads to good bodily condition and is an aid to knowledge only because bad physical condition leads us to commit mental mistakes. At the same time, proponents of the traditional program of music and gymnastic typically stressed the physical and moral effects of their program without assigning responsibility for the two types of effects separately, the former to gymnastic and the latter to music. In *The Clouds*, the *Dikaios Logos* praises the traditional Athenian system of education through music and gymnastic for the bodily strength and temperate character it produced; see *Clouds* 961-1009. Of course, Aristophanes is concerned to satirize and not just to describe the traditional education here; the *Dikaios Logos* exhibits an intemperate erotic interest in the bodies of the young boys who are shaped by gymnastic. See Marrou (1956, 36–45) for an account of traditional Athenian education and the place of physical training within it.

is both spirited and philosophic, able to fight against enemies while still loving reason. Music without gymnastic leads to a "feeble warrior"; gymnastic without reason leads to brute savagery. When both crafts perform their characteristic tasks or functions of cultivating the philosophic and arousing the spirited parts of the soul, they produce a harmonious, courageous, and temperate soul. This result follows from the best application of music and gymnastic. These factual and normative claims are the full extent of the argumentative support that Socrates provides for his claim that the founders of gymnastic and musical education put forward their innovations for the sake of the soul. Socrates follows the pattern already described of pointing to a particular result of actions, namely the production of psychic harmony, a result which follows from the performance of a function and the production of which is a necessary condition of the best performance of that function.[18]

Precisely because Socrates cannot tell us much about the conscious goals of the founders of Greek educational practices but can identify the purpose of those practices, he supplies a mythic origin for these practices. After setting forth the factual and normative claims identified above which support the identification of psychic harmony as the purpose of education, he summarizes at 411e4-7 his account of education: "It seems, then, that a god has given music and physical training to human beings not, except incidentally, for the body and soul but for the spirited and wisdom-loving parts of the soul itself…." This attribution of educational institutions to divine gift is not a mere pious fiction. Socrates is aware that at some unknown date, human beings began to practice education in music and gymnastic; regardless of the intentions of the first human practitioners of this schooling, it was done for the sake of psychic harmony and virtue. This whole scheme may be safely attributed to the divine since the result is divine and since no one human being can be identified as the inventor of the scheme. But Socrates' argument for the claim that gymnastic education has the purpose of fostering psychic harmony arrives before this divine attribution and stands or falls independently of it as an instance of the functional teleology of action.

---

[18] Again, the claim that we have an instance of the functional teleology of action can be given more definite shape by spelling out a different completion of the formal schema of Chapter 1. The claim that gymnastic and musical education is practiced for the sake of psychic harmony amounts to the following four conditions:

1) Students of music and gymnastic perform actions of performing music and physical training under the direction of teachers in these crafts, actions which are of lesser value than psychic harmony in the young
2) The actions of performing music and physical training under the direction of teachers in these crafts causally contribute to psychic harmony in the young in virtue of performing the functions of music and gymnastic
3) The value of the actions of performing music and physical training under the direction of teachers derives in part from their producing psychic harmony in the young
4) The actions of performing music and physical training under the direction of teachers in these crafts perform the functions of the crafts of music and gymnastic in the best way only if they causally contribute to psychic harmony.

These discussions of Class 3 goods suggest a general description of what makes for a Class 3 good: such a good is a rational practice conceived on the model of a craft which, when performed in the best way, produces a Class 2 good such as health or psychic harmony. Class 3 goods are performed for the sake of Class 2 goods, a process which may be a matter of consciously intending to promote a Class 2 good (as when a doctor aims to produce health) or a matter of acting for the sake of an unintended end (a weaver makes beautiful fabrics for the sake of psychic harmony in the young). Given that Class 2 goods are the ends for the sake of which Class 3 goods are performed, we can treat Class 2 goods as measures for the value of Class 3 good: a Class 3 good has its own particular sort of value because and to the extent that it promotes some Class 2 good.

These passages indicate that the best city is strongly unified by the role of Class 2 goods as ends and measures for Class 3 goods. Without explicit planning being required for this level of unity, the city is composed of activities and parts that interact organically. The result is the only city that is in fact one city: all other cities are composed of factions of rich and poor, dominating and dominated that are at war with each other (422e-423a). That this best city is unified results from its observance of the principle of specialization, especially with regard to the guardians. Speaking of the need to ensure that each person in the city does his or her own work, the task for which he or she is best suited, Socrates at 423c6-d6 connects the observance of the principle of specialization with the unification of the city:

And the [order] we mentioned earlier is even easier, when we said that, if an offspring of the guardians is inferior, he must be sent off to join the other citizens and that, if the others have an able offspring, he must join the guardians. This was meant to make clear that each of the other citizens is to be directed to what he is naturally suited for, so that, doing the one work [ergon] that is his own, he will become not many but one, and the whole city will itself be naturally one not many.

This passage links the actions of single individuals, each doing their own work or characteristic activity, to the unity of the whole city. The causal linkages between the two levels, that of individual actions and habits, and that of the city, we may suppose, are provided by the teleological patterns of crafts being carried on within the best city for the sake of psychic harmony and virtue. Thus the unity and harmony of the best city can be traced back to the parts of the city and to the actions of the individuals who make up those parts. Because Socrates introduced the city as a means to gain insight into the soul, we should expect that this pattern of action linking parts to whole through teleological structures will reveal itself again at the level of the individual soul. This is one theme of the next chapter, which is devoted to the parts of the soul.

6

Teleology and the Parts of the Soul

6.1 Introduction

Socrates introduces the political inquiry into the best city in order to see more clearly what justice means for the human soul. To recall his words at 368d, he wants us to view the word "justice" written in large letters so that we are better able to read the same word written in smaller letters. We should inquire into justice as it is present in the best city so that we are better able to understand the nature of justice in the soul. As we have seen, the best city is constituted by different parts which engage in partnerships and associations with each other. In this chapter, our attention turns from the city to the soul. We will consider the manner in which Socrates argues in *Republic* 4 that the soul has roughly the same parts as the best city. Our concern is not only to describe accurately the course of Socrates' reasoning; it is also to portray the soul described in *Republic* 4 as capable of acting for such ends as pleasure, honor, and knowledge. A further end for the sake of which the soul acts is, in the case of the virtuous soul, a hard-won unity.

Socrates' strategy for understanding justice in the soul requires that he first come to understand a more evident case of association, namely a city, and then apply what he learns there to the less evident case of association, the soul. Thus, we find Socrates in Books 2, 3, and 4 describing the best city as an association of citizens who fall into three classes, namely the wage earners, the auxiliaries, and the guardians. After setting forth this structure of the best city, he is able at 427c-434c to provide an account of the four cardinal virtues present in this city, namely wisdom, courage, temperance, and justice. His goal is to apply the resulting account of justice in the city to determine what justice is in the soul. This procedure requires that Socrates confirm and strengthen his original claim, first presented only in the most indeterminate form at 368-9, that the city is like the soul. This is what occurs at 434c-441c, where Socrates argues that the human soul is a complex whole composed of roughly the same parts as are present in the best city. He claims that, just as the city is made up of the wage-earning, auxiliary, and guardian classes, so is the soul made up of appetitive, spirited, and rational parts. Once the city-soul analogy has thus been reaffirmed in a more detailed form, Socrates is ready to apply the results of his investigation of justice in the city to the investigation of the nature of justice in the soul.

Socrates' division of the soul into three parts at 434c-441c provides commentators with a full budget of problems, of which two will be discussed in detail here.[1] The most basic issue is the nature of the psychic conflict that plays a key role in Socrates' argument. His demonstration that the soul has more than one part relies on pointing to the possibility of conflict or opposition within the soul, as in the case of people who are thirsty and desire to drink but do not drink. The nature of the conflict or opposition that requires partition of the soul has been the subject of controversy. Terence Irwin and Anthony Price hold that the sort of psychic conflict that leads to soul-partition is best characterized as one part of the soul taking up a second-order attitude of opposition toward another part of the soul. By contrast, Hendrik Lorenz denies that this second-order attitude of opposition is characteristic of the sort of conflict that reveals different parts of the soul. Lorenz proposes the "Simple Picture," according to which soul-partition in *Republic* 4 arises out of attraction to and aversion to the same action. Call this debate over the proper interpretation of psychic conflict the What-Sort-Of-Conflict Problem.

Second, commentators have noted that Socrates seems to describe the soul as composed of agent-like parts each of which is capable of desire, belief, and instrumental reasoning. If this is so, then the chances for the unity of the soul and of the human being may be vanishingly small. This interpretive problem, which may be termed the Unity Problem, has been posed in the strongest form by Christopher Bobonich: if the soul is composed of three parts, how can Plato think of the soul as a unified whole which is the bearer of moral responsibility for action?

The present chapter will set forth an interpretation of Socrates' division of the soul using teleological concepts of activity and the completion of an activity first discussed in the previous chapter. Having described and defended this interpretation, it will be possible to provide principled solutions to the What-Sort-Of-Conflict Problem and the Unity Problem. According to the present interpretation, the different parts of the soul should be conceived of as groupings of impulses to motion which share similar ends and which are stirred into motion by particular fields or types of objects. When the activities of the different parts of the soul are completed in the best way through access to the right sort of objects, the result is unity of the soul. This will allow us in the final section of the chapter to notice a further case of the functional teleology of action. In addition to the proper ends of the different parts (bodily pleasure, honor, the overall good of the agent), the soul's unity is one end for the sake of which all the parts operate, even though they may not conceive of this result as a goal to be pursued.

---

[1]   Two further problems will not be addressed in detail here. The first is the question of whether the parts of the soul qualify as freestanding agents. Those who describe the parts of the soul resulting from the partitioning arguments of Book 4 as agent-like parts include Moline (1978); Annas, (1981, 109–53); Irwin (1995, 203–42); and Bobonich (2002, 219–57). Opposed to this agential interpretation of the parts of the soul are Price (1995, 53–7) and Price (2009); Stalley (2007). A final problem is whether Plato in *Republic* 4 recognizes weakness of will, a thesis represented by Cooper (1984); Irwin (1995, 205–9); and Bobonich (2002, 216–47). This thesis is opposed by Carone (2001) and Shields (2007).

6.2 Parts of the Soul: Activities, Fields, Ends

Socrates begins his investigation of the soul by asking whether we act through a single thing, the soul, or whether we act on one occasion with one part and on another occasion with another. After contrasting the spiritedness of the Scythians with the love of money of the Egyptians and the love of learning of the Athenians, he asks at 436a8-b4 whether these different motivations and patterns of life come from one or more parts of the soul:

> Do we do these things with the same part of ourselves, or do we do them with three different parts? Do we learn with one part, get angry with another, and with some third part desire the pleasures of food, drink, sex, and the others that are closely akin to them? Or, when we set out after something, do we act with the whole of our soul, in each case? This is what's hard to determine in a way that's up to the standards of our argument.

After presenting these two options, he proceeds to argue for the second. To summarize his argument, he proposes the so-called Principle of Opposites: "It's clear that the same thing will not be willing at the same time to do or undergo opposites with respect to the same thing [*kata tauton*] and in relation to the same thing [*pros tauton*], so that if we ever find this arising in things, we will know that these are not the same but many."[2] Cases in which a thing seems simultaneously to do or undergo opposites in the same respect and in relation to the same thing are to be reconciled with the Principle of Opposites by attributing a plurality of parts to the thing in question. It happens in our experience that human beings do or undergo opposites in relation to the same possible course of action, as when a thirsty man desires to drink, has the option to drink some potable liquid, and yet does not drink. In such a case it is reasonable to attribute to the man some desire or impulse not to drink that opposes or blocks the postulated desire to drink. The desire to drink and the opposing desire or impulse not to drink fall under the more general categories of assent and dissent, acceptance and rejection of a course of action. If a human soul performs or undergoes both of these paired opposites in the same respect and in relation to the same thing, then that soul is composed of at least two distinct parts. The case of the thirsty man who abstains from drinking (hereafter TM) is offered to illustrate the opposition of appetite and reason: he both assents and dissents from drinking, and accepts and rejects the act of drinking. The appetitive part assents to and accepts the act of drinking while the rational part dissents from and rejects the same act (439c3-e2). Two other examples of opposing impulses are put forward. As Socrates explains these cases, Leontius is a man whose spirited part opposes his appetitive part's desire to look at corpses (439e5-440a7) while Odysseus is one

---

[2] 436b9–c2, revising the Grube-Reeve translation, which gives *kata tauton* at 436b10 as "with the same part." This translation takes a stand on the interpretation of the Principle of Opposites by presenting the phenomenon of undergoing opposites with respect to different aspects, a phenomenon apparently on display in the spinning top described at 436d4–e5 which is in motion with respect to its circumference and at rest in respect to its axis, as directly a case of different parts. The preferred translation leaves this interpretive question open.

whose rational part opposes his spirited part's desire to slaughter his maidservants for their service to Penelope's suitors (441b3-c2). Given the Principle of Opposites and the particular sorts of opposition alleged to occur in these cases, Socrates claims that we must recognize the existence of the appetitive, spirited, and rational parts of the soul.

This suffices to indicate the broad outlines of Socrates' argument. One basic task for the interpreter of this argument is that of characterizing the different parts of the soul. A first observation is that Socrates conceives of these distinct parts as responsible for different types of actions. In the passage 436a8-b4 quoted above, he asks whether we act through a single thing, the whole soul, or whether we act sometimes through one part of the soul, at other times through a second part of the soul, and on a third occasion through a third part of the soul. Socrates opts for the second alternative, according to which each part of the soul is a principle of a distinct sort of action. A part of the soul is that by which we desire, or become angry, or learn. Apparently Socrates takes our desiring, becoming angry, and learning as examples of our acting or doing (*prattomen*, 436a8-9) quite distinct sorts of activities.

If each part of the soul is a principle for action of a distinct sort, we may inquire as to how precisely this occurs. We might at first assume that the role of these parts as springs of action can be read off directly from their names. On this approach, the appetitive part serves as a principle of action by drawing upon desire while the rational part bases itself upon reasoned belief and other cognitive faculties. We need only find a third motivational source to assign to the spirited part in order to complete the proposed explanation, perhaps the emotion of anger or the drive for honor. But this approach will not succeed, since all three parts in fact generate action by evincing beliefs and desires.[3] We read in *Republic* 9 that each part of the soul has its own pleasures and desires (581a3-c8), and even the spirited and appetitive parts seem to rely upon beliefs as they orient themselves to act. The spirited part is softened by proper education in music and poetry to the effect that the auxiliaries and guardians in the best city will achieve temperance (410a-411b). The spirited part draws upon beliefs about what is fine and shameful inculcated in it by its education and can serve as the locus for the virtue of courage when it preserves true beliefs about what is to be feared and what is not (441a3, 442b10-c2). The appetitive part is described as the money-loving part because its desires find the easiest satisfaction through money (580d5-581a1). It is reasonable to assume that the appetitive part loves money not simply by desiring money for its own sake but by forming the belief that money secures the optimal satisfaction of bodily desires.

A better account of the fact that the parts of the soul serve as principles of action will portray the parts as directed impulses to motion where each part is responsible for a

---

[3] Moline (1978) and Bobonich (2002, 219–23) give detailed accounts of the quasi-agential character of the three parts of the soul in the *Republic*: each part exhibits beliefs and desires, communicates with the other parts, and is capable of persuading and being persuaded. Even if we do not go so far as Moline and Bobonich in affirming the agential character of the parts, it is clear that each part is associated with characteristic beliefs and desires.

distinct type or sort of motion. This conception of the parts starts from the observation that Socrates distinguishes parts of the soul in cases where he finds two opposed motions occurring in the soul. The first such case is that of the people who are thirsty but refuse to drink. While the rational part of the soul prevents the soul from drinking, the same soul insofar as it thirsts wishes to drink and rouses itself to drink (439a9-b1). Each part is identified by linking it with some motion toward or away from a single course of action, in this case drinking, and the parts are compared to the two hands of an archer exerting force in different directions (439b8-c1). This conception of the parts as directed impulses would allow Socrates to draw upon the view put forward in the *Phaedrus* and the *Laws*: that the soul is characterized essentially by motion and in particular self-motion, so that it can be defined as a principle of motion.[4] The soul moves itself in a number of different ways, and since this self-motion is an essential property of the soul we may speak of different forms (*eidē*, 435c1, 439e1, 440e7) or types (*genē*, 441a1, 443d3) of soul just as naturally as we may speak of the parts of the soul. The fact that the soul has different types based on the different types of motion of which it is capable can then be illustrated by the example of the spinning top which is at motion and at rest in the sense that it undergoes circular motion but lacks a different type of motion, the inclination of the top away from an axis drawn through its center (436d-e).

If the parts are characterized as impulses to different types of motion, this requires a more detailed account of these different types of motion. As ways in which the soul can generate motion, the parts can be described in terms of the types of things that rouse the soul to move itself, the activities which the parts carry out, and the ends toward which they move. In effect, Socrates specifies the three parts appetite, spirit, and reason as aroused by different fields or types of things, as carrying out different actions, and as arriving at different ends or satisfactions. This amounts to taking the distinction between different types of motion arising within the soul as arising not simply out of the different directions of motion through space or from whether such motion in space follows a straight or curved line. More important for Socrates' purposes is whether the motion is toward money, honor, or learning: the ends that define the motions ascribed to Egyptians, Scythians, and Athenians by Socrates' amateur ethnography. This pattern of motion toward an end is manifest in the appetitive part. This part is illustrated by the workings of thirst, which is by its nature a desire for drink or potable liquid. In relation to its object, potable liquid, thirst moves the soul to drink; drinking is the activity for which thirst is responsible. By gaining access to its object and carrying out the action of drinking, thirst achieves its particular pleasure, the pleasure of quenching thirst. Two other desires that Socrates mentions as relatively clear examples of the appetitive part are hunger, and eros or sexual desire. For hunger, we may supply the field or object of food, the activity of eating, and the pleasure that results from eating

---

[4] *Phaedrus* 245c–246a, *Laws* 895a–896b. This feature of Plato's conception of the soul is explored briefly in Miller (1999, 90–1).

when hungry. For eros, the field or object is the body of the beloved, the activity is sexual intercourse, and the end is sexual pleasure.

The spirited part of the soul also can be described in terms of a field in relation to which it is aroused, the activity it carries out, and the end it pursues. To judge from the examples given in *Republic* 4, the spirited part of a person is aroused when the person carries out actions or endures events that are shameful or when the person envisions such a prospect. Leontius feels shame at his looking with pleasure on the corpses piled up by the side of the road, and Odysseus sees his maidservants sleeping with the suitors as an event that brings shame upon him, the head of the household. These two examples also show the spirited part of the soul carrying out its distinctive activity of resisting what is shameful. This occurs in two different ways, with the spirited part either reacting to the activities of the other two parts within the soul or reacting to external events. In the Leontius case, the spirited part acts as a police force within the soul, in particular by supervising and disciplining the appetitive part. The Odysseus case shows how the spirited part acts in relation to the outside world: it resists the actions of others that would inflict dishonor on the soul. Common to both cases is a commitment to fight against what is shameful. In response to this perception of shamefulness, the spirited part acts out of anger to prevent or beat back the shameful act or event, either by Leontius holding himself back from gazing at the corpses or by Odysseus slaughtering the maidservants. If this typical pattern of action is carried out successfully by the spirited part, then the spirited part gains its ends of honor and self-esteem and avoids blame and ill repute.[5]

The rational part is identified first as the part that opposes thirsty people's desire to drink. On the basis of calculation, the rational part forbids such people to drink (439d1). This part is responsible for calculating what is better and what is worse, according to Socrates' commentary on Odysseus' refraining from slaughtering the maidservants (441c1-2). He claims that it is appropriate for this rational part to rule,

---

[5] This presentation of the spirited part of the soul accords in its general outline with the accounts given by Brennan (2012) and Singpurwalla (2013). Brennan describes the spirited part as pursuing honor through two complementary activities. First, it monitors the distribution of appetitive goods among and between persons to ensure that the individual obtains its proper share of these goods. Second, it maintains order between the different parts of the soul within the person, in particular by ensuring that the appetitive part does not overstep its bounds. For Brennan the spirited part carries out these tasks while operating at a distinct cognitive disadvantage. Its capacity to invest real features of the world with the predicate "honorable" is an artifact of culture and education and not a genuine way of knowing the world: "But spirit is constitutionally incapable of grasping such things [as the Form of the Good or of Beauty]. It is the constant dupe of culture, with no internal capacity to imagine that the noble is other than what its training and environment tell it to admire"; Brennan (2012, 111). By contrast, Singpurwalla assigns to spirit the capacity to perceive society-independent facts about what is honorable: "…there is a fact of the matter about what it is to be fine and honourable, and it is this fact that shapes the individual's conception of the fine and honourable. I argue that being fine and honourable involves living up to your rational views about how you should behave, despite appetitive temptations to the contrary"; see Singpurwalla (2013, 42–3). Brennan and Singpurwalla disagree on the degree of cognitive achievement to be ascribed to the spirited part, but share a basic conception of the spirited part as pursuing honor by resisting demeaning conduct on the part of others toward the soul or on the part of the appetitive part of the soul. This is the core of the present account of the spirited part.

"since it is really wise and exercises foresight on behalf of the whole soul…." (441e3-4). Given these comments on what the rational part does, we can identify as the field or object of the rational part the prospect of benefit or harm for the whole soul. Such a field lacks the specificity of the field associated with thirst/ potable liquid, and is defined not by its relation to such a natural kind but by the general property of being beneficial or harmful to a human soul. Any event or object that is apt to yield benefit or harm for the whole soul will show up on rational part's radar screen. In response to this field, the activity proper to the rational part is calculating or reckoning the benefit or harm for the whole soul that is achieved by a prospective course of action or event. More will be said about this activity of calculation, but at the least, it involves gaining insight into the positive and negative outcomes of potential courses of action. It is by calculation that the thirsty man realizes that he will suffer serious harm if he drinks water while suffering from dropsy. By calculation, Odysseus understands that he stands to lose his chance to gain revenge on the suitors if he slaughters the maidservants and thus drops the guise of being a harmless beggar. Finally, if the rational part carries out its activity of calculating, it achieves as its end the overall benefit for the whole soul at which it aims in its calculations.

This description of the different parts of the soul diverges from some commentary on the parts of the soul by requiring a three-fold specification of each soul-part. A part of the soul is defined as a grouping of motions or desires each of which has an activity, an object or field, and an end. At times commentators discuss parts of the soul as defined by their orientation to activities and ends, leaving out the notion of the object or field of a part.[6] Some explanation of the field or object of a part is in order, then, to clarify the notion. Actions such as drinking or eating or being angry or learning require something in relation to which these actions take place. The desire that is thirst motivates a person to drink, and in this context I use the term "object" to refer to a general type, potable liquid, tokens of which make the activity of drinking possible. The appetitive part drinks when it thirsts and has access to potable liquid, the spirited part becomes angry in reaction to some shameful act being perpetrated, and the rational part calculates concerning the benefit of the soul by considering existing things under the aspect of their being beneficial or harmful to the soul. The appetitive part is a cluster of desires similar to thirst, each with its own object, so that the object of the appetitive part is

---

[6] For example, in discussing Socrates' claim at 437d that thirst is the desire for drink and not for good drink, Lorenz has this to say: "…[I]f someone has a desire that is fully specified simply as thirst, the object of that desire is fully specified simply as drink, or drinking…. If so, the principle requires that there are in fact cases in which a desire occurs the object of which is fully specified as drink or drinking. What such a desire is for is, simply and without qualification, drinking"; see Lorenz (2006, 28–9). In his exposition of the Simple Picture, Lorenz in effect collapses the object or field of a desire (for example, drink or potable liquid as the object of thirst) into the activity which the desire carries out (drinking). Similarly, Irwin omits the object in relation to which opposing actions take place from his statement of the Principle of Opposites, or as he terms it the Principle of Contraries: "The same thing cannot do or undergo contraries in respect of the same aspect of itself"; see Irwin (1995, 204). Tad Brennan speaks of honor as the object of the spirited part of the soul, meaning that honor is what the spirited part pursues as its end; see Brennan (2012, 110).

a field or range of such objects.[7] The spirited part has as its field those states of affairs that bring dishonor to an agent, while the rational part has the field of those states of affairs that harm or benefit the soul as a whole.

To further specify this account of the object of a part, it will be helpful to compare the present account of drink, the object of thirst, with Gabriela Roxana Carone's treatment of the same. Carone offers her account of the object of thirst in the course of arguing that Plato's description of thirst and other appetitive desires does not amount to a rejection of the Socratic view that all desire is desire for good things found in the *Meno*, *Gorgias*, and *Protagoras*.[8] When Socrates asserts that thirst is of drink and not good drink, this is part of "a 'theory of intentionality' by which every mental faculty is indi-viduated and defined by its own distinctive object."[9] On Carone's account and on mine, Socrates' claim at 439a4-7 that thirst is of drink and not of good drink is meant to delineate the sort of thing in relation to which thirst operates. And on both accounts that claim does not commit him to rejecting the claim that all desire is desire for good things. Thus, Socrates' claim at 439a4-7 does not commit him to affirming the possibility of *akrasia* through the presence of good-independent desires in the soul. The accounts differ in the way in which thirst is related to drink. For Carone, this relation is one species of the intentional relation between mental entities and the world. In my view, this intentional relation is not the proper model for describing the relation between a part of the soul and the object that makes possible that part's activity. Socrates at 438a-c explicates the object of thirst in part by reference to such non-intentional relations as the faster being faster than the slower and the double being double the half. This should warn us away from Carone's approach to understanding the relation between thirst and its object. In addition, the intentional attitude of desire toward the thing desired typically involves conceiving of the desideratum as satisfying some description: good or pleasant or useful. This implication of the intentional attitude of desire works at cross-purposes to Socrates' claim that the object of thirst is simply drink and not any particular kind of drink. The better way to conceive of the object of thirst is as the potable liquid in the world that is necessary for thirst to move an agent to drink. This relation of a desire to its object is a non-intentional relation, since the desire moves the agent to drink only if the object of drink, potable liquid, is actually present. By contrast, the intentional relation between mental states and their intentional objects does not require the existence outside the mind of objects answering to these mental states.

---

[7] On this description of the appetitive part, it is a cluster of desires (thirst, hunger, sexual desire, the desire for money) which do not share a strong unity. Their objects are a somewhat disparate lot (water, food, the body of a beloved, money) united by their ability to afford pleasure when the soul carries out the activities of drinking, eating, and sexual intercourse. Apparently, the fact that the pleasures pursued by the appetitive desires are related or akin (*adelpha*, 436b1–2) is responsible for this part achieving a limited unity. It is an advantage of this account that it assigns to the appetitive part only a limited unity, since Socrates at 588c7-10 compares this part to a "multicolored beast with a ring of heads that it can grow and change at will – some from gentle, some from savage animals."

[8] Carone (2001).   [9] Carone (2001, 118).

In support of defining a soul-part in this way by reference to the field or object of the part, I would point to two considerations. First, the discussion of the natural object of a desire at 437d5-439b1 contains a series of comparisons between thirst and a range of disparate relations, comparisons which require us to distinguish between the activity, the object, and the end of thirst. The comparisons in question range widely: just as thirst is of drink, so the greater is greater than the less, the double is double the half, the heavier is heavier than the light, the faster is faster than the slower, knowledge is knowledge of what is learned, and carpentry is knowledge of the production of buildings. If these comparisons are to shed light on what thirst is "of," then we should not take thirst's object to be simply the thing desired or the thing that satisfies desire. Socrates sees the greater being greater than the lesser and the faster being faster than the slower, and takes these relations to be comparable to thirst being "of" drink. With regard to the greater and the faster, a relational property takes some object in relation to which the property is realized. The faster needs the slower to exist in order to be faster than something. To extrapolate from these cases, what thirst is "of" is the thing that the thirsty person requires in order to engage in the activity of drinking. Without the notion of the object of a desire as that thing in relation to which desire occurs, and which allows the desire to generate its characteristic activity, such comparisons between thirst and the greater and the faster will seem abstruse. In addition, the object of thirst, potable liquid, is not the same as that which thirst seeks as its end. The end sought by the appetitive part is bodily pleasure. A person can drink liquid without deriving pleasure from it, as when the person is hot and thirsty and drinks a cup of hot coffee instead of the cold drink that would be pleasing. The object of thirst is drink and not hot drink or cold drink or much drink or little drink (437d7-e6). For thirst to achieve its end, pleasure, it must have hot drink or cold drink or much drink or little drink, depending on the condition of the thirsty person.[10] In the case of the hot and thirsty person drinking hot coffee, the characteristic activity of thirst is present, as is thirst's object, potable liquid, but the lack of pleasure indicates that thirst's end is not achieved. So the object of a desire such as thirst is distinct from both its activity and its end.

Second, the notion of the object of a part allows us to make sense of the precise wording of the Principle of Opposites. That principle sets out the sort of scenario that will force us to attribute a plurality of parts to a thing that seems to exhibit opposite

---

[10] This account of pleasure following upon or being constituted by a desire finding a particular sort of object goes beyond what can be found in the text at 437d5-439b1. However, it is consistent with the account of the pleasures that follow upon eating and drinking found at *Gorgias* 496c-e and *Republic* 585b-d. Such bodily pleasures are or follow upon the filling of a deficiency or lack in the body. The *Philebus* provides a more nuanced account of such pleasures; the pleasures of food and drink are the processes of restoring the body to a natural state of equilibrium (*Philebus* 31d-32b, 42c-d). From the perspective afforded by this later dialogue, thirst has as its object drink, but thirst achieves pleasure when a deficiency or excess in the body of some quality is balanced by taking in food or drink with the properties required to affect a restoration of the natural equilibrium of the body (e.g., too much dryness and heat in the body is balanced by drinking a cold liquid).

actions. The principle tells us, in its literal wording, that the same thing will not simultaneously undergo or perform opposites with respect to the same thing [*kata tauton*]
and in relation to the same thing [*pros tauton*]. We should expect the last phrase, "in
relation to the same thing," to make its own contribution to the meaning of Principle of
Opposites. The preceding phrase, "with respect to the same thing," seems to indicate
that we are not forced to attribute a plurality of parts if an object exhibits opposites of
assenting to and rejecting an action but exhibits these opposites through different
aspects of itself. The man who moves his head and hands while standing in the same
spot moves some of his parts but does not move others. The spinning top is both at rest
and moves, but it is at rest with respect to its axis (*kata men to euthu*, 436e1) while it
moves as a whole with respect to its circumference (*kata de to peripheres*, 436e2) by
rotating. No reference so far is made to anything outside either the man or the top. But
the cases of psychic conflict that concern Socrates, especially the case TM, involve the
soul of an agent experiencing opposites in relation to something outside of the agent.
People who are thirsty have a desire which has an external object, potable liquid, and
those who are thirsty but do not drink seem to undergo opposites in relation to a single
instance of that object: their soul simultaneously bids and forbids them to drink a
given instance of potable liquid. Even after we distinguish parts of the soul, it is necessary to maintain a single thing to which the different parts take up opposed relations of
desire and aversion. The object of a part is a type of external thing, an instance of which
arouses desire in one part. At the same time, this instance draws the opposition of
another part in virtue of its posing a threat to the honor of the agent or to the good
of the whole soul. Seen in this light, the "in relation to the same thing" clause in the
Principle of Opposites is not simply a reiteration of the content of the "with respect
to the same thing" clause. This is confirmed by the restatement of the Principle of
Opposites at 439b5-6. There, Socrates confirms his claim that in the TM case we have
two parts within the one who is thirsty yet refrains from drinking by reminding
Glaucon of their support for the Principle of Opposites: "It can't be, we say, that the
same thing, with the same part of itself, and in relation to the same [*peri to auto*], at
the same time, does opposite things." The notion expressed in the first statement of
the Principle of Opposites by "with respect to the same" is here expressed by "with the
same part," while the notion of "in relation to the same," first expressed by the preposition *pros*, is now expressed by the preposition *peri*. In this second formulation of
the Principle of Opposites, the two notions "with the same part" and "in relation to the
same" are clearly different from each other. Since it is the same principle that is
expressed in both formulations, the notions expressed by "with respect to the same"
and "in relation to the same" in the first formulation must also differ from each
other. The object of a part of the soul helps to determine the referent for the expression
"in relation to the same." In the case of psychic conflict, two parts of the soul take up
different stances in relation to a single token falling under two types. This allows
each part of the Principle of Opposites to make its unique contribution to the meaning
of the whole.

6.3 The Rational Part: Calculation and Practical Judgment

In this discussion of the parts of the soul and their respective activities, objects, and ends, the rational part in particular deserves closer consideration. Its success or failure in achieving its end of benefit for the whole soul is clearly decisive for the well-being of the person. Yet we gain surprisingly little information about how this part of the soul does its job from *Republic* 4. We know that we learn by this part of the soul (436a): that it uses calculation to oppose harmful desires of the appetitive part; that spirit normally aligns itself with the rational part against the appetitive part (440a-b); that the rational part calms the spirited part by its pronouncements like a shepherd calling his dog to heel (440d); that its operation of calculation appears in most people only in maturity and fails completely to appear in some (441a-b); and that its calculations amount to having foresight concerning whether prospective courses of action are better or worse for the soul of the agent considered as a whole (441b, 441e). The tasks of the rational part are alternately described at 442a-c as deliberating to keep the soul and body in good condition and passing on instructions to the spirited part as to which actions or events are to be feared and which are not to be feared. These descriptions of the rational part amount to a description of what it produces, benefit for the whole soul or person, but say relatively little concerning how exactly it achieves this important result. Recent publications by Jessica Moss and Todd Ganson have shown that the rational part (the *logistikon*) engages in the activity of calculation (*logizesthai*) in order to provide reliable assignments of value to proposed courses of action. The rational part of the soul differs from the other two parts by its ability to aim at and locate the truth about what is good as opposed to being deceived by appearances. These contributions by Moss and Ganson point us in the right direction, but they leave open how exactly the rational part carries out its activity of calculation.[11] In order to characterize the rational part more fully, it is necessary to look to other passages in the *Republic* where the rational part and its operation of calculation appear.

The first text is the description of calculation (*logistikē*) and arithmetic in Book 7 of the *Republic* (522c1-526c5). This passage will be discussed in more detail in Chapter 10, but a quick summary of the passage will help to guide our sense of what the rational (*logistikon*) part of the soul does. Calculation for Socrates is of the utmost importance; it is employed in every craft and every type of thought (522c1-2), and it is a required course of study for the philosophers who will serve as guardians in the best city (525b1-c6). Its importance suggests that calculation does not consist merely in the addition and

---

[11] See Moss (2008) and Ganson (2009). One strength of these treatments of the rational part of the soul as engaging in calculation and aiming explicitly at truth is that they allow us to conceive of the appetitive and spirited parts as capable of a range of cognitive activities. If we link the rational part to the operation of calculation in particular, this allows us then to affirm that the other parts of the soul possess lower-level cognitive abilities (belief, the ability to communicate with other parts, instrumental reasoning) while still emphasizing their distinction from the rational part. They do not calculate and so are prey to deceptive appearances unless they are securely guided by the rational part.

subtraction of mathematical quantities. Rather, calculation supports the soul's drive to find definitions of the opposite qualities that are found together in perceptible objects. We perceive ordinary objects such as fingers as both big and little, hard and soft, and any object or number presents itself to perception as both one and many (523e1-524b5). In this context, a number must be understood not as an abstract and indivisible object but as a collection of units. Such objects are summoners, in that they summon the intellect to use calculation to find the truth about the opposite qualities presented to sense-perception. Calculation allows the soul to determine whether these opposite qualities are two or one. Once calculation tells the soul that they are different and separate from each other, then the understanding is able to pursue the question of what each is and to see them as separate entities (524c6-11). After we are in possession of definitions, we are able to recognize in what way things are both big and little, hard and soft, and one and many. This puts us in a position to understand how a finger can be both big and little, and hard and soft. In particular, Socrates treats calculation as the faculty that allows us to examine any quantity as a thing that is both one and many, a single collected entity and a plurality of units. The most characteristic feature of calculation is its preoccupation with number and the task of determining the quantity of a given thing (525a10-11). When faced with a thing that is both one and many, calculation sets an intelligible unit, a "one" that cannot be divided within the given context of finding the quantity of a particular object (525d5-e3). By setting this basic unit, calculation allows us to answer the question "How many?" with regard to such a plurality. The unit measures the plurality in question a determinate number of times, so that a tree is so many branches, a herd of cattle is so many cows, and an army is so many soldiers.

This thumbnail sketch of calculation or *logistikē* as it appears in *Republic* 7 can be used to explicate the workings of the rational or *logistikon* part of the soul in *Republic* 4. Apparently, Socrates saw important similarities between calculation, understood in this way as a process of discrimination of opposite aspects leading to definitions of these aspects, and the activity of the rational part of the soul, making a practical judgment to engage in or avoid a particular course of action. Such practical judgments can be seen most clearly when they are given in opposition to the urgings of appetitive desire or spirit. In such cases of psychic conflict, the rational part may consider the fact that a proposed course of action seems both good and bad, and desirable and undesirable. The thirsty man who refrains from drinking must be capable of considering the action of drinking as both good *qua* pleasantly thirst-quenching and bad *qua* unhealthy. The rational part of the soul may then take up the considerations that speak in favor of drinking and may gain insight into the ends that would be promoted by this action, namely bodily pleasure. The rational part will also survey the considerations that speak against drinking and the ends that refraining from drinking will promote, namely health. This consideration of the opposed motives in play in such a case of psychic conflict corresponds to one aspect of calculation in *Republic* 7, namely its ability to direct the soul toward comprehension of the two opposing qualities whose compresence characterizes summoners (big and small, hard and soft, etc.). Situations of psychic conflict such as the thirsty man who refrains from drinking or Odysseus' restraining his anger are practical summoners, so to speak. They provide the rational part of the soul with the task of determining what is desirable and what is undesirable, harmful and beneficial, good and bad in some possible course of action.

A second aspect of calculation in *Republic* 7 is the ability of the calculator to find a basic unit that measures any quantity that can be described as being both one and many. The provision of this basic unit allows for accurate measurement of the original quantity and allows that quantity to be described as five feet long or two thousand soldiers. A practical judgment put forward by the rational part of the soul will not in every case turn on assigning such a quantitative measurement to a proposed course of action. However, it will relate that course of action, drinking this liquid for instance, to a single value, the overall good of the whole soul. At 441b, Socrates speaks of the rational part as calculating what is better and what is worse. This apparently means that the rational soul characterizes different courses of action as better or worse for the whole soul; soon after, Socrates says that the rational part ought to rule because it exercises forethought on behalf of the whole soul (441e3-4). The good of the whole soul, however conceived, is apparently the basic value in reference to which the rational soul characterizes different actions as better or worse. Although the man is thirsty and can expect pleasure from drinking, not drinking is better for the whole soul because drinking, though pleasant, will cause sickness. Not drinking, though painful, preserves health. The good of the whole soul must be conceived in sufficient detail for the rational soul to rank the preservation of health as better for the soul than achieving bodily pleasure at the cost of health. In such cases, the rational soul exercises forethought by describing a proposed course of action in terms of its positive or negative effect on some basic good to which the agent is committed. The rational part does this on behalf of the whole soul by forming some conception of the good of the whole soul and by taking this good condition of the soul as the basic value in relation to which proposed actions are evaluated as better or worse. To make a fully rational judgment to act or not to act, then, is to calculate by evaluating the action in terms of its relation to the good of the whole soul.

This pattern of judgment may be illustrated by considering Socrates' refusal to escape from prison in the *Crito*. Socrates' discussion with Crito about the advisability of escape serves as a dramatic enactment of relations between the rational and the spirited parts of the soul. Crito attempts to convince Socrates to escape by drawing the latter's attention to the harm that will be done to Crito's reputation and that of other friends of Socrates. The ordinary person in Athens will believe that Socrates' friends were unwilling to spend the money necessary to ensure his escape, and so Crito will gain the worst reputation of all, that of one who values his money more than his friends. Socrates compliments Crito on his spirited zeal or eagerness (*prothumia*, 46b1), but cautions that this eagerness is valuable only if it is directed correctly. Socrates himself is one who is always persuaded by the argument that seems best to him as he calculates (*moi logizomenōi*, 46b6).

Socrates engages in calculation in the *Crito* in a two-stage process. He begins by taking up the considerations that Crito puts forward as most salient in characterizing escape from prison as good and remaining in prison as bad, namely honor and ill repute. He reasons that honor and ill repute are not, merely as such, good and bad; the only honor that is valuable is that awarded by those who know, not honor awarded by those who are ignorant (47a-48a). This leads Socrates to reject Crito's belief that we should concern ourselves with the opinion of the many about what is good, fine, just, and their opposites. This first stage of Socrates' calculations corresponds to the aspect of calculation in the *Republic* that involves separating the opposed qualities that are present together in a given action. The same action may be shameful and fine, in that it appears shameful to the many who are ignorant, and fine to the one who knows. Next, Socrates at *Crito* 48b4-c2 proposes a single value in relation to which the rightness or wrongness of escaping from prison may be reliably determined. The good life, the beautiful life, and the just life are the same, so the crucial question for Socrates is whether his escaping from prison is a just action or not. Here Socrates dismisses the considerations in favor of escaping which Crito brought forward, namely that staying in prison will lead to his death and dishonor for his friends. Once it is decided that it is unjust for him to escape from prison, these considerations will not be included in his calculations (*hupologizesthai*, 48d4). The bulk of the *Crito* is then devoted to considering whether it is just or unjust for Socrates to escape from prison, as Socrates argues that it would be unjust for him to escape from prison and thus break the agreement he made to obey the laws. This argument may be disputed, especially since Socrates' position comes uncomfortably close to giving the state unlimited authority over the lives of its citizens. Nevertheless, it is clear that Socrates in the *Crito* attempts to carry out the second aspect of the activity of calculation present in the *Republic*: having settled on a single basic value, he determines the rightness or wrongness of an action by its positive or negative influence on that value. That single value mentioned in the *Crito*, the good and just life, will coincide with the single value which calculation in *Republic* 4 takes as its end, the overall benefit of the soul. Living a just life improves the soul while unjust action harms the soul (*Crito* 47d-48a).

6.4 What Sort of Conflict? Partition of the Soul in *Republic* 4

This discussion of texts from *Republic* 7 and the *Crito* is intended to shed light on the particular activity that is characteristic of the rational part of the soul. In cases of psychic conflict, the rational part is capable of considering a possible course of action and distinguishing between the good and bad, beautiful and shameful, desirable and undesirable aspects of that action. It attempts to define as best it can these opposed properties. And it evaluates the proposed course of action by placing it in relation to a single value, described either as the good life or as the benefit of the soul as a whole.

Having achieved this description of the rational part's activity, we can profitably take up the What-Sort-Of-Conflict Problem arising from the tripartition of the soul. As Terence Irwin and Anthony Price have noted, it is not just any sort of conflict of desires that gives rise to Socrates' partition of the soul. It is possible to be torn between two desires such that acting on one desire rules out acting upon the other, but we do not for this reason expect that the soul should be divided. Terry Penner describes such a case: a thirsty man lying in bed on a cold morning desires both to remain in his warm bed and to get a drink of water. The man can act upon only one of these desires and so experiences a conflict of desires, but we do not think this should give rise to a partition within the soul, perhaps into a warmth-seeking part and a drink-seeking part.[12] To address this problem, Irwin seeks to describe a special type of contrariety of desires which will divide the appetitive from the rational and spirited parts but will not subdivide the appetitive part. His solution relies on presenting the spirited and rational parts as not merely generating desires that work at cross purposes to appetitive desires but also as taking a stand against acting on appetitive desire as such:

Opposition 'to an appetite' may be simply an aversion to this appetite for this object; alternatively, it may be opposition to acting on appetite as such. In the second case, the opposition presupposes some grounds for objection to following appetite. Since no appetite can itself be opposed to acting on appetite, the sort of desire that opposes acting on appetite must be some non-appetitive type of desire. Plato's position is reasonable if he takes the desires that are contrary to appetite to be those that are opposed to acting on appetite as such.[13]

This strategy explains partition of the soul by reference to a special type of opposition between desires, namely the sort of opposition where at least one desire is opposed in principle to acting upon the other desire.

Price adopts a variant of this strategy as well. He distinguishes between the weak contrariety between two desires that in particular cases cannot both be acted upon, and the strong contrariety of desires found in a person who is actively set upon pursuing two incompatible courses of action. In addition, such strong contrariety of desires may be the scene of confrontation, when one desire takes up a negative attitude toward the other desire:

Plato has in mind a rejection of a desire to drink that entails a desire not to drink. There will then be both a *contrariety* of desire, and a *confrontation* of desire: I not only want to act in a certain way and to act otherwise, but further have one desire that adversarily confronts another, a desire that looks another in the face and recoils from it.[14]

As in Irwin's discussion of soul-partition, the crucial ingredient for division into parts is the fact that the desire of one part takes up opposition not just to the particular action proposed by the desire of another part, but to the other desire's role in giving rise to action.

---

[12] Penner (1971, 109–111).   [13] Irwin (1995, 207–8).   [14] Price (1995, 47).

This strategy for explaining soul-partition faces an important objection: it ascribes to the rational part too general an opposition to acting on appetite. According to Irwin, the rational part opposes acting upon appetitive desire as such. This is objectionable both from the point of view of attributing to Socrates a cogent position and from the point of view of interpreting his position in a way that is consistent with other passages in the *Republic*. To attribute to Socrates the notion that the rational part is opposed to acting on appetitive desire as such is to saddle him with an unattractive conception of the relations between the rational and the appetitive parts. If thirst bids me to drink the glass of water before me and I am not aware of any special circumstances present that speak against drinking (I am not suffering from dropsy, no drops of deadly poison have been mixed into the water, etc.), then I normally follow my appetite and drink the water. It would seem obtuse for Socrates to hold that acting upon appetitive desire in normal circumstances is opposed by the rational part, at least until the rational part can intervene and supply its own desire to drink, one that has been derived from pro-cesses of reasoning and is thus untainted by appetite. In addition, later passages in the *Republic* dealing with appetitive desire and bodily pleasure do not support the notion that the rational part opposes the appetitive part as such. In normal circumstances, when a man drinks water because he is thirsty, the appetitive desire in play will qualify as a necessary desire. Necessary desires are described at 558d-e as the sort of desire which cannot be eliminated by habituation and whose satisfaction benefits the person who acts upon it (in normal cases, it is good for a thirsty person to drink water). Following such necessary desires leads to harmless pleasures, which are goods of the first class in the division of goods proposed by Glaucon and accepted by Socrates. Saying this much does not deny that the rational part has the task of supervising and guiding the appetitive part. Under the guidance of reason the appetitive part gains what is best for it, the truest pleasures open to it (586d-e). This indicates that the appetitive part stands in need of the rational part, but it is quite distant from the claim that the rational part opposes the appetitive part as such. When the appetitive part follows the guidance of reason and gains the truest pleasures possible for it, this is a matter of the appetitive part gaining its own pleasures (586e1, 587a1-2) and gaining what is most related to it (*oikeiotaton*, 586e2). If the rational part opposed the workings of appetitive desire as such, the scenario in which appetite gains what is best for it under the guidance of reason would not be described as a matter of appetite gaining its own pleasures or gaining what is most related to it.

With regard to the TM case, it is necessary to clarify why it is that reason opposes the impulses of the appetitive part. This opposition may be based on a contingent feature of the workings of desire in a particular case, or reason may oppose appetitive desire in a more fundamental way. I hold that the former option is the better description of the TM case. There is nothing objectionable *per se* in desiring to drink when thirsty; in most cases, this is an impulse worth supporting. It is only in the exceptional cases where the would-be drinker is ill or where the water has been poisoned that reason must step in to oppose desire. For Irwin, reason opposes simply following the impulses of desire, while for Price reason confronts desire. There may be desires worth opposing as such or worth confronting, but the TM case does not seem to justify this sort of opposition.

At this point one who supports Irwin and Price's strategy may defend that strategy as follows. The sort of opposition between desires that leads to partition of the soul in a case such as TM is not the rational part's opposition to acting on appetitive desire as such, but its opposition to acting upon appetitive desire when doing so is harmful and runs counter to the purposes of the rational part.[15] This is a sensible approach to describing the conflict between reason and appetite; when the rational part opposes the appetitive part in the case TM, we should understand the rational part objecting not to the general phenomenon of drinking water when thirsty or acting upon appetitive desire, but drinking water when doing so damages the agent's health (e.g., when the drinker suffers from dropsy). But this strategy would amount to an essential change in Irwin and Price's approach to describing the sort of conflict that generates partition of the soul. What the rational part thus opposes or confronts is not the desires of the appetitive part as such, but those appetitive desires which happen to conflict with the rational desire for health and the overall good of the agent. On this modified version of Irwin and Price's approach, what the rational part opposes is not the appetitive part's standing as a source of action, but simply acting in ways that are harmful.

In light of this objection to Irwin and Price's solution to the What-Sort-Of-Conflict Problem, I propose a different solution. According to the account of the parts of the soul offered previously, each part is best described as a type of motion by which the soul acts. Different motions are distinguished by their objects or fields, the activities that the parts carry out in relation to those objects, and the ends they pursue. In the case of TM, the appetitive part responds to an instance of its object, drink, by prompting the agent to drink the quantity of potable liquid before it in order to achieve its end of pleasure. The appetitive part will respond to the possible course of action positively; it sees this prospect as pleasant and so pursues it. The rational part on the other hand generates opposition to this course of action by responding to its field or object, those objects or events that yield benefit or harm to the whole soul. In the case of TM, one instance of the object of the rational part is the quantity of water that the appetitive part hankers for. In considering the water, the rational part is aware of two aspects. The water promises pleasure, but it also will do harm to the person's health. The rational part engages in the first part of its characteristic activity of calculation by becoming aware of both aspects of the water, the aspect under which drinking the water is pleasant and desirable and the aspect under which drinking the water is harmful and undesirable.

---

[15] This option is present in the following comment from Price: "Rejection of a desire may take various forms: I may recoil from having it; I may recoil from ever fulfilling it; I may recoil from fulfilling it here and now"; see Price (1995, 57). Price might choose the third alternative in describing the rational part's rejection of appetitive desire. If he were to do so, however, he would depart from the spirit of the strategy of explaining soul-partition by reference to one part rejecting another part in principle as a worthy source of action.

It sees the proposed course of action as a practical summoner, the sort of situation that carries both positive and negative aspects. The rational part then resolves this conflict by engaging in the second part of calculation: it refers the proposed course of action, drinking the water, to the single value of the good of the whole soul. From this perspective, drinking the water is rejected, since the pleasure that follows upon drinking is judged less good for the whole soul than the health that would be lost by drinking. In pursuit of its end of overall benefit for the soul, the rational part dissents from the activity of drinking, and so enters into opposition to the appetitive part. To use the metaphor of the archer whose hands pull and push in opposite directions, the appetitive part draws the water to itself while the rational part pushes it away.

On this account of the TM example, we can specify exactly where the conflict between the parts is located. The two parts take opposing stances toward the action of drinking the water: the appetitive part seeks to drink the water for the sake of pleasure, while the rational part seeks not to drink the water for the sake of health and the good of the whole soul. The two parts are reacting to the same particular thing, the water, though they will react to it under different descriptions. The appetitive part will see the water as pleasant while the rational part will see it as unhealthy. The fact that they take up opposing stances with regard to the same action, drinking, is explained by the different descriptions each part gives of the water. These different descriptions in terms of health and pleasure stem from the two parts being devoted to different ends, pleasure in the case of the appetitive part and the overall good of the whole soul in the case of the rational part.

We may extrapolate from the analysis of TM to a general description of the conditions that, according to *Republic* 4, will require partition of the soul. Partition of the soul is necessary, Socrates will say, just in case

1) there are opposing motions within the soul with regard to the same action (assent and dissent with regard to drinking water in the case of TM);
2) the opposing motions arise in reaction to a single particular (a portion of water in the case of TM) which falls under two types (pleasant to drink and unhealthy);
3) these opposing motions are explained by different descriptions of the single particular as falling under the two types mentioned in condition #2.

Penner's example of conflicting bodily desires, the desire to drink and the desire to be warm, does not lead to partition of the appetitive part on this account because the different desires, though they motivate opposing stances toward the same action of getting up out of bed, do not occur with regard to a single particular object which falls under two types. The desire to drink is a reaction to the prospect of water, its object, while the desire to be warm is a reaction to a different object, the cold of the morning. The desire to be warm does not see the water in any particular light, while the desire to drink does not see warmth as desirable or undesirable. As a result, conditions 2 and 3 above are not satisfied. The question of which bodily pleasure to seek is an intramural dispute for the appetitive part, one that does not involve competing descriptions of a single token of two types. Thus, no partition of the appetitive part is required.[16]

This general account of when and how partition arises may be applied to the other two examples of psychic conflict present in *Republic* 4, namely Leontius and Odysseus. Before considering these, it is worth remarking that they differ in an important respect from TM. TM is a generic example that illustrates a simple case of conflict of motivations that we all experience: that between bodily desires and our rational awareness of what is in our best interest to do. On the other hand, the Leontius and Odysseus examples deal with very specific, unusual cases of conflict experienced by named individuals, one an historical personage and the other a fictional character. After first employing a quite generic example of the conflict between appetite and desire in TM, Plato has chosen to illustrate the conflicts of spirit and appetite and reason and spirit with two unusual and complex cases of conflicting motivations. We should assume that Plato chose these particular examples because the detailed motivations and circumstances they involve allowed him to convey important points about the sort of psychic conflict that leads to partition of the soul. A satisfactory account of these cases of conflict must make sense of these specific motivations and unusual circumstances.

The case of Leontius is one that gives a quite determinate description of a struggle between appetite and spirit. When Leontius notices the corpses being disposed of by the public executioner, he experiences a desire to look upon them. His spirited part resists this desire, but ultimately the desire to look becomes too strong. As described at 440a, he runs up to the corpses and says, addressing his eyes: "Look for yourselves, you evil wretches, take your fill of the beautiful sight [*tou kalou theamatos*]!" The desire that drives Leontius to look upon the corpses must be an appetitive desire if the case is to function as a conflict between appetite and spirit. Given Leontius' angry description of the corpses as a "beautiful sight," the appetitive desire in question should be identified as an erotic desire. It is a desire that seeks sexual pleasure by gazing upon the corpses, perhaps because the pale skin of the corpses answers to his

---

[16] Nicholas D. Smith proposes an example which, in his view, threatens to generate further partition of the appetitive part of the soul: "Jones finds himself caught between a strong desire to drink the water he sees in front of him, on the one hand, and his aversion to the pain he anticipates if he were actually to attempt to drink the water, since he notices that it is boiling hot. He desires to drink, but holds back"; see Smith (1999b, 36). This sort of example differs from Penner's case in that it does involve opposing descriptions of a single token falling under two types: the water is pleasant as quenching thirst and painful as boiling hot. However, I find implausible the description of such a case as one where Jones is genuinely caught between a desire to drink the boiling hot water and a desire not to drink the water. In my experience, the anticipation of pain from drinking boiling hot water effectively removes the desire to drink, even when I am thirsty; I am more than willing to allow the boiling water to cool sufficiently to make drinking pleasurable. Similarly, when I take a baked potato out of the oven, my desire to eat is momentarily stilled by the anticipation of the pain that would arise were I to eat the potato immediately. Such common cases of desire biding its time, as it were, do not require partition of the appetitive part because the first condition mentioned above, the presence of two opposing motions within the soul, is not satisfied.

sexual predilections.[17] That is, Leontius' appetitive part moves him to gaze upon the corpses in pursuit of sexual pleasure. This part will describe the pale-skinned corpses as beautiful and pleasant to look at. At the same time, Leontius' spirited part moves him to refrain from gazing upon the corpses. The spirited part considers deriving sexual pleasure from gazing upon a corpse to be shameful and dishonorable. It resists the desire to gaze upon the corpses for the sake of the end of retaining honor and avoiding shame. In the process, the spirited part offers its own description of the particular things that the appetitive part views as beautiful and pleasant: speaking of the corpses, it says, "Take your fill of the beautiful sight!" Taken in context, we should understand this to be said ironically and even sarcastically; the spirited part is in fact rebuking the appetitive part for wanting to gaze upon something that is not beautiful but ugly and shameful. If it is the pale skin of the bodies in particular that draws Leontius' erotic attention, then this particular color is present because the bodies are rotting corpses. This would help explain why the spirited part sees the pale skin as something ugly and shameful to look at, a "beautiful sight" indeed. Thus, we have in the Leontius case the essential elements needed for partition of the soul. The appetitive and spirited parts in this example take up opposing stances of assent and dissent toward the action of gazing at the corpses, and in doing this each part is reacting differently to the same particular things, the pale corpses. The parts take their opposing stances toward the action because they offer different descriptions of these things: the corpses are described as beautiful and pleasant to look at or as ugly and shameful to look at. In this account of the Leontius example, the third condition of the analysis of psychic conflict leading to partition finds clear application in the spirited part's ironic description of the pale corpses as a beautiful sight.

The third example, that of Odysseus refraining from killing the maidservants, also fits the analysis of the conditions which require partition of the soul. As in the Leontius example, a fuller account of the example helps us to understand the precise nature of the psychic conflict depicted. At the start of Book 20 of the *Odyssey*, Odysseus is posing as a beggar in order to find a likely occasion to strike at the suitors who are consuming his household. He settles down to sleep on the floor of the entry hall of his own household, in itself a shameful condition for the head of the household. At this point he hears the laughter and conversation of the maidservants who have become accustomed to sleep with the suitors, and at this his heart or *thumos* is stirred. Presumably, it is his situation as a whole, sleeping like a beggar on the floor of his house while his servants

---

[17] This possibility would be supported if we accept a speculative emendation of a fragment of the comic poet Theopompus, a contemporary of Plato's. As amended, the fragment mentions Leontius as enjoying the sight of a young man who is "as pale as a corpse"; see Theodorus Kock, *Comicorum Atticorum Fragmenta*, vol. I (Leipzig: Teubner, 1880), p. 739. If the emendation is accepted, then we have reason to think that Leontius was known for his attraction to pale-skinned youths, and Plato mentions Leontius with the expectation that his audience will readily connect the appetitive desire to gaze at corpses with this particular form of sexual desire. But even independently of this proposed emendation, it is reasonable to identify Leontius' desire to gaze at the corpses as sexual in order to allow his case to be one of conflict between appetite and reason.

consort with the enemy, which moves his spirited part to kill the maidservants. This situation is the particular thing, here an event, which the spirited part sees as shameful. His rational part takes a stand against killing the maidservants, but it does so by addressing the spirited part and offering its own description of Odysseus' predicament. The full text of the rational part's speech to the spirited part runs as follows:

> Bear up, heart. You have had worse to endure before this
> On that day when the irresistible Cyclops ate up
> My strong companions but you endured it until intelligence [*mētis*]
> Got you out of the cave, though you expected to perish.[18]

The strategy of the rational part here is to offer to the spirited part a different understanding of Odysseus' situation. The situation is bad, indeed, but even worse was the time when Odysseus had to watch as six of his comrades were eaten by Polyphemus (*Odyssey*, 9.285-346). The hero had it in mind to kill the Cyclops as he slept, but he realized that if he were to do this then he and his remaining comrades would perish, unable to move the giant stone blocking the entrance to Polyphemus' cave (9.299-305). As the rational part reminds the spirited part, it was intelligence (*mētis*) that allowed Odysseus to escape from the cave and to take revenge upon the Cyclops. Thus, the rational part asks the spirited part to reconceive the present situation by placing it in relation to its earlier experience in the Cyclops' cave. Both situations are shameful and inimical to Odysseus' honor, but in both cases acting on the desire for immediate revenge would only make matters worse. The better course, as in the cave, is to trust in Odysseus' cunning and wait for the suitable occasion to attack the suitors and regain one's honor.

If this is the substance of the rational part's address to the spirited part within Odysseus, then we have another example that fits the analysis on offer of psychic conflict leading to partition of the soul. The spirited part and the rational part exhibit different motions or stances toward the same action, killing the maidservants. These opposed motions arise in reaction to a single particular, the situation in which Odysseus finds himself at the start of Book 20, posing as a beggar and sleeping on the floor of his house while his maidservants go to the beds of the suitors. The opposed motions arise because the different parts offer different descriptions of this situation. The spirited part sees it as overwhelmingly shameful, the sort of situation that calls for immediate violent action in support of one's honor. The rational part is aware of this feature of the situation, but it engages in calculation by finding a different aspect of the situation. This is the sort of situation that, like Polyphemus' cave, calls for patience and cunning. If Odysseus can restrain his anger, he will be able both to restore his honor and to defeat his enemies; if he acts immediately, his enemies may gain the upper hand. The spirited part assents to killing the maidservants in order to gain its end of honor; the rational part dissents from this action in order to gain its end of the good of the

---

[18] *Odyssey* 20.18-21, translation by Lattimore with minor changes.

whole soul. The third condition of the analysis of psychic conflict leading to soul-partition again fits the particular words that the rational part within Odysseus addresses to the spirited part: the spirited part describes its situation as shameful while the rational part describes that same situation as rewarding cunning and patience.

This analysis of the sort of psychic conflict that is involved in soul-partition suggests an important respect in which Lorenz's Simple Picture must be qualified. According to Lorenz, all that is required for soul-partition is conflict between two opposed motivations taking up stances of desire and aversion toward the same course of action.[19] However, the details of the Leontius and Odysseus cases suggest that soul-partition involves more than just desire for and aversion to the same action. In these cases, a crucial ingredient is the different descriptions given of the particular token of two types (the corpses described as beautiful and shameful, and Odysseus' situation described as shameful and as rewarding patience). These different descriptions explain the opposing motions of assent and dissent in the soul. With Irwin and Price and against Lorenz, I hold that it is only for some cases of direct conflicts of desire and aversion toward the same course of action that Plato will accept soul-partition. That restricted range of cases that qualify as revealing soul-partition is set not by the phenomenon of second-order confrontation of one desire by another, though; it is the different descriptions of the same token that qualifies a conflict of desires as apt to lead to soul-partition.

6.5 The Unity Problem

The second problem for Socrates' partition of the soul, the Unity Problem, arises from the following question: in what sense is a soul composed of three parts also a single thing? Christopher Bobonich in particular has raised this problem as a pressing one for Plato. He emphasizes two sorts of concerns linked to conceiving of the soul as an association of parts. One area of concern relates to communication between the parts: "First, all the parts seem to share some information, for example, they are aware of the person's environment. But how are we to explain this? ... [E]xactly how does communication between the parts happen?"[20] As a second area of concern, Bobonich raises the prospect of alienation between parts. He poses two problems for the person who identifies with the rational part, as Plato advises us to do. By identifying with the rational part we lose our grip on the idea that the person as a whole is responsible for the actions that result from the lower parts exercising undue authority. In addition, we have no non-instrumental reason to care for the good of these lower parts; my appetitive and my spirited parts are not in the full sense part of me.[21] If reason is the "real" self, then we may find ourselves cutting ties of responsibility and concern with the other parts.

---

[19] "According to [the Simple Picture], it is the simultaneous occurrence of a desire and an aversion towards one and the same object that, Plato thinks, reveals a partition of the soul"; Lorenz (2006, 41).
[20] Bobonich (2002, 254).   [21] Bobonich (2002, 255–6).

The account of the rational part's activity of calculation developed previously allows for a fitting response to the first set of issues contained within the Unity Problem, namely concerns about the prospects for genuine communication between the parts. As we have seen, the rational part is capable of calculating, where this activity involves the discernment of different aspects of a single object. The rational part is able to discern the ambiguous character of summoners, which in the practical realm involves seeing a glass of water as both pleasant to drink and unhealthy. Having seen these different aspects and thus comprehending both the reasons for and against a given action, it is well placed to speak persuasively to the lower parts. Odysseus' speech in Book 20 of the *Odyssey* provides a model of this sort of interaction. His rational part is able to acknowledge the shameful aspects of his situation and to allow that the spirited point has its reasons. At the same time, the rational part is able to move the spirited part to conceive of the situation in a different light, namely by recalling the situation in Polyphemus' cave and the need for intelligence to guide the desire for revenge. The values of the spirited part are not dismissed out of hand; Odysseus eventually does see to the slaughter of the maidservants (*Odyssey* 22.430-446). But the spirited part is persuaded to pursue its goals under the guidance of the rational part. In dealing with the appetitive part, presumably, the rational part has less room to invite its interlocutor to reconceive the object of its desire; the appetitive part's desires are less flexible. Here the rational part must appeal more to the appetitive part's interest in long-term satisfaction of desires: given what both parts know about health and disease, drinking the water now may bring immediate pleasure but will cause a greater amount of pain in the long run. The general features of these interactions are clear: the rational part discerns the value to which the other part of the soul responds, determines the proper weight to be given to the ends pursued by the other part in terms of the good of the whole soul, and then persuades the other part that it will achieve those ends best when it obeys reason. Clearly, this pattern does not lead in every case to unification under the guidance of reason, but we have a model for how this can occur, according to which the values of each part are affirmed and measured by a single end, the good of the whole soul.

The second aspect of the Unity Problem, namely concerns about alienation between parts, is addressed by setting out Socrates' conception of how a complex whole such as a city or a human being can be unified. In passages from Books 4 and 5, Socrates proposes that the unity of such complex wholes is achieved when each part of the whole identifies with and promotes the interests of the whole in the conviction that what is good for the whole is also good for the part. Such identification based on a convergence of interests between the different parts is spoken of as each part loving or engaging in friendship toward the other parts and toward the whole. In Book 4, Socrates at 412d-e describes the character of the guardians who will rule the city by noting that they must be the ones among the citizens who most care for and love the city. As he says at 412d4-7, this love is expressed in the conviction that the guardian's interest is the same as the city's: "And someone loves something most of all when he believes that the same things are advantageous to it as to himself and supposes that if it does well, he'll do well, and that if it does badly, then he'll do badly too." The guardians' ability to put this conviction into practice ensures that the city will be unified; as Socrates says at 424d, when the guardians rule well by ensuring that each citizen performs the task for which he or she is well suited, the result is unity in citizens and city: " . . . each of the other citizens is to be directed to what he is naturally suited for, so that, doing the one work that is his own, he will become not many but one, and the whole city will itself be naturally one not many." Finally, unity based on convergences of interests characterizes not only cities but also the different parts of a single human being. When Socrates in Book 5 attempts to show that the city is benefited by the community or association of women and children among the guardians, he asserts that the greatest benefit to the city is whatever binds it together by making all the citizens rejoice at the well-being of one of their number and feel distress at the sufferings of a different one. The best city is the one that carries this pattern to such a degree that it is like a single person: "What about the city that is most like a single person? For example, when one of us hurts his finger, the entire association [koinōnia] that binds body and soul together into a single system under the ruling part within it is aware of this, and the whole feels the pain together with the part that suffers."[22] A human being is a whole consisting of parts bound together by this interweaving of interests: the weal of one part is the weal of all the parts just as the woe of one is the woe of all.

The three passages quoted in the previous paragraph suggest that the parts of a complex but unified whole satisfy two distinct conditions. First, the parts must instantiate structural properties that evidence the adjustment of the parts to their role within the whole to which they belong. Put in another way, each part must be capable of doing its own task. The hands and feet of a human body are both appendages at the end of limbs, but they show different structural properties that reflect their different functions within the human body. Second, the parts must exhibit causal properties such that each part benefits or harms the other parts. In particular, each part benefits the other parts when it performs its function well and harms the other parts when it performs that function badly.[23] If the feet perform their functions of supporting the body and

---

[22] 462c9-d2. The term used by Socrates to denote the community of women and children among the guardians and the association of body and soul is koinōnia, the term for association or partnership. In Chapters 3 and 4, I have argued that this term denotes the activity of engaging in partnerships and associations that is the function that is perfected by the virtue of justice. This is consistent with Socrates' recommendation of the community of women and children in the kallipolis. The goodness of his best city is located in the way in which its leaders engage in partnership with regard to conceiving and raising their children.

[23] The formulation of these two conditions for the unity of a complex whole derives from Brown (2012). Brown gives a relatively hopeful account of the prospects for unity of the tripartite soul by arguing that the level of systematic organization found in the soul allows it to exist at least as a minimally united thing in all humans and, in the case of the virtuous, to exhibit a stronger unity. The first, structural condition for the unity of a complex whole covers roughly the same ground as Brown's description of the unearned unity shared by all human souls. The second condition is intended to explicate what Brown mentions but does not expound, namely the earned unity that characterizes virtuous souls.

allowing locomotion, this contributes to the well-being of the other parts within the body. If the feet are malformed or injured and so are not able to support the body or allow locomotion, the other parts of the body suffer from this defective performance of function. In sum, Plato will see the parts of the soul as forming a single complex whole to the extent that the parts exhibit properties which allow them to play distinct and mutually supporting functions within the soul and to the extent that the good condition of one part, defined in terms of good performance of function, causes benefit to the other parts. Similarly, in a unified whole the ill condition of one part, defined as poor performance of function, makes the other parts worse off.

This analysis of the notion of the unity of a complex whole suggests a response to Bobonich's concern regarding alienation between parts. On Bobonich's account, if we identify with the rational part of the soul, we have no non-instrumental reasons for caring for the interests of the two lower parts. In Socrates' view, a well-unified soul that satisfies both of the two conditions for complex unity will have instrumental but genuine reasons for caring for the two lower parts. Each part will see the well-being of the other two parts as indispensable to its own well-being. It will love and see as its own those parts that are thus accommodated to its well-being. This attitude is unambiguously self-interested, and thus will fail to satisfy one who expects altruistic concern to hold between different parts of the soul. However, the convergence of interests between parts serves as a powerful source of unity and one that captures our actual attitudes toward the different parts of our bodies and our selves. As Diotima instructs Socrates in the *Symposium*, we desire and love what is good and not simply what belongs to us or what makes us whole. As an instance of this pattern, she notes that we are willing to amputate limbs from our bodies which have become diseased and harmful (*Symposium* 205d10-206a1). Socrates can claim as well that by identifying with the rational part we commit ourselves to loving and caring for the other parts under the condition that they promote the good of the whole soul. But Socrates will not countenance a scenario in which one part promotes its own good by neglecting the good of the other parts. He conceives of a unified soul as one whose parts share a common good. This attitude is based on instrumental reasons, if by that we mean that each part has reason to promote the good of the other parts as a way of promoting its own good. But the final purpose that such instrumental reasons serve is not the domination of the rational part but the good of the whole soul.

A similar response is available to Socrates in reply to Bobonich's claim that the tripartition of the soul prevents a satisfying account of moral responsibility:

[I]t seems to undermine the idea that the person is responsible for actions resulting from the lower parts winning out. The problem is not just that the strength of the lower parts' desires might be so great that the person could not do otherwise, but the more basic worry that the akratic desires and emotions are not really his desires and emotions. All that it seems the person is responsible for is how he responds to these alien forces, not for having them.[24]

---

[24] Bobonich (2002, 255–6).

These comments raise the problem of how we should identify with reason without disavowing responsibility for those parts of the soul that may depart from reason's guidance. Socrates' solution, I would suggest, will draw upon the fact that the different parts of the soul do not merely represent distinct styles of action; they are causal forces which, in pursuit of their ends, influence the other parts of the soul. In the best case, the parts support each other in pursuit of their ends; this is the pattern described by the second criterion for being a complex whole. In particular, the rational part offers its recommendations in order to promote its end of the good of the whole soul. Although the lower parts may at times ignore the guidance of the rational part, this does not mean that the rational part has taken on the role of merely offering informed commentary on what the lower parts do, as if they were external agents. The rational part must influence the lower parts to pursue their ends in the proper way as part of its characteristic role of ruling and directing the soul as a whole. Although the lower parts may be alien to the rational part in the sense of failing to comprehend or heed its directives, even so the lower parts are not alien to reason in the sense that the rational part can achieve its ends simply by ignoring their conduct. The rational part is responsible for them in the sense that it must bring them into accord with reason if it is to achieve its own ends. The sense of responsibility in play here is perhaps not what Bobonich has in mind, the direct responsibility of an agent for those actions which she performs intentionally. The rational part cannot determine by itself the nature of the desires that drive the spirited and appetitive parts. But even so, the rational part cannot regard these lower parts as simply alien to it in the full sense; their success in carrying out their rationally approved functions partially determines the rational part's success in its project of achieving the good of the whole soul.

These reflections on how best to resolve the Unity Problem have led us to a distinct picture of the interactions between the parts of the soul and the ways in which these interactions can hinder or promote the unity of the soul. Each part can harm the unity of the soul by obstructing the other parts in their attempts to gain their own ends. The appetitive part can force a thirsty man to drink against the recommendations of the rational part, thus harming the person's health and frustrating the rational part's drive toward the good of the whole soul (439b3-5). The appetitive part can suborn the rational part and allow it to perform only the uninspiring tasks of instrumental reasoning, as when the appetitive part within the oligarchic man forces the rational part to find the means by which a little money can become a lot (553c-d). The rational part can offer mistaken advice to the other parts so that they do not achieve the pleasure or honor they desire. A badly educated spirited part may resist the beneficial discipline of the rational part, perceiving such supervision as shameful. Clearly, a fully unified soul will not feature such obstruction. But the achievement of full unity requires not only that each part avoid this obstruction but also that it provide aid to the other parts as they pursue their ends.

In order to see how this positive contribution to unity of the soul occurs, we may consider the ways in which the appetitive part contributes to the rational part achieving its end, the good of the whole soul. The appetitive part contains many unnecessary desires, those which come to the fore in the democratic man and the city to which he corresponds, but also necessary desires. The latter are defined as those desires that cannot be removed from us by processes of habituation and that benefit us when they are satisfied (558d11-e2). However we may reshape or mold them by habituation, basic desires for food, drink, and sexual intercourse are ineliminable. This fact is a benefit to us, since their operation has the function of promoting self-preservation and the reproduction of the human race. Because such desires have the potential to grow out of all proportion to their benefit, Socrates supplies a measure for the best state of such desires at 559a11-b6: "Aren't the following desires necessary: the desire to eat to the point of health and well-being and the desire for bread and delicacies? – I suppose so. The desire for bread is necessary on both counts; it's beneficial, and unless it's satisfied, we die. – Yes. The desire for delicacies is also necessary to the extent that it's beneficial to well-being." The same measure holds for sexual desire, says Socrates, and so we can assign to the clearest examples of appetitive desires a common measure for the good performance of their activities: achieving health and bodily well-being. Enjoying the pleasures that result from such necessary desires will qualify as a Class 1 good, the enjoyment of harmless pleasures mentioned at 357b4-8. The necessary desires themselves appear as Class 3 goods, in that the experience of the desire is painful but produces a Class 2 good, being healthy.

A similar account can be given of the spirited part's relations with the rational part. As is the case with the appetitive part, the spirited part enables the rational part to achieve its end by refraining from conflict and waging civil war within the soul. In addition, the spirited part has a distinctive role to play as reason's helper. It wards off shameful events or actions by fighting against external enemies and by preventing the appetitive part from acting upon base desires. Its role as reason's auxiliary may be expressed by noting that, as in the *Crito*, the spirited person will have beliefs about what is fine and shameful, about what brings honor and ill repute. These beliefs direct spirit toward honor, but the value of this honor is a matter of being honored by those who know, not by those who are ignorant. To gain honor from those who know, the spirited part must take its beliefs from the rational part. When the spirited part acts in this way upon well-founded beliefs about what is fine and shameful, it gains honor for itself, guides the appetitive part in its pursuit of its own pleasures, and helps the rational part achieve what is best for the whole soul. Here, as in the case of the appetitive part, the spirited part relies upon the rational part for its proper functioning and contributes to the rational part achieving its own end.

6.6 Unity of the Soul as End of Action

In order to provide a fitting response in the previous section to the Unity Problem, we have developed an account of the way in which the different parts of the soul in the *Republic* may form a complex unity. In the virtuous soul each part pursues its own ends and at the same time makes a positive contribution to the other parts' achievement of their ends. The result of each part "doing its own" in this way is the unity of the soul in the strong sense, the achievement of a whole in which all the parts support and gain support from the other parts. To conclude the discussion of the parts of the soul, I argue that this achievement of unity serves as a further example of the functional teleology of action. The parts of the soul, considered as principles of action, act for the sake of their particular ends but also contribute to the unity of the soul. In the best case, the actions that arise from the parts of the soul are carried out for the sake of the unity of the soul even when the actions do not involve any intention or plan to achieve the unity of the soul.

To demonstrate that the parts of the soul act for the sake of the unity of the soul, it suffices to show that the four conditions are satisfied which feature in the analysis of the functional teleology of action. As an example, we imagine a person acting on a range of desires for food, drink, and sex in ways that achieve the end of pleasure and also cooperate with the rational part's drive for promoting the good of the whole soul. These actions constitute a series of actions $A_1, A_2, \ldots, A_N$ motivated by necessary appetitive desire. Such desires and the beliefs accompanying them are capable of motivating action in their own right. As necessary desires, the desires in play adhere to the measure of the good of the whole soul and thus will be approved by the rational part of the soul. The resulting actions $A_1, A_2, \ldots, A_N$ bring about the unity of the soul, since these actions allow the different parts of the soul to benefit each other. The appetitive part confines itself in these actions to necessary desires and harmless pleasures, which helps the rational part to achieve its end of the good of the soul. The rational part oversees the workings of the appetitive part and thus helps it to achieve the truest pleasures available to it. The actions in question also achieve harmless pleasures, a Class 1 good, but unity of the soul is by far the higher good. Thus the first condition is satisfied, since the actions $A_1, A_2, \ldots, A_N$ bring about a result E which is of greater value than the actions themselves.

The second condition requires that the actions $A_1, A_2, \ldots, A_N$ bring about the result E (here the unity of the soul) by carrying out some function or set of functions F. In the case of the appetitive part of the soul, the actions of drinking, eating, and sexual intercourse are motivated by a range of bodily appetites (thirst, hunger, eros or sexual desire) each of which has a particular function. The function of such a bodily appetite is to move the person who feels the desire to pursue the object of that desire (drink, food, the body of the beloved) and to secure self-preservation and the survival of the species. The actions of drinking, eating, and sexual intercourse promote the unity of the soul in the course of carrying out these functions. This addresses the second condition in the analysis, which requires that the actions $A_1, A_2, \ldots, A_N$ produce the result E in virtue of carrying out their functions.

To see that the third and fourth conditions of the analysis are satisfied by the case of necessary appetitive desires helping to bring about the unity of the soul, it is helpful to recall aspects of the account of the nature of a complex unity. The soul is a unity in the strong sense because its parts cooperate harmoniously, with each part helping the other parts to achieve their ends. Actions motivated by necessary appetitive desires exhibit this pattern, as their pursuit of pleasure promotes bodily health, one of the ends of the rational part of the soul. The value of such actions motivated by necessary appetitive desire consists in part in this causal contribution they make to the unity of the soul, as the third condition suggests. Finally, making this contribution to achieving the unity of the soul is a necessary condition of carrying out the functions of appetitive desire in the best way. Clearly, it is possible to carry out the functions of appetitive desire in a variety of ways, some good and most bad. Appetitive desire is a many-headed creature, to use the image from *Republic* 9, and it is a standing challenge for the rational part to cultivate the tame and gentle aspects of the beast while eliminating the savage and cruel. To cultivate appetitive desire in the best way is to encourage those desires that, like the necessary desires, work for the good of the whole soul and accept the guidance of reason. Desires that carry out their function in the best way will be those that promote the unity of the soul by accepting the authority of the rational and the spirited parts. This amounts to satisfying the final condition for actions motivated by necessary appetitive desires to be performed for the sake of the unity of the soul.

The claim that the appetitive part of the soul acts for the sake of achieving unity of the soul illustrates some of the salient themes of Plato's functional teleology of action. As in the ascent passage in the *Symposium*, where we find the claim that all stages of erotic desire in the ascent are for the sake of the vision of the Form of Beauty, the *Republic* suggests that actions motivated by appetitive desire serve purposes beyond the immediate ends of that desire. The agent who acts upon necessary appetitive desire may conceive of her goals simply as gaining the pleasures that come from the objects of that desire. However, the actions that flow from this sort of desire find their fuller purpose in achieving the unity of the soul. Another aspect of the city-soul analogy emerges; just as the best city included craftsmen exercising their functions for the sake of unintended ends of psychic harmony and friendship with reason, so the soul consists of parts which carry out their functions for the sake of the unintended end of unity. Serving this purpose marks an important sense in which all action for Plato is oriented toward the good, since unity is a characteristic mark of goodness for souls and indeed for all complex entities. The claim that actions motivated by necessary appetitive desire are carried out for the sake of unity of the soul is thus one articulation of Socrates' oracular claim at *Republic* 505e1-2 that every soul pursues the good and does all that it does for the sake of the good.

7

The Defense of Justice and the Teleology of Action

7.1 *Republic* 4: Just Souls, Just Actions, and the Just City

As we saw in Chapter 5, Socrates is faced with a particular task in the body of the *Republic*. Glaucon and Adeimantus tell Socrates to praise justice for itself, which he may accomplish by setting forth the nature of justice as an activity of the soul and the benefits which are constituted by that activity. He may also mention the criterial benefits of justice, those beneficial consequences of being just that testify to the completion or perfection of the activity of being just. To praise justice in this way will be to draw attention to its status as a good of the second class in Glaucon's division of goods. He may not bring in the fringe benefits of justice, the central case of which is the reputation for being just and its attendant benefits. By describing the nature of justice and its criterial benefits, Socrates should give definitive support to the claim that the life of the just person is better and happier than the life of the unjust person.

The current chapter is devoted to an examination of the arguments that Socrates provides in fulfillment of this task. As described previously, Book 1 contains a series of arguments that, though rough and inconclusive, direct us to conceive of justice as a psychic power of a particular sort, one that benefits the just person by making her more capable of action in partnerships and then transmits itself to the groups to which she belongs. In Book 4, Socrates sets forth a fuller account of what justice is that confirms this preliminary description of justice as a self-transmitting power. In accordance with the task set for him by Glaucon, he then explains how justice benefits the just person chiefly in terms of benefits constituted by being just, though he also brings to our attention some of the criterial benefits of being just. This account of Socrates' defense of justice is used to reply to the concern raised by David Sachs in his influential paper "A Fallacy in Plato's *Republic*" that Plato commits a fallacy of equivocation in Book 4. The larger topic raised by Sachs, namely the relation between justice as a psychic state and just actions, can be described as a matter of justice transmitting itself to the city by way of just actions.

Following this exposition of the main argument of the *Republic*, the focus shifts to a set of interpretive questions that have played a prominent role in the secondary literature on this dialogue. In the wake of Sachs' article, a generation of scholars has sought to bridge the gap between what Glaucon supposedly requested, a defense of justice construed as the performance of moral action, and what Socrates actually provides, a defense of justice construed as a psychic state of harmony. The result of these scholarly efforts has been greater insight into the moral psychology of the *Republic*, as commentators have shown that the ideally rational philosophers described by Socrates will be motivated by their insight into the Form of the Good to perform moral actions. However, this reaction to Sachs' problem does not give a satisfactory interpretation of Book 4, as it appeals to concepts and arguments developed later in the *Republic*. In addition, this approach to Socrates' defense of justice alters the terms of that defense markedly by shifting the center of concern from the just soul to just actions. The presentation of justice as a self-transmitting power allows us to describe Socrates' Book 4 defense of justice in terms of concepts accessible within this book while giving priority to the just soul over just actions.

7.2 Justice as a Class 2 Good in *Republic* 4

In Book 4 Socrates completes the account of justice first sketched in Book 1. He describes justice, both in the city and in the soul of human beings, as a power capable of maintaining the different parts or aspects of city and soul in proper balance, with each part doing the work that is its own. This definition of justice serves Socrates as an essential step in the process of praising justice for itself, as it allows him to describe the characteristic activity associated with being just and on this basis to set out the benefits constituted by being just.

Before considering the particulars of this argument in favor of justice, it will be helpful to present a short sketch of the account of justice developed between 432b and 445b. The account of justice in this stretch of text falls naturally into two parts: a first part, 432b-434c, generates the account of justice in the city as a power by which each class in the city does its own task; a second part at 441b-445b applies the account of justice to the soul. This second part concludes with an analogy between justice and health and the assertion that justice is always preferable to injustice. The two parts are separated by the passage 434d-441c, discussed in Chapter 6, in which Socrates demonstrates that there are the same parts in the soul as in the best city.

The accounts of justice in the city and in the soul follow the same rough pattern. The definition of justice is first announced without elaborate preparation and without constructing this definition anew; previous discussions of the structure of the best city provide the necessary starting points. The definition of justice is then confirmed by appeal to ordinary intuitions about justice in political affairs and in the doings of individuals. Finally the benefits of justice for cities and souls are described, so that we are led to the conclusion at 445b that acting justly and being just are always more profitable than their opposites. The account of psychic justice is longer and richer in content, including as it does a fuller description of how justice in the soul preserves the other cardinal virtues (441e-442d), an extended metaphorical description of how justice operates in the human soul, and an account of just action derived from the account of justice as a state of the soul. An outline of the two parts of the discussion of justice follows:

I. Justice in the City (432b-434c)
   A. Statement of definition of justice: justice is doing one's own and is opposed to meddling (432b-433b)
   B. Confirmation of the definition of justice (433b-434a)
      1. Use of the method of elimination—justice is what is left in city when courage, wisdom, and temperance have been defined (433b-e)
      2. Appeal to judicial practices: judges promote just outcomes by seeing that citizens have their own and not another's (433e-434a)
   C. Benefit and harm to city are justice and meddling (434a-c)
II. Justice in the Soul (441c-445c)
   A. Application of the definition of justice to the soul (441c-442d)
      1. As city is just by classes doing their own, the soul is just when three parts of the soul do their own tasks (441d-e)
      2. Description of three parts of the soul and their operation in just soul (441e-442b)
      3. Review of courage, temperance, wisdom (442b-d)
      4. Formal announcement of what it is for a human being to be just (442d)
   B. Confirmation of the definition of psychic justice (442d-443b)
      1. The just person is least likely to commit fraud, to betray friends and city, to fail to show respect for parents and the gods, etc. (442d-443a)
      2. The cause of this just behavior is the fact that each part of the just person's soul does its own task (443a-443b)
   C. Benefit of justice in the soul: justice is harmony and health, injustice is disorder and disease (443c9-444e4)
   D. Final agreement: given what justice and injustice are, it is always more profitable to be just and to act justly (445a-b)

   A noteworthy aspect of the treatment of justice here is the brevity of several crucial steps in the argument. Socrates announces his proposed definition of justice in the city (I.A) not by providing a novel account of justice but by bringing back on stage an idea introduced earlier in the *Republic*. In the best city, each person will perform one and only one of the tasks that make a contribution to political life, namely the task for which he or she is by nature best suited. This principle, first presented in Book II in the construction of the healthy city, is now identified as justice or some form of it. Much of the following discussion of justice consists of showing how it applies to the city and the soul. The account is confirmed as a description of justice in the city and in the soul by showing that it conforms to our understanding of how justice in present in a city and in the actions of a just person (I. B, II. B). The point of this investigation of the nature of justice is to guide us in judging whether the just life is better than the unjust, but hardly has this question been posed than it is answered emphatically at 445a5-b1 by Glaucon: "But Socrates, this inquiry looks ridiculous to me now that justice and injustice have been shown to be as we have described.... [H]ow can it be worth living when his soul – the very thing by which he lives – is ruined and in turmoil?" The final agreement is given immediately (II. D), and no further argument is given in Book 4 to support the judgment that justice is preferable to injustice.

A plausible explanation for this brevity of argument at crucial steps is that Socrates relies on previously developed results. The description of what justice and injustice are and the depiction of just and unjust action as producing justice and injustice respectively suffice to convince Glaucon and Socrates that justice is to be preferred over injustice without exception. The grounds for preferring justice in this way are likely present in the preceding accounts of justice and injustice. Similarly, when Socrates introduces justice at 433a as the principle of specialization in another guise, he must expect his previous application of this principle to guide our evaluation of this proposed definition of justice. This principle was proposed to ensure that each craft provides its product in the best condition possible for the common use of all the members of the city. Following the principle of specialization will require that the most spirited citizens serve as auxiliaries, that those most devoted to the good of the city will rule as guardians, and that the craftsmen of the moneymaking class will be satisfied with the amount of money and creature comforts that will allow them to be good carpenters, farmers, smiths, etc. When the principle of specialization is thus implemented, it will perform the role assigned to justice: according to Socrates at 433b9-c1, it will be "a power that makes it possible for [wisdom, temperance, and courage] to grow in the city and that preserves them when they've grown for as long as it remains there itself."

This power present in the just city is generated by an analogous power present in the soul of the citizens of this city. At the explanatorily basic level, justice is a trait of individual humans. This trait is then passed on to the city to which these humans belong. For Socrates, justice is a self-transmitting power, one that moves from the souls of humans to their cities. That Socrates conceives of justice as rooted in the individual soul is indicated by his observation at 435e1-3: "Well, then, we are surely compelled to agree that each of us has within himself the same parts and characteristics as the city? Where else would they come from?" Although Socrates discusses justice in the city first in order to see justice writ large and then passes on to the smaller letters of justice in the soul, this order of inquiry reverses the order of explanation, according to which the traits of souls explain the traits of cities.

A first description of the process by which justice transmits itself from the soul to the city can be found in the opening lines of the second part of the account of justice. After the tripartition of the soul provides Socrates with reason to believe that the soul has the same number and types of parts as does the city, he is ready to assert that a human being is just in the same manner as a city (441d5-e2). The rational part of the soul considers what is best for the whole soul, and the spirited part acts as ally to the rational part in governing the appetitive part (441e-442a). The result is that the character of doing one's own, present first in the relation between the different parts of the soul, is transmitted to the soul as a whole. Socrates remarks at 441d12-e2, "Then we must also remember that each one of us in whom each part is doing its own work will himself be just and do his own." The actions that typically result from this state of justice are described as follows: the person the parts of whose soul do their own work will refrain from dishonesty, embezzling money, adultery, and betrayal of friends and fellow citizens (442e-443a), and will engage in financial affairs, private contracts and political office in such a way as to preserve this inner state of justice (443e). These actions attributed to the just person draw her into a range of associations with others, from private financial agreements to family relationships to carrying out political offices. We can expect that when the citizens of the city are just by doing their own in such dealings with each other, the city as a whole is just as a consequence.

   In this discussion of justice, we see justice in the soul expressing itself in the sort of just action that promotes a just city. One particular section of this passage, from 442d to 443a, requires close examination due to the role it has played in the secondary literature. After Socrates and Glaucon agree that justice in the soul is no different from justice in the city, they proceed to test and confirm this account of justice by examining whether such a just person would be likely to commit typically unjust actions. This passage at 442d9-443b4 (section II. B) plays a starring role in David Sachs' criticism of Plato's procedure in defending justice. For convenience, I will refer to this as the test passage. According to Sachs, Plato commits the fallacy of irrelevancy in that he is asked to defend "vulgar justice," understood as performing various actions conventionally understood as just and refraining from performance of actions conventionally under-stood as unjust, but actually provides a defense of something else, psychic justice. This is the state exhibited by a soul, each part of which does its own task. The vulgar concep-tion of justice, says Sachs, is shared by all of Socrates' interlocutors, including Glaucon in the important passages in Book 2 in which Socrates is charged with defending justice. For Socrates' account of psychic justice to be relevant to his assigned task of defending vulgar justice, it must be the case that a person who exhibits psychic justice will also exemplify vulgar justice. It is in the test passage that Plato shows an awareness of the need to connect psychic justice with vulgar justice. According to Sachs, in this passage Plato has Socrates assert that a man who is just according to the theoretical account of psychic justice will also be just according to the vulgar conception: "The passage shows that Plato supposes that the just man – as he conceives him – is less likely than anyone else to perform those acts, to embezzle, thieve, betray, behave sacrilegiously, fail to keep oaths or agreements, commit adultery, neglect his parents or the service he owes to the gods. Plato thinks the conduct of his just man, far from being at variance with the vulgar conception of justice, will exemplify it."[1] But, according to Sachs, this claim that the psychically just man will exemplify vulgar justice is only an assumption

[1] Sachs (1963, 143).

that is never supported with further argument. It is an implausible assumption to make, because there is nothing to prevent a psychically just man from committing an act commonly recognized as unjust in an intelligent, courageous, and self-controlled way. Sachs raises this possibility in order to suggest that Plato's proposed definition of justice as a state of psychic harmony will diverge in significant ways from the definiendum, the actions which show proper regard for the interests of others and which Sachs refers to as vulgar justice.

This objection to Plato's procedure has set the agenda for a generation of scholars by directing them to consider the relation between psychic justice and the type of other-regarding action that Sachs associates with vulgar justice or conventional morality. As we will see later, these scholars react to Sachs' article by seeking to close the gap between Plato's description of psychic justice and his alleged conclusion that the psychically just person will act in accordance with conventional morality. However, as Jerome Schiller notes, it is also possible to react to Sachs' charge by denying that the gap exists.[2] I propose to take this path by arguing that the charge of committing a fallacy of irrelevancy is mistaken. For this charge to stick, the following two assertions must be true. First, Socrates is expected to defend the position that vulgar justice, or acting in accordance with conventional morality, is more profitable than injustice. Second, Socrates' defense of justice includes the claim that Sachs finds asserted in the test passage, namely that the psychically just person will exemplify vulgar justice or conventional morality.

Both assertions involved in the charge of fallacy of irrelevancy are false. With regard to the first, Socrates may reply that he has not been charged by Glaucon with the task of demonstrating that vulgar justice or any conception of justice built around the performance of actions endorsed by convention is more profitable than injustice. Sachs' charge of fallacy of irrelevance is built in part on a particular reading of Socrates' task and hence of what is relevant to accomplishing that task. In his view, all of Socrates' interlocutors accept the vulgar conception of justice, though Glaucon and Adeimantus also work with the Platonic conception of justice as a state of the soul. Given the presence of the vulgar conception of justice, Plato's arguments to the effect that a state of psychic harmony promotes happiness more than psychic disharmony will be relevant to justice only if he can bring this state of harmony into relation with vulgar justice. This relation will be secured by demonstrating that a man who possesses psychic harmony will not commit vulgar injustice.[3]

According to Sachs, Plato fails to bring the two conceptions of justice into relation with each other; this is the point of his remark that vulgar injustice can be performed in

---

    [2] Schiller (1968).
    [3] "What Plato tries to establish . . . is that a man each of the parts of whose soul performs its own task . . . leads a happier life than any men whose souls are not thus ordered. Regardless of Plato's success or failure in this endeavor, for it to be at all relevant he has to prove that his conception of the just man precludes behavior commonly judged immoral or criminal; that is, he must prove that the conduct of his just man also conforms to the ordinary or vulgar canons of justice"; Sachs (1963, 152–3).

an intelligent and self-controlled manner. But there is good reason to question Sachs' claim that Socrates must show that the just person will refrain from vulgar injustice if his discussion of psychic harmony is to be relevant to justice. Although Cephalus and Polemarchus do treat justice as vulgar justice, this is not the case with Glaucon. He describes what the many say when they treat justice as a Class 3 good, something worth having only for its consequences. On the view of the many, justice is faithful adherence to a set of laws or conventions agreed upon by those who perceive their own weakness and inability to defend themselves satisfactorily against the pleonectic desires of others (358e-359a). These laws condemn the actions forbidden by vulgar justice, such as stealing, adultery, and lying. But Glaucon does not require Socrates to accept this contractarian account of justice, which he ascribes to the many and which is associated with treating justice as a Class 3 good; it is allowed and expected that Socrates will defend his conviction that justice is a Class 2 good by developing his own account of justice and then arguing that justice so conceived is rationally preferable to injustice. As we saw in Chapter 5, Socrates' task includes giving an account of justice as a power in the soul analogous to other Class 2 goods such as health and seeing. If Socrates succeeds in this task by giving a new and more insightful definition of justice, one that gets closer to the essence of justice than does the vulgar conception of justice, then he does not need to show that one who possesses this psychic power will also exemplify vulgar justice. His task need not involve defending the benefits of vulgar justice.

A second flaw in Sachs' interpretation of Plato's defense of justice is his misunderstanding of the role of the test passage, as reflected in the second assertion mentioned above. The interpretation of this passage will play a key role in assessing Sachs' charge of a fallacy of irrelevancy, so it is worth quoting the passage at 442d-443b in full:

If there are still any doubts in our soul about this [whether justice in the soul differs from justice in the city], we could dispel them altogether by appealing to ordinary cases.

Which ones?

For example, if we had to come to an agreement about whether someone similar in nature and training to our city had embezzled a deposit of gold or silver that he had accepted, who do you think would consider him to have done it rather than someone who isn't like him?

No one.

And would he have anything to do with temple robberies, thefts, betrayals of friends in private life or of cities in public life?

No, nothing.

And he'd be in no way untrustworthy in keeping an oath or other agreement.

How could he be?

And adultery, disrespect for parents, and neglect of the gods would be more in keeping with every other kind of character than his.

With every one.

And isn't the cause of all this that every part within him does its own work, whether it's ruling or being ruled?

Yes, that and nothing else.

Then, are you still looking for justice to be something other than this power, the one that produces men and cities of the sort we've described?

No, I certainly am not.

According to Sachs, the test passage mentions the actions typical of vulgar justice (not stealing, not betraying friends and city, not lying, avoiding disrespect to family and the gods) in order to assert that the man who exhibits psychic justice will exemplify these actions. On this view, the function of the test passage is to bridge the gap between psychic justice and vulgar justice. An immediate problem for this view of the test passage is that the passage does not, in fact, perform its assigned function. The test passage does not assert that the psychically just man will always meet or exemplify the criteria of vulgar justice. It asserts only that the psychically just man will be less likely than anyone who is not psychically just to commit acts such as embezzling deposited money, adultery, and neglect of family and the gods.

Socrates asks four questions in the test passage, questions that list types of action typically recognized as unjust. Based on the first and fourth questions Socrates asks, at 442e4-443a1 and 443a9-10, we can assert only the comparative claim that the psychically just man is less likely than any other sort of person to perform such actions. The closest we come to a universal claim that the psychically just man will never commit unjust acts comes in the second question, which literally asks whether the just man will be outside (*ektos*) temple robberies, thefts, and private and public betrayal. This metaphor amounts to saying that the psychically just man would be far from committing such acts. The third question, asked at 443a6-7, does not ask whether the psychically just man always keeps his agreements. It asks instead whether he is the sort of person we ought to trust when it comes to agreements: "And he'd be in no way untrustworthy in keeping an oath or other agreement." As Socrates' discussion with Cephalus makes clear, the just person who is trustworthy when it comes to keeping agreements is the one who also knows when it is time to act against the letter of an agreement in order to keep to its spirit. As a result, the test passage does not assert that psychic justice rules out vulgar injustice categorically. And in fact, the psychically just man of the *Republic* will at times commit acts of vulgar injustice. He will refuse to return deposited property to its owner if this return is harmful to the owner, he will on occasion tell lies in his capacity as ruler in the *kallipolis* (382c-d, 414b-415d, 459c-e), and the rulers in the best city enjoy family relations that would scandalize the proponent of vulgar justice. As a result, we cannot accept Sachs' view that Plato uses the test-passage to assert that the psychically just man will always follow vulgar justice.

A better understanding of the test passage emerges from a closer examination of what the passage is supposed to test or confirm. According to Sachs, the passage lists criteria for vulgar justice and asserts that whoever possesses psychic justice will pass these tests. The test passage tests whether possession of psychic justice is sufficient for possession of vulgar justice, or whether a person with a certain psychic constitution meets the requirements for vulgar justice. But if we look at the passage preceding the four questions about the behavior of the just man, we find a different answer to the question of what is being tested. At 442b-d (section II.A.3), Socrates and Glaucon agree that the tripartite psychology developed in Book IV allows for convincing accounts of the three cardinal virtues other than justice: a person is courageous because of her spirited part's holding on to beliefs about what is and is not to be feared, wise because of her rational part ruling for the good of the whole soul, and temperate because of the agreement between parts of the soul as to which part should rule. Then Socrates and Glaucon agree at 442d5-10 on what it is for a human being to be just and assert the identity of psychic justice with justice in the city: "And, of course, a person will be just because of what we've so often mentioned, and in that way." "Necessarily." "Well, then, is the justice in us at all indistinct? Does it seem to be something different from what we found in the city?" "It doesn't seem so to me." In these lines, Socrates is concerned to arrive at a correct account of the four cardinal virtues in the human soul. He uses the tripartite psychology to give plausible accounts of courage, wisdom, and temperance, and then refers back to what he has "so often mentioned," apparently the account of justice in a human being provided at 441d4-e1 according to which a person is just by virtue of the fact that each part of her soul does its own work. Having asserted a candidate definition of justice in the soul, he moves on in the test passage to seek confirmation of this theoretical account of justice in the soul and its coincidence with the previous definition of justice in the city. The test passage begins at 442d11-e2 as follows: "If there are still any doubts in our soul about this [i.e., whether justice in the soul is the same as justice in the city], we could dispel them altogether by appealing to ordinary [or vulgar, *fortika*] cases." It is the correctness of the theoretical account of justice in the soul and the identity of justice in the soul with justice in the city that is being tested in the test passage.

When Socrates appeals to ordinary cases, then, he is not asserting the extensional equivalence of two distinct concepts, psychic justice, and vulgar justice. Rather, he is testing the success of his account of psychic justice as each part of the soul doing its own task and its convergence with the prior account of justice in the city. The appeal to ordinary or vulgar cases, what a just person is normally expected to do, is not a scientifically precise test, because as noted above a just person may in particular cases lie or refuse to return deposited property to its owner as agreed. A more insightful description of just actions will describe them as those actions which flow out of and help to sustain the state of psychic balance that is justice, as Socrates will go on to argue at 444c2-d11. However, the appeal to cases of just and unjust action understood in the ordinary way serves to give preliminary confirmation of the proposed definition of justice. A person who enjoys the described state of each psychic part doing its own task is described as a person "similar in nature and training to our city" (442e5-6). This just person will be ruled by reason, and will not allow the appetitive or the spirited part of the soul to usurp the leading role in the soul. Such a person will be least likely to steal money or commit adultery and will be least tempted to betray her comrades or her city, the stereotypical acts that undermine cities. This does not indicate a distinct vulgar conception of justice; rather, Socrates is making the claim that justice as a state or power of the soul will usually result in the actions that we typically associate with law-abiding behavior demanded by cities. The content of this claim is not simply a highly reliable correlation between psychic justice and acts conventionally recognized as just, but the idea that psychic justice is responsible for those acts. As Socrates says at 443b1-2, "Isn't the cause [*aition*] of all this that every part within him does its own work, whether it's ruling or being ruled? – Yes, that and nothing else." Socrates takes the results of the test passage, namely that the person with psychic justice is the one we least expect to sin against the laws of the city and more importantly that psychic justice is the cause of this lawful behavior, to be clear confirmation of his definition of justice. He and Glaucon reach agreement at 443b4-6: "Then, are you still looking for justice to be something other than this power, the one that produces men and cities of the sort we described? – No, I certainly am not." This passage articulates the real result of the test passage: it provides supporting evidence for the identity of justice in the city and justice in the soul, where both of these are defined as all parts doing their own task. The justice of the soul is not to be distinguished from the justice of the city. The function of the test passage is not, as Sachs claims, to assert that the person who possesses justice in the soul will in all cases conform to a separate conception of justice.[4]

Two aspects of the test passage should be noted here. The first is its assertion that justice understood as a state of psychic harmony is the cause of a type of actions commonly accepted as just. The psychically just person is treated as the last person we would expect to embezzle gold or silver, to commit robbery and theft, to commit adultery, or to betray friends and city. Why exactly we ought to expect the just person not to act in these ways is not clear from the test passage alone, but Socrates and Glaucon agree readily that the cause of this fact is the internal state of each part of the just person's soul doing its own work. We may supply the thought that the stereotypical acts of injustice mentioned in the test passage are the outward manifestations of inner disorder. Theft, adultery, and betrayal of friends are tempting to people with excessive and unruly appetitive and spirited desires. The just person avoids such inner disorder and so is the last person we would expect to find embezzling money, committing adultery, and betraying allies. Second, the result of this internal state of the soul is that the just person acts in a way that promotes the good of others. By not embezzling gold or silver

---

[4] Stephen Everson (2011) presents a similar criticism of Sachs' claim that Socrates has committed a fallacy of irrelevancy. According to Everson, Sachs operates with an understanding of definitions of properties such as justice informed by the techniques of ordinary language philosophy. Definitions were taken to be statements expressing the content of a notion to be defined, such as justice, where a valid test of the worth of a definition was to consider whether the content of the defining statement matched exactly the content of our beliefs about the definiendum. Plato's procedure in defining justice as a state of psychic harmony should not be held to this standard, argues Everson; it is closer to the model of definition seen in the definition of gold as the element possessing a particular atomic structure. This is an a posteriori definition which arises out of scientific discovery and not from faithful transcription of our beliefs about the definiendum.

deposited with him, the just person acts in a way that respects the interests of the one who deposited the money. By refraining from theft and robbery, the just person allows the owners of property to keep whole what belongs to them. Not committing adultery is a way to ensure that the just person's family life and the family life of her neighbors are given their best opportunity to flourish. By not betraying friends and fellow citizens, the just person serves as a reliable companion in social life for others in her city. In whatever way the causal process operates so that the state of psychic justice leads to these actions, the actions themselves are ways in which the just person promotes the interests of others and refrains from doing harm to those interests. I will refer to such actions as actions that promote the good of others.

The test passage thus asserts that the just person, the one who possesses and acts from a state of psychic harmony, will be more likely to act so as to promote the good of others than any person who lacks justice. Closer inspection of the test passage will help clarify what sort of good of others it is that is promoted by the just person. At first sight, the just person benefits others simply by keeping hands off their possessions and spouses. But a better way of characterizing the actions mentioned in the test passage is to note that they strengthen and make more effective the associations we maintain in society. By not embezzling deposited money, by keeping one's oaths and promises, and by not betraying friends and city, the just person strengthens the expectation of mutual support that is part of life in a good city or society. We live in cities and engage in political and social life in part to meet our immediate needs for food, shelter, and clothing, and we will achieve these goods more securely and easily while sharing society with someone who acts in the ways described in the test passage. The city and political life is also a venue for the shaping of character and the acquisition of virtue, and we will have a better chance at acquiring virtue if our fellows do not betray their friends and their community and do not violate the obligations of family life. The benefits of society (security of material possessions, cooperation and trust in common endeavors, aid and support from others in acquiring virtue) will be achieved more certainly as a result of the actions mentioned in the test passage. This is the type of good of others produced by the just person's actions.

It is fitting for Socrates to present the just person as one who reliably produces this sort of good for others, namely the benefits of society. He associates justice with the characteristic activity of forming and maintaining partnerships, and so the just person will be the one who acts as a good and beneficial partner by refraining from the acts of injustice mentioned in the test passage. A partnership such as a city will not survive long if its members regularly fail to act in ways that promote the good of others. The just person is the one who shows herself to be a good partner by acting in ways that allow others to achieve the benefits of society. Socrates' description in the test passage of what we can expect from the just person can be seen as a delayed answer to the question put to Polemarchus in Book 1: "What about the just man? In what action and in what work [*ergon*] is he most capable of benefiting friends and harming enemies?" The just man benefits friends and fellow citizens by acting in ways that promote the good of others in the context of forming and maintaining partnerships, in particular the partnership of political life.

This discussion of the test passage leaves us with an important question. How exactly does justice understood as a psychic state lead to actions that promote the good of others? The test passage asserts that psychic justice leads to such action but does not explain how this will happen. To attempt to answer this question I turn to the following passage, 443c-444a (II.C in the outline), which for convenience I will refer to as the harmony passage. This passage contains the most detailed exposition of the workings of psychic justice in Book 4:

One who is just does not allow any part of himself to do the work of another part or allow the various classes within him to meddle with each other. He regulates well what is really his own and rules himself. He puts himself in order, is his own friend, and harmonizes the three parts of himself like three limiting notes in a musical scale – high, low, and middle. He binds together those parts and any others there may be in between, and from having been many things he becomes entirely one, moderate and harmonious. Only then does he act. And when he does anything, whether acquiring wealth, taking care of his body, engaging in politics, or in private contracts – in all of these, he believes that the action is just and fine that preserves this inner harmony and helps achieve it, and calls it so, and regards as wisdom the knowledge that oversees such actions. And he believes that the action that destroys this harmony is unjust, and calls it so, and regards the belief that oversees it as ignorance.

This passage asserts a distinctive connection between justice as an internal psychic activity and external actions affecting other persons. Being just is a particular way of ruling oneself and ordering the different parts of oneself. It is compared to musical harmonies between varied musical notes and the achievement of friendship with one-self; this comparison recalls the band of thieves argument of Book 1, which associated justice with friendship between different elements of a group. As in the band of thieves argument, this state of order internal to a person generates a distinctive way of acting with others in partnerships and associations. Justice begins with the task of self-rule: the just person harmonizes and binds together the three parts of her soul under the leadership of reason. The three parts of the soul described functionally are three parts which enter into specified associations with each other: reason has the role of ruling and looking after the interests of the whole soul, spirit is properly the ally and helper of reason in disciplining appetite, and appetite does its own task by obeying the directives of reason as it pursues its desires (441e-442b). This internal association then provides the basis for acquiring money, entering private contracts, and engaging in politics. These actions affecting others should be understood as ways of continuing the activity of forming partnerships. Acquiring money involves taking up one of the occupations or crafts. In practicing this occupation the one who makes money provides some benefit to others in exchange for money. Practicing such an occupation is one way of contributing to one's city, which is itself a partnership (369b-c). A private contract is a small-scale partnership, in which each side agrees to provide some specified service or good to the other. Engaging in politics means taking an active role in the large-scale partnership that is a city, either by fulfilling the duties of a citizen or by filling a political office. These actions mentioned in the harmony passage are all ways of carrying out the function associated with justice, namely forming and maintaining partnerships.

By using the harmony passage's description of forming and maintaining partnerships, we can provide an answer to the question that arises from the test passage. The earlier passage asserted that psychic justice is the cause of the just person carrying out actions that promote the good of others, but did not explain how psychic justice is responsible for these actions. The harmony passage in effect traces the activity of forming and maintaining partnerships from the interaction between parts of the soul to the interaction between parts of a city. If the just person remains a private citizen, then her psychic justice will remain localized in her private friendships and in the practice of her occupation, the moneymaking and private contracts mentioned in the harmony passage. To the extent that the just person gains prominence in political life, she will be able to enter into the partnership of ruling. In the best case, Socrates will say, the just person becomes a guardian in the just city. In this city, she is able to transmit the order and harmony of relations between appetite, spirit, and reason to the relations between workers, auxiliaries, and guardians. When Socrates speaks of justice as the power that is responsible for just men and for just cities (443b), he apparently has this sort of case in mind: the activity of forming partnerships and associations transmits itself from the soul of the just person to the relations of ruling and being ruled that obtain between different classes within the just city.

The harmony passage also contains a description of the principle that guides the just person in acting. She will act in ways that affect others and will enter into partnerships with them only if these actions preserve and foster the state of inner harmony that is psychic justice. Under such conditions, she will give such an action the title of fine or beautiful (*kalēn*). This indicates that the just person will not take as decisive for selecting actions such criteria as their conformity with conventional morality or production of pleasure or gaining external goods such as honor or victory in battle. The deciding factor for the just person in her choice of action will be the effect of that action on the correct balance and order of the parts within her soul. We may formulate this as a principle on which the just person relies as she deliberates about how to act, the Harmony Principle:

HP   Choose the act which preserves and promotes harmony in one's own soul

Like all principles which purport to guide action, this principle does not apply itself and so must be supplied with several qualifications. The principle HP presupposes that the agent who uses it is already just to some extent, i.e., already possesses to some degree psychic harmony, perhaps by keeping the appetitive part of the soul minimally compliant with the directions of reason. The point of the harmony principle is to guide the agent toward actions which preserve and further improve this harmony. In addition, the principle does not tell the agent how to determine which action will preserve and promote psychic harmony and which will destroy it. Some insight into this question must be supplied from elsewhere; looking backward in the *Republic* we may mention education in music and poetry and looking forward we may anticipate the philosopher's knowledge of the Form of the Good. Finally, this principle guides an agent only when she is in a situation of choice between actions which have different effects on her psychic harmony. If two actions are identical in their effect on psychic harmony, then the principle HP is indifferent with respect to those actions. Subject to these qualifications, though, HP tells a person who is just what to take into account when deciding to act: she should focus on the role of her action in fostering harmony in her soul.

Justice as a psychological state is both the causal origin and a crucial consequence of just actions that satisfy HP. These actions mentioned in the harmony passage—gaining money, entering into private contracts, and engaging in political affairs—involve the just person in dealings with others in which the good of those others is promoted. Acquiring money will involve providing some good or service to others in exchange for money, contracts and private associations with others have their point in the provision of benefit for both parties, and engaging in political affairs leads to providing services to the city, perhaps by holding public office. Only in the suitable environment of the best city will the just person be able to act justly in such a way as to rule as a guardian. In this best case, the performance of just actions flows from and preserves the justice of individual souls, and this justice of souls is also responsible for the justice of the city formed by these individuals. The best city in which each class does its own work will be constituted by the farmers, smiths, and carpenters of the moneymaking class who acquire money in a just manner, by auxiliaries who take up the political task of fighting for the city, and by guardians who exercise wisdom in directing these activities. Only the guardians will possess justice in the full sense of possessing the psychic state of each part of their soul doing its own work. Only in the soul of a guardian does reason achieve its proper task of ruling the other parts for the good of the whole soul. But the other classes can exhibit justice in a qualified sense when they act in ways that obey and give support to the orders of the guardians. In this way, the moneymaking class and the guardians can aid in the transmission of justice from the soul of the guardians to the city. As Socrates summarizes the results of this paragraph, both the just man and the just city have now been identified, along with the justice that is present in both (444a4-6). Just actions have served as the necessary means for justice to transmit itself to the city.

With this account of the relation between psychic justice and just action in hand, we can review quickly the substance of Socrates' defense of justice in *Republic* 4. The core of justice in the soul is the activity of ordering the different parts of the soul, allotting to each its proper task and its place in the natural hierarchy of ruling and being ruled. This activity constitutes the benefit of having a well-ordered and harmonious soul. According to Socrates, this is a benefit which is great enough to make being just always preferable to being unjust regardless of any gain of political power, honor, and external goods resulting from being unjust. Glaucon agrees to this claim at 445a-b; once one understands what justice and injustice are, and the analogy they bear to health and sickness, then it is clear that being just always benefits the just person more than being unjust. There is no sense in gaining lesser goods while losing justice and thus ruining the soul, that by which one lives. In addition, justice is a Class 2 good comparable to health, the sort of good that is an activity that is valuable for its own sake, and also produces criterial benefits. While justice operates at the most basic level within the soul of the just person, as the harmony passage attests, it also expresses itself through just action on its way to making the city just. Just action clearly benefits other people who associate themselves with the just person, but the just person can also benefit from imparting justice to her city. Not only do citizens of a just city gain protection from harm inflicted by tyrannical rulers; in addition, their individual plans for happiness gain support from the associations they form with others. And citizens of a just city can reflect that this gain in individual happiness is made possible by a system that benefits all, a system that does not rest on the exploitation of the weak and unfortunate. This allows citizens to combine private happiness with merited self-esteem. This beneficial result of being a member of a just city is not a necessary consequence of being just; external circumstances must cooperate in order for this consequence to arise. But when it does arise, it is a sign of the proper functioning of the just person's soul and a criterial benefit of being just.

To summarize Socrates' treatment of justice as a Class 2 good, he describe justice as the activity of rational and wise self-rule exercised within the soul. Like being healthy, seeing, and being wise, the activity of being just is desirable for the benefit it constitutes, a soul that is harmonious and unified. This activity is also desirable for the criterial benefits it generates with the aid of other cooperating causes, such as the help of fellow citizens who aid in the project of making a city just. The creation of a just city is a key instance of the criterial benefits of psychic justice. It is not one that results necessarily from the possession of psychic justice, since the creation of a just city requires a supportive social environment and the presence of fellow citizens who will aid in the creation of the just city. But when the just city does flow from the presence of harmonious self-rule in the soul of just individuals, this is a genuine benefit and one that testifies to the good condition of the activity of harmonious self-rule operating within these just persons. This is the sort of defense of justice we expected to find on the basis of the division of goods and Glaucon's challenge in Book 2.

7.3 Justice and Just Actions

Although Sachs' charge of committing a fallacy of irrelevancy does not stand up to close examination, his paper raises a larger issue which requires consideration. This larger issue is the relation between justice defined as a state of psychic order and justice defined in terms of actions that promote the good of others. Socrates recommends to us a state of psychic order as an essential component of our happiness and as a good which benefits us more than anything we could ever achieve without this good. Precisely how this recommendation of psychic order is intended to carry over to a recommendation of the sorts of actions mentioned in the test passage remains unclear. These actions—showing respect for the property of others, refraining from theft and betrayal, keeping promises, and the rest—are typical examples of promoting the good of others. Yet Socrates traces these actions back to the just man's concern to promote and preserve his internal state of psychic order. Without accepting the details of Sachs' charge of irrelevancy, we may well wonder whether Socrates has solved his problem by changing the subject. If Socrates is required to defend the value of justice, where justice is seen most clearly in action that promotes the good of others, then it will seem unsatisfactory to receive praise of a state of psychic harmony. As Sarah Waterlow puts it,

[M]oral goodness is one thing and one's own welfare another, and how can Plato manage to define the first so that it approximates to the second without letting slip some of the conceptual content of the first, in particular its connexion with moral *action*? Yet this is a connexion he needs for the sake of his main thesis, since what he means to equate with the individual's own welfare is a state of being which although it lies beyond what common sense thinks of as moral goodness, includes and even explains the latter; for which reason it must maintain, in some sense, the common sense connexion with moral action. Having himself, first, cut this required connexion (or so it is claimed), Plato can now do no more than *assert* that it holds, hoping perhaps that it somehow still does or that no one will notice that it doesn't.[5]

If moral action is action undertaken expressly for the good of others, then Plato's praise of justice as a state of psychic order and his description of the just man's concern to promote this state threatens to render mysterious the connection between justice and moral action.

Terence Irwin presents a different version of this problem, one that clearly articulates the challenge of connecting psychic justice with concern for the good of others. After rehearsing Sachs' objection, namely that Socrates has given us a defense of psychic justice (p-justice) when a defense of conventional or common justice (c-justice) was in order, Irwin notes that common justice can be understood either in terms of the common description of justice or in terms of the common intuition concerning justice. The common description of justice is often beset by contradiction and imprecision, but the common intuition is associated with a coherent understanding of the virtuous person and her willingness to respect the needs and interests of others.[6] Socrates (and in turn Plato) are committed to showing that the just person is happier than the unjust, and this entails showing that one who is concerned to promote the good of others is happier than one who lacks this characteristic motivation of the just:

It is fair, then, by Plato's own standards as well as the standards of common sense, to expect him to vindicate an other-regarding virtue of justice. If p-justice does not imply regard for the

---

[5] Waterlow (1972, 24); italics in original.   [6] Irwin (1995, 256–9).

interests of others, we have good reason to infer that it is not justice and that therefore a proof that the p-just person is happier than anyone else does not prove that the just person is happier than anyone else. If Plato's argument about p-justice is to prove that justice promotes happiness, he must prove that p-justice is other-regarding.[7]

In these lines derived from reflection on Sachs' objection, Irwin presents a basic condition for the defense of justice: any defense of justice must acknowledge that justice entails a concern to respect and promote the needs and interests of others.

As a result of forty years of Platonic scholarship, it should be clear that Socrates is on firm ground when he asserts in the test passage that the just person will normally perform stereotypically just actions and will do so in a way that promotes the good of others. Although Sachs is right to note that in Book 4 the claims set forth in the test passage are asserted without further argumentative support, the assertions in question have been defended numerous times by commentators. These commentators have shown that the moral psychology contained in other parts of the *Republic* provides more than enough support for the claims made in the test passage that the just person can be relied upon to act in a way that promotes the good of others by refraining from embezzlement, theft, adultery, etc.[8] But a different solution, one that draws more directly upon the defense of justice in Book 4, exploits the resources of Plato's functional teleology of action. A notable feature of Socrates' description of the just man taking action in the harmony passage at 443c-444a is that the just man seems to pay more attention to the quality of his action and its relation to his internal state of psychic order than he does to the positive effect of this action on others. As Sachs, Waterlow, and others have rightly perceived, these and other lines from Book 4 do not ascribe to the psychically just man an explicit concern to promote the good of others in the way that is supposedly required by vulgar justice or common morality. The content of the just man's intention in acting justly is best described as the wish to preserve and reproduce the state of psychic harmony in his soul; the good of others is not included in the content of this intention. However, the just actions performed with this intention are actions by which, in the best case, the citizens of the *kallipolis* produce a just city and thus promote the good of others. In less than optimal circumstances, just actions performed with the intention of maintaining the agent's psychic harmony secure for others the benefits of society and thus promote the good of others. As a further example of the functional teleology of action, I will argue, just actions are performed for the sake of promoting the good of others as an unintended end.

As discussed in section II, the test passage attributes to the just person actions of truth-telling, keeping oaths, honoring family obligations, and refraining from theft and betrayal. The harmony passage traces the generation of just actions from an internal

---

[7] Irwin (1995, 259–60).

[8] Instances of this sort of response to Sachs are found in Demos (1971); Vlastos (1971); Kraut (1973b); Cooper (1977); Brown (2004); and Singpurwalla (2006). Notable exceptions to this body of literature are Annas (1978) and Smith (1999b), which do not construe the arguments of *Republic* 4 as attempts to connect two distinct conceptions of justice.

state of proper self-rule to moneymaking, care for the body, engaging in private contracts, and holding political office. These just actions will involve craftsmen providing their services to the city and fulfilling their contractual obligations as well as auxiliaries and guardians executing political duties. All such actions are cases of maintaining partnerships with others and thus helping others to enjoy the benefits of society. Just actions are thus cases of promoting the good of others, even if the just agent chooses them under a different description, that of promoting the state of inner harmony in his soul as specified by HP. More importantly, the harmony passage speaks of such actions as ways in which the just man does his own, the formula that expresses an individual citizen's contribution to the justice of the city. As expressions of each citizen doing his own, these actions allow the just person to constitute and maintain partnerships with other citizens. These partnerships include the associations we form in our ordinary, flawed societies. They can also include the special partnership that is Socrates' kallipolis. In all such cases, just actions transmit justice from the soul to the partnership that is formed.

The distinctive Platonic functional teleology of action provides a way to connect psychic justice, just actions, and the good of others. If it can be shown that the four conditions of the for-the-sake-of relation elaborated in Chapter 2 hold for just actions and the creation of just partnerships, this would be a way of showing that just actions are performed for the sake of the good of others. Just actions that flow out of a state of psychic justice would find their purpose in establishing just partnerships, and this is an important way for the just person to promote the good of others. In the formal terms of the analysis of the for-the-sake-of relation, the actions $A_1, A_2, \ldots A_N$ are the just actions described at 443c–444a and in the test passage: carrying out the ordinary moral duties of truth-telling and family life, making money, engaging in private contracts, and holding political office. Establishing a just partnership is a result E that is produced by these actions. Given this specification of actions and end, it is necessary to show that the four conditions hold which ensure that the actions $A_1, A_2, \ldots, A_N$ are performed for the sake of E.

First, the just actions in question are of lesser value than the result they produce, the just city. These actions may be onerous in themselves, and may be instances of Class 3 goods in Glaucon's division of goods. Acquiring money, for instance, would involve the practice of a craft such as weaving or medicine. Holding political office and ruling benefits the ruled and not the ruler, as we learn in the conversation between Thrasymachus and Socrates in Book 1. These actions have value in virtue of the good they produce: the products of the various crafts, for instance, or living in a well-administered city. A just partnership, on the other hand, is something valuable in itself. Its promise of harmonious participation in social and political life qualifies it as an end worth pursuing for its own sake and not merely a means to a further end.

Second, just actions produce or contribute to a just partnership by carrying out one or more functions. The just agent acts out of her internal state of psychic justice, in which each part of her soul performs its own function. As Socrates says at the end of the test passage, the cause (*aition*) of a just person carrying out various just actions is that each part of the just person's soul does its own task with regard to ruling and being ruled (443b1-2). The harmony passage makes a similar assertion at the level of the whole person: the just actions mentioned in this passage are ways in which a person "does his own" in the sense of carrying out the function which belongs to him as moneymaker or in carrying out the political tasks of an auxiliary or guardian. Thus, the second condition is fulfilled, since the just actions in question produce a just partnership by carrying out one or more functions (the functions of the parts of the soul and the function of one of the three classes in the city).

The final two conditions associated with the functional teleology of action are also satisfied. The just actions described in the test passage and in the harmony passage are valuable in part because they contribute to establishing just partnerships such as a city. This may not be the aspect of these actions that attracts the just person to them, but their role in establishing just partnerships is part of their total value. Finally, the fourth condition requires that the just actions in question perform the functions mentioned in the second condition in the best way only if they contribute to establishing a just partnership. That is, the just actions perform in the best way the functions of the appetitive, spirited, and rational parts of the soul and the functions of the various classes in the city only if they help to bring about a just partnership. This can be shown by noting that the different classes within the just city have been defined in relation to each other in such a way that mutual support from all the classes, as is found in a just partnership, is required for optimal performance of function by any one class. The guardians can do their job of ruling in the best way only when they receive material support from the moneymaking class and when the auxiliaries execute the directives of the guardians. The auxiliaries also require material support from the moneymakers as well as rational guidance from the guardians. The workers in the city can perform their functions optimally only if the guardians and auxiliaries maintain the proper education in the city and safeguard the proper assignment of worker to task in accordance with the principle of specialization. As we saw in Chapter 5 in the account of the unity of a city, the different classes form a single whole when each helps the others to carry out their own task. The prerequisite for these functions being carried out in the best way will be each class within the city doing its own, which is another way of saying that the just city, a particular sort of partnership, will be established.

These comments concern the particular functions that Socrates assigns to the classes within the best city and their role in creating his ideal city. However, these observations about the creation of the kallipolis illustrate an underlying principle that holds of all social roles and their role in supporting partnerships. As social and political animals, we perform a range of functions: the function of a brother, sister, parent, or child within a family; the function of a doctor, farmer, cobbler, or insurance salesperson within our professional lives; and the function of a citizen within a political community, which is a matter of ruling and being ruled in turn. In all these cases, good performance of function is indicated by the fact that our actions underwrite strong associations and partnerships with family members, with work colleagues and employers, and with our fellow citizens. The best way of performing these functions will lead to the creation of just partnerships of various kinds. The establishment of just partnerships is part of the point of our performance of these functions, and as a result, the best performance of function requires the establishment of just partnerships.

This set of reflections on passages in Book 4 is meant to secure the claim that just actions lead to the formation of just partnerships in a way that satisfies the four conditions of the for-the-sake-of relation. This amounts to the claim that, when circumstances cooperate, the just person performs just actions for the sake of establishing just partnerships. A striking instance of this pattern is the case where the just person performs just actions for the sake of establishing Socrates' kallipolis. Although the just person may perform these actions intending only to preserve the harmony of his soul by carrying out the terms of a contract or by defending his city, such actions may be performed also for the sake of an unintended end, a just and harmonious political community. This analysis of the functional teleology of just action suggests the following reply to the concern raised by Waterlow and Irwin. As noted earlier, it is not enough for Socrates merely to assert that the just person will act justly and in doing so promote the good of his own soul. The just person must show the right sort of orientation toward the good of others. But this correct orientation, as Socrates would describe it, need not be that of explicit and altruistic concern for the good of others. The correct orientation to the good of others need not involve acting with the intention to promote the good of others. To judge from the harmony passage, the intention with which the just person acts is preservation of his own inner state of psychic order and harmony. For some, this suffices to convict Socrates of missing the point of justice; from their perspective, justice must issue in an explicit commitment to uphold the legitimate interests of others. However, Socrates can provide a strong rejoinder to this position, one that draws upon the role of justice in the city and other partnerships as the end of just action. Just partnerships are clearly a great benefit for all its citizens, so that any action that promotes such partnerships in the city will also work for the good of others. According to Socrates, just actions are performed for the sake of establishing just partnerships. While justice at its core is a structure or power lodged in the soul of the individual human being, this power can express itself in the best way only if it promotes the good of others by creating just partnerships.

This conception of the relations between justice, just action, and the good of others rejects the intuition that the correct orientation of justice toward the good of others must be that of altruistic concern for the good of others and an associated intention to promote the good of others. Socrates may go on the offensive and ask why it must be central to justice that the just person intends to promote the good of others. The *Republic*'s pervasive discussion of justice in terms of structural relations and harmony between parts of the soul and classes in the city will underwrite the following piece of counsel from Socrates: if we want to be just, we should pay less attention to promoting the interests of this or that part of the soul, this or that person or group of persons within the city, and focus instead on maintaining a certain delicate harmony between the parts of the soul and the parts of the city.[9] Success in achieving this harmonious balance will in fact promote the interests of all parts of the soul and all classes within the city, but it is not necessary and may even be imprudent to require that the just person aim to promote the good of others. The good of others enters into Socrates' defense of justice at a different point. It is not a goal that guides the just person in action but is part of the end for the sake of which the just person acts. As such, it serves as a standard for evaluating the worth of just actions. This draws justice as a state of psychic order into an appropriate relation to the good of others. We evaluate a person's actions and psychic states as just or unjust by considering whether those actions and psychic states issue in the good of others. But this criterion for justice need not be a goal of the just agent.

It should be noted that this account of the relation between justice and just actions does not commit Socrates to an egoistic theory of motivation. So far, this account of justice and just actions in Book 4 contains the following two claims: first, that the just agent acts justly by selecting those actions which preserve and promote his inner state of justice, and second, that the good of others need not be an intended goal of the just agent in these actions, even if the good of others is bound up with the formation of just partnerships, that for the sake of which the just person acts. Given that these or similar claims are intimately involved in the defense of justice in Book 4, it has seemed to commentators such as H. A. Prichard that here Socrates assumes that the motivating force behind just action, and indeed behind all action, must be self-interest.[10] But this is not required by the present account of just action. Socrates says that the just agent selects the action which preserves his inner state of harmony and calls that action just and

---

[9] This counsel appears first in reaction to Glaucon's protest that the healthy city does not allow its citizens to live better than pigs do (372d), then in response to Adeimantus' worry that the guardians in the best city will not be happy living in communal housing without any private property beyond what they need to do their job (419a), and finally as an answer to Glaucon's concern that compelling the philosophers to return to the cave of political life is unjust (519d). Socrates treats Glaucon's request for delicacies and desserts as a request for a luxurious and fevered city rather than a healthy city, one motivated by the desires of the appetitive part of the soul. This request is "cured" by Socrates' program of education in music and poetry, especially by the reduction of music to the Dorian and Phrygian modes of harmony (399a-e). This imposition of harmony and temperance on the appetitive part of the soul is presented as a gain in health for the citizens and the city. Similarly, Socrates responds to the concerns of Glaucon and Adeimantus about the happiness of the guardians in part by making the point that justice requires making the whole city as good and as beautiful as possible, not focusing on the interests of any one element in the city. As Socrates says to Glaucon at 519e1–520a2, "You are forgetting again that it isn't the law's concern to make any one class in the city outstandingly happy but to contrive to spread happiness throughout the city by bringing the citizens into harmony with each other through persuasion or compulsion and by making them share with each other the benefits that each class can confer on the community."

[10] This understanding of Socrates' defense of justice is reflected in Prichard's comments: "There is no escaping the conclusion that when Plato sets himself to consider not what *should*, but what *actually does* as a matter of fact, lead a man to act, when he is acting deliberately, and not merely in consequence of an impulse, he answers 'The desire for some good to himself and that only'. In other words we have to allow that, according to Plato, a man pursues whatever he pursues simply as a good to himself, i.e. really as something that will give him satisfaction, or, as perhaps we ought to say, as an element in what will render him happy"; see Prichard (2002, 33). Italics in original.

beautiful (*kalēn*, 443e5-6). This account of the just person's action allows the just person to see his actions as having inherent beauty and dignity and to be motivated by this aspect of a proposed action. If Socrates understood the motive for all action to be self-interest, it would be natural for him to present the just person as conceiving of his action as useful or beneficial. In addition, the present account seeks to clarify the typical way in which justice, a psychological state, issues in just action that ultimately promotes the good of others. This is not the same as proposing a general theory of motivation for all actions, according to which all action is motivated by the agent's concern for his own interest. The pattern of justice transmitting itself from soul to city leaves room for the temperate craftsman to fulfill his promise to weave a cloak out of a sense of duty, for the courageous auxiliary to die in battle for the good of the city, and for the wise guardian to rule because she is convinced that it is just for her to do so. Such actions do not conform to an egoistic theory of motivation according to which all action is motivated by the desire to promote one's own interests.

This description of the relation between justice, just action, and the good of others rests upon the conviction that a satisfactory account of this relation can be formulated using passages in Book 4 and earlier in the *Republic*. In this respect, it differs from the usual approach to this issue. Under the stimulus provided by Sachs' article, an impressive series of papers has sought to show that Plato possesses the resources to bridge the gap between psychic justice and conventional morality. These resources are to be found in Books 5 to 7 with their discussion of the forms and the philosopher-kings. Raphael Demos first set the trend by accepting the substance of Sachs' criticism and by having recourse to the doctrine that reason takes the forms as its objects, especially the Form of the Good. He accepts that justice as Socrates defines it is essentially self-regarding, since it takes the ordering of one's own soul as its main task. "But so defined, justice is self-regarding. How then can it possibly imply a concern for other people (rendering to everyone his due)?"[11] To answer this question, Demos develops a more high-powered conception of reason, one that draws upon the central books of the *Republic*. Reason is not simply bare calculation of what is good for the individual soul; it is cognition of the forms and involves a distinctive type of desire. This desire drives the one whose soul is ruled by reason to know and also to embody the forms. "To aim at the good is also to aim at the production of good things; thus for an individual to aim at justice means that he cares not only for justice in the abstract, but also that justice should be embodied in human beings in general."[12] This gap-filling approach to the problem set by Sachs is characterized by four central themes. First, justice as defined in Book 4 is self-regarding and so cannot address the legitimate expectation that justice entails promotion of the good of others. Second, the fully just person is the philosopher; the one whose soul is ruled by reason is the one who knows the forms. Third, to know the forms is to evince concern for justice and goodness in all places and persons.

---

[11] Demos (1971, 54).   [12] Demos (1971, 55).

Fourth, concern for one's own justice implies a generalized concern for all to be just and good.

A distinguished array of scholars has improved on Demos' sketch of a reply to Sachs by restating many of the themes above with greater rigor. John Cooper, Richard Kraut, and Norman Dahl agree that the just person envisioned in the *Republic* will achieve insight into the forms and will thereby be motivated to act morally with no special concern for his own interest. Cooper focuses on the claim that the just person serves the form of goodness, the source of rational order, and not his own happiness:

[A] just person is a devotee of *the* good, not *his own* good; and these are very different things. Knowing the good, what he wants is to advance the reign of rational order in the world as a whole, so far as by his own efforts, alone or together with others, he can do this. He recognizes a single criterion of choice: What, given the circumstances, will be most likely to maximize the total amount of rational order in the world as a whole?[13]

Richard Kraut pursues a similar interpretation of why the just person will make moral decisions:

Someone who has been fully prepared to love the orderly pattern of the Forms will be free of the urge to seek worldly advantages over other human beings or to engage in the sort of illicit sexual activity to which people are led by unchecked appetites. Furthermore, such a person is in the best possible position to make wise political decisions; having understood the Forms, she can see more clearly than others what needs to be done in particular circumstances (500d–501a).[14]

With the philosopher's knowledge of the forms comes a willingness to act as morality requires. Concern for justice and goodness itself constitutes a motivation to act in other-regarding ways, ways consistent with the rough descriptions of just actions given by Cephalus and Thrasymachus in Book 1: telling the truth, returning what one owes, and in general refraining from selfish gain.

This body of scholarship has improved our understanding of the moral psychology implicated in the central books of the *Republic*. It has effectively disproved the claim found in Prichard that Plato is an egoist by marshalling superior textual support for a non-egoistic theory of moral action in the dialogue. Despite these manifest strengths, the gap-filling interpretation should not be accepted as the canonical statement of the relation between justice, just action, and the good of others. This is so for two reasons. First, the gap-filling interpretation concedes too much to Sachs when it accepts that the account of justice in Book 4 does not provide a defensible connection between justice and the good of others. If the basic problematic posed by Sachs is accepted, then Socrates, Glaucon, and Adeimantus are not justified in the agreements they reach by

---

[13] Cooper (1977, 155–6).
[14] Kraut (1992, 323–4). Other works which describe the philosopher-rulers of the *Republic* as motivated by knowledge of the forms to act without special concern for their own interest include Kraut (1973a); Dahl (1991), and White (1979, 43–54).

the end of Book 4. They believe that they have gotten clear on the nature of justice, the virtue that promotes the good of others. If the gap-filling interpretations are right, these agreements are premature. Socrates is not yet entitled to claim that he has identified justice, and he will need to give further support to his claim that the cause of the just acts detailed in the test passage is the state of harmony within the just man's soul. If it is possible to provide an interpretation of justice and its relation to the good of others that does not put the agreements reached in Book 4 in such a doubtful light, then it is to be preferred to the gap-filling interpretation. The interpretation of justice provided here fits the bill: the just person acts for the sake of establishing just partnerships and thus uses her justice in a way that promotes the good of others. We can affirm the agreements reached by Socrates and Glaucon in Book 4 as giving insight into the nature of justice, the virtue that promotes the good of others.

Second, the gap-filling interpretations propose a new description of the principle that guides the just man in his actions. According to the harmony passage, the just man selects actions on the basis of the principle HP: he goes for those actions that preserve and promote the state of harmony in his soul. The gap-filling interpretations replace this principle with various principles that allow the philosopher to bring the forms to bear on the world as a whole. Such a principle instructs the philosopher to embody justice in all human beings (Demos) or to maximize rational order in all things (Cooper). But Socrates does not direct the philosopher-rulers to impress the Form of the Good on the world in general. The closest thing to such a wide-ranging principle comes in Book 7 at 540a8-b4: "And once they've seen the good itself, they must each in turn put the city, its citizens, and themselves in order, using it as their model. Each of them will spend most of his time with philosophy, but, when his turn comes, he must labor in politics and rule for the city's sake ...." This passage at 540a-b can be construed as a variation on the main theme of the Harmony Principle: the philosopher-ruler selects those actions that ensure an orderly state of soul for herself. In her capacity as guardian, she will also seek to transmit this order to the soul of her fellow citizens. In doing so, she will spread the same state of order and harmony to the city. Within the best city, the philosopher's knowledge of the Form of the Good generates order and harmony. But there is no mention of the philosophers turning to the larger world outside of the city to generate justice in all humans or to maximize rational order.

Similarly, when he concludes his defense of justice at the end of Book 9, Socrates relies on metaphorical statements of the Harmony Principle and not on principles that tell the philosophers to shape the wide world. At 588c-89b, he compares the human soul to a composite of serpent, lion, and human being. The point of this image is to clarify what is being said by the proponents of injustice and justice: the former recommend to us that we strengthen the serpent and the lion, weaken the human being within us, and make the various parts enemies, while the latter tells us to place the human in control of the bestial parts of our nature and to promote friendship among all the parts. This reworking of the advice given to us by the supporters of justice obviously draws upon the concern to promote internal order that motivates the Harmony Principle. Similarly,

Socrates finds a rationale for conventional moral judgments and laws in the effects of these on the relations between the parts of the soul; both serve to restrain the serpent and lion within us and make them obedient to the human (589c-591a). Finally, he recommends that we regulate the activity of each of the three parts of the soul by aiming at maintaining the proper order and constitution in the soul (591b-592a). These reiterations of the Harmony Principle come at the end of Book 9, after the rich discussion of forms and the rule of reason in the soul of the philosopher. If the gap-filling interpretations provided the correct account of how the just man seeks to impress justice and rational order on the world as a whole, we would expect to find Socrates concluding his defense of justice with a statement of how the just man consults the forms and then shapes all the various items of his world in accordance with them. Given that Socrates does not do this but instead repeats the line of thought found in the harmony passage, we have reason to reject the gap-filling interpretations as statements of the relation between justice and moral action. The just man's goal is not the maximization of rational order in the world but the preservation of harmony in his own soul.

8

The Form of the Good I
Vision and Knowledge in Three Images

8.1 Introduction

In a passage that introduces the *Republic*'s discussion of the central metaphysical and epistemological principle, Socrates draws our attention at 505d11-506a2 to the need for the best people in the city, the philosopher-rulers, to gain insight into the Form of the Good:

Every soul pursues the good and does whatever it does for its sake. It divines that the good is something but it is perplexed and cannot adequately grasp what it is or acquire the sort of stable beliefs it has about other things, and so it misses the benefit, if any, that even those other things may give. Will we allow the best people in the city, to whom we entrust everything, to be so in the dark about something of this kind and of this importance?

As he describes the Form indirectly through the three images of the Sun, the Divided Line, and the Cave, Socrates also provides clues about how it is possible to draw closer to the Form through an intellectual ascent from sensible objects to forms. After presenting these three images, Socrates in Book 7 describes the education of the philosopher-rulers with special attention to the role of mathematics (521b-531d). Taken together, these texts allow us to discuss the way in which philosophers act and learn for the sake of the Form of the Good. Their education is presented in the image of the Cave. This image sets forth a turning of the soul from darkness and shadows to confrontation with the sun, which here stands for the Form of the Good. The mathematical program of study described at 521b-531d gives a less figurative account of parts of this process, as it details a path of study meant to prepare potential philosophers for the greatest study, the Form of the Good. The rigorous study of advanced mathematics that forms an essential part of the education of the philosopher-rulers is one case of acting for the sake of the Form of the Good.

In this and the following two chapters, an examination of a cluster of issues introduced by the passage above will conclude our investigation of Plato's functional teleology of action. Understanding the Form of the Good is the unintended end or purpose of philosophic inquiry in the sense indicated by our previous account of Plato's functional teleology of action. The present chapter begins the presentation of this theme by introducing the three images that Socrates uses to convey his beliefs about the Form of the Good: the Sun, the Divided Line, and the Cave. An important motif in these images is the presence of vision as an analogue to knowledge. Because vision plays an important role in the three images of Sun, Divided Line, and Cave, it will be profitable to examine Plato's theory of vision in the *Timaeus* in some detail. Having considered this theory of vision, we will be in a better position to understand several puzzling features of these images of the Form of the Good. The image of the Divided Line in particular conveys the thought that we exercise vision for the sake of directing our thought toward intelligible objects; in this respect, the *Republic* echoes one of the striking claims made in the *Timaeus*, namely that we have vision for the sake of practicing astronomy and becoming philosophers (*Timaeus* 46e-47c). The present chapter will conclude with an overview of the comparison Plato frequently employs between vision and knowledge.

Two qualifications must be made in order to delimit the scope of this investigation of the Form of the Good as the end of philosophic inquiry. As with all attempts to investigate the Form of the Good, interpretive limits are set by Socrates' refusal to state his beliefs about the Form in so many words. He offers us instead the three images of the Sun, the Line, and the Cave. These images provide suggestive glimpses of the way in which the Form of the Good is the end of philosophic inquiry, but any conclusions on this subject must rest on the interpretation of these complex images. Second, this discussion of Books 6 and 7 does not contain a comprehensive interpretation of the Form of the Good. A complete treatment of the Form of the Good would require extensive discussion of Plato's ontology and theory of knowledge. Our attention will be restricted here to the Form of the Good *qua* end of action for the philosopher-rulers as they make the intellectual ascent from the world of sense through their mathematical studies to the forms. The scope of these final three chapters may be delimited as follows: given that there is such a thing as the Form of the Good that is a first principle for ethics, epistemology, and ontology, how do philosopher-rulers-in-training act for the sake of this thing?

The answer to this question is contained in the account of the guardians' intellectual ascent toward the Good at the end of Book 6 and in Book 7. Socrates' discussion of the Form of the Good in these pages is less a theoretical account of a single object of knowledge and more a description of how human beings can move through different states of cognition for the sake of knowledge of one fundamental principle. The Divided Line distinguishes between four different states: imagination or eikasia, belief or pistis, thought or dianoia, and dialectic. These states are arranged in ascending order of cognitive accomplishment. In each of the first three states, one uses images for the sake of gaining knowledge of the objects of the next higher state. The exposition of this process of ascent will begin in the present chapter, which focuses on vision as an analogue to knowledge and the role of eikasia in the Divided Line and in the Cave. The following chapter, Chapter 9, will focus on the role of dianoia in the Divided Line. Here again the distinctive feature of the movement upwards from visible to intelligible objects is the use of images to gain insight into the next higher level. The final chapter, Chapter 10, attempts to trace the final step in the ascent toward the Good, namely the transition from dianoia to dialectic. The Divided Line and the Cave provide scant details on this final stage of the ascent, but close attention to the propaedeutic studies described in Book 7 will help to fill out our understanding of this final movement upwards. The transition from dianoia to dialectic is made by reflection on the objects of dianoia, in particular by formulating more explicitly the notions of commensurability and harmony used by mathematicians at the level of dianoia. To describe this whole intellectual ascent toward the Form of the Good more simply, it is like climbing a ladder: one starts at the bottom and goes upward step by step until one reaches the top.

8.2 Three Images of the Form of the Good: An Overview

Glaucon puts Socrates on the spot at 506b. Socrates has told the assembled company that the philosopher-rulers in the best city must gain insight into the greatest study, the Form of the Good, in order to fulfill their role as guardians of the well-being of their fellow citizens. He has also criticized the opinions of others on the content of this greatest study: it cannot be pleasure, as the majority think, nor can it be knowledge, as some more cultivated types suppose. But Glaucon is not content with a review of what other people think: "Well, Socrates, it doesn't seem right to me for you to be willing to state other people's convictions but not your own, especially when you've spent so much time occupied with these matters." Socrates declines to state his own opinions, either stated baldly or in the shape of a well-developed theory. Even the best opinions stated without knowledge are shameful and ugly; like blind men who happen to find their way correctly to their desired end, such opinions reflect true belief without understanding (506c6-9). Apparently because he wishes neither to expose his friends to such opinions nor to run the risk of appearing ridiculous himself, Socrates declines to state his opinions about the highest good. Instead, he offers an image of the Good Itself: an image in words of the Form of the Good, an image described as an offspring of the good and similar to it (506e3-4). This description apparently applies to all three images of the Good which follow, the first of which is the image of the Sun.

At the heart of this first image is a comparison between the sun in the visible world and the Form of the Good in the intelligible. Even if the power of sight is present in the eyes and color is present in visible things, the eyes will not see unless the sun provides a link between sight and the visible. Light from the sun is this link; it makes sight to see in the best way possible for it and makes visible things to be seen in the best way (507d-508a). Parallel to this is the role of the Form of the Good in the intelligible realm: whenever the soul is turned in the right way toward the Good Itself, then the mind understands. Knowledge and truth are not the Good Itself, but are similar in form to the Good (*agathoeidē*, 509a3), just as sight and light are not the sun but are similar in form to the sun (*helioeidē*, 509a1). The sun provides birth and growth and nourishment to visible things, but is not itself subject to such changes. Similarly, the Form of the Good provides existence and being to things that are known but is itself beyond being, surpassing it in dignity and power (509b).

In this powerful image, emphasis falls on the central role of the Form of the Good in our attempts to know the world and on the dependence of all things on this form. We find that sight, the analogue to knowledge in the visible world, is set in relation to or toward (*pros*) the sun (508a9). This statement of sight's orientation toward the sun is not elaborated in detail, beyond the observations that sight is similar in form to the sun and that sight receives its power from the sun. This might be taken as the claim that sight operates for the sake of perceiving the sun and other heavenly bodies, as at *Timaeus* 47b-c, or it might be only the weaker claim that sight operates successfully in virtue of the eye's similarity to the sun and the sun's provision of light. In any case, all of reality is divided into two classes or "places" (*topoi*, 509d2-3), the visible and the intelligible, with each ruled by a central principle.

Immediately after the image of the Sun comes that of the Divided Line. To continue the exposition of the Good Itself that began in the image of the Sun, Socrates proposes that we consider a line divided first in two sections. These sections, La and Lb, represent the visible and intelligible realms introduced in the first image. Each of the two sections is then divided a second time in accordance with the ratio employed in making the first division. Imagining that the line is drawn vertically and moving from the bottom upwards, the first subsection of the visible realm (L1) contains images and reflections of visible objects, while the second subsection of the visible (L2) contains these visible objects themselves. The third segment of the line (L3), or the first subsection of the intelligible realm, contains the objects associated with dianoia while the fourth subsection (L4) contains those understood by dialectic. The objects associated with dianoia include the mathematical objects that geometers and arithmeticians study on the basis of their hypotheses, while the objects associated with dialectic include the forms.[1] Study of these forms leads to insight into the unhypothetical principle, which is the most important entity within the subsection L4.

---

[1] One terminological point should be addressed here. Socrates associates the different segments of the line with different cognitive states of the soul and assigns different entities to the different segments. For instance, shadows and reflections are contained in L1, and the state of imagination or eikasia is also associated with L1. Animals and plants and manufactured objects are contained in L2, and the state of pistis or belief is associated with L2. Here it is tempting to assume that, since eikasia involves the viewing of shadows and reflections in some way, eikasia takes as objects of visual perception these shadows and reflections. Similarly, pistis or belief is connected in some way to the external objects copied by shadows and reflections, and so it is natural to say that belief is about these external objects. However, this manner of speaking goes beyond what we are told explicitly at 509d-510a, where the different visible entities are simply assigned to the two line segments. Whether the states of eikasia and pistis engage in various intentional relations of perception or belief in relation to the objects contained in L1 and L2 remains to be seen from a closer examination of the text. In order to keep a range of options open for understanding the relations between state and entities, I will say that states such as eikasia or dianoia are associated with or linked with various entities or objects.

Through understanding this principle, it is possible to know the hypotheses employed by mathematicians; without such a principle, full understanding of these hypotheses is impossible.

In addition to dividing the line into two main sections and four subsections, Socrates sets these elements of the line in proportional relations. In its original construction the line is cut into two unequal sections, the intelligible and the visible, each of which is divided again in accordance with the same ratio. The result is a line with two sections (La, the visible section, and Lb, the intelligible section) and four subsections (L1-L4) which stand in relation to each other as follows: as the intelligible section Lb is to the visible section La, so L4 is to L3 and so L2 is to L1. These proportional relations are meant to illustrate not simply the relative lengths of line segments but the fact that the objects associated with the different segments have different shares of truth. Commenting on the division of the visible section into subsections L2 and L1, pistis and eikasia, Socrates poses this question at 510a8-10: "Would you be willing to say that, as regards truth and untruth, the division is in this proportion: As the opinable is to the knowable, so the likeness is to the thing that it is like?" In speaking of different shares of truth and untruth, we may rely on the conception of truth as genuineness or reality; the man who looks into a mirror is the real thing in relation to which the image in the mirror is only a copy or likeness. The ratio between eikasia and pistis is one example of this relation between a likeness or copy and the thing to which it is like, an original. This ratio between eikasia and pistis is identified in terms of truth and untruth with that between the opinable or visible and the knowable. Thus the ratio in terms of truth and lack of truth between eikasia and pistis is the same as the ratio between the visible and the intelligible realms, which we know from the original construction of the line is the same as the ratio between dianoia and dialectic. It follows from this set of proportional relations that the subsections L2 and L3 will be equal in length, though it is not clear whether this aspect of the Divided Line is intended by Plato to indicate important truths about the relation between pistis and dianoia or between the entities associated with each.[2]

Two aspects of the image of the Divided Line distinguish it from the image of the Sun. The image of the Sun provides a profound yet simple mapping of the two realms, the visible and the intelligible: vision and visible objects are linked by the light of the sun in the one realm, knowledge and knowable objects are linked in some way by the Form of the Good. Much remains to be said about the Form of the Good after the image has been set forth, but we feel that the heart of the matter is before us. By contrast, the meaning of the image of the Divided Line threatens to escape us with its multiple levels and distinctions of different affections in the soul (imagination, belief, dianoia, dialectic) each with its own set of objects. Instead of the simple pattern of a single principle uniting the soul with its objects in the two realms of the visible and the intelligible, we have a complicated scheme of cognitive faculties with illustrations

---

[2] See Foley (2008) for a discussion of the equality of L2 and L3 within the Divided Line.

drawn from the practice of mathematicians. The different sections and their objects stand in proportional relations to each other in a way that is meant to represent different levels of truth in the states or their correlated objects. In addition to this first contrast between the Sun and Divided Line, a second is the introduction in the Divided Line of the relation of image and original. While the Line threatens to escape the reader's understanding with its multiplication of states, it also employs this relation of copy and thing copied to connect the different levels of cognitive achievement. The first affection of the soul, imagination or eikasia, is linked with images of physical objects, while physical objects in turn serve as images of the entities linked with dianoia. The objects linked with dianoia are in some way images of the objects linked with dialectic: if we connect the Divided Line with a later commentary provided by Socrates, we can assert that dianoia itself only dreams of the reality in relation to which dialectic provides genuine insight (533b6-c5). In other words, dianoia is like imagination in providing us with images of the originals grasped more fully by the faculty set above it, namely dialectic.

After the Divided Line's articulation of various states of soul and their objects, we are placed in a narrative of movement and progression through stages of unfreedom and freedom, lack of education and education: the image of the Cave (514a-521c). This image conveys the need to turn the soul away from the visible world to the intelligible as part of an ascent to the Form of the Good. Socrates offers us an image of our nature with regard to our education and our lack of education (514a1-2) as he describes a group of prisoners bound with chains at the bottom of a cave and unable to understand the reality of the world around them. They are able only to see shadows cast on the rear wall of the cave, shadows created by other cave dwellers who carry statues and puppets in front of a fire burning in the cave. One prisoner is freed and is turned around toward the puppets and the fire, neither of which he is able to see due to the poor state of his eyesight and his conviction that the shadows he saw previously are more real than these new objects before him. The prisoner is then brought up out of the cave, a transition that corresponds to the transition from the visible realm to the intelligible (517a8-b6). At first, he is unable to see in the light of day, but he begins to accustom himself to his new surroundings by viewing shadows and reflections in water of plants and animals. The act of viewing reflections and images prepares him to look upon the real plants and animals. Ultimately, the freed prisoner develops the ability to see the sky, the stars, and finally the sun. The sun appears in this image as an analogue to the Good Itself, as it did in the image of the Sun. Having seen the real objects outside the cave and the sun, the former prisoner returns to the cave. After a period of adjustment in which he is unable to see due to the gloom of the cave, he is better able with the benefit of his experience of the outside world to see and identify the shadows he encounters.

This image concerns the turning of the soul away from the visible world and the realm of the senses to the intelligible world. Immediately following the image, Socrates discusses the five propaedeutic studies that are capable of turning the soul. The excursus on the propaedeutic studies is abstract and intended to draw out the finer points of mathematical practice, while the image of the Cave is concrete and direct. Even with these differences in style, it is clear that Plato wishes us to understand the two passages as making the same point: in order to arrive at an understanding of the Form of the Good, the soul must turn from preoccupation with sensible things to the understanding of intelligible realities. The Cave presents this message in figurative terms, while the five mathematical disciplines in fact accomplish this turning of the soul, according to 532b6-d1:

Then the release from bonds and the turning around from shadows to statues and the light of the fire and, then, the way up out of the cave to the sunlight and, there, the continuing inability to look at the animals, the plants, and the light of the sun, but the newly acquired ability to look at divine images in water and shadows of the things that are, rather than, as before, merely at shadows of statues thrown by another source of light that is itself a shadow in relation to the sun – all this business of the crafts we've mentioned has the power to awaken the best part of the soul and lead it upward to the study of the best among the things that are, just as, before, the clearest thing in the body was led to the brightest thing in the bodily and visible realm.

The prisoner's ascent out of the cave involves the development of the power of sight for the sake of seeing the brightest thing in the visible realm, and similarly education in the propaedeutic disciplines involves the strengthening of the rational part of the soul for the sake of knowing the Form of the Good. Here as in the other images, the ability to see is an analogue to the soul's ability to know reality.

8.3 Vision in the *Timaeus*

In order to make sense of the images of Sun, Divided Line, and Cave with some confidence of fidelity to Plato's intention, it is necessary to inquire into his conception of vision as a perceptual power. Materials for this inquiry will be found in the writings of Empedocles and in Peripatetic testimony concerning Democritus as well as in the *Timaeus*. The most important text for surveying Plato's theory of vision is *Timaeus* 45b-47c. Here Plato puts in the mouth of his character Timaeus an account of the mechanism of seeing: the eye sends forth a stream of fire, the process of extromission, which during daytime coalesces with the sun's fire. The result is a body stretching between the eye and the object of sight which conveys motion from visible objects back into the eye, into the body, and then into the soul. This is the process of intromission. He also attaches to this account two apparently tangential topics, the appearance of images in dreams and in mirrors. The discussion of vision ends with Timaeus revealing the true purpose of our power of vision: the divine fashioned our vision to the end that we engage in astronomy, inquire into the nature of the universe, and become philosophers.

This quick survey of *Timaeus* 45b-47c may suggest at first that it is a skein of loosely related topics: first the bodily mechanism of vision, then digressions on dreams and mirrors, and finally an injunction to practice philosophy. The section on mirrors,

46a2-c6, seems to break the development of Timaeus' account of seeing; according to Cornford, "A short appendix on mirror images is added here, seemingly for its own sake rather than as contributing to the main argument."[3] In fact, as we will see, the passage on mirror images continues the task of specifying the bodily mechanism of vision. The entire passage 45b-47c is unified by Timaeus' observation at 46c7-e7 that the whole inquiry into the process of seeing, from the discussion of fire sent out of the eye to images to mirrors, dealt with the auxiliary causes of vision: the operations of fire, earth, and other elements without which one cannot see. As Timaeus tells us, the intelligent cause of vision still required unfolding; without understanding how these necessary processes of interaction between bodily elements work to the benefit of human beings, one will fail to grasp the genuine cause of the phenomena of vision. From the perspective offered by this observation, Timaeus hopes to show how fire being emitted from the eye, the construction of the eye, and the appearances of images in mirrors all work toward the beneficial effect of better equipping the human soul to practice philosophy.

Timaeus' account of the processes of vision begins with a description of the activity of seeing in the normal case. The eye contains pure fire, akin to the fire of the sun. When we use our vision during daytime, the sun provides this pure fire to the air around us to give us daylight. The eye is made "close-textured, smooth, and dense" (*leion kai puknon*, 45b7-8) so as to let the pure fire within it flow out while fencing out the coarser stuff in the surrounding environment. The emitted fire makes a stream or ray which, if it meets with kindred fire from the sun, forms a continuous and homogenous body extending from the eye. The body of fire meets external objects and transmits motion from those objects back to the eye. These motions make their way into the eye, further into the entire body, and ultimately to the soul. This transmission of motion is what we call seeing (45d3). When night arrives and the kindred fire is absent from the surrounding air, we cannot see because the extromitted fire from our eyes is quenched and the body extending from the eye is cut off (45d3-6).

In this account of vision, Plato employs existing accounts of vision inherited from Presocratic investigations of nature. Empedocles and Democritus are likely the chief sources for these materials. Like the Timaean account, the fragments of Empedocles contain a description of the eye as a carefully wrought container for fire, one that allows fire to be sent out from the core of the eye while keeping off the water and coarser elements that would extinguish the eye's fire. Thus, Empedocles in fragment B84 compares the eye to a lantern with panels crafted to shelter the fire from wind while allowing the fire to pass through:

> As when one who purposes going abroad prepares a lantern,
> A gleam of fire blazing through the stormy night,
> Adjusting thereto, to screen it from all sorts of winds, transparent sides,
> Which scatter the breath of the winds as they blow,

[3] Cornford (1937, 154).

> While, out through them leaping, the fire, i.e. all the more subtle part of this,
> Shines along his threshold with incessant beams:
> So the primaeval fire, fenced within the membranes.
> And delicate tissues gave birth to a round-eyed daughter –
> Tissues bored through with wonderful channels –
> And these fended off the deep surrounding flood,
> While letting through the fire, i.e. all its more subtle part.[4]

Along with this extromission of fire, an important factor in explaining vision is the intromission of bodily traces issuing from visible objects.[5] According to Empedocles, we see and perceive in general when external objects send effluences to the pores that exist throughout our body for receiving these effluences. As Socrates relates at *Meno* 76c-d, Empedocles considers visual perception to occur when external objects give off effluences that enter the pores that are fitted to receive them.

It is clear that Plato's theory of vision is indebted to Empedocles, namely in the conception of the eye as a source for the extromission of fire and in the use of intromission of motions from external objects. However, Plato chooses to depart from Empedocles in at least two important ways. First, he makes the sun a crucial factor in the occurrence of vision. In the fragment B84, Empedocles compares the eye to a lantern that a man prepares to light his way in the wintry night. Even in the cold and dark of a winter's night, the lantern emits its untiring rays. Empedocles' image of the lantern suggests that the fire coming forth from the eye will not be affected by the surrounding air as long as the eye shields its source. Yet Plato describes the fire of the visual ray as quenched by the night air that lacks the kindred fire provided by the sun. This is a point on which Aristotle at *De Sensu* 437b10-24 takes Plato to task, pointing out that light is not extinguished by darkness but by cold or wet things attacking the fire that is the source of light. Apparently, Plato took the evident fact that we do not see well at night as signaling the dependence of the eye, the organ of sight, on the sun infusing its kindred fire into the air. By adding this element to his account of the process of vision, Plato makes the process of vision dependent on the eye's likeness to and familial relation to the sun, an eternal and divine reality. And second, Plato introduces the novel idea of a body formed between the eye, the organ of sight, and the object seen. As far as we can judge on the basis of the surviving fragments and testimony relating to

---

[4]   See H. Diels and W. Kranz, *Die Fragmente der Vorsokratiker* (Berlin: Weidmann, 1951–2), fragment 31 B84 (DK 31 B84). Translation by J. I. Beare from Aristotle, *Sense and Sensibilia*, 437b26-438a2 in *The Complete Works of Aristotle*, ed. Jonathan Barnes (Princeton, New Jersey: Princeton University Press, 1984).

[5]   Exactly how and whether the extromission of fire plays a role for Empedocles in vision is unclear. O'Brien (1970) argues that extromission plays no explanatory role in Empedocles' account of vision, while Long (1970), defends the thesis that both intromission and extromission are causes in the process of seeing. Although the latter view represents something of a scholarly consensus, Rudolph (2016) sides with O'Brien in treating Empedoclean vision as explained by intromission as perceptible objects send effluences to the surface of the eye.

Empedocles, he did not require a body to exist between the seer and the object seen.[6] In effect, Plato construes vision on the model of the sense of touch: seeing an object requires that the seer make literal bodily contact with it.[7] The ability to make bodily contact with the object of vision, of course, is dependent on the sun shedding its light in daytime. This allows fire from the eye to coalesce with fire from the sun to form the body uniting seer and thing seen.

A further source for the Timaean account of vision is Democritus' account of the appearance of an image of the object seen on the pupil of the seeing eye. Immediately after quoting the passage from Empedocles, which presents the eye as a lantern, Aristotle at *De Sensu* 438a5-12 gives a condensed sketch of Democritus' contributions to the account of vision:

Democritus, on the other hand, is right in his opinion that the eye is of water; not, however, when he goes on to explain seeing as mirroring [*to horan einai tēn emphasin*]. The mirroring that takes place in an eye is due to the fact that the eye is smooth, and it really has its seat not in the eye, but in that which sees. For the case is one of reflexion [*anaklasis*]. But it would seem that in his time there was no scientific knowledge of the general subject of the formation of images [*tōn emphainomenōn*] and the phenomenon of reflexion. It is strange, too, that it never occurred to him to ask why the eye alone sees, while none of the other things in which images are reflected do so.

According to Aristotle, Democritus understood well that the eye is made of water but mistakenly identified seeing with the mirroring or reception (*emphasis*) of an image in the eye. Apparently, here Aristotle refers to the fact, well known to Plato and his contemporaries, that an image of whatever objects we look at directly will appear on the surface of our eyes. So when we look at some object, for instance the face of another person, an image of that object appears on the surface of the pupil of the eye.[8] This phenomenon is the source for the poetic description at *Alcibiades* 133a of a man seeing himself by looking at the eye of another and seeing there his own face. The phenomenon of mirroring or the reception of an image in the eye was one common Presocratic strategy for explaining vision, a strategy first employed by Alcmaeon and later by Anaxagoras.[9] Aristotle criticizes Democritus for making this phenomenon of the eye's reception of an image the important factor in seeing. According to Aristotle, what Democritus is thinking of is only

---

[6] Anne Merker points out that Empedocles provides a detailed analysis of the structure of the eye, as in fragment B84, but does not mention an exterior body conveying effluences to the eye; see Merker (2003, 27–8).

[7] On this point, see Ganson (2005).

[8] See von Fritz (1953) for an overview of Democritus' approach to vision. In particular, von Fritz discusses the sense of the term *emphasis*. Modern readers are tempted to find in *emphasis* a case of reflection, as in Beare's translation of *De Sensu* 438a5-12. However, von Fritz notes that Democritus is concerned with images being received into the eye and thus allowing the person to see as opposed to the reflecting back of an image. David Lindberg makes a similar point: "If we are to understand what Democritus meant by it, we must construe reflection (*emphasis*) not according to our modern understanding, as a process of rebound or deflection, but simply as visibility or presence in something"; see Lindberg (1976, 2–3).

[9] See Rudolph (2016) for a discussion of *emphasis* in Presocratic explanations of vision.

a reflection (*anaklasis*), an affection (*pathos*) of the eye, and not the act of seeing present in that which sees. Aristotle comments drily that apparently Democritus was not clear on the facts concerning images and reflections in general.

From Aristotle's point of view, some necessary distinctions have not yet been drawn. In particular, the use of mirroring or *emphasis* to explain vision seems to run together the distinction between the intentional content of perception, how things seem to the perceiver, and whatever part of the perceiver's physiology functions to allow perception to arise. The similarity of the pupil of the eye to a mirror and its reception of an image of an object is taken as a key stage in the perception of that object. As a result, the physiological state of a reflection appearing on the surface of an eye can be confused with the intentionality-laden fact that the soul sees by means of an image or appearance being received in some manner in the eye.

This is Aristotle's evaluation of the use of *emphasis* or the reception of an image in a smooth surface to explain vision. I suggest that Plato in the *Timaeus* makes use of *emphasis* in this way. According to the Timaean picture, seeing involves the transmission of motions through the eye into the soul, motions that are capable of producing appearances (*phantasmata*, 46a2) within the soul. The first step in this production of images by which one sees would be the reception of the image in some way into the eye. One candidate for this reception of images is the phenomenon of *emphasis*. In taking the reception of a mirror image on the eye to be an essential step in the process of seeing, Plato would be continuing a pattern within Presocratic theories of vision that started with Alcmaeon and continued in Democritus. If this is the case, then the apparent digression on mirrors at *Timaeus* 46a2-c6 is in fact not a departure from the main theme of the passage. The reception of mirror images is one of the auxiliary causes of vision, one of the natural phenomena that allow the soul to see.

The discussion of mirrors and other similar surfaces beginning at 46a2 focuses on the different inversions of images possible with different mirroring surfaces. At 46a2-b6, Timaeus accounts for the left-to-right inversion of a face seen in a mirror:

And so there is no longer any difficulty in understanding how images are produced in mirrors or in any other smooth reflecting [*emphanē*] surfaces. On such occasions the internal fire joins forces with the external fire, to form on the smooth surface a single fire which is reshaped in a multitude of ways. So once the fire from the face comes to coalesce with the fire from sight on the smooth and bright surface, you have the inevitable appearance of all images of this sort. What is left will appear as right, because the parts of the fire from sight connect with the opposite parts of the fire from the face, contrary to the usual manner of encounter.

Following this passage, Timaeus deals at 46b6-c6 with further inversions produced by concave mirrors.[10] For our purposes, we should observe that the account of left-to-right inversion at 46a2-b6 applies as much to the appearance of an image on the surface of the

---

[10] See Kung (1988) and Merker (2003, 39–43) for more detailed discussion of the inversion of images described at *Timaeus* 46a2-c6.

eye of the sort referred to at *Alcibiades* 133a as to the appearance of an image on a bronze mirror. Timaeus' account of image-inversions is applied to images produced in any smooth surface that is reflective, or to speak more precisely, receptive of images [*emphanē*]. The eye is such a smooth surface; as Aristotle notes at *De Sensu* 438a6, the eye is apt to undergo the affection of *emphasis* because it is smooth. After an image is received on the surface of the eye, it is capable of entering the eye as part of the process of seeing.

On this interpretation of *Timaeus* 46a-c, Plato takes up the discussion of mirror images because one of its instances, the reception of an image on the surface of the eye, is part of the process of visual perception. This allows us to explain why Plato devotes a significant amount of space to the discussion of mirror images (46a2-c6), roughly the same number of lines as are devoted to the discussion of the normal case of seeing (45b2-d2). We can also give a fitting sense to Timaeus' summary of his discussion of the auxiliary causes of vision at 46c7: "Now all of the above are among the auxiliary causes employed in the service of the god as he does his utmost to bring to completion the character of what is most excellent." What is brought to completion by the god is the soul, which is brought to the practice of philosophy in part by the function of seeing (47a7-c4). The phrase "all of the above" is taken most naturally to refer to the whole passage dealing with vision, from the discussion of the eye to the passage on mirrors and other smooth surfaces. If the phenomenon of images appearing in smooth surfaces applies only to images in mirrors and not in the eye, it is difficult to explain why Timaeus sees this phenomenon as one of the auxiliary causes of vision.

A later passage in the *Timaeus* confirms this interpretation of the discussion of mirrors at 46a2-c6. According to our reading of this passage, the reception of a mirror image on the eye is one part of the process by which the soul sees. In a discussion of the liver, Timaeus treats the reception of a mirror image on the surface of the liver as one way in which the appetitive part of the soul undergoes quasi-perceptual experience. Thus, at *Timaeus* 71a3-b5:

[The gods] knew that this [appetitive] part of the soul was not going to understand the deliverances of reason and that even if it were in one way or another to have some awareness of them, it would not have an innate regard for any of them, but would be much more enticed by images and phantoms day and night. Hence the god conspired with this very tendency by constructing a liver, a structure which he situated in the dwelling place of this part of the soul. He made it into something dense, smooth, bright [*puknon kai leion kai lampron*] and sweet, though also having a bitter quality, so that the force of the thoughts sent down from the mind might be stamped upon it as upon a mirror that receives the stamps and returns visible images.

Due to the construction of the liver after the model of the eye (dense, smooth, and bright), the mind is able to use the liver to provide images to the appetitive part of the soul. When the mind feels the need to frighten the appetitive part of the soul, bilious colors appear in the liver (*khrōmata emphainoi*, 71b7-8), while it paints opposite images on the liver (*enantia phantasmata apozōgraphoi*, 71c3-4) when it wishes to calm the appetitive part. Here the presence of color and images in the liver is not simply a physiological change in the liver of which the soul is not immediately aware, as when a person suffers from cirrhosis of the liver. The reception of images and colors in the liver allows the appetitive part of the soul to become aware of these colors and shapes. Here the phenomenon of *emphasis* leads to perceptual awareness of colors and images. If the reception of images on the surface of the liver leads to perceptual awareness on the Timaean account, we should expect that the appearance of an image on the surface of the eye likewise would lead to visual perception of the object which produces the image.

Thus, Plato in the *Timaeus* seems to incorporate a central theme of earlier Presocratic theories of vision, and in particular Democritus' theory of vision: vision takes places through the reception of images of external objects into or on the eye, the phenomenon that Aristotle refers to as *emphasis*. However, Plato reshapes this Democritean material by making it part of an explicitly teleological account of vision. Where Democritus portrays a universe in which vision, like all physical processes, occurs as a result of unguided necessity, Plato treats vision as supported by the influence of the sun. He also associates vision with a number of large-scale purposes at 47a4-b1: "Our ability to see the periods of day and night, of months and of years, of equinoxes and solstices, has led to the invention of number, and has given us the idea of time and opened the path to inquiry into the nature of the universe." Taken together these intellectual pursuits have led to the practice of philosophy. We may explain the Timaean claim that vision serves the purpose of allowing us to practice astronomy by observing that the mechanisms of seeing laid out at 45b-47c are such as to facilitate the viewing of fiery and bright objects, such as the sun, the stars, and the planets. The eye has its own native fire, which allows it to see fiery objects easily by an application of Empedocles' principle that fire is seen by fire. The visual stream of fire allows fire from the heavenly objects to transmit motions to the eye, whose smooth and mirrorlike surface is apt to receive the image of bright objects. The particular composition of the eye and the mechanics of seeing promote the viewing of the sun, stars, and planets, which Timaeus would present as an instance of the divine fashioning of auxiliary causes to promote the end of coming to know the nature of the universe.

8.4 Vision and the Images of the Good

Our discussion of Plato's theory of vision in the *Timaeus* is intended to deepen our understanding of the three images of the Good in *Republic* 6 and 7. A review of these images will show how each employs vision as an analogue for or comparison term in relation to knowledge.

8.4.1 Vision and the Image of the Sun

The image of the Sun turns on Socrates' observation that the ability of sight to see and the capacity of visible things to be seen stand in need of a third item connecting them, the "yoke" of light provided by the sun. Similarly the soul's power to know and the capacity of intelligible things to be known require a linkage provided by the Form of the Good. Socrates' assertion of the need for a yoke in the visible realm bears an obvious similarity to the Timaean theory that we see when fire from our eyes coalesces with the sun's fire to form a body connecting the eye with visible objects. The Timaean theory will also explain why Socrates speaks of the eye as the most sun-like of all the organs: the eye imitates the sun by emitting fire as part of its function of seeing. The sun allows sight to carry out its function in the best way (508a) by emitting the gentle, non-burning fire found in daylight (*Timaeus* 45b). The eye can see at night, though not as well, by the light of the moon or other sources of illumination used at night, such as a torch or manmade fire.

8.4.2 Vision and the Divided Line

In order to pursue the theme of the analogy between vision and knowledge, we can turn to the image of the Divided Line. The leading theme of this reading of the Divided Line is that seeing and knowing are activities in which images or copies at one section of the line are used for the sake of gaining insight into an imaged or original object which stands in the next higher section of the line. In addition, all the activities of seeing and knowing are carried out for the sake of insight into the unhypothetical principle mentioned at 511b5-6. We use shadows and reflections for the sake of perceiving visible objects, we study visible diagrams in mathematics for the sake of knowing intelligible realities, and we investigate forms for the sake of insight into the unhypothetical principle. At each level of the Divided Line, humans use images introduced at one level of the line for the sake of gaining insight into the inhabitants of the next higher level. The unhypothetical principle is to be identified with the Form of the Good: it is that for the sake of which philosophers carry out their characteristic devotion to knowledge. This devotion to knowledge is expressed through the pursuit of various crafts and sciences, especially the mathematical sciences. Socrates draws our attention to geometry in the image of the Line with a two-fold purpose: he wishes both to point out the limitations of mathematics and to explain how mathematics can contribute to understanding of the Form of the Good. The limitations of mathematics are emphasized in Socrates' distinction between thought or dianoia, the faculty exercised in mathematical study, and the more advanced faculty of dialectic. At the same time, mathematical studies provide images that are used by dialectic to gain insight into the forms, especially the Form of the Good. Because they prepare the way for the study of the Form of the Good, mathematical studies are carried out for the sake of coming to know the Form of the Good. This is the case even though mathematicians do not intend to gain knowledge of the Form and need not see the objects of their study as good.

Section L1 is described briefly at 509d9-510a3: "In terms now of relative clarity and opacity, one subsection of the visible consists of images. And by images (*eikonas*) I mean, first, shadows, then appearances (*phantasmata*) in water and in all close-packed, smooth, and shiny (*pukna te kai leia kai phana*) materials, and everything of that sort, if you understand."[11] The state of the soul that corresponds to this subsection of the line is imagination or eikasia (511e1-2). The things populating this lowest section of the line include shadows and reflections cast in bodies of water and mirrors. But also, I claim, the things populating section L1 include the visible images that are received in the eye and that we use in order to perceive external objects. As we saw in reviewing the Timaean account of seeing, the eye is something that is made smooth and close-packed (*leion kai puknon*, *Timaeus* 45b7-8). That is, the eye is the sort of smooth and close-packed object that, according to *Republic* 510a, is apt to receive appearances or *phantasmata*. When Socrates speaks of the images of L1 as including the *phantasmata* that appear in close-packed, smooth, and shiny surfaces, he is referring in part to the images that are received in the eye as part of the process of visual perception.

Interpreting the section L1 in this way has the advantage of providing a rationale for the inclusion of this section within the Divided Line. The image of the Line appears to provide a classification of all intelligible and visible items in existence, including the unhypothetical first principle of all things situated either at the top or just beyond the end of the line. It would be strange for Plato to devote one out of the four sections to such trivial things as shadows and reflections in mirrors or in puddles and lakes. One could well suspect that the inclusion of L1 was motivated simply by the desire to find items for L1 that would extend the pattern of one section serving as an image of the next higher section, as in the case of L2 in relation to L3. Julia Annas comments as follows: "... [T]he lowest stage of the line, *eikasia*, is not a significant state in its own right. How much time do we spend looking at images and reflections, and how interesting is this? It has a point only as illustrating the relation of imaging holding between the contents of [L1] and [L2] (which in turn illuminate the upper part of the line)."[12] But if we interpret the contents of L1 in the context of the Timaean account of seeing, we can find a strong rationale for including this section. The line's main division is between intelligible and visible things. If L1 includes the appearances which are received in the eye and by means of which we perceive external objects, then every case of seeing a visible thing in L2 depends upon the human soul's use of some member of L1. The main contents of the visible part of the line are found in L2: these are the external objects about which our visual experience of the world informs us. But the workings of the power of vision require the reception of images in the eye, and such images are among the contents of section L1. To answer Annas' question as to how much time we spend looking at images and reflections, the

---

[11] Here I alter the Grube-Reeve translation; in place of "reflections" for *phantasmata* I give "appearances". Translating *phantasmata* as "reflections" unnecessarily restricts the range of entities that belong in L1 to images cast upon mirrors and bodies of water, while the translation with "appearances" leaves open the possibility that the images in question are received in the eye and then become part of the mechanism of visual perception as described at *Timaeus* 45-7.

[12] Annas (1981, 248-9).

short answer is "Not much time at all." But a longer and more informative answer will state that, while we do not spend much time *looking at* images and reflections in the sense of directing our attention to reflections, still every case of looking at an external object is a case of *looking by means of* an image or reflection of that external object. Whenever we see or look at a tree, we do so by the reception in the eye of an image of a tree. To reply to the second half of Annas' question, this is a matter of no small importance, and it would explain why Plato assigned one of the four subsections of the line to visible images and reflections.

The normal use of such appearances received in the eye allows us to perceive and to be aware of external visible objects. To speak of the normal or proper use of such appearances suggests that there is also an abnormal or improper use. This is found in dreams and hallucinations, the cases in which an appearance is present in the soul but the appearance is not connected in the normal way to an external visible object. The normal sort of connection to an external object is set forth in the *Timaeus* at 45b2-d3: fire in the eye is sent out to coalesce with the sun's fire, forming a continuous body that conveys motions from the object into the eye and then into the soul. The normal connection is lost at night, when the surrounding night severs the body of fire connecting the eye and the external object. When the eyes close and strong motions continue to agitate the soul during sleep, this leads to the phenomenon of dreaming, in which it is possible for a person to have the appearance of a tree outside their window. The person may believe that she is seeing a tree outside their window, even though there is no such tree. This case in which the normal connection between items in L1 and items in L2 has been lost recalls Socrates' description at 476c1-d2 of dreaming in contrast to waking vision: a dreamer is one who thinks that a likeness is not a likeness but rather the thing itself that it is like.

With this contrast in place between the normal and the abnormal use of appearances, we can understand how the soul uses the appearances that are received in the eye for the sake of gaining insight into external objects. As the Timaean account of seeing indicates, the function of the appearances received in the eye is to allow the soul to perceive external objects. In the normal case, the presence of appearances in the eye produces a particular benefit for the larger organism: the human being is able to see a tree by "looking through" the appearances of a tree received in the eye. There are non-standard cases, such as dreaming, and cases in which the external environment does not support the use of these appearances, as when night defeats our ability to see. In these non-standard cases, the benefit that is proper to the use of appearances is lost. We can say, then, that the appearances in the eye perform their function in the best way only if they help to cause the result of the human being seeing an external object such as a tree, a member of section L2 in the line. This result of seeing an external object is the end for the sake of which the soul uses the appearances.

This brings us to section L2. The contents of section L2 are described briefly at 510a5-6: "In the other subsection of the visible, put the originals of these images, namely, the animals around us, all the plants, and the whole class of manufactured things." These provide the standards by which we may measure the accuracy or truth of the images contained in L1. If there is a divergence between the information conveyed by an image of a tree and the reality of the tree as an external object, the problem lies in the image and not in the tree. This much is implied by the relation between image and original.

Although the relation between the objects in L1 associated with eikasia and the objects in L2 associated with belief or pistis is an instance of the relation between image and original, we should not conclude that Plato expects us to dispense with eikasia in order to benefit from pistis. The normal process by which we see the objects linked with pistis is through the use of the objects linked with eikasia. We see external objects through the images received on the surface of the eye and transmitted into the soul. As a result, we should understand eikasia and pistis as two mutually supporting states of the soul. The text of the Divided Line at 509d8-510a6 might suggest that we exercise eikasia just in that amount of time that we spend looking at reflections in mirrors and puddles, and that we leave eikasia behind when we turn our gaze to the objects which cast those reflections and thus employ pistis. Instead, the present interpretation proposes that the use of eikasia is part and parcel of the use of pistis: the first state of the soul is not left behind when we have recourse to the second, but is incorporated into the second.

Here the nature of eikasia is ambiguous, in that it admits of both a normal use and a degenerate variety. The normal use of eikasia involves the use of images as a way of perceiving the originals of those images. If the Timaean account of vision is assumed here, this is a case of (literally) making contact with the originals of those images: there is a continuous body stretching from the tree that I see to my eye, a body that transmits motions and appearances into my soul. Whether or not we assume the details of the Timaean account of vision, though, the normal use of eikasia leads to pistis, the belief in or conception of external realities. In the degenerate use of eikasia, I apprehend the image of a tree, but in this case it is only an image and nothing more. I take myself to be seeing a tree because of the presence of an image of a tree in my soul, where there the right sort of causal connection between the image of a tree and a tree is lacking. Dreaming is one instance of this degenerate use of eikasia, in that a dreamer is aware of an image that lacks the proper connection to an external original and takes this image to be an external object. As Vasilis Karasmanis puts it, "...the dreamer a) sees an image instead of a reality, and b) takes this image to be the reality that is apprehended."[13] This is an accurate description of dreaming and of the degenerate use of eikasia due to the presence of the first condition, namely that what a dreamer takes to be real is an image and not a reality. At the same time, the normal use of eikasia involves something quite close to Karasmanis' condition b): the person who sees rather than dreams takes herself to be seeing a tree due to the presence within her of the image of a tree. As Plato is ready to admit, the difference between dreaming and

---

[13] Karasmanis (1988, 152).

seeing is not something that we always grasp with immediate certainty. We may not be able to discern accurately whether we are dreaming or seeing simply by inspecting the content of our experience.[14] The difference between dreaming and seeing, the degenerate and the normal use of eikasia, depends on the right sort of causal relations holding between external objects, the eye, and the soul such that fire or light transmits motions between visible objects and the eye. But in either case, the person who uses eikasia will take herself to be in contact with external objects and not merely with images or reflections.[15]

I have spoken of the normal use of eikasia, that in which the presence of images of visible objects in the eye of a person helps that person to see external visible objects. One way to describe this normal case is the claim that the person makes use of eikasia and its associated images for the sake of having belief or pistis about external objects. As part of developing a conception of a particular tree, for example the birch tree I see from my kitchen window, I collect different visual impressions or images through eikasia. Using a range of these images, I can say how the tree looks from my window as well as from the opposite end of the garden, how the tree looks both in spring and in late October. Through the use of momentary visual images I am able to gain the conception of the tree as an enduring, three-dimensional object which is the source of but not identical to the different images I have of it. Only by developing such a conception through pistis or belief can a person judge reliably which of his momentary impressions are likely to be accurate. The use of images in eikasia thus produces or helps to bring about the result of pistis concerning the tree, and only by gaining this result can one make the best use of these images. That is, we use the images associated with eikasia for the sake of gaining pistis.

---

[14] See Gallop (1971, 189–90). Gallop refers to *Theaetetus* 157e-158e, where Socrates claims that the content of our present experience cannot disprove the supposition that we are in fact dreaming at any given moment.

[15] This conception of eikasia is similar in rough outline to the accounts of eikasia given by Paton (1922) and Hamlyn (1958). Paton and Hamlyn emphasize the similarity between reliance on eikasia and our use of sense-perception; eikasia is characterized as an acquaintance with appearances or sense-data which does not involve an awareness of the difference between appearances and the reality which the appearances depict. However, Paton and Hamlyn present eikasia as similar to sense-perception as a whole and do not present the particular connection between eikasia and the reception of images in the eye in *emphasis*. Without this connection, their interpretations of eikasia are vulnerable to the objection presented succinctly by Yancey Dominick, namely that the description of eikasia in the Divided Line makes it highly implausible that anyone would consistently mistake images for reality, as when someone mistakes a reflection of a tree in a puddle for a tree; see Dominick (2010) for a helpful overview of different interpretations of eikasia in the secondary literature. Dominick presents an alternative approach to eikasia, according to which it is typical of the use of eikasia that a person is aware of the difference between image and original and uses the image with the intention to gain information about the original. The current interpretation of eikasia agrees with Dominick's in asserting that eikasia is, at least sometimes, a reliable means to gain insight into the originals that generate the images that are the objects associated with eikasia. On my interpretation, this is the function of the eye receiving images and does not require intentional action on the part of the one who sees external objects. Hence, even if the person seeing is not aware of the difference between image and original, it is possible for the person using eikasia to use images for the sake of gaining insight into the originals to which the images correspond. This is what occurs in the normal case of seeing an external object.

8.4.3 Vision and the Image of the Cave

The image of the Cave follows a single prisoner who moves from a state of captivity at the bottom of the cave to the freedom of the realm outside the cave. There he is able ultimately to gaze upon the sun. In this progression, the prisoner's starting point is a state in which he is able only to see shadows of objects cast upon the back of the wall of the cave. Once freed, he is turned toward the puppets that are the source of the shadows and toward the fire in the cave, though he is unable to see them well and does not succeed in understanding them. He strengthens his ability to see once he reaches the realm outside the cave by looking at shadows and reflections in water in the light of day. At last, he is able to look upon the originals of these copies and upon the sun itself.

From this brief review of the Cave we may distinguish four levels at which it is possible to view objects and to exercise vision: viewing shadows cast upon the back wall of the cave, viewing the puppets and the fire within the cave, viewing shadows and reflections outside the cave, and viewing living creatures, stars, planets, and the sun. A common interpretation of the cave matches these four levels of objects and of the use of vision to the four segments of the Divided Line. The state of viewing only shadows cast upon the wall of the cave corresponds to eikasia, viewing the puppets corresponds to pistis, viewing shadows and reflections outside the cave corresponds to dianoia, and gazing upon the originals of these copies corresponds to dialectic.[16] This standard interpretation seems to me to be correct; as we will see, our discussion of eikasia and pistis in the Divided Line will help to resolve one important problem that has been posed for this interpretation of the Cave.

This standard interpretation of the Cave in relation to the Divided Line is faced with the difficulty of matching the existence of the bound prisoners at the bottom of the cave with eikasia. We are told at 517b in the image of the Cave to fit together the life and experiences of prisoners in the cave to the visible section of the line. This leads readers to correlate eikasia, the lowest level of the Divided Line, with the lowest level of the Cave, the stage at which the bound prisoners can see only shadows. But Socrates tells us at 515a that the bound prisoners are like us: they mistake the shadows that they are accustomed to see for the whole of reality. This presents a problem for the identification of the bound prisoners' experience with eikasia, for no one spends their entire life gazing upon images in water and in mirrors. Similarly, no one is at all likely to think that such reflections constitute the whole of reality. If the prisoners' experience is correlated with eikasia, then it seems that they are not very much like us.

This problem can be resolved cleanly by our proposed interpretation of eikasia. If eikasia is not simply a matter of looking at mirrors or puddles of water but is employed every time we use our vision to see an external object, then there is a straightforward sense in which the bound prisoners are like us. At the start of our ethical and cognitive education, we take our sense experience at face value: the world simply is for us

---

[16] See Raven (1953) and Karasmanis (1988).

whatever the senses show us. In the case of vision, this is a matter of believing to be real whatever we see with our eyes. This "seeing with our own eyes," on the present reading of Plato's theory of vision, necessarily involves reliance on images. These images enter our soul via the mechanism of *emphasis*, the reception of images on the surface of our eyes. We see external objects only through the medium of these images. Similarly, the bound prisoners in the cave have access to the puppets behind them only through the shadows cast on the wall facing them. They attempt to determine the reality of the objects passing before them, but these attempts necessarily involve reliance on images. We are like these prisoners in our lack of education, namely to the extent that we are unable to go beyond the limits set by our visual experience and the images through which we perceive the world.[17]

The second stage of the Cave illustrates the difficulty of attempting to break with the assurances provided by immediate visual experience. A prisoner is freed from his bonds and forced to turn toward the puppets and the fire behind him. This turning is a case of gaining contact with a greater level of being (*pros mallon onta*, 515d3) and is accompanied by a process of elenctic questioning. As Socrates puts the question at 515d4-7, "...if we pointed to each of the things passing by, asked him what each of them is, and compelled him to answer, don't you think he'd be at a loss and that he'd believe that the things he saw earlier were truer than the one he was now being shown?" Socrates expects that the typical prisoner freed from the state of being able to view only shadows will seek to return to the certainty afforded by this limited view of reality. The prisoner is able to see well only after he is compelled to leave the cave and there, in the light of the sun, trains his eyes to see reflections of real trees, animals, and planets. These reflections are cast as shadows or as images in water. I take this to indicate that in the image of the Cave Plato portrays humans in their lack of education as unable to grasp the nature even of simple physical objects once they have been shown that the images provided by their visual experience are not fully reliable as a guide to reality. Even Socratic elenchus does not by itself provide satisfactory answers to the questions it poses. Only outside the cave can the freed prisoner develop his faculty of vision, which indicates that stable understanding of the world requires the guidance of the sciences, especially the mathematical studies whose procedures are sketched in the Divided Line and will be described more fully in Book 7 immediately after the

---

[17] This interpretation is compatible with those readings of the Cave which describe the experience of the bound prisoners as shaped by the moral conventions and cultural prescriptions of their society; see Smith (1999a) and Tanner (1970). It is characteristic of Plato's use of images that a single feature of one of his images can bear a multiplicity of meanings. Thus, the fact that the bound prisoners take the shadows before them to be the whole of reality can mean both that they give credence in an uncritical manner to their visual experience and that they accept too readily a wide range of moral and cultural judgments, judgments propagated by those who hold the puppets and who are thus responsible for the shadows cast on the back wall of the cave. I claim only that the current interpretation of eikasia allows us to forge a more direct connection between the description of the bound prisoners in the Cave and the description of eikasia in the Divided Line than is possible on readings similar to Smith's and Tanner's. Once this basic similarity between the situation of the prisoners and those who rely uncritically on eikasia is accepted, further correspondences a là Smith and Tanner may be explored.

image of the Cave. The transition from lack of education and consequent inability to understand to education and ability to understand is signified in the Cave by movement out of the cave into the light of day; this corresponds to utilizing dianoia and dialectic, the states of the soul associated in L3 and L4 with the intelligible section of the line.

8.5 Vision and Knowledge

After reviewing the three images of the Form of the Good, it is worthwhile to pause to reconsider the analogy between vision and knowledge. In all three of the images, vision operates as an analogue to knowledge. Reliance on this analogy presupposes that vision and knowledge share important features and that the analogy between vision and knowledge is not misleading. Having surveyed Plato's account of vision in the *Timaeus*, we are now in a position to consider the value of this analogy. As with any analogy, there are limits to the similarities between the two items compared; our task in evaluating the analogy involves setting out the relevant similarities between the items compared and noting the significant differences between them. One important difference between vision and knowledge as powers is that most human beings enjoy full vision from infancy on, while those who exercise knowledge by grasping Beauty Itself and other forms are relatively few, according to Socrates (476b9-10). Presumably, these few exercise knowledge in the full sense only in adulthood. This first difference indicates that the power of knowledge is not, like vision, something that is activated without conscious effort in the presence of what it is set over and when the right background circumstances are met. If a person with normal sight stands in front of a visible object in the light of the sun, she will see as long as she opens her eyes. The power of knowledge does not operate of itself in this way; the potential knower must search for good answers to questions like "What is beauty?" or "What is justice?". The opening books of the *Republic* illustrate through Socrates' conversations with Polemarchus, Thrasymachus, and Glaucon how difficult the search is and how various attempts to answer these questions can go astray. Even if all humans possess the basic capacity for knowledge, this does not mean that attempts to exercise it are infallible or that humans possess a capacity of intellectual intuition that simply opens itself to the truth.

   With these qualifications, though, we can affirm important elements of the analogy between vision and knowledge. When vision and knowledge operate successfully as powers, they allow us to recognize independently existing elements of reality. This successful operation of a power shows itself in contact with an object commensurate with the power, a visible color or shape in the case of vision and a form in the case of knowledge. Both vision and knowledge involve active engagement on the part of the seer and the knower. On the Platonic conception of vision, the eye must send out its inner fire to coalesce with the fire infused in daylight to form the body of the visual ray that conveys motions to the surface of the eye. Similarly, the soul of the knower must engage in inquiry, the sort of search we see exemplified in conversations which center on the Socratic "What is F?" questions. Whether these powers of vision and knowledge operate well or badly depends in part on whether they are trained on the right sort of objects and whether they obtain support from the environment. To specify this last point, we can spell out how vision and knowledge need to be directed to the right things and to derive support from external sources. We are best able to read the word "justice" when the letters are written in large type and when they are viewed in the light as opposed to darkness. We can know the forms when our souls are turned away from the sensible world by training in mathematics and other disciplines and when the Form of the Good provides the connecting bond of truth to link the soul's power of knowing and the power of the forms to be known.

The description of the visible realm in the image of the Sun is intended to guide our thoughts in the attempt to comprehend the Form of the Good. As the sun is responsible for our ability to see, so the Good is in some manner responsible for the soul's ability to make contact with the thing known. In providing an exposition of these and other passages in which knowledge is elucidated by a comparison with vision, commentators have at times attributed to Plato the conception of knowledge in its highest form as direct and unmediated intuition of being.[18] However, one implication of the Timaean theory of vision is that the force of the analogy between vision and knowledge points in the opposite direction. In vision, we have literal, bodily contact with visible objects. Our awareness of those objects is indirect and mediated by the transmission of motions from the visible object, through the body of fire leading up to the eye, into the eye, into the body, and finally into the soul. The result is the reception of images or appearances (*phantasmata*) into the soul. To the extent that knowledge operates in a fashion similar to that of vision, the knowing soul will also rely on images and appearances to mediate its contact with intelligible objects. Saying this does not amount to the claim that for Plato all knowledge of intelligible objects is indirect and mediated by the use of images; we should not assume that by employing the analogy of vision and knowledge Plato meant to assert that vision and knowledge operate in exactly the same way. But those who rely on the comparison between vision and knowledge to make inferences about the nature of knowledge in the *Republic* should be aware that vision does not provide an example of direct and immediate intuition of being.[19]

[18] Robinson (1953, 172–6); Cross and Woozley (1964, 252–3); Cooper (1966, 65–9); and Halfwassen (1992, 231).

[19] The reading provided here of the Sun image provides support to the main point of Horn and Rapp (2005), namely that the text of the *Republic* does not support the attribution to Plato of an intuitionistic epistemology. Where Horn and Rapp point to the lack of fit between such an epistemology and the express terms used by Plato to describe the methods of knowing, I claim that the nature of vision itself blocks the inference from the claim that knowing is like seeing to the conclusion that knowledge is direct intuition of being. And where Horn and Rapp attempt to minimize the undeniable presence of the language of seeing as mere metaphor that does not express the substance of Plato's conception of knowledge, I claim that the use of seeing as an analogue to knowing, rightly understood, represents a successful use of metaphor to express doctrine. For Plato seeing involves the use of images to develop a belief about an external object, a process that is analogous to the methodical use of images in the intelligible section of the Divided Line.

One important implication of the vision-knowledge comparison in the image of the Sun is the insight that knowledge is more stable than belief due to the stability of the objects with which it is in contact. At 508c-d, Socrates draws out some of the parallels between vision, with its dependence on the sun, and knowledge with its dependence on the Form of the Good. When we turn our eyes toward colored objects at night and without the light of day, they are almost blind; when we turn them toward things on which the sun shines, they see clearly. Similarly, when the soul is fixed upon things on which truth and being shine, then the soul knows and understands; when we fix the soul on the realm of becoming and passing away, then the soul has beliefs and wavers. To call on the Timaean account of vision, we may explain the success and failure of vision and knowledge in these lines as a matter of contact and lack of contact with stable reality. In the daytime, the eye is able to maintain reliable contact with visible objects due to the fact that fire from the sun is available in abundance to build the connecting body between objects and the eye. At night, the lack of fire from the sun means that the eye's external body is cut off. At best, the eye can see indistinctly by the dim light of the moon or with the shifting light of a torch or manmade fire. In the intelligible realm, the comparison to vision suggests that success in knowing depends on maintaining secure contact with the object of knowledge. Socrates describes success in knowing as a case of the soul resting on or being fixed upon (*apereisētai*, 508d5) the object of knowledge. When the soul turns itself to objects that come to be and pass away, the many just and beautiful and good things, then the soul engages in belief. Such a person who acknowledges only the images of the forms and whose contact with being has been cut off can be compared to one who dreams at night but does not see (476c5-7). What this person comprehends may be quite similar to the reality, even indistinguishable from it in ordinary experience, just as a dream-image may be indistinguishable from an external object. Even so, the one who recognizes only visible and sensible objects lacks the contact with reality required of knowledge, just as the dream-image lacks the contact with external objects required of vision. A person who has belief without this contact with reality will typically lack stability of belief: his beliefs will move "up and down," to use the literal translation of the phrase used at 508d8, a phrase often used by Plato to describe the fluctuations of a person who lacks knowledge of what it is to be just or beautiful or good (*Hippias Minor* 376c1-3; *Gorgias* 481d7-e1; *Ion* 541e6-8).

One issue that remains unclear in the three images is how exactly the Form of the Good draws the knowing soul together with intelligible objects. The Timaean theory of vision is of little help in dealing with this question. In the case of vision, the sun and the eye emit fire that constitutes a body linking sight and the thing seen. No such body can find its place in the intelligible realm. Socrates does not specify exactly what the link is which yokes the soul and the intelligible objects, unless we follow Rafael Ferber in taking the Form of the Good to be itself the third item which connects knower and known.[20] However, this option disturbs the parallelism between the visible and the

---

[20] Ferber (1989, 57–66).

intelligible realms: in the visible realm light is the connecting third item, and it is said to be similar to the sun in form, but not itself the sun (509a1). From this, we should expect the link between the knower and the known to be provided by the Good Itself and to be similar to the Good in form, but not itself the Good. Truth seems to be a likely candidate, as it is said to be like the Good in form (509a3). The truth referred to here seems to consist in the stability and genuineness of the object of knowledge, rather than in a property of propositions or linguistic items. Truth is provided to the objects of knowledge by the Good at 508e1-2, which suggests that here Plato operates with an "ontic" conception of truth as that which is grasped by knowledge and which is present in particular to the forms.[21]

A final issue concerning the comparison between vision and knowledge is whether vision suffers or benefits from the comparison. Following A. S. Ferguson, we may see the comparison as working to place vision and knowledge in a close, symbolic connection: as vision stands to visible objects under the influence of the sun, so knowledge stands to the forms under the influence of the Form of the Good. Especially in the image of the Sun, it seems that vision plays a positive role in our understanding of the world.[22] In the Divided Line, by contrast, the visible realm is referred to as the realm of opinion at 510a9, which suggests that understanding commences only when we gain access to objects of mathematics that are not seen. The image of the Cave compounds the ambivalent character of seeing. Life in the cave, which we are told to associate with the visible section of the Line, is a scene of illusion, manipulation, and lack of understanding, while at the same time the training of vision outside the cave is a symbol of education leading to understanding of the Good Itself.

Without attempting to resolve the ambiguity of the comparison between vision and knowledge, I wish to close this chapter by commenting on the role of eikasia and pistis in the Divided Line in helping us to achieve dianoia, the first state associated with understanding of intelligible objects. As we have seen earlier, eikasia and pistis are two complementary states that allow us to gain a rough conception of external, visible things as enduring, three-dimensional objects. Eikasia is used for the sake of pistis, in that our use of images received on the eye allows us to see external objects. In turn, the entities associated with pistis, those objects for the sake of which we employ eikasia, are themselves used as images to allow mathematicians to gain insight into the objects of dianoia. To anticipate the contents of the next chapter, Socrates speaks at 510d-511a of geometers using diagrams in order to think about a square or a diagonal that is not drawn and seen but understood. In such a case, the geometer will construct an argument that involves referring to different parts of a visible diagram and drawing conclusions about the square or diagonal depicted in the diagram. In this process, eikasia, pistis, and dianoia are in play with the first two operating for the

[21] See Kahn (1981) and Szaif (1996) for fuller accounts of Plato's tendency in the *Phaedo*, *Symposium*, and *Republic* to associate truth with the forms as objects of knowledge.
[22] See Ferguson (1921).

sake of the third. The student who follows the geometrical demonstration will use eikasia in order to perceive the diagram as an external object, the sort of thing present to pistis. The demonstration succeeds when the student uses the drawn square as an image to gain insight into the square that is not drawn but thought about. Here eikasia and pistis operate for the sake of understanding intelligible objects. Eikasia and pistis are clearly deficient in comparison to dianoia as ways to understand the world. In the best case, though, these states contribute to the understanding of intelligible objects. The two states associated with the visible world are used for the sake of giving us access to intelligible objects.

9

The Form of the Good II
Dianoia in the Divided Line

9.1 Introduction

The previous chapter introduced one particular way of understanding the Form of the Good in the *Republic*. The Form of the Good is the greatest study which the philosopher-rulers must come to know. Because it is required of the philosopher-rulers that they understand this basic principle, their education must help them win insight into this most important form. Insight into the Form of the Good, that which is the end or purpose of the philosopher-rulers' education, is described figuratively in the three images of the Form of the Good, the Sun, Divided Line, and Cave. In reviewing these three images, we noticed in the image of the Divided Line a pattern of using images for the sake of insight into the originals of those images. The four states of the soul (eikasia or imagination, pistis or belief, dianoia, and dialectic) mentioned in the Divided Line were drawn into relation by this pattern: in each of the first three, the soul uses images for the sake of gaining insight into the objects of the next higher state. This pattern came to the fore in particular in discussing the visible section of the Divided Line and in advancing an interpretation of eikasia and its relation to pistis.

The current chapter continues to set forth this interpretation of the Form of the Good by considering the intelligible section of the Divided Line. In reviewing the image of the Line, we will seek to determine how the activities of seeing and knowing are carried on for the sake of the Form of the Good. Typically, commentators have sought to resolve puzzles related to the distinctions Socrates draws between the different states of the soul. In particular, dianoia has provided a raft of problems: its relation to pistis below it and to dialectic above it in the line, the identity of the objects linked to dianoia, and the epistemological status of mathematics.[1] These are worthy topics for study, and in the present chapter, I will attempt to gain some measure of insight into them. However, these questions do not fully address the issue of what the Divided Line tells us about the Form of the Good. A full interpretation of the Divided Line will seek satisfactory resolution of these disputed questions, but it must also integrate these particular issues into a larger conception of the Line. That larger conception must show

---

[1] For a helpful overview of problems generated by the Divided Line and dianoia in particular, see Smith (1996).

how the Line serves Socrates' original purpose in fashioning the three images: he wishes to convey his sense of the Form of the Good and its role as that for the sake of which philosophers are to be educated. Accordingly, we must seek to determine what Socrates accomplishes in the Divided Line with his distinctions between different ways of seeing and knowing and what these distinctions add to his presentation of the Form of the Good.

To pull together the main results of this chapter, we will see that dianoia illustrates one of the chief distinguishing features of the Divided Line, namely the use of the image-original relation. Dianoia employs visible objects such as the diagrams used in geometry and uses these visible objects as images for the purpose of gaining insight into intelligible objects. In the process of making its inquiries, dianoia employs hypotheses as starting points. These hypotheses include definitions of the entities associated with dianoia. Examples of these definitions include the definitions which mathematicians set forth as they make their demonstrations. These procedures are discussed in the Divided Line in relation to the third section of the line, L3. Philosophers are expected to make a further transition from dianoia to dialectic and thus to move from L3 to L4, the highest section of the line. In making this transition, the hypotheses or definitions fashioned by dianoia are taken over by dialectic and used as images of the objects associated with dialectic, the forms. One mark of making this transition to dialectic is the activity of giving an account of the hypotheses previously employed by dianoia. The transition from dianoia to dialectic is described only briefly in the Divided Line; a fuller account of the transition and how dialectic uses as images the definitions provided by dianoia will be the subject of the final chapter, which takes up the account of the propaedeutic sciences in Book 7.

Having thus accounted for the different sections of the Divided Line, we can hazard an interpretation of the whole line as an image of the Good. The line as a whole is unified by the image-original relation: the objects associated with each of the first three sections are used as images for the sake of gaining insight into the objects associated with the next higher section. Success in reaching the top of the line is marked by understanding the unhypothetical first principle mentioned at 511d. Because each lower section of the line contributes to the understanding of the higher sections, each part of the line is present for the sake of understanding the unhypothetical principle, which is the highest object of dialectic. All acts of seeing and knowing reach their highest purpose in helping us to gain insight into this principle. Once an understanding of the unhypothetical principle is gained, every other part of the line is best understood by relating it back to that principle. The organization of the visible and intelligible sections of the line around this single principle is an image of the dependence of the visible and intelligible realms on the Form of the Good.

9.2   Some Questions about Dianoia

The previous chapter unfolded an interpretation of eikasia in relation to pistis in the lower section of the Divided Line. The two subsections L1 and L2 of the visible section of the line were associated with eikasia and pistis respectively. The objects linked with eikasia were identified as visible images and reflections, including the images received in the eye in the process of visual perception. The objects linked with pistis are the external objects which provide the originals for the images associated with eikasia. These contents of L2, the objects linked with pistis, do not require much discussion; they are simply the middle-size objects which we see as we direct our sight to the world around us. The philosophical significance of the first two sections of the line consists not so much in the listing of the entities in a given section as in the soul's use of those entities to gain an understanding of the objects at the next level up. It is the relation of imaging between L1 and L2 which is of interest.

The same holds for L2 in relation to L3: their importance for the Divided Line consists in the use that the soul makes of them as images of intelligible objects. The entities mentioned as belonging in L2 include manufactured objects, and one particular sort of manufactured thing, a geometrical diagram, allows the soul to gain access to the intelligible realm. The soul takes visible objects which previously served as the originals for items in L1 and uses them now as images of intelligible objects. This is the work of dianoia, the faculty associated with L3, which is first described summarily at 510b4-9. Socrates tells Glaucon the following:

In one subsection [of the intelligible part of the line], the soul, using as images the things that were imitated before, is forced to investigate from hypotheses, proceeding not to a first principle but to a conclusion. In the other subsection, however, it makes its way to a first principle that is not a hypothesis, proceeding from a hypothesis but without the images used in the previous subsection, using forms themselves and making its investigation through them.

This highly compressed presentation contains three points about dianoia: it is compelled to use hypotheses, it uses as images the visible objects belonging to the second section of the line, and it does not ascend to an unhypothetical first principle.

Glaucon (understandably) confesses that on the basis of such a brief statement he does not understand exactly what Socrates has in mind. In reply, between 510c2 and 511b1 Socrates amplifies his comments by giving as illustrative examples of the procedures used in L3 the practices of geometers and other mathematicians who make use of visible things from L2 as images of intelligibles. A careful unpacking of this description of mathematical practice will help us to understand this second instance of using images for the sake of insight into an imaged object. Practitioners of these mathematical sciences set forth as hypotheses such entities as the odd and the even, different geometrical shapes, and the three types of angles. They do not consider it necessary to offer an account of these hypotheses, as if they were evident to all, but carry out their investigations on the basis of these hypotheses in order to arrive at a conclusion which answers the question that originally roused them to their inquiries (510c2-d3). This explanation of dianoia's reliance on hypotheses in terms of the procedures of mathematicians is echoed in the following section, which explains dianoia's use of images by referring to the use of diagrams in geometry. A geometer will draw a diagram featuring a square and a diagonal and will make arguments about the drawn figures (510d6), but he will do so for the sake of the square itself and the diagonal itself (*tou tetragōnou autou heneka . . . kai diametrou autēs*, 510d7-8) to which the drawn figures are similar and of which the drawn figures are images. Diagrammed squares and diagonals are employed in the attempt to grasp the square and the diagonal of which the diagrams are images, a cognitive task that is accomplished by dianoia (511a1-2). Finally, at 511a4-b1 Socrates links dianoia's reliance on hypotheses and images to its inability to reach an unhypothetical principle. He says that in this section of the line the soul is not able to rise above its hypotheses but instead employs as images those things which were copied in the section below. Presumably, he means that visible diagrams are images of the type of entity contained in L3. Diagrams are visible objects which can generate reflections and shadows and appearances of the sort contained in L1, but when employed as images they allow the geometer to grasp entities belonging to L3.

This summary of the crucial passage 510c2-511b1 reports but does not interpret Socrates' description of the workings of dianoia. It is still unclear what the description of dianoia and mathematical study is supposed to tell us about the Form of the Good, that of which the Divided Line is an image. Working on the assumption that mathematical study is to be pursued for the sake of learning about the realm of being and the Form of the Good, though, we may inquire into the cognitive strengths and limitations of mathematical study. Three lines of investigation will be pursued here out of the many questions that arise from reflection on this passage. The first concerns the hypotheses mentioned at 510c and 511a. What precisely are these hypotheses, reliance on which characterizes dianoia? Why is the soul that employs dianoia compelled to use them, and how does reliance on hypotheses limit dianoia? A second line of investigation will clarify the reliance on images, which is an essential feature of dianoia. The nature of one sort of image which dianoia employs seems clear enough, as we are familiar with the use of diagrams in geometry, but we may ask whether and how dianoia's reliance on images limits its cognitive reach. Third, we will investigate the nature of the objects associated with dianoia and the manner in which these objects can serve as images of the objects associated with dialectic, namely the forms. An important goal here is to understand what is involved in making geometrical claims about visible, drawn squares and diameters for the sake of knowledge of the square itself and the diameter itself.

One feature of the image of the Line provides welcome aid in addressing these interpretive challenges. Socrates begins his explanation of dianoia's procedures by relating them to the methods used in geometry and calculation or arithmetic: "I think you know that students of geometry, calculation, and the like hypothesize the odd and the even, the various figures, the three kinds of angles, and other things akin to these . . ." (510c2-5). Glaucon answers that he does indeed know that students of mathematics proceed in this way. After Socrates concludes his exposition of the methods of dianoia, Glaucon reiterates the link between dianoia and the methods of the mathematical sciences of his day: "I understand that you mean what happens in geometry and related sciences" (511a10-b1). The exposition of dianoia and its methods is thus framed by explicit links between dianoia and the methods employed in mathematics at the time of the dramatic date of the *Republic*, namely sometime in the last quarter of the fifth century BCE.[2] However we understand the hypotheses and images mentioned in this passage and however we understand the limitations these place on dianoia, this interpretation must accord with contemporary Greek mathematical practice.[3] Our knowledge, let alone our reliable conjecture, about ancient Greek mathematical practice is limited; as Myles Burnyeat notes, Glaucon understands a lot more about mathematicians and their methods than we do.[4] However, we can speak with reasonable certainty about some features of the methods used by Socrates' mathematically minded contemporaries, and our account of dianoia's use of hypotheses and images and its being unable to arrive at an unhypothetical principle must agree in rough outline with these features. Of course, the resulting critique of dianoia delivered by Socrates need not agree fully with the accounts that contemporary mathematicians would give of their own practice. Socrates does not simply report what mathematicians do but also evaluates their habits of thought in light of his own exacting epistemological criteria. However, our account of Socrates' critique must show how he is reacting to modes of thought current in the mathematical practice of his day. We can formulate the following interpretive principle: Socrates' description of dianoia as used by mathematicians should be explicable as an informed observer's evaluation of mathematical practice in the last quarter of the fifth century BCE.

9.3 Hypotheses

The first line of investigation to be pursued focuses on the hypotheses which mathematicians are said at 510c to employ. I take it that the hypotheses which dianoia employs are propositions put forward as starting points for focused inquiry. This general conception of what a hypothesis is reflects Plato's use of the term in such dialogues as the *Meno*, the *Phaedo*, and in the *Parmenides*.[5] In these texts we find such hypotheses as: that virtue is knowledge (*Meno* 87c5); that virtue is good (*Meno* 87d2-3); that forms

---

[2] Nails (1998).

[3] The mathematical practice with which Plato invites comparison is at least that of the last quarter of the fifth century BCE but perhaps even later, up to 360 BCE. Books 6 and 7 include references to research in harmonics and stereometry attributed to Archytas, who was born sometime between 435 and 410 and who made many of his mathematical discoveries after the death of Socrates. See Huffman (2005, 5–8).

[4] Burnyeat (2000, 24).

[5] Richard Hare argues that the hypotheses in the Divided Line must be objects and not propositions, because "they must be things of which (or about which) it is possible to give a *logos*; and this...means to 'say what they are'" (1965, 22). However, Taylor (1967) assembles convincing evidence from the Platonic dialogues and other ancient sources that the normal sense of "*hypothesis*" indicates a proposition which serves as a basis for focused investigation. Further research into what it means to put forward a hypothesis, both in Plato and in pre-Platonic scientific sources, supports Taylor's claim that the Greek term "*hypothesis*" usually refers not to an object but to a proposition put forward as a starting point for inquiry. See Huffman (1993, 78–92); Wolfsdorf (2008a); and Baltzly (1996).

such as the Beautiful Itself and the Good Itself exist (*Phaedo* 100b5-7); and that seeing is knowing (*Theaetetus* 165b7). In this context a hypothesis need not be a claim put forward merely as conjecture or one whose truth is open to question; the hypothesis that virtue is good is one whose truth Socrates will affirm with certainty. Such hypotheses may be assertions of existence, as in the hypothesis of the forms in the *Phaedo*, or they may be predications of some property of a subject, as in the hypothesis that virtue is good. A special sort of hypothesis is the definition or attempt at a definition, as in the proposal that virtue is knowledge. These examples of hypotheses are taken from ethical and metaphysical investigations, but the use of hypotheses in a mathematical context requires special consideration. The mathematicians mentioned in the Line do not give an account of their hypotheses, and this suggests to C. C. W. Taylor that the hypotheses in question will be similar to those unproved propositions which Euclid sets out at the beginning of different books of his *Elements*: in Book I, definitions of point, line, surface, and of figures such as circle and isosceles triangle; postulates such as that which licenses the geometer in extending a finite line indefinitely; and common notions such as that equals subtracted from equals result in equal remainders. Taylor claims that these hypotheses used by practicing mathematicians include definitions as well as existential assertions, so that the hypotheses mentioned at 510b will presumably include statements of what it is to be an odd or even number and claims that such entities as squares or right angles exist.[6]

In addition to the points which Taylor makes concerning the normal sense of *hypothesis* in Plato and other authors, we may observe that research into the practice of ancient Greek mathematics indicates that even at the time of the dramatic date of the *Republic* mathematicians did offer definitions in propositional form of the basic elements of their subject, such as the odd and the even and the different types of geometrical figures.[7] Aristotle speaks of the Pythagoreans who pursued mathematical research as

---

[6] For Taylor the hypotheses include existential assertions as well as definitions, apparently on the basis of Aristotle's distinction at *Posterior Analytics* I.2 72a 18-21 between hypotheses and definitions. On the basis of this distinction, a definition says that an F is such-and-such a thing while a hypothesis claims that some F exists; see C. C. W. Taylor (1967, 198–9). But this interpretation of mathematical starting points, either in Euclid or in earlier mathematical practice, as involving existential assertions is dubious. See Mueller (1991, 70–6) for a careful treatment of the passages in Aristotle which influence Taylor's approach, a treatment which avoids classing mathematical hypotheses with existential assertions. For present purposes, what is important is that hypotheses include definitions.

[7] Ian Mueller writes as follows: "I suggest then that if we take what Plato says about mathematical hypotheses in the *Republic* at face value, then the mathematics, or at least the geometry, with which Plato was familiar contained as starting points at most, and probably at least, definitions"; see Mueller (1991, 83). Netz (2003) argues that making a hypothesis in the mathematical practice of Socrates' day was a concrete practice typically used by mathematicians at the start of their proofs. The practice was that of setting out a diagram, taking the diagram to exemplify the mathematical entities with which the proof is concerned, and making the assumptions necessary to generate the proof. Netz's proposal is compatible with the thesis that the hypotheses mentioned in the Divided Line include definitions; indeed, without the use of some definitions, the practice of setting out diagrams would not contribute to the solution of problems and the proof of theorems. Netz's proposal should thus be seen not as contradicting the thesis that the hypotheses of the Divided Line include definitions but as providing a richer sense of what it is to hypothesize the odd and the even, the three types of angles, and the different geometrical figures, in contrast to Mueller's claim that

innovating by taking numbers as the first principles of things and offering definitions of numbers and the types of number, such as the odd and the even.[8] As a result, we can say confidently that the mathematicians known to Socrates and Glaucon did give definitions of such things as the odd and the even and various geometrical figures, and that these definitions formed a crucial subset of their hypotheses.

The present claim is that Socrates' mathematicians formulate definitions as part of setting out their hypotheses. This claim is not contradicted by the observation that these mathematicians probably did not formulate their definitions so deliberately and fully as one might assume on the basis of inspection of the first pages of a modern edition of Euclid's *Elements*.[9] Heath's translation of the *Elements* begins with twenty-three numbered definitions, while Socrates in his informal mathematics lesson with the slave boy in the *Meno* gives a partial definition of squares at the start of the lesson and introduces the key concept of a diagonal when the lesson is almost over.[10] Even when definitions are introduced casually and on an ad hoc basis, as in the *Meno*, they serve as starting points for mathematical proof by providing required characterizations of named elements of geometrical figures. Due to the rough definition given of the diagonal as a line stretching from one angle of a square to the opposite angle, it is relatively easy to prove that a diagonal of a square divides the square into two equal halves; this is proved in Proposition 34 of Book I of the *Elements*.

The inclusion of definitions in the hypotheses of the mathematicians explains why mathematicians are compelled to use hypotheses. Once the mathematicians have made or established their hypotheses, they are said at 510d1-3 to proceed to the object of their concern, what drove them to engage in this particular piece of reasoning: "…starting out from these [hypotheses], and moving on through the rest, they conclude in agreement at that for the investigation of which they roused themselves." The goal of the mathematicians' investigation is successful completion of a mathematical proof, which in a geometrical context would be the proof of a theorem asserting that a geometrical figure possesses a specified property or the construction of a figure with a specified property. Successful completion of such a proof in good deductive order requires a preliminary statement of what is to be proved, a statement which relies on a definition of the property in question. For instance, the first proposition of Euclid's *Elements* sets the task of constructing an equilateral triangle starting from a given

---

these hypotheses do not go beyond propositions that function as definitions. Netz's larger point, as elaborated both in Netz (2003) and in Netz (1999), is that ancient Greek geometry draws its characteristic marks from its reliance on the practice of drawing visual diagrams within the context of mathematical proof.

   [8] Aristotle, *Metaphysics* 986a16-21, 987a20-8.

   [9] Netz observes that Greek mathematicians offer comments and explanations as introduction to the real work of mathematical demonstration: "Most definitions do not prescribe equivalences between expressions (which can then serve to abbreviate, no more). They specify the situations under which properties are considered to belong to objects.… There is no metamathematical theory of definition at work here. Before getting down to work, the mathematician describes what he is doing – that's all" Netz (1999, 95).

   [10] Squares are identified loosely at *Meno* 82b9-c2 as having all four sides equal; something like a definition of the diagonal of a square is introduced at 84e4-85a1.

finite line. This is a mathematically trivial task whose accomplishment dates from the prehistory of Greek mathematics, but it is one that presupposes some statement of what it is to be an equilateral triangle. Without a definition or similar clarification of what is meant when one speaks of an equilateral triangle, it is impossible to recognize with certainty what is to be constructed and at what point such a triangle has been successfully constructed. Thus, achieving the goals of inquiry in the deductive manner characteristic of dianoia in the Divided Line compels the soul to employ at least one sort of hypothesis, namely definitions.

Given that the identity of the hypotheses has been thus clarified, we can turn to another aspect of our first investigation: how does dianoia's reliance on hypotheses limit its cognitive reach? It cannot be the case that dianoia is limited simply by having to do with hypotheses, since dialectic also deals with hypotheses and is not thereby constrained from reaching the heights of knowledge. The important contrast between dianoia and dialectic has to do with their different attitudes toward giving an account of the hypotheses they employ. Mathematicians do not think it worthwhile to give an account of their hypotheses, while practitioners of dialectic are spurred to investigate these hypotheses. While mathematicians employ hypotheses as necessary preliminaries to achieving a proof of that which roused them to inquiry (510d2-3), dialectic arises when these hypotheses serve as spurs to inquiry (511b5). The hypotheses become one focus of inquiry rather than preliminaries to the goal of inquiry. Because hypotheses do not become a focus of inquiry in this way within dianoia, the mathematician is not able to rise above the hypotheses he employs in order to reach the goal of his inquiry (511a6-7). Exactly what it would be to rise above the hypotheses by giving an account of them will be discussed in the following chapter, in an examination of the contributions made by mathematical studies to an understanding of the Form of the Good.

9.4   Images and Intelligibles

The second investigation concerns a central aspect of this Socratic commentary on mathematical practice: the use of visible images to gain insight into intelligible objects. At 510d5-511a2, Socrates claims that geometers use dianoia to learn about entities other than the visible diagrams they draw. I translate this passage as follows, inserting numbers into what is one long Greek sentence to mark what I take to be distinct units of sense:

Then also you know that (1) they make use of visible forms and make their arguments about them, although they are not thinking about these but about those things to which they are similar, (2) thus making their arguments for the sake of the square itself and the diagonal itself but not [for the sake of] this [diagonal] which they draw, and similarly with the others, (3) thus making use of these things as images, those which they shape and draw and of which shadows and reflections in water are images, thus seeking to know those very things which one would not know other than by the faculty of dianoia.

This passage establishes a contrast between, on the one hand, mathematicians' manipulation of visible diagrams and the arguments they make about these drawn diagrams and, on the other hand, their thinking about intelligible objects. Using visible diagrams and making arguments about them will include drawing squares and tracing the diagonal of a given square, much as Socrates does in the *Meno* at 82b-85b as he leads the slave boy through the steps of an argument in support of the conclusion that the square with area twice the area of a given square is constructed on the diagonal of the given square. Such a procedure does not require any reference to intelligible squares and may involve only true beliefs (*doxai*), as Socrates indicates at *Meno* 85c4-7. Mathematical practice typically involves more than this, though; when mathematicians use visible diagrams as images, they are able to think about an intelligible square and an intelligible diagonal, what Socrates refers to as the square itself and the diagonal itself.[11]

To use visible squares as images in this context seems to be a case of employing diagrammed squares in the context of a proof whose conclusion holds true, strictly speaking, not of the diagrammed square but of another, intelligible square. As Burnyeat points out, the mention of the square itself and the diagonal itself should lead us to think of an early proof of the existence of incommensurable magnitudes, a proof which was executed by comparing the length of a side of a square and the length of the diagonal of that square.[12] The conclusion of this proof indicates that the side and the diagonal of the given square do not share a common measure, a result that means that the ratio of these two lines cannot be represented as the ratio of two lines measured exactly by a common unit. This is a result that is both surprising and apparently falsified by empirical inspection of any visible square; as Ian Mueller says, this is a result that is "always disconfirmed by careful measurement."[13] Yet this result must be accepted as a valid deduction from accepted starting points. Its truth, Socrates would assert, holds not of the visible square but of an intelligible square to which the visible one is similar. Dianoia uses visible objects as images by constructing diagrams that serve as steps in a train of reasoning that establishes truths about intelligible objects distinct from the diagrams. The visible diagrams are images in part because, if a discrepancy is pointed out between the visible object and the result proved by reflection on the object, the flaw is located in the visible object, not in the train of reasoning or in the intelligible object

---

[11] With regard to the square itself and diagonal itself mentioned at 510d7–8, I am persuaded by Moon-Heum Yang's argument to the effect that Socrates speaks here not of the Form of Square and the Form of Diagonal but of intelligible originals of which visible squares and diagonals are images. The intensive pronoun "*autos*," "itself," is used at 510e1 to refer to visible objects in their capacity as originals for shadows and reflections. Its use at 510d7–8 thus is no guarantee that we are dealing with forms, but rather points to the status of these intelligible objects as paradigms for visible squares and diagonals. See Yang (1999) and Yang (2005). See also Myles Burnyeat (2000, 35–7).

[12] Burnyeat (2000, 27–8). A proof of incommensurability *per impossibile* is mentioned by Aristotle in the *Prior Analytics*, 41a29, and a proof which fits this description was included at the end of manuscripts of Book X of Euclid's *Elements*; see Becker (1936, 533–4). This proof shows that if the diagonal and side of a square are commensurable then the same number is both odd and even; it is given as an appendix to this chapter.

[13] Mueller (1980, 115).

to which the visible object is similar. The visible square whose side is commensurable with its diagonal is only an imperfect copy of the square itself.

Recent articles by Burnyeat and Moon-Heum Yang provide explications of the manner in which visible diagrams are similar to intelligible objects. Burnyeat proposes that the intelligible objects may be conceived of as ideal exemplifications of the definitions contained in the hypotheses that mathematicians put forward and that govern the items they draw. Even in the sort of entry-level mathematics practiced by Socrates and the slave-boy in the *Meno*, mathematical inquiry will begin by drawing a figure and laying down some rough-and-ready definitions: a square is a rectangular figure that has four equal sides, while a diagonal is a line that connects the opposite angles of a square. The term "the square itself" is employed in such a context of mathematical inquiry because drawn squares do not fit these definitions perfectly; the sides of a drawn square will not be perfectly straight or equal in length. "It is to mathematics ... that we should look to judge the effect of the word 'itself'. In [510d-e] it tells us to ignore the wobbles in the drawing and the fact that the line has breadth. . . . What remains when [we] do so is not a Form, but an ideal exemplification of the relevant definition."[14] Visible squares are imperfect realizations and intelligible squares perfect realizations of these definitions. Yang describes the notion of structure as the root of the similarity between visible diagrams and intelligible objects. Starting from definitions and drawn diagrams, mathematical argumentation establishes certain relationships between the entities and their parts and between the parts themselves as they are depicted in visible diagrams. For instance, we can establish that the square that has as one of its sides the diagonal of a given square has an area twice that of the given square. These relationships define the structure of geometrical objects, a structure that is only imperfectly present in the visible diagrams. "When the mathematicians in the Line are said to argue about visible figures but think about intelligible objects they resemble, what is meant should be that the structures the mathematicians prove by using diagrams may be most exactly applied to mathematical objects of which they want to reach knowledge."[15]

9.5   Images for the Sake of Intelligibles

So far our discussion of the Divided Line and the crucial passage 510d5-511a2 has followed a straightforward reading derived from the commentary offered by such scholars as Burnyeat and Yang. Geometers use visible diagrams as images by making arguments about these diagrams, where the conclusions of the arguments hold true not of the visible objects drawn but of intelligible objects to which these visible objects are similar. Because their conclusions hold true of these intelligible objects, we may say that mathematicians are thinking about intelligible squares and diagonals. On this straightforward reading, making arguments for the sake of the square itself and the diagonal itself is a matter of reasoning with the intention of establishing truths about

---

[14] Burnyeat (2000, 36–7).   [15] Yang (2005, 302).

intelligible objects distinct from the squares and diagonals that are drawn. Yang explains clause (2) in 510d5-511a2 as follows: "In this part, mathematicians – geometricians in particular – are said to 'make their arguments' about visible figures. But, as Socrates unambiguously says, they argue so with a definite intent, that is, *in order to* know intelligible objects such figures resemble. This is exactly what the little word *heneka* ('for the sake of') at 510d8 indicates."[16]

This is the straightforward reading of 510d5-511a2 and of the notion of using visible objects for the sake of understanding intelligible objects. In response to this straightforward reading, I wish to make one observation and to present an objection. As an observation, I note that the straightforward reading is crafted to fit the use of dianoia in geometry. If dianoia is used in other forms of reasoning using hypotheses and images for the sake of understanding intelligible objects, then it may be necessary to supplement this straightforward reading. As an objection, I argue that the straightforward reading goes against the interpretive principle mentioned earlier that Socrates' account of dianoia as used in geometry should be explicable as an informed observer's description of mathematical practice in the late fifth century BCE. The straightforward reading proposes that when mathematicians use visible diagrams as images for the sake of understanding intelligible objects, they use visible diagrams with the intention of gaining insight into intelligible objects and they use visible diagrams while thinking about these intelligible objects. This ascribes to mathematicians a Platonizing impulse toward the immaterial and away from the world of sense-experience. In the passage in question, Socrates sets out to describe the actual practice of the mathematicians of his day and Glaucon agrees that Socrates has described what they actually do. If we consider what mathematicians of Socrates' day actually did, we will not find that they set out to learn about intelligible objects such as the square itself. The development of geometry in the late fifth and early fourth centuries BCE gives evidence of great increase in the range and strength of results proved, of the desire to present these results as part of an axiomatic structure flowing from a restricted and well-defined set of definitions, and of an increasing awareness of the methods of proof used in deriving these results. This is the stream of mathematical inquiry that culminated after Plato's lifetime in the *Elements* of Euclid. But ancient Greek mathematical practice shows no desire to gain insight into intelligible objects as such: that is, the square itself or the diagonal itself as distinct from the diagrammed squares and diagonals that, according to Socrates, serve as visible images of these non-visible originals. Mathematical practice in Socrates' day made no essential use of the distinction between a visible and an intelligible realm, a distinction that is of no help in solving the problems mathematicians set for themselves.

Nor does this fact escape the attention of Socrates and the author of this dialogue, Plato. Socrates' main criticism of mathematical practice in *Republic* 7 is that it is too preoccupied with sensible magnitudes, visible planetary motions, and audible harmonies

---

[16] Yang (2005, 291).

and does not seek out non-sensible units and ratios (*Republic* 527a, 529a-d, 531a-c). In Plato's other central depictions of mathematical practice, in the *Meno* and the *Theaetetus*, no mention is made of intelligible objects standing behind the diagrammed squares employed by mathematicians. In the latter dialogue, the brilliant young mathematician Theaetetus improves on his teacher Theodorus by providing a general definition of power or square root as a prelude to a general proof that, for any square equal in area to a non-square number, the side of that square (i. e., a power) will not be commensurable with the side of a square equal in area to a square number. But even the mathematically astute Theaetetus is too focused on the visible realm; when Socrates asks him to provide a fittingly general account of knowledge as he did for the powers, he can only offer the proposal that knowledge is perception (*Theaetetus* 151e).

In light of these facts, Glaucon could not affirm truly that Socrates has given an accurate account of mathematical practice if this account ascribes to mathematicians the awareness that the objects of their mathematical knowledge are intelligible squares, diagonals, and so on. In addition, insight into the square itself would mean, in the best case, knowledge of the essence of the square. But mathematicians in Socrates' day were not concerned to learn the essential nature of squares; they hoped instead to prove certain necessary properties of squares and other figures: that it is possible, for any rectilineal plane figure, to construct a square equal in area to that plane figure, or that for any right-angled triangle the square on the hypotenuse is equal to the sum of the squares on the other two sides. To put this point in a different way, the square itself mentioned at 510d7-8 would be one of the entities the definition of which is one of the hypotheses that form the starting points of the mathematicians. But these mathematicians do not think it worthwhile to give an account of the hypotheses, and thus of what it is to be a square. Their focus is not on the square itself but instead on the theorems about squares to be demonstrated and the figures to be constructed, "that for the investigation of which they roused themselves" (511d2-3). Thus, when mathematicians are described as using diagrams as images, this cannot mean that they draw figures with the intention of gaining insight into intelligible objects such as the square itself and the diagonal itself. Actual mathematical practice did not reveal this conscious, intentional commitment to gaining knowledge of intelligible objects. Following the interpretive principle mentioned above according to which Socrates' comments must be explicable as the comments of an informed observer of mathematical practice of the late fifth century BCE, we should reject this implication of the straightforward reading of clause (2).

I propose a different interpretation of the statement that mathematicians make their arguments for the sake of the square itself and the diagonal itself. Mathematicians succeed in thinking about intelligible objects, but they do this only in virtue of fashioning images of these objects. The images that mathematicians fashion are the arguments or discussions (*logous*) that they present as they demonstrate particular truths about squares, triangles, and numbers. These images include as one constitutive part the diagrams of squares mentioned at 510d-e, but they include also the definitions of such entities as odd and even numbers, geometrical figures (circle, triangle, square, etc.), and the three types of angles. Finally, their images include the particular conclusions about these hypothesized entities that mathematicians demonstrate. Having set forth a definition of a square and then drawn a square with its diagonal, the geometer will demonstrate that the square on the diagonal has an area twice that of the original square or that the diagonal is incommensurable with the side of the square. The entire argument constituted by definition, visible image or diagram, and conclusion is an image in words of the square itself.

On this account, the use of dianoia in geometry and related sciences is marked by a mixture of cognitive success and failure connected to the use of images. Mathematicians succeed in thinking about intelligible entities when they demonstrate the particular properties that hold true of the entities they hypothesize and define (squares, triangles, odd and even numbers). These properties do not hold true of the visible diagrams they draw. However, mathematicians gain only a limited conception of these hypothesized entities because they fail to give an account of their hypotheses. To take up Burnyeat's example of the proof that the side of a square is incommensurable with its diagonal, the mathematicians who arrive at the proof of this theorem have proven a conclusion that does not hold true of a drawn, visible square. The mathematicians know that their conclusion holds true of the square depicted by the diagram; in this sense they are knowing the intelligible square by means of dianoia, as clause (3) of 510d5-511a2 suggests. But the typical mathematician does not care to examine the nature of the square itself. Squares are among the things for which he provided definitions in the course of setting out his hypotheses. He takes these as fully known and in need of no further investigation, although he does not give an account of them (510c3-d1). His intention in using dianoia is to prove mathematically significant truths about squares, not to move in thought to the intelligible square or to examine the nature of squares and thus to arrive at an explanation of the fact that the diagonal and side of any square are incommensurable. Those who use dianoia are able to think about intelligible objects, but they have only a limited conception of these objects, one that falls short of understanding the nature of these objects. Mathematicians make their arguments for the sake of the square itself and the diagonal itself not because they are thinking directly about these intelligible objects but because they devise images of those objects.

To understand in what sense mathematicians think about intelligible objects, it will be helpful to consider more closely the proof *per impossibile* of the incommensurability of the side and diagonal of a square. Close examination of this proof (see the appendix at the end of the chapter) will show both the difficulties of the straightforward reading of 510d5-511a2 and the limited nature of the understanding gained by dianoia. The proof apparently takes over the definition of a square given in the 22nd definition of Book 1 of Euclid's *Elements*, namely that a square is a quadrilateral figure that has right angles and is equilateral. The proof proceeds by assuming, contrary to fact, that the ratio between the diagonal and the side of a square can be expressed as a ratio between two numbers, i. e., that the diagonal and the side are commensurable. The proof also involves setting forth a ratio between the square on the diagonal and the square on the side; as we know from the demonstration given by Socrates at *Meno* 84d-85b, this ratio is equal to the ratio 2:1. Once these preliminary steps have been made, including the assumption that the diagonal and the side are commensurable, it is demonstrated that the number corresponding to the side of the square is both odd and even. It follows that the assumption is false, and that the diagonal and side of a square are incommensurable. In such a proof, the point of setting forth a ratio between side and diagonal of a square is not to suggest by visual inspection of the two lines and of the ratio between them the real features of the square itself. Rather, the geometer draws impossible consequences from the assumption that the ratio is one that holds between commensurable magnitudes or lines, given that the ratio of the squares on the two lines is equal to 2:1. Although careful inspection of a diagram of the squares thus constructed could suggest that one square is twice the size of the other, no visual inspection or measurement could suggest the incommensurability of the lines in question. We are simply left with the result that, if we assume that the side and the diagonal of an arbitrary square are commensurable, a contradiction results. From this piece of mathematical reasoning and from the use of diagrams as images, we know an important property of all squares, namely that the diagonal and the side of a given square are incommensurable. We do not know whether the original definition of a square as a plane figure with four right angles and four equal sides is a good definition of a square, one that states the essence of squares. And we do not know why all squares exhibit the incommensurability of side and diagonal. In this sense, the proof gives us a limited conception of the square itself, or the Form of Square. The mathematicians who develop such a proof have fashioned an image of the square itself.

The development of mathematical proofs in the practice of geometry is one instance of the use of dianoia. As was observed earlier, the straightforward reading is crafted to fit the practice of geometry. However, we may also point to non-mathematical examples of argumentation from the *Republic* that fit the summary description of dianoia provided in the Divided Line at 510b4-9. To recall, dianoia involves arguing on the basis of hypotheses, it uses as images the visible objects associated with L2, and it does not connect its hypotheses with an unhypothetical first principle. Socrates at 510d-511a illustrates the use of dianoia by reminding Glaucon of the typical practice of geometers, but we should not assume that dianoia consists only of mathematical reasoning. In Book 2, Glaucon describes the lives of the completely unjust man and of the just man, starting from a definition of the essence of justice (359a4-5, b4-5). Justice consists in compliance with the laws and agreements put in place by social convention to restrain our natural tendency to commit injustice (358e-359a). Because justice has this nature, the life of the completely just man is a poor second in comparison to the life of the completely unjust man. To demonstrate that no one is just willingly and that the successfully unjust person lives a life of freedom and well-being, Glaucon relates the story of the ancestor of Gyges, who used the power to do injustice without penalty to become king (359c-360b). Glaucon assures Socrates that every person will act similarly if given the same power to act unjustly without fear of penalty. He also tells Socrates to shape his conception of the unjust man after the model of the skillful craftsmen; like a helmsman or doctor, the completely unjust man will discern what he can accomplish and what he cannot and will make the most of the first option. Thus, Glaucon fills out his portrait of the completely unjust man with statements about the behavior of ordinary human beings and with comparisons to craftsmen. Socrates compliments Glaucon at 361d4-6 for his skill in portraying the unjust and the just man: he has presented the men as if he were scouring statues for judging in a competition. In this example of dianoia, Glaucon begins by setting forth a hypothesis, namely a definition of justice. He then points to the behavior of human beings in daily life so that we can understand two intelligible objects, the completely just man and the completely unjust man. The result is the presentation of two statues or images, ready for judgment in the competition for the best life. He draws the conclusion that complete injustice is more beneficial for a human being than is complete justice. Although Glaucon cannot claim mathematical certainty for his conclusion, he is employing a general method of argumentation of which mathematical reasoning is another, related species.[17]

In reply to this provocative praise of injustice, Socrates responds with his own use of dianoia. As he sets out to construct the best city, he and Glaucon and Adeimantus agree that in such a city each person will carry out the task for which he or she is best suited by nature to perform. It turns out that this, or some form of it, is justice (433a3), since they established the just city by following the principle that each citizen should do his or her own affair. With this principle in hand, Socrates has secured an image (*eidōlon*, 443c4-7) of justice, namely a conception of a just city. The possession of this image points him toward the corresponding conception of justice in the soul. The just person is the one who enjoys psychic health with each part of her soul performing the task or function that it is best suited to perform. Having gained agreement with this conception of justice, Socrates can then proceed to show that the life of the just man is better than the life of the unjust man. His argument does not meet the highest standards of precision (435c9-d5, 504b1-7), presumably because he has not given an account of his definition of justice by relating it to the Form of the Good. Even so, Socrates aims to improve on Glaucon's use of dianoia by developing a better hypothesis or definition of justice, namely the principle that each part of a city or of a soul must perform the task for which it is best suited by nature. By following the consequences of this principle, he is able to point to images of justice: the city in speech and the nature of health in the body provide suggestive pictures of what it is to possess justice in the soul. On the basis of these images, Socrates claims to demonstrate the truth of the claim that the just man is happier than the unjust.

---

[17] Cambiano (2005) describes Glaucon in Book 2 as using a method of hypothesis related to the procedures of mathematicians described in the *Meno*. In particular he points to similarities between Glaucon's instructions to Socrates to construe the just and the unjust man in particular ways and the language used in geometrical proofs to set hypotheses and to deduce conclusions from these starting points; see Cambiano (2005, 15–16).

On this account, dianoia in its various usages exhibits certain key features.[18] The one who uses dianoia formulates arguments that are images of some intelligible reality, such as the square itself or the Form of Justice. Socrates at *Phaedo* 99d-e compares this use of arguments to the practice of viewing the sun in eclipse by looking at its reflection in a body of water. The arguments generated by dianoia provide us with intelligible images of intelligible objects, as the *Phaedo* passage suggests. These arguments include as a starting point one or more hypotheses, including a provisional definition of the object of inquiry. These arguments also include demonstrations of various properties ascribed to that intelligible reality, such as the incommensurability of the side and diagonal of a square or the benefit for a person's life that follows upon being just. Visible objects or properties (diagrams of squares, the actions of humans in society, health) may be incorporated into these arguments to help us understand the properties that follow from the provisional definitions of the intelligible objects (incommensurability of side and diagonal, the benefit that justice brings). At best, this gives us a reliable but limited conception of an intelligible object (the square itself, the Form of Justice): our understanding of the intelligible reality in question is limited by the use of visible objects to convey part of the truth about that reality, and the provisional definition is not founded upon a more fundamental first principle. These limitations ensure that the products of dianoia serve, at best, as images in words of intelligible realities. However, the provision of such an image is a genuine contribution to the understanding of intelligible realities. When geometers prove the incommensurability of side and diagonal, they have at least gained a secure understanding of a quality of the square itself, if not the essence of the square itself. Their arguments can achieve their full value when they contribute to our understanding of the square itself.

This account of dianoia as the state associated with images in words of intelligible realities has the advantage of preserving the analogies that Socrates sees between dianoia and other subsections of the line. In the original construction of the line, we are told to divide a line into two unequal sections and then to divide each section again in the same ratio. The result is a series of identical ratios between sections and subsections of the line: as the intelligible is to the visible, so is pistis to eikasia and so is dialectic to dianoia. The ratio between eikasia and pistis is identified with that between the opinable or visible and the knowable, which we know from the original construction of the line is the same as the ratio between L3 and L4, or between dianoia and dialectic. That ratio between a likeness and the thing to which it is like is present in the relation between a verbal image of an intelligible reality, the sort of object associated with dianoia, and the intelligible reality itself, which is associated with dialectic. Just as eikasia

---

[18] The account of dianoia here developed is closest to that in Gallop (1965) and Gallop (1971). Like Gallop, I take dianoia to be associated with verbal images of intelligible objects. Gallop draws attention to a wide range of images used by Plato as part of moral argumentation.

provides us with visible images of visible originals, so dianoia provides us with intelligible images of intelligible realities.

Later in Book 7, in reviewing the distinction between dianoia and dialectic, Socrates speaks as follows at 533e7-534a5:

It will therefore be enough to call the first section [L4] knowledge, the second [L3] thought [dianoia], the third belief, and the fourth imaging [eikasia], just as we did before. The last two together we call opinion, the other two, intellect. Opinion is concerned with becoming, intellect with being. And as being is to becoming, so intellect is to opinion, and as intellect is to opinion, so knowledge is to belief and thought to imaging.

As Nicholas Smith observes, the correspondence asserted here causes problems for many interpretations of dianoia. Socrates associates dianoia with the lowest section of the line, eikasia, which traffics in visible images. The natural inference is that dianoia uses intelligible images.[19] The present account of dianoia allows us to affirm Socrates' statement at 533e-534a, as there are several clear parallels between dianoia and eikasia. Just as eikasia provides us with images of the objects which we take to be real in the visible world, so dianoia generates images in speech or intelligible images of intelligible realities. Like eikasia, dianoia generates images which fall short of the full reality of the originals to which they are similar. In the typical use of eikasia, a person uses a visible image to perceive an external object and is not aware of any contrast between image and original; the image is that through which one sees the original. Similarly, the mathematicians who construct a proof of the incommensurability of the side and diagonal of a square take themselves to be knowing a particular feature of the square itself. Of course, they are in contact with the square itself only through an image. A person who attempts to make contact with reality through such an image can be described as dreaming. As Socrates recalls at 533b6-c3:

And as for the rest, I mean geometry and the subjects that follow it, we described them as to some extent grasping what is, for we saw that, while they do dream about what is, they are

---

[19] See Smith (1996, 30). Smith proposes that the objects associated with dianoia are the visible objects of L2 as they are used as images to gain insight into forms. I do not think this can be true in light of 510e3–511a1, where Socrates says that geometers who use visible forms as images are trying to see or know those things which one cannot see or know except by the use of dianoia. The items that one cannot see except by dianoia cannot be visible forms, which are grasped by pistis. Thus, the objects which dianoia allows us to see or know cannot be the same as the objects linked with pistis. Smith rejects the idea that the objects of dianoia include the hypotheses that geometers set forth because, he says, these hypothesized entities are forms: "It seems, then, that the geometer hypothesizes mathematical Forms, such as the odd, the even, the 'three Forms of angles', the square, and the diagonal. Can these be the objects Plato sees at the second highest segment [L3]? Plainly, they cannot, for the simple reason that the geometer's Forms are not images"; Smith (1996, 33). But in fact, the geometer's hypothesis is a provisional definition of squares. It is unclear whether such a definition states the essence of squares and thus allows us to know the Form of Square, since the geometer does not give an account of her hypotheses. Such a provisional definition of justice, as in Socrates' defense of justice in *Republic* 4, is described as an image (443c4).

unable to command a waking view of it as long as they make use of hypotheses that they leave untouched and that they cannot give any account of.

A dreamer is one who sees the images provided by eikasia without the proper connection to external objects; similarly geometers who rely on hypotheses without the ability to give an account of them are employing images of intelligible realities without the proper connection to a more fundamental first principle.

9.6 Dianoia and Dialectic

The preceding section contained an account of dianoia and the objects linked with it: it is the state associated with the fashioning of intelligible images, as when a geometer proves the incommensurability of side and diagonal of a square or when Socrates argues on the basis of the construction of the ideal city that justice is more beneficial than injustice. By fashioning such images, the practitioner of dialectic gains genuine insight into intelligible objects. However, it is left to the highest state in the Divided Line, dialectic, to improve on the results of dianoia. This brings us to the final transition in the Divided Line, that between L3 and L4. At this point the text of the Divided Line gives us relatively little direction to determine how this transition is made. In the first summary description of the intelligible section of the line, we read as follows:

In the other subsection, however, [the soul] makes its way to a first principle that is not a hypothesis, proceeding from a hypothesis but without the images used in the previous subsection, using forms themselves and making its investigation through them.

Here, the movement of the soul in thought has both a starting point and a final destination; the soul starts from a hypothesis, one of those mentioned in L3, and ends in the unhypothetical first principle. It deals with hypotheses in some way but does not concern itself with the visible images used in making the transition from L2 to L3. If we continue to treat the hypotheses mentioned in L3 as including definitions of mathematical entities, we may spell out the procedure applied in this step as a matter of turning away from visible diagrams of squares and diagonals and turning toward definitions of squares and diagonals. In some way yet to be described, the soul works with these definitions to arrive at the unhypothetical first principle.

A slightly more detailed account of this procedure arrives at 511b2-c2. After Socrates describes the faculty of dianoia that is associated with L3, he turns to L4 and its counterpart, understanding:

I mean that which reason itself grasps by the power of dialectic. It does not consider these hypotheses as first principles but truly as hypotheses – but as stepping stones to take off from, enabling it to reach the unhypothetical first principle of everything. Having grasped this principle, it reverses itself and, keeping hold of what follows from it, comes down to a conclusion without making use of anything visible at all, but only of forms themselves, moving on from forms to forms, and ending in forms.

As in the earlier summary of L4, the starting point for this investigation is the hypotheses. In some unspecified way, the hypotheses support the soul's movement to the unhypothetical first principle; in figurative language, Socrates speaks of the hypotheses used in L3 as stepping stones or steps on a ladder which make possible the dialectician's progress to the unhypothetical first principle. Exactly how this is to happen is left unsaid.

One plausible supplement to Socrates' words builds upon the observation that the hypotheses used in L3 include definitions used by mathematicians. Mathematicians do not give an account of these definitions, but it is part of the nature of dialectic to make them the subject of inquiry and to give an account of these definitions and in general of the hypotheses used by dianoia. Mathematicians employing dianoia are concerned primarily to prove conclusions about the entities defined by their hypotheses, for instance the incommensurability of the side and diagonal of a square. The dialectician turns from these particular facts about mathematical entities to reconsider the definitions and other hypotheses that the practitioner of dianoia employs but neglects to consider further. The dialectician may propose a definition of a class of entities that were previously discussed one by one, or she may criticize the definitions previously used and propose new and better ones. This is part of the task of giving an account of the hypotheses used by dianoia. What the dialectician does in giving an account of these hypotheses cannot be specified on the basis of the slim evidence provided by the Divided Line; this will be one of the topics discussed in the next and final chapter.

The Divided Line also suggests that this critical examination of definitions will yield knowledge in the full sense only if the dialectician relates the forms known and the definitions formulated to a first principle. As long as one definition is given in terms of another hypothesis which is itself not known, the result is not knowledge in the full sense. As Socrates will say later in Book 7 at 533c2-6, mere agreement between hypotheses and conclusions is not enough to secure knowledge: "What mechanism could possibly turn any agreement into knowledge when it begins with something unknown and puts together the conclusion and the steps in between from what is unknown?" Knowledge in the full sense requires recourse to some principle that is a first principle and hence does not need support from another source. Exactly how this happens is, to say the least, left unclear in the Divided Line. We do not know what the content of this first principle is, only that it is not a hypothesis, that by recourse to it things that previously could not be known are knowable, and that the "way" to it involves consideration of forms without dependence on visible images.

The Divided Line gives us only sparse information on the methods used by dialectic in L4 and on the content of the unhypothetical first principle. Having said this, though, one characterization of dialectic in relation to the unhypothetical first principle is possible: dialectic examines the hypotheses found in L3 for the sake of insight into the unhypothetical first principle. The hypotheses present in L3 serve as stepping stones that make possible the dialectician's insight into the unhypothetical first principle. The dialectician's inquiry into the hypotheses helps to produce or bring about understanding of the unhypothetical first principle, where this inquiry is an instance of the function of the rational part of the soul. The dialectician's inquiry is of lesser value than the insight into the first principle that it produces, and the value of this inquiry consists in part in its contribution to understanding that first principle. Finally, performing the rational function of the soul in the best way requires insight into the unhypothetical first principle. As Socrates tells Glaucon at 511c7-d2, any rational study that, like geometry and the other mathematical sciences, does not make its way back to this first principle fails to qualify as understanding and does not succeed in knowing its basic elements. With recourse to this first principle, those same basic elements can be known. The fourth and final condition for the presence of the for-the-sake-of relation is present, since the best way of knowing the hypotheses which are the objects of dialectic involves gaining understanding of the unhypothetical first principle and using this grasp of the first principle to achieve full knowledge of these hypotheses.

The preceding paragraphs provide only a sketch of the way in which the dialectician uses the definitions provided by dianoia as images for the sake of understanding the unhypothetical principle. The Divided Line simply does not provide a detailed and informative account of how dialectic operates. In order to supply this lack we must turn to the description of the propaedeutic sciences in Book 7 following the image of the Cave. This will be the focus of the final chapter; as we will see there, Socrates treats these mathematical sciences in a manner that accords with his discussion of dianoia in the Divided Line. The propaedeutic sciences have the important benefit of turning the mind from visible things to intelligibles. They bring us this benefit in part by employing hypotheses, including definitions, which serve to define on a provisional basis the objects of these sciences. Such hypotheses provide the starting points for the activity of the dialectician, who is capable of reviewing these hypotheses and drawing out for further study the concepts employed in these hypotheses.

The activities of seeing and knowing thus have their highest purpose in the understanding of a single reality, the unhypothetical first principle. This provides a fuller explanation of the sense in which the Divided Line is an image of the Form of the Good. All the contents of the Line are oriented toward a single end, the unhypothetical first principle. All the contents of the Line, both the individual entities distributed into the different sections and the states associated with these entities, are tightly organized in relation to each other. In each of the lower sections, the objects associated with that section are used as images for the sake of gaining insight into the objects associated with the higher sections. The different perceptual and cognitive powers described in the line are fulfilled ultimately by the contributions they make to understanding the unhypothetical first principle. The pervasive organization of the Line into sections oriented toward a single end provides an image of the influence of the Good Itself on our world.

Appendix to Chapter 9

The Received Proof of the Incommensurability of the Diagonal and Side of a Square[20]

Let it be proposed to us to prove that in square figures the diameter is incommensurable in length with the side.

Let ABCD be a square, of which AC is the diameter. I say that AC is incommensurable in length with AB.

For if possible, let it be commensurable. I say that it will follow that one and the same number is odd and even. Now it is manifest that the square on AC is the double of that on AB. Since AC is commensurable with AB, then AC will have the ratio to AB of one number to another. Let these numbers be ef and g, and let them be the least numbers in this ratio. Then ef is not a unit. For if ef is a unit and has the ratio to g which AC has to AB, and AC is greater than AB, then ef is greater than the number g, which is impossible. Thus, ef is not a unit; hence, it is a number. And since AC is to AB as ef is to g, so also the square on AC is to that on AB as the square of ef is to that of g. The square on AC is double that on AB, so the square of ef is double that of g. The square of ef is thus an even number; thus, ef itself is even. For if it were odd, the square on it would also be odd, since, if an odd number of odd terms is summed, the whole is odd. So ef is even. Let it be divided in half by h. Since ef and g are the least numbers of those having this ratio, they are relatively prime. And ef is even; so g is odd. For if it were even, the dyad would measure ef and g. For an even number has a numerical half. Yet they are relatively prime; so this is impossible. Thus, g is not even; it is odd. Since ef is double eh, the square of ef is four times the square of eh. But the square of ef is the double of that of g; so the square of g is double that of eh. So the square of g is even, and g is even for the reasons already given. But it is also odd, which is also impossible. Hence, AC is incommensurable in length with AB. This was to be proved.

---

[20] See Knorr (1975, 23).

10

Studying Mathematics for the Sake of the Good

10.1 Introduction

The two previous chapters discussed the image of the Divided Line and its presentation of the Form of the Good. The Divided Line lays out a range of cognitive states and associated entities, from *eikasia* or imagination to belief to dianoia to dialectic. It proposes that the end or purpose of these cognitive states is insight into the Form of the Good, which appears in the Divided Line in the guise of the unhypothetical first principle. The image of the Line allows us to speak in some detail of how Plato understands the transition from belief to dianoia: mathematicians use visible objects such as geometrical in order to learn about intelligible objects, and they construct intelligible images in words of such intelligible objects as the square itself and the diagonal itself. The use of visible objects as images marks the transition from section L2 to section L3 in the Line and from pistis to dianoia. The Line is less forthcoming with regards to the transition from L3 to L4 and the movement from dianoia to dialectic. Socrates says that the dialectician differs from the practitioner of dianoia by being able to give an account of the hypotheses employed in dianoia, but he does not explain in any detail how the dialectician is supposed to give an account of these hypotheses. This final chapter will address these topics by focusing on the program of mathematical study which Socrates prescribes for the philosophers-in-training in his ideal city.

The five propaedeutic studies discussed at 521c-531c—arithmetic, plane geometry, solid geometry, astronomy, and harmonics—are intended to turn the soul toward the intelligible realm and in particular to support the soul's search for the Good Itself. Describing the rationale for studying the most advanced forms of geometry available in his day, Socrates speaks to Glaucon at 526d7-e8 as follows:

> What we need to consider is whether the greater and more advanced part of [geometry] tends to make it easier to see the form of the good. And we say that anything has that tendency it if compels the soul to turn itself around towards the region in which lies the happiest of the things that are, the one the soul must see at any cost.... Therefore, if geometry compels the soul to study being, it's appropriate, but if it compels it to study becoming, it's inappropriate.

Here and elsewhere, Socrates advances the claim that the philosophers-in-training should study mathematics for the sake of knowing the Form of the Good. That is, the correct use of dianoia in the five propaedeutic disciplines will strengthen the soul for the highest achievements of dialectic, namely gaining understanding of the Form of the Good.

Clearly, Socrates expects the study of higher mathematics to pay off in the form of insight into the Good Itself. Why this should be the case and how precisely the study of mathematics will lead to this effect is not immediately apparent, to say the least. The chief task of the present chapter is to provide a detailed account of how Socrates' program of mathematical study supports insight into the Form of the Good. To sketch the account to be developed in this chapter, it will be helpful to recall certain features of our interpretation of the Divided Line in the previous chapter. The mathematicians who employ dianoia rely on hypotheses that include definitions of the basic entities studied in their discipline: odd and even numbers, the different types of angles, and the various plane figures. Turning to the five propaedeutic studies surveyed at 521c-531d, Socrates in effect evaluates these studies in terms of their efficacy in turning the souls of the guardians toward the Form of the Good. The mathematical studies contribute to this turning by formulating definitions of mathematical entities that employ the notions of ratio and commensurability. As mathematicians work with visible figures and diagrams to prove their conclusions, they will come to see ratios as a central aspect of their field. Definitions that express this awareness of the importance of ratios then become the basis for dialectical inquiry leading to an awareness of the Form of the Good. The propaedeutic studies are carried out for the sake of understanding the Form of the Good in the sense that they stimulate the formulation of definitions of mathematical entities, where these definitions become the raw material for the dialectical understanding of the Form of the Good.

10.2 The Propaedeutic Studies

By the end of the image of the Cave, Socrates has given more explicit articulation to his conception of the philosopher-rulers. Philosophers are the only ones fit to rule in the ideal city because they are the only ones who can appreciate a life better than ruling, the life of beholding the Good Itself. The philosophers will prefer this life to the cave of political life. That preference marks them as the only people who may be trusted to administer political life in the cave out of a sense of justice and not out of delight in the political life with its concern for honor, triumph, and bodily pleasure. The task incumbent upon Socrates and Glaucon is to devise an educational program that will foster such people who prefer a life directed toward knowing the Form of the Good over a life that promises political rule as its highest achievement. The propaedeutic studies arrive on stage at this point: Socrates hopes to turn the prospective philosopher-rulers toward the Form of the Good by immersing them in the most advanced study of mathematics available at the time. This is the subject that is capable of "turning a soul from a day that is a kind of night to the true day – the ascent to what is, which we say is true philosophy" (521c6-8). To understand how the propaedeutic studies accomplish this goal, it is necessary to examine the contributions made by individual sciences. The present discussion focuses on arithmetic, plane geometry, and astronomy as providing illustrations of the way in which these disciplines generate new definitions of mathematical entities, definitions which make use of the notions of ratio and commensurability.

10.2.1 Arithmetic

Socrates' discussion of arithmetic at 522c-526c reveals an emphasis on making arguments about visible objects for the sake of insight into intelligible objects. Arithmetic, the simple matter of the one and the two and the three, is important for the guardians not for the sake of numbering ships and troops but as dealing with the unit and with the numbers, which are among the most powerful summoners. Summoners are those properties and objects that present opposing perceptions to the senses and thus engage the intellect in the quest for definitions. Sight perceives a finger to be both big and little, and to resolve this conflict the mind is summoned to discriminate between bigness and littleness and to ask what the big and the little are (524c2-11). The one and the numbers count as summoners because sight always perceives the same thing to be both one and indefinitely many, a condition which befalls every number as well (525a5-8). Socrates describes the connection between these numerical summoners and the search for definitions at 524e4-525a3: "The soul would then be puzzled, would look for an answer, would stir up its understanding, and would ask what the one itself is. And so this would be among the subjects that lead the soul and turn it around towards the study of that which is."

As this passage shows, Socrates wishes to attribute to mathematics the role of directing the soul to the realm of being in consequence of dealing with problems set by numerical summoners. Arithmetic engages the soul in the project of making arguments about visible objects that present simultaneously the properties of being one and being many. In order to deal with such problems posed by summoners the soul resorts to definitions of the one. This is consistent with Socrates' treatment of mathematics in the Divided Line as an illustrative case of dianoia, a state that provides definitions of the entities concerning which it furnishes arguments. In Book 7 Socrates adds that arithmetic in dealing with the problems set by summoners (a finger that is both large and small) serves as a preparation for insight into the forms. Socrates owes us a justification for this view of arithmetic, since it is not self-evident that arithmetic or any mathematical discipline will deal with the problems set by summoners by leading the soul on to the forms. Even allowing that sight perceives each visible object as no more one than many, as Socrates asserts at 524e, it is not clear that arithmetic is the proper discipline to deal with this problem set by numerical summoners. James Adam's comment (1963, Vol. 2, 113) on this passage points to problems of conceptual analysis, not to the sort of problems recognized by mathematicians: "A visible *hen* [one] is always seen both as *hen* and *polla*

[many] (one wood, many trees; one tree, many branches, etc.)." The solution for such problems would seem to come not from mathematics but from philosophy; in connection with the concept "tree" the Japanese maple outside my window counts as one, while in connection with the concept "branch" the same thing counts as many. The young Socrates responds to Zeno's paradoxes in the *Parmenides* in somewhat this manner. Without showing any special mathematical expertise, he proposes that one human being can partake of unity as one person while partaking of plurality in virtue of the different parts of his body.[1] If arithmetic is the study which responds to the summoning problems brought up by the one and by the numbers, Socrates must explain how it does so.

The passage 525d5-526a7 addresses this problem directly. Here Socrates describes patterns of thought typical of mathematicians as they deal with objects that are both one and many and links these patterns of thought to the understanding of intelligible objects. For convenience, I will refer to this as the Ideal Numbers passage:

[Calculation] leads the soul forcibly upward and compels it to discuss the numbers themselves, never permitting anyone to propose for discussion numbers attached to visible or tangible bodies. You know what those who are clever in these matters are like: If, in the course of the argument, someone tries to divide the one itself, they laugh and won't permit it. If you break it, they multiply it, taking care that the one never be found to be many parts rather than one.[2]

That's very true.

Then what do you think would happen, Glaucon, if someone were to ask them: "What kind of numbers are you talking about, in which the one is as you assume it to be, each one equal to every other, without the least difference and not having a single part within itself?"

I think they'd answer that they are talking about those numbers that can be grasped only in thought and can't be dealt with in any other way.

This passage has played a starring role in the controversy over whether Plato's ontology includes the so-called mathematical intermediates, that is, a plurality of intelligible twos and threes existing between sensible pairs, triples, etc. and the Form of Twoness and Form of Threeness.[3] I wish to remain neutral on this issue and to focus instead on the way in which properly mathematical conceptions of number lead to the conception of intelligible objects, the "numbers themselves" which are the objects of dianoia alone. In particular, the notion of a number having a part or parts as developed in the definitions put forward in ancient Greek number theory helps us to understand why Socrates would say that mathematicians are thinking of intelligible objects when they discuss numbers.

[1] *Parmenides* 128e–129d.
[2] Here I revise the Grube-Reeve translation, substituting "the one" for "one thing" as a translation of *to hen*. The preferred translation is both more literal and fits better with a mathematically motivated reading of the passage, according to which the mathematicians are concerned to preserve the one or the unit as a single part of a number rather than many parts.
[3] Mohr (1981).

Much of the Ideal Numbers passage concerns mathematicians' opposition to the proposal that the one itself can be cut or divided. Such a proposal would lead to the result that the one contains parts. In response to this proposal, mathematicians take care to avoid the result that the one has many parts. They choose to describe numbers that are collections of units each of which is equal to every other unit and each of which lacks any part within itself. It is instructive to compare the patterns of thought ascribed here to mathematicians with the first five definitions presented in Book VII of Euclid's *Elements*:

1. A unit is that by virtue of which each of the things that exist is called one.
2. A number is a multitude composed of units.
3. A number is a part of a number, the less of the greater, when it measures the greater;
4. But parts when it does not measure it.
5. The greater number is a multiple of the less when it is measured by the less.[4]

These definitions form the basis of Euclidean number theory, which in the context of *Elements* VII means the nature and properties of the odd and even numbers, prime numbers, square and cube numbers, and perfect numbers. We cannot assert that the mathematicians of Socrates' day used or had formulated exactly these definitions; such a claim would reduce the role of Euclid in setting down definitions to that of a mere stenographer and would impute to Socrates' contemporaries an explicit interest in formulating definitions. Such an imputation is not supported by the ideal numbers passage itself, which does not describe mathematicians appealing to definitions. Even so, similar concepts of number and of a part of a number show up in the definitions of *Elements* VII and in the Ideal Numbers passage. Numbers are collections or multitudes of countable units. Since they are multitudes of units, numbers have various parts, but this straightforward observation leaves obscure a distinction between two different ways of "having parts," a distinction clarified by Definitions 3 and 4 above. 4 is a part of 12 and 5 is a part of 12, but for Euclid it is more illuminating to say that 4 is *a part* of 12 while 5 forms *parts* of 12. The number 4, taken three times, measures the number 12 without remainder while the number 5 does not. If we conceive of numbers as represented by lines of different lengths, as was typically done by the mathematicians of Socrates' day, then the notion of one number measuring another becomes clear: the line that is the number 12 will be covered exactly by matching to it three times the line that is the number 4, just as a yardstick will be measured three times by a foot-long ruler. The line that is the number 5 can be laid twice against the line that is the number 12, but a remainder that is less than 5 will be left; in this sense, the number 5 represents parts of the number 12. 12 is a multiple of 4 but not of 5 because it is measured by 4 but not by 5, as Definition 5 tells us. With these basic notions of unit, number, part of a number, and one number measuring another, it is possible to provide definitions of

---

[4] All quotations from the *Elements* are taken from Heath (1956).

odd numbers, even numbers, prime numbers, and perfect numbers, as Euclid does in Definitions 6-22 of Book VII.

This understanding of a part or parts of a number allows us to provide a properly mathematical motivation for the resistance to dividing the one itself on display in the ideal numbers passage. We do not need to ascribe to the mathematicians metaphysical commitments to the one as the ultimate and irreducible source of reality or contentious views about indivisible lines or ambitious theories of anthyphairetic ratios, the procedure in Euclid for finding the greatest common measure of two quantities.[5] The mathematicians are committed rather to conceiving of numbers as multitudes of units where each number is measured by one or more of its parts: 12 is measured by the unit and also by the part 2 and by 3, 4, and 6. This conception of number allows for a straightforward definition of prime numbers, which are measured only by the unit, or the one. The viability of this conception of number is necessary for the further development of definitions of composite numbers and perfect numbers. When the mathematicians in the Ideal Number passage do not allow an imagined interlocutor to divide or cut the one itself, they do not raise metaphysical objections; instead, when the interlocutor "breaks" it they multiply it, i.e., they treat the newly derived fragment of the one as the basis for a new number which is measured by that fragment and thus is a multiple of that fragment.[6] This procedure shows the mathematicians as "taking care that the one never be found many parts rather than one." This phrase need not entail a refusal to predicate of the one any quality other than oneness; it commits the mathematician only to describing the one as a part of the number to which it belongs and not as parts. Similarly, the emphasis on the one not being many parts but only one does not reveal a doctrinaire refusal to countenance the division of the one, but an insistence that the end result of such a division be a final unit which measures the number to which it belongs and does not form parts of that number.

This insistence that the unit be conceived as a part of a number rather than parts of a number also stands behind the question posed to the mathematicians at 526a1-4: "What kind of numbers are you talking about, in which the one is as you assume it to be, each one equal to every other, without the least difference and not having a single part within itself?" The unit or the one, construed as a single part of a number, will be exactly equal with or will measure every other single part of that number, just as the line representing the number 12 will be measured by its part 4 because it contains three segments of exactly equal length, namely 4 units. For the mathematicians, the unit or

---

[5] For this last option, see Fowler (1999).

[6] Suppose that a mathematician starts with a line composed of three units or three "ones." The interlocutor divides one of the units in a particular ratio, perhaps 5/7. The new unit that results is not a part of the original number 3; it is parts of 3, since the new unit does not measure the original line. In contemporary terms, we would say that the fraction 5/7 does not go into 3 without remainder. In reply to the interlocutor's move of cutting the original unit, the mathematician multiplies the new unit: by multiplying 5/7 by 7, the mathematician produces a new number that has the original unit as a part and also has the interlocutor's unit 5/7 as a part. This account of the mathematicians' procedure of multiplying in response to cutting is inspired by the account of the Ideal Numbers' passage in Mendell (2010).

the one does not have a single part within itself not because it is uncuttable in some metaphysical sense, but because a number conceived of as a collection of units presupposes some initial countable unit. This unit will be held fixed for this particular context of counting; it serves as the basic unit that measures the number and all its other parts but is not itself measured by a more basic unit. Such a unit may never be found in the realm of sense; any attempt physically to break or cut a yardstick into three exactly equal foot-long rulers will be limited by the imperfections of our knives, saws, and measuring instruments. But this limitation on our ability to produce the sort of units that make up the mathematicians' numbers is beside the point, of course; they will laugh and protest that they are dealing with units or ones that can only be dealt with by the understanding.

On this reading of the ideal numbers passage, the impulse behind the mathematicians' recourse to non-sensible objects of dianoia is the emerging structure of ancient Greek number theory. In order to investigate systematically the properties of odd and even numbers, of prime and composite numbers, mathematicians require a simple way of characterizing these different groups of numbers. The notions of part of a number, parts of a number, and measuring a number supply this need. Even numbers are those that are divided into two equal parts, each of which is a single part of the original number, while odd numbers are those that cannot be so divided. Prime numbers are those measured only by the unit while composite numbers are those that are measured also by some other number. The basic notions of a part of a number and parts of a number are present already in the Ideal Number passage as the expert mathematician replies to a troublesome interlocutor. We can surmise, then, that the mathematicians of Socrates' day employed these basic notions as hypotheses, in the sense of useful starting points, in the constructions of the proofs that later came to form Book VII of the *Elements*. More systematic reflection on number theory and the role of these hypotheses would normally lead to explicit statement of definitions similar to those that open *Elements* VII.

Two points may be drawn out here before passing on to plane geometry, the second of the propaedeutic studies. First, the mathematicians in the Ideal Number passage employ conceptions of numbers that rely on notions of ratio and commensurability. They conceive of numbers as assemblages of units, where these numbers can be divided into units that stand in whole-number ratios to the original numbers. Their units are commensurable with each other and with the numbers they compose. The mathematicians resist the division of numbers into units that cannot stand in such ratios to the original numbers (that is, their numbers lack parts in the sense of Definition 4 in Book VII of the *Elements*). Second, the mathematicians in the Ideal Number passage employ such concepts of number as hypotheses or definitions, but they are not capable of giving an account of their hypotheses. When the troublesome interlocutor asks the mathematicians at 526a1-4 what sort of numbers they have in mind, the mathematicians do not give a further explanation of the nature of numbers; they simply say that they are talking about numbers that can be grasped only in thought (*dianoēthēnai*, 526a6). As Socrates has warned us in the Divided Line, mathematicians as practitioners of dianoia employ hypotheses but cannot give an account of them. It seems that for Socrates the practice of arithmetic is in good order in that it has recourse to the right sort of hypotheses. Still there is work to be done in the context of inquiry into the basic concepts employed in arithmetic, inquiry that is carried out by question and answer between expert mathematician and interlocutor.

10.2.2 Plane Geometry

The second propaedeutic study is plane geometry. At 526d-527b, Socrates justifies the place of geometry as one of the five propaedeutic studies by emphasizing its capacity to direct the soul to the study of being as opposed to becoming. This, rather than practical benefits such as surveying land more accurately, is the genuine rationale for the study of geometry. In this short passage, Socrates' most explicit description of what geometers do comes at 527a6-10:

They speak on the one hand [*men*] in a way that is quite ridiculous and forced upon them; for they speak as if they are making all their accounts [*pantas tous logous poioumenoi legousin*] as men who are acting and for the sake of action, calling it squaring and applying and adding and all such things; but [*de*] the whole field of study is in a way practiced for the sake of knowledge.

After Socrates gains Glaucon's assent to this interpretation of the study of geometry, an interpretation which seeks to correct the literal meaning of the geometers' words, he adds a clarificatory remark on the sort of knowledge for the sake of which geometers carry out their investigations. The knowledge in question is knowledge of what exists always and not of what comes to be at some time and passes away (527b4-7).

The passage 527a6-10 quoted above deserves close study, as it is the most detailed treatment of plane geometry in Book 7. On a simple reading of these lines, the account at 527a6-10 of what geometers do consists in a contrast between what geometers say as they practice their craft and what their field actually does. These lines contain a single sentence which follows the structure of a typical "*men . . . de . . .*" construction, an arrangement of Greek particles often indicated in translation by "one the one hand . . . on the other hand. . . ." The first clause seems intended to report on how geometers talk: on the one hand, they speak as if they are engaged in a practical project centered on action, one that results in producing squares and other geometrical figures. But the second clause corrects this first impression: on the other hand, the point of geometry is not to make anything or to carry out an action but to gain knowledge.

The simple reading is not misguided. Socrates does want to correct the impression that geometry is valuable for its practical utility, and he does point to a contrast between the language of squaring and applying areas and the epistemic contributions of geometry. Socrates is correct to note that the language used to describe geometrical techniques carries the literal implication of making figures by manipulating and stretching and combining areas. Squaring here refers not to the multiplication of a number by itself, a procedure at home in arithmetic, but the practice in geometry of constructing a square equal in area to a specified plane figure. Applying an area is the technique of transforming squares, triangles, and any other rectilineal areas into rectangles stretched along a line. These procedures basic to ancient Greek geometry are employed in Euclid's *Elements* and, as we will see, were familiar to Plato and his audience, though not necessarily precisely as given by Euclid.[7] For example, Proposition 44 of Book I of the *Elements* is a construction problem: to apply a parallelogram equal in area to a given triangle to a given straight line in a given angle. That is, if the geometer is supplied with an arbitrary triangle and an arbitrary line, he should be able to transform the triangle into a parallelogram with the same area as the triangle and with base equal in length to the given line. The parallelogram should also be constructed with an interior angle equal to whatever angle is chosen. A special case of this assignment would be the common task of constructing a rectangle stretched along a given line; in this case, the angle is specified as a right angle. The following proposition, Proposition 45, builds upon 44 by assigning the task of applying to a given line a parallelogram equal not just to any triangle but to any rectilinear figure, no matter how oddly formed. Such a rectilinear figure is first decomposed into a number of triangles, for each of which a parallelogram of equal area is constructed. These parallelograms can also be constructed to a set height and then arrayed together or added to form a single parallelogram with area equal to the original rectilinear figure.[8] And Proposition 14 of Book II extends the results of Book I, Propositions 44 and 45 by transforming any parallelogram into a square of equal area. These central results of Books I and II of the *Elements* illustrate the procedures mentioned in 527a6-10 of squaring, applying, and adding areas in the course of demonstrating that any rectilinear figure can be transformed into a square of equal area. As this quick summary of geometrical construction techniques shows, it is quite natural if not inevitable to describe these techniques in language that, taken literally, suggests the manipulation of some quasi-material stuff to make different shapes. So we may understand why Socrates chooses to describe the geometers' use of language as "forced upon them" (*anagkaiōs*, 527a6); when we seek to put into words what happens in a proposition such as *Elements* I, 45, we find ourselves speaking willy-nilly of the reshaping and manipulation of areas. Socrates draws attention in 527a to the contrast between what geometers say they are doing and the real point of what they are doing. They say they are constructing squares and parallelograms, but they are in fact gaining knowledge of unchanging being.

---

[7] Plato uses *parateinein* at 527a to refer to the operation of applying an area where Euclid uses different forms of the verb *paraballein*. That *parateinein* refers to applying an area is shown by *Meno* 87a, where Socrates uses this verb to refer to application of a triangular area to a line in the form of a rectangle. Similarly, Plato uses *prostithenai* to refer to the addition of areas where Euclid uses *proskeisthai*. Beyond these terminological issues, Euclid first presents the operation of squaring at *Elements* II.14 in a proof that does not employ proportions. As we will see, we have good reason to expect that Plato and his audience were familiar with squaring as an operation carried out using proportions.

[8] See Mueller (1981, 16–18) for a discussion of the centrality of I, 45 in Book I of the *Elements*.

Thus far, we have a simple reading of 527a6-10. I see two problems for the simple reading. First, it allows Socrates only to make a rather pedantic point about how geometers speak. He says that geometers speak quite ridiculously (*mala geloiōs*) in making their accounts or arguments, and this ridiculousness apparently stems from the contrast between what they say they are doing, manipulating and reshaping areas, and the real purpose of their field, gaining knowledge. But it seems quite unlikely that any geometers were so ridiculous as to fixate on the literal meaning of their words and to take their discipline to have its point in constructing figures rather than gaining knowledge. Second, the reading presented so far of 527a6-10 does not allow Socrates' description of what geometers do to support his larger program of recommending geometry for its efficacy in turning the soul toward the Form of the Good. If the arguments used by geometers refer largely to the tasks of constructing squares and applying areas, as Socrates suggests, then his claim that it is carried out for the sake of knowledge of eternal being appears unmotivated. It is unclear how the activities of squaring and applying and adding areas make a positive contribution to gaining knowledge of unchanging being, such that these activities can be carried out for the sake of such knowledge. In addition, Socrates has not said anything in the present context to support his idea that mathematical knowledge puts the mathematician in contact with non-sensible, intelligible entities. Anyone who prior to reading 527a was unconvinced of Socrates' claim that geometry has as its highest result the knowledge of eternal being will remain unconvinced after reading this passage.

In light of these problems that face the simple reading of 527a, I present a complex reading of the passage. This reading starts from the observation that the term *logos*, the accusative plural of which appears at 527a7 as *logous*, can bear a wide range of meanings. One common meaning is that of argument or account. The word "*logous*" appears as the direct object of the verb *poieisthai*, to make. On the direct reading of the passage, this verb combines with "*logous*" to signify the action of making arguments or speeches. On this reading, geometers are said to offer accounts or make arguments in the course of their inquiry as if they were interested in the practical task of making figures. But "*logos*" can also mean "ratio" in mathematical contexts. For instance, when Socrates directs his listeners to construct the Divided Line at 509d, he tells them to imagine a line cut into unequal segments and then to cut each segment again in the same ratio—in accordance with the same *logos* (509d8)—as was applied to the whole line. Given this possible meaning of "*logous*" at 527a7, we may consider how our understanding of the whole passage 527a6-10 is affected if "*logous*" is taken to mean "ratios." If "*logous*" has the meaning of "ratios," then Socrates is asserting that geometers make or devise ratios as they carry on their activities of squaring and applying and adding areas. Making ratios is a matter of drawing two or more lines to represent quantities that stand to each other in determinate ratios, as occurs at the start of many passages in Euclid's *Elements*.[9]

---

[9] For instance, Book VI, Proposition 12 is a construction problem: "To three given straight lines to find a fourth proportional." The proof begins, "Let A, B, and C be the three given straight lines; thus it is required to find a fourth proportional to A, B, C." In this step we should imagine the geometer drawing three lines

Socrates comments that geometers make these ratios and set out these lines as if they were motivated by the purpose of constructing figures. This second reading of 527a6-10 is more complex in the sense that it presents Socrates as making two different claims when he says that geometers make *logous*. They are said to make arguments in the course of their investigations, but they are also said to make ratios as they carry out the operations of squaring, applying areas, etc.

This complex reading has the virtue of allowing Socrates to provide a more detailed and insightful description of what the geometers of his time were doing as they set about solving construction problems. As already mentioned, a central achievement of Books I and II of Euclid's *Elements* is the demonstration that for any rectilinear figure, a square of equal area can be constructed. This result can be proved using ratios and proportions, and such a procedure is used in *Elements* VI. However, this is not the method used in *Elements* II. Euclid sets about proving this result in his first two books without employing ratios and proportions; for his own reasons he introduces these notions only in Book V of his *Elements*. However, we have good reason to believe that this approach to proving the results of Books I and II was a relatively late development; earlier in the fourth century BCE, when Plato wrote the *Republic*, the normal procedure would have involved using ratios and proportions to show that a given parallelogram is equal to a square, as in *Elements* VI.[10] Euclid employs ratios and proportions in Book VI, Propositions 13, 14, 16, and 17 to show that a square can be constructed

---

A, B, and C where A and B stand in a particular ratio to each other, and then setting out to find the fourth line D such that the proportion A:B::C:D holds of all four lines.

[10] This claim is based on several pieces of historical evidence. First, the use of proportionals to solve construction problems can be traced back to the fifth century BCE, when Hippocrates of Chios (active in Athens from 430) reduced the problem of the duplication of the cube to the problem of finding two proportionals between two given lines; van der Waerden (1961, 136–41, 159–61). Many of the theorems presented in Books I and II of Euclid's *Elements* can be proved more simply with the use of proportionals, as Proclus observes in discussing *Elements* I, 47, the Pythagorean Theorem, and its more general counterpart VI, 31: "How [Euclid] proves the theorem in the sixth book will be evident there. But now let us consider how he shows the theorem before us to be true, remarking only that he does not prove the universal proposition here, since he has not yet explained similarity in rectilinear figures, nor proved anything in general about proportion. Hence many of the things here proved in a partial fashion are proved in that book more generally through the use of the above method [i. e., using notions of similarity between figures and proportions]"; see Proclus (1970, 338). If proportionals were commonly used by the mathematical contemporaries of Plato to solve construction problems including the squaring of a parallelogram, this suggests that Euclid took it upon himself to demonstrate the propositions in the first books of his *Elements* without employing proportionals, putting off such use of proportionals until the definition and introduction of this material in Book VI. Apparently Euclid made such a choice to employ one of the methods of arranging elementary material mentioned by Proclus, drawing upon Eudemus' third century BCE history of geometry: "It is a difficult task in any science to select and arrange properly the elements out of which all other matters are produced and into which they can be resolved. Of those who have attempted it some have brought together more theorems, some less; some have used rather short demonstrations, others have extended their treatments to great lengths; some have avoided the reduction to impossibility, others proportion…"; see Proclus (1970, 60). Artmann (1985) credits Theudios, a mathematician younger than Plato and active in the Academy, with authorship of a treatment of elementary geometry without use of proportionals. From these observations we may suppose with a high degree of probability that the method of squaring a rectangle in Plato's day involved proportions, namely finding a mean proportional between the two sides of the rectangle.

equal in area to a given parallelogram. Given the two lines A and B which define the parallelogram as its two sides, it is possible to find a mean proportional C between these two lines (i.e., a line C which is related to A and B such that A:C::C:B), according to Proposition 13. Given this proportion A:C::C:B, Proposition 17 tells us that the rectangle which has A and B for its sides is equal to the square with side C. Presumably this was the procedure for squaring which the geometers of Socrates' day commonly used, and this allows us to see how ratios and proportions would be used in carrying out the operation of squaring. Applying areas would also commonly involve setting out proportions, as the operation of applying areas was used in the task involved in Book VI, Proposition 25, "To construct one and the same figure similar to a given rectilineal figure and equal to another given rectilineal figure." In carrying out this construction task, a new figure must be constructed similar to a given figure, where two figures are similar if their angles are equal and the sides about the equal angles are proportional. Given the importance of working with ratios and proportions in the operations of squaring and applying areas, we can say that making *logous* was part and parcel of the geometrical practice in Socrates' day; it is the technique of setting out the ratios and proportions involved in squaring and applying areas. On the complex reading, Socrates is alluding to this fact.

If we accept the complex reading of 527a6-10, we can also connect this passage to a fourth-century discussion of how best to define the operation of squaring. Aristotle in Book II, chapter 2 of *De Anima* (413 a11-20) uses the example of squaring to illustrate more and less insightful ways of giving a definition:

For it is not enough for a definitional account to express as most now do the mere fact; it must include and exhibit the cause also. At present definitions are given in a form analogous to the conclusion of an argument; e.g., What is squaring? The construction of an equilateral rectangle equal to a given oblong rectangle. Such a definition is in form equivalent to a conclusion. One that tells us that squaring is the discovery of a mean proportional discloses the cause of what is defined.

Here Aristotle contrasts two sorts of definitions. The first contains the statement of a fact of the sort mentioned in a conclusion to some stretch of argumentation, namely the fact that an equilateral rectangle, or square, has been constructed equal to a given oblong rectangle. The second sort of definition points to the cause of the fact along with the fact itself. The key insight which allows the mathematician to assert that the constructed square is equal to the oblong rectangle is grasping the fact that the constructed square is built on a line which is the mean proportional between the sides of the oblong rectangle. This fact is the cause of or explanatory factor behind the conclusion that the constructed square is equal to the oblong rectangle. Aristotle's clear preference for the latter sort of definition in the context of defining the soul is illustrated by his praise of the method of defining squaring by reference to the discovery of a mean proportional between two lengths. Apparently, Aristotle expects his audience to be familiar with the difference between the two sorts of definitions in the case of squaring, and he has recourse elsewhere to this example of two sorts of definition.[11] So we may expect this illustration of how best to define squaring to have been a textbook example of proper definition for the audience of the *De Anima*. Aristotle would expect his audience to accept readily his point that defining squaring not in terms of constructing a figure but in terms of finding a particular proportion between lines is a case of epistemic best practices; he then hopes to find a related way of defining the soul. Socrates anticipates Aristotle's point about the proper way to define squaring in 527a6-10. He suggests that geometers misunderstand the point of their activity if they think that the essence of squaring is the construction of a square figure or the proof that a square can be constructed equal in area to a given rectilineal figure. The essential step in squaring, that which a definition of squaring should place in the foreground, is the discovery of a mean proportional between two lines such that the square takes this length as its side.

The complex reading of 527a6-10 also allows us to understand why Socrates might claim that geometry produces knowledge of eternal being. On the simple reading of this passage, Socrates does not say anything in 527a6-10 to motivate his claim that geometry is for the sake of knowledge of eternal being. But according to the complex reading, Socrates wishes to say that geometers in the course of squaring take on the task of finding ratios which employ mean proportionals: given two lengths A and B which form the sides of a rectangle, it is necessary to find a length C such that the proportion A:C::C:B holds. These ratios and proportions are, on one view congenial to Socrates and Plato, eternal. Although a particular rectangle may be constructed or destroyed, it is always the case that its lengths provide the extreme members of a proportion, the mean member of which defines a square equal in area to that rectangle. The fact that it is possible to transform a rectilineal area of any shape into a square is underwritten in part by this unchanging relationship between individual rectangles and squares. One characteristic mark of unchanging being is its unifying presence in a wide range of changing phenomena.[12] An example of this aspect of unchanging being is the role of ratios and proportions in showing that any rectilineal area can be converted into a square. By making ratios, geometers achieve knowledge of these unchanging realities, even if they mistakenly consider the discovery of such ratios merely as a means to their ultimate ends. Geometers think that the real point of their inquiries lies in the conclusions that they can prove, such as the conclusion that, for any rectilineal figure, it is possible to construct a square of equal area. But in fact, the important aspect of their study is the discovery of ratios that indicate the presence of eternal being.

---

[11] *Metaphysics* 996b20-2; here Aristotle mentions as an example of knowing what a thing is the knowledge that squaring is the finding of a mean proportional.

[12] Burnyeat (2000, 19–22) proposes a similar reading of unqualified or eternal being, namely as context-invariance: in all cases, the sum of two odd numbers is an even number. To move from arithmetic to geometry, we can say that ratios reveal eternal being by showing that any rectilineal figure can be matched with a square of equal area.

A final application of the complex reading comes in spelling out the sense in which geometry is a field of inquiry carried out for the sake of knowledge of eternal being. Socrates justifies the place of geometry in the structured education of the philosopher-rulers by claiming that it is practiced for the sake of such knowledge, but it is clear by now that this cannot be established simply by asking geometers what they intend to achieve by their inquiries or the manifest purpose of a construction in geometry. If we rely on the statements of geometers, we will be directed toward the processes of constructing figures and toward the solution of construction problems rather than gaining knowledge of eternal being. But as Socrates reinterprets geometrical practice, the use of the techniques of squaring and applying areas in the course of solving construction problems carries an unexpected payoff, namely greater understanding of the ratios and proportions that determine the relations between rectangles, squares, and similar figures. In his view, this insight into ratios and proportions is not a happy accident or side effect of solving construction problems; it is that for the sake of which geometers carry out their investigations.

As in previous cases of acting for the sake of an unintended end, it is possible to spell out the conditions that justify us in treating an unintended result of certain actions as an end or purpose of those actions. In this case, the actions in question are the actions of solving construction problems: for instance, proving that for any rectilineal figure it is possible to construct a square of equal area. The unintended result of carrying out this proof is gaining understanding of the ratios and proportions that relate squares, rectangles, and similar figures. To adapt the formal account of the for-the-sake-of relation set out in Chapter 1 to the particular case at hand, we have the following four conditions:

1) Geometers perform actions of constructing squares and rectangles which are of lesser value than understanding the ratios and proportions between the sides of squares, rectangles, and similar figures,
2) The actions of constructing squares and rectangles causally contribute to understanding ratios and proportions in virtue of performing the function of the craft of geometry,
3) The value of the actions of constructing squares and rectangles derives in part from their producing understanding of ratios and proportions,
4) The actions of constructing squares and rectangles perform the function of the craft of geometry in the best way only if they causally contribute to understanding ratios and proportions.

In these four conditions, mention is made of the function or characteristic activity of the craft of geometry. We do not find in the *Republic* an explicit description of the function of geometry, but intuitively it is reasoning about the properties of lines, angles, and plane figures such as circles, triangles, and squares, and providing demonstrative proofs of those properties. Conditions 1 and 2 are met if in the performance of this function geometers construct various figures and in doing so produce the more valuable result of learning about the ratios between the sides of these figures. The third condition asserts that part of the value of the process of constructing figures is the contribution it makes to this insight into ratios and proportions. As we have seen, these three conditions are part of the complex reading of 527a set forth above. The fourth condition asserts that a necessary aspect of carrying out the geometrical task of constructing figures in the best way is the production of insight into ratios and proportions. That this fourth condition is met can be seen from consideration of Euclid's procedure in II, 14 of the *Elements*. There he sets out a procedure for constructing a square equal in area to a given rectangle without using ratios. His procedure is flawless, in the sense that for any rectangle a line is constructed which serves as the basis for a square that is in every case equal in area to the original rectangle. But any bright geometer will want to know the relation between the two lines defining the rectangle and the constructed line on which the square is built; the ratio-less procedure of II, 14 raises a question that Euclid will eventually answer by setting forth the ratios and proportions of *Elements* VI. Failure to do so would leave incomplete the geometer's investigation of the procedure of squaring.

We may conclude this discussion of plane geometry and its role in the education of the philosopher-rulers by restating the main results of the section 526d-527b. Socrates is concerned to correct two distinct misapprehensions about the subject, one held by those outside the field, and one held by those adept in it. He cautions Glaucon not to fall into the common error of thinking that study of plane geometry is justified by the practical use of the field for such endeavors as farming and military strategy. But he also warns that those proficient in geometry may overestimate the worth of the conclusions they prove (that for any rectilineal figure a square can be constructed equal in area) and overlook the importance of the concepts and definitions developed in the course of establishing those results (the ratios and proportions established between the sides of squares, rectangles, and similar figures). Geometry is practiced for the sake of knowledge of eternal being, not because geometers understand themselves as seeking such knowledge, but because in the best case it will produce understanding of those ratios and proportions that reveal the eternal structure of geometrical objects. These ratios and proportions are mentioned in the proper definition of squaring. It is this best-case result, namely the formulation of definitions employing notions of ratio and proportion, which justifies the place of plane geometry in the education of the philosopher-rulers. As was the case with arithmetic, the practitioners of geometry employ the right sort of hypotheses, but they do not give the right sort of account of the significance of these hypotheses.

10.2.3 Astronomy

Taking up Socrates' treatment of astronomy, we find another instance of the pattern of studying visible images for the sake of insight into intelligible objects. The actual practice of astronomy fails to achieve this end, says Socrates, because astronomers commit themselves to finding the truth of the heavens in visible phenomena. Attempts by astronomers to deal successfully with problems set by sensible phenomena ought to lead to the positing of intelligible objects, namely the "true motions" (529d) of heavenly bodies posited by astronomers. These true motions ought to be among the hypotheses posited by mathematicians as they attempt to solve problems relating to the commensurability of the sensible world. Positing these hypotheses and thus gaining access to intelligible objects is one aspect of "making the ascent to problems" which, according to Socrates, is necessary for perceiving the truth about the motions of the heavenly bodies and their commensurable relations to each other.

This short and compressed description of astronomy stands in need of fuller explication. Here it is necessary first to acquaint ourselves with the usual practice of the science in Socrates' day in order to grasp the import of his prescriptions for the discipline. Socrates' contemporaries would understand astronomy as the craft or science that observes and predicts the risings and settings of the sun, moon, planets, and the other stars at different times of the year. In addition to predicting the risings and settings of the heavenly bodies, astronomers were understood to chart their paths in the sky. These tasks were connected with that of determining the seasons of the year by reference to the summer and winter solstices and to the vernal and autumnal equinoxes. This conception of astronomy as tracking the appearances of the heavenly bodies and using these appearances to fix the seasons of the year stands behind Glaucon's first reaction at 528d2-4 to Socrates' proposal to include astronomy in the education of the philosopher-rulers: "That's fine with me, for a better awareness of the seasons, months, and years is no less appropriate for a general than for a farmer or navigator." While today we might see the function of the theoretical astronomer and that of the maker of almanacs as quite different, this was not the common view in Socrates' day. In the second half of the fifth century BCE we find a series of proposals for describing the cycles of seasons and years, proposals motivated in part by confusion over the length of the year and the placement of solstices and equinoxes in relation to lunar months and festivals within the calendar. The birth of scientific astronomy in ancient Greece is often dated to the observation at Athens of the summer solstice in 432 BCE by Euctemon and Meton. Meton went on to propose a calendaric cycle of nineteen years in order to bring into rough agreement the cycle of lunar months and the solar year.[13] Emerging at roughly the same time was the conception of the universe as a sphere upon which the sun, moon, and stars described orbits. An example of the mixture of theoretical astronomy with the tasks of calendar-making is Oinopides of Chios, active at around 450 BCE, to whom is attributed the application of geometrical construction techniques to problems in astronomy and the discovery of the ecliptic (the great circle on the heavenly sphere followed by the sun in its annual motion through the heavens). Oinopides is also credited with an estimate of the length of the year at 365 and 22/59 days

---

[13] See Evans (1998, 20–2, 182–90) for a detailed description of Meton's development of a luni-solar calendar.

and an estimate of the Great Year at fifty-nine years. The Great Year is the shortest amount of time that would contain a whole number of days, months, and years. That is, Oinopides was recognized as an astronomer both for his description of the paths of the heavenly bodies and for his proposal of fifty-nine years as the length of time in the Great Year.[14]

If this mixture of calendaric reform and empirically based model-building represents the accomplishments of the actual astronomers of Socrates' day, then his recommendations for the practice of astronomy amount to a redirection of the astronomer's attention. The real astronomer will use visible phenomena of the sky as images that suggest the reality of true motions, and it is in these intelligible objects and not in empirically measured days, months, and years that we should expect to find the sort of commensurability that Meton and Oinopides sought in their calendaric proposals. As Socrates says at 529c6-d5:

We should consider the decorations in the sky to be the most beautiful and most exact of visible things, seeing that they're embroidered on a visible surface. But we should consider their motions to fall far short of the true ones – motions that are really fast or slow as measured in true numbers, that trace out true geometrical figures, that are all in relation to one another, and that are the true motions of the things carried along in them. And these, of course, must be grasped by reason and thought, not by sight....

The true motions mentioned here will apparently be motions of uniform speed in circular orbits.[15] These differ from the observed motions of the planets, which occur at non-uniform speeds and which include so-called retrograde motion, in which the planets appear to reverse their progress across the sky.

Although we have become accustomed to thinking of the positing of circular or elliptical orbits as the natural task of the astronomer, we should note that Socrates sees this "ascent to problems" as a marked departure from the conventional astronomy of his day. As we have seen, that practice of astronomy included the examination of the observed positions of sun, moon, stars, and planets to find whole-number ratios of days to months and months to years. According to Socrates, this focus on visible objects will never allow the astronomer to find the truth about the proportions between days, months, and years:

Therefore, we should use the embroidery in the sky as a model for the sake of learning about those other things. If someone experienced in geometry were to come upon plans very carefully drawn and worked out by Daedalus or some other craftsman or artist, he'd consider them to be very finely executed, but he'd think it ridiculous to examine them seriously in order to find the truth in them about the equal, the double, or any other commensurable proportion.... Then

---

[14] Oinopides is discussed by Dicks (1970, 88–9) and by Evans (1998, 57–8).
[15] See Mourelatos (1981, 2–7); according to Mourelatos, the real motions studied by astronomy differ from the motions observed in the heavens by their standing in ratios to each other. They are faster and slower circular and concentric motions carried within a single motion, all of which motions are coordinated with each other according to determinate ratios.

don't you think that a real astronomer will feel the same when he looks at the motions of the stars? He'll believe that the craftsman of the heavens arranged them and all that's in them in the finest way possible for such things. But as for the commensurable proportion of night to day, of days to a month, of a month to a year, or of the motions of the stars to any of them or to each other, don't you think he'll consider it strange to believe that they're always the same and never deviate anywhere at all or to try in any sort of way to grasp the truth about them, since they're connected to body and visible?[16]

Socrates' contemporaries in the field of astronomy took as one of their goals the description of whole-number ratios or commensurable proportions between days, months, and years, leading to the estimation of the Great Year. In his eyes, this endeavor is doomed to failure by the imperfection of the sensible realm: the relative length of nights and days changes throughout the year, the lunar month does not stand in any whole-number ratio with days, and the year similarly stands in a whole-number ratio neither with days nor with lunar months. The only way to represent the truth of commensurability is to leave behind the visual phenomena associated with days, lunar months, and years by ascending to problems. This is a matter of positing intelligible, non-sensible motions of the heavenly bodies, namely orbits of uniform circular motion.[17] Positing these "true motions" will allow the astronomer to give a new definition of the Great Year, one based on the commensurability of these motions. Assuming that the speeds of the different motions maintain the proper proportions relative to each other, the Great Year is completed when all the circular orbits of the heavenly bodies simultaneously complete a whole number of revolutions and all the heavenly bodies return to their original starting points.[18] The hypothesis of uniform circular motion thus allows for a new definition of the Great Year, one which allows the astronomer to exhibit the truth of commensurability which more empirically minded astronomers vainly sought to describe. The real astronomer will not ignore the visible phenomena to be seen in the sky, but he will employ them as images or models, studying them and the problems of commensurability they generate for the sake of insight into

---

[16] 529d7–530b4. The translation departs from the Grube-Reeve in two respects, first by giving a literal translation of *tēs pros ekeina mathēseōs heneka* at 529d8 and second by translating *summetria* at 530a1 and a8 as "commensurable proportion" rather than as "ratio." On the proper translation of *summetria*, see Mourelatos (1980, 39–41). Mourelatos argues that this term does not signify for Plato simply any ratio between two quantities, commensurable or incommensurable. The term denotes a ratio between two commensurable quantities sharing one or more common sub-multiples. In addition to this mathematical sense, the term is used synonymously with a range of value-laden terms connected with notions of measure, fittingness, and beauty.

[17] For an extended examination of what it would be to ascend to problems in the context of astronomy, see Mueller (1980, 103–22).

[18] See *Timaeus* 39c1-d7: "As for the periods of the other bodies, all but a scattered few have failed to take any note of them.... And so people are all but ignorant of the fact that time really is the wanderings of these bodies [the seven planets], bewilderingly numerous as they are and astonishingly variegated. It is none the less possible, however, to discern that the perfect number of time brings to completion the perfect year at that moment when the relative speeds of all eight periods [of the seven spheres of the planets and the sphere of the fixed stars] have been completed together and, measured by the circle of the same that moves uniformly, have achieved their consummation."

the true motions mentioned at 529d1. Because the work of studying visible phenomena helps to cause the more valuable result of positing true motions, and because positing these hypotheses is necessary for astronomers to succeed in performing their function of finding the commensurability of the motions of the heavenly bodies, Socrates may assert that astronomers study visible motions for the sake of insight into intelligible objects. In particular, astronomy correctly pursued can offer a better definition of the Great Year, now understood in terms of the period required for commensurable "true motions" to complete simultaneously their circular orbits and to return the heavenly bodies to their original starting positions. According to this revised definition of the Great Year, it is possible to describe the ratios between the various times required for the different bodies to return to these original positions.

10.3   Commensurability, Dialectic, and Giving an Account of the Hypotheses

In our review of three of the five propaedeutic studies, the concepts of ratio and commensurability have emerged as a key feature of the hypotheses and definitions which these studies employ or which they ought to employ. Practitioners of arithmetic and calculation conceive of numbers as composed of units which stand in whole-number ratios to each other and to the numbers which they compose; they resist the common attempt to divide the one and thus to produce units which do not stand in such ratios with each other and with the numbers they compose. Geometers use the techniques of squaring and applying areas, techniques which involve finding mean proportionals between two lines. They misunderstand the point of their procedures when they speak of squaring as the construction of a square and neglect the essential step of finding a mean proportional. Astronomers attempt to find the proper conception of the Great Year; they fail because they are looking for it in the wrong place, in the commensurability of days, months, and years. The real astronomer will use a different conception of the Great Year, namely the simultaneous completion of eight circular orbits. These orbits follow the "true motions" of the heavenly bodies grasped by reason and not by sight. Commensurability and incommensurability have emerged as important traits of the mathematical entities thus defined and classified. All numbers and their parts are commensurable with each other if they are treated as the Ideal Number Passage recommends; squaring in the sense of finding a square equal in area to a given rectangle presupposes that the sides of the square and the rectangle are commensurable with each other; and the true motions of the Great Year are commensurable with each other.

The notion of commensurability is not merely an implication of the definitions that mathematicians develop or ought to develop. It is also part of the knowledge that Socrates expects the philosopher-rulers to master as part of their education. That this is the case can be seen in a passage that describe the abilities of the fully trained guardians.

At 534d3-6, Socrates makes a pun in describing the prerequisites for the guardians to engage in dialectic and to rule the city: "Then, as for those children of yours whom you're rearing and educating in theory, if you ever reared them in fact, I don't think that you'd allow them to rule in your city or be responsible for the most important things while they are as irrational [*alogous*] as incommensurable lines." The pun depends on the fact that *logos* can mean both reason and ratio and that incommensurable lines were defined as those lines whose lengths relative to each other could not be described as a ratio or *logos* of whole numbers. To be irrational thus means to lack *logos* in the sense of failing to partake in reason, but also to lack *logos* in the sense of lacking ratio. To lack ratio in turn will have different possible meanings; one possible way of lacking ratio is to possess a soul whose parts do not preserve the correct order in their relations to each other, but another possible way is to lack understanding of commensurability defined as the relation between numbers and magnitudes having a common unit or measure. The requirement that the philosopher-rulers not be irrational or *alogos* thus involves the requirement that they possess an understanding of commensurability.

This understanding of commensurability bears a particular significance in *Republic* 7 as a bridge between dianoia and the mathematical sciences on the one hand and dialectic and the study of the Form of the Good on the other. When Socrates finishes his comments on harmonics at 531c9-d3, he gives a final observation on the need for reflection on the results of the mathematical sciences: "Moreover, I take it, if inquiry into all the subjects we've mentioned brings out their association and relationship with one another and draws conclusions about their kinship, it does contribute something to our goal and isn't labor in vain, but that otherwise it is in vain." This discovery of an underlying unity in the different mathematical sciences is said to be the prelude to the song that dialectic sings as it investigates the being of each thing (531d6-8). A further confirmation of this link between synthetic reflection on the mathematical sciences and dialectic is found at 537b8-c7. As he describes the stages of the education of the philosopher-rulers, Socrates says that after being released from physical training in their early twenties they must achieve a unified grasp of the mathematical subjects they learned first as children:

Moreover, the subjects they learned in no particular order as children they must now bring together to form a unified vision of their kinship both with one another and with the nature of what is. . . . It is also the greatest test of who is naturally dialectical and who isn't, for anyone who can achieve a unified vision is dialectical, and anyone who can't isn't.

We are not told exactly what the content of this unified vision is, but it is reasonable to suppose that it will involve the notion of commensurability. As we have seen, this notion characterizes many of the elements of the mathematical sciences and is presupposed by various hypotheses employed in the propaedeutic sciences as these appear in *Republic* 7. Given these indications in *Republic* 7 that the notion of commensurability is woven throughout the different mathematical sciences, the dialectician's task of finding a unified vision of the kinship of the different mathematical sciences will include finding a unified account of commensurability.

The concept of commensurability accessible to the dialectician is in part a mathematical notion, but also one that conveys aesthetic and ethical value. As we have seen in Socrates' pun at 534d, insight into commensurability is expected to equip the philosopher-rulers for the practical tasks of maintaining order within the *kallipolis* and preserving harmonious relations within the souls of its citizens. As we read at 540a4-b1, the philosopher-rulers are expected to use the Form of the Good as a model to put in order their city, their fellow-citizens, and themselves:

Then, at the age of fifty, those who've survived the tests and been successful both in practical matters and in the sciences must be led to the goal and compelled to lift up the radiant light of their souls to what itself provides light for everything. And once they've seen the good itself, they must each in turn put the city, its citizens, and themselves in order, using it as their model.

One explanation for Socrates' requirement that the philosopher-rulers acquire scientific knowledge of commensurability is that this knowledge will equip the philosopher-rulers to promote order and harmony within the city and in its citizens. This reflects the association Plato sees between commensurability and broader, normative notions of measure and order.[19]

On the present account, mathematicians employ as hypotheses definitions that, once mathematical study has reached some level of sophistication, include definitions employing notions of commensurability. If mathematical study is pursued for the sake of insight into these definitions, including definitions employing the value-laden topic of commensurability, then we have found a new way to express the thought that mathematical study is pursued for the sake of insight into the Form of the Good. Mathematics is especially relevant for the education of the philosopher-rulers because the intensive study of high-level mathematics yields new definitions of number, figures, ratios, and commensurability. These definitions are themselves in need of investigation and conceptual clarification, a service provided by dialectic as it gives an account of the hypotheses developed by mathematicians. The result is an understanding of the nature of commensurability and whatever other subjects account for the underlying unity of

---

[19] Looking beyond the *Republic*, a signal instance of this association is a passage from the *Philebus* in which Socrates describes the best human life as a mixture of pleasure and reason. Any mixture depends for its value on the role of commensurability between elements of the mixture: "But it is certainly not difficult to see what factor in each mixture it is that makes it either most valuable or worth nothing at all.... [a]ny kind of mixture that does not in some way or other possess measure or the nature of proportion [*tēs summetrou phuseōs*] will necessarily corrupt its ingredients and most of all itself"; *Philebus* 64d3-11. The role of commensurability in generating and maintaining valuable mixtures is meant to justify Socrates' claim that measure and commensurability reveal themselves as virtue and beauty (*Philebus* 64e6-7). In a passage where Socrates perhaps comes closest to spelling out his conception of the good, he says that the nature of the good has commensurability as one of its aspects: "Well, then, if we cannot capture the good in one form, we will have to take hold of it in a conjunction of three: beauty, commensurability, and truth. Let us affirm that these should by right be treated as a unity and be held responsible for what is in the mixture, for its goodness is what makes the mixture itself a good one"; *Philebus* 65a1-5. See also *Timaeus* 69b and 87c-d for other references to the role of commensurability in constituting objects as good and beautiful.

the mathematical sciences. Commensurability, as the dialectician understands it, is either an aspect of the Form of the Good or is analogous to the Form of Justice or the Form of Beauty by being one of the intelligibles which require explanation by reference to the Form of the Good.[20]

We have proposed that the results of the use of dianoia in Book 7 include definitions of mathematical entities and procedures developed in such fields as arithmetic, geometry, and astronomy. These definitions and procedures will employ concepts of ratio, proportionality, and commensurability. Dialectic then follows a method different from that of dianoia, one that consists centrally of the examination and evaluations of definitions. The philosopher-in-training who has completed the intensive study of mathematics prescribed by Socrates will arrive at the end of this immersion in mathematical inquiry with a number of different definitions employing commensurability as this important concept appears in different fields. This is precisely the sort of situation in which progress depends on comparison of different definitions in search of an underlying, unified account of commensurability. The elenctic examination of definitions will serve to point out the strengths and weaknesses of partial definitions and their relative suitability for incorporation into a unified account. The dialectician will seek a definition of commensurability itself, a statement of what it is to be commensurable which will find application across all the different types of commensurable objects and quantities. Success in finding this synoptic vision of commensurability will be indicated by the ability to explain why the unified account of commensurability is superior to other, partial definitions. This non-deductive, elenctic testing of definitions is different in nature from the deductive procedures of dianoia. As used in mathematics, dianoia constructs chain of deductive reasoning starting from hypotheses, including definitions of mathematical entities, and leading to conclusions about the entities defined. Mathematicians who employ dianoia may revise their definitions and generate new ones so as to prove their conclusions in more general and rigorous fashion. Even so, the conscious examination and critique of these definitions, and attempting to define

---

[20] This account of commensurability as a concept employed both in mathematics and in ethics owes much to the illuminating account of *Republic* 7 given by Burnyeat (2000). According to Burnyeat, Plato requires the philosophers-in-training to study the most advanced mathematics of his day because they are expected to gain an understanding of commensurability, a concept basic to ethics and aesthetics as well as to mathematics. On this account, grasping the content of mathematics is "a constitutive part of ethical understanding"; Burnyeat (2000, 6). Although Burnyeat's article provides great insight into the individual mathematical sciences and their role in supporting the dialectician's understanding of commensurability, I wish to reject his attribution to Plato of the view that mathematics is a constitutive part of ethics. Potential philosopher-rulers pursue mathematical study in the propaedeutic sciences for the sake of understanding the Form of the Good, but the functional teleology of action allows us to affirm this while preserving the separation between mathematics and ethics as distinct fields of inquiry. Practitioners of arithmetic, geometry, and astronomy are motivated by properly mathematical concerns as they develop their hypotheses and definitions of the basic entities in their fields: proving theorems rigorously and in the most insightful way. These definitions then may be taken over by the dialectician, who develops a synthetic conception of commensurability, the sort of general conception that must be explicitly related to the Form of the Good. Mathematical inquiry can thus follow its own imperatives even as its products serve the end of understanding the Form of the Good.

the key terms used in those definitions, is the province of dialectic. To put the idea in a different way, dialectic and not dianoia gives an account of the hypotheses employed in dianoia.

As was noted in the previous chapter, the Divided Line says precious little about the final step of the intellectual ascent that takes the soul from dianoia to dialectic and from the use of hypotheses to an understanding of the unhypothetical first principle. As a result of our discussion of the propaedeutic studies, it is possible now to characterize the transition from dianoia to dialectic. This step of the intellectual ascent occurs through critical and elenctic discussion of the fruits of dianoia, namely the definitions of mathematical entities generated by high-level mathematical study. Dialectic involves an explicit focus on the hypotheses which dianoia used previously without giving an account of them, it uses these hypotheses in some manner as steps on a ladder to gain insight into the unhypothetical first principle, and it relies on forms rather than on visible images. The hypotheses which dianoia uses include the definitions of mathematical entities which the propaedeutic studies formulate or ought to formulate. In pursuit of their own desiderata of providing rigorous deductive proofs of its results, the propaedeutic studies generate definitions of their subject matter. These definitions, especially those which employ the key notions of commensurability and ratio, are the steps on the ladder which dialectic climbs in order to gain a better understanding of the Form of the Good. In seeking a general account of commensurability and other notions, the dialectician is in effect giving an account of the hypotheses that result from the use of dianoia. Because the dialectician reflects on, critiques, and pulls together into synthetic unity the definitions provided by the mathematicians, she directs her attention to forms as these are described by definitions. While the mathematician uses dianoia to move from visible images (lines representing numbers, diagrammed squares and rectangles, the visible motions of the heavenly bodies) to intelligible objects (numbers construed as assemblages of ideal units, the square itself, the diagonal itself, the true motions of the heavenly bodies), the dialectician begins and ends her inquiry with forms. That is, she attempts to unify the different definitions provided by the use of dianoia by achieving a synthetic understanding of commensurability.

From these observations, we can draw out three properties which characterize dialectic in contrast to dianoia. First, dialectic gives an account of the definitions provided by dianoia in the propaedeutic studies, while dianoia cannot give an account of its hypotheses. Second, dialectic arrives at an understanding of a first principle that is not an hypothesis; dianoia is not capable of rising above the hypotheses it employs. Third, dialectic engages in successful elenctic defense of the accounts it provides; dianoia follows the deductive pattern set by geometry but does not provide the capacity to defend in elenchus the definitions it provides. Even if the practitioner of dianoia uses the right sort of hypotheses, as do the practitioners of arithmetic and calculation in the Ideal Numbers passage, he will not be able to answer questions about the nature of the entities hypothesized and so lacks full knowledge of them.

These three properties appear together in a passage which is perhaps the most informative description offered in Book 7 of the achievements of dialectic. Socrates and Glaucon converse as follows at 534b3-c5:

Then, do you call someone who is able to give an account of the being of each thing dialectical? But insofar as he's unable to give an account of something, either to himself or to another, do you deny that he has any understanding of it?

How could I do anything else?

Then the same applies to the good. Unless someone can distinguish in an account the form of the good from everything else, can survive all refutation, as if in a battle, striving to judge things not in accordance with opinion but in accordance with being, and can come through all this with his account still intact, you'll say that he doesn't know the good itself or any other good.

The dialectician gives an account of the being of each thing, in the sense that he works with the definitions thrown up by dianoia, definitions which purport to state the essence of numbers, squares and other plane figures, and justice. Because he gives an account of these definitions, the dialectician can claim to know the being of each defined entity and not simply to have true opinion about these things. The dialectician's ability to give an account extends all the way to the Form of the Good. In some way that is left vague, the dialectician gives an account of this most important form. One plausible specification is the description of the dialectician as giving a synthetic account of the notion of commensurability that is employed differently in the various definitions employed in the propaedeutic studies. Finally, the dialectician defends these accounts in elenchus. Socrates uses the elenchus to indicate promising avenues of investigation, as in Book 1 of the *Republic*, but he does not achieve knowledge. The dialectician's account of the being of each thing survives the test of the elenchus, while the accounts of Socrates and other practitioners of dianoia do not.

This account of dialectic as differing in nature from dianoia may be contrasted with the account of dialectic given by Hugh Benson in his recent book *Cleitophon's Challenge*.[21] Benson's goal in this book is to give a unified account of Plato's preferred philosophic method in the *Meno*, *Phaedo*, and *Republic*, namely the method of hypothesis. The method of hypothesis is a general procedure for finding the answer to some question. One begins by identifying a hypothesis H1 from which an answer to the question can be derived. This first stage involves demonstrating that the answer to the question follows from H1. This is the proof-stage of the method. As a second step, one confirms H1. This involves examining the consequences of accepting H1 and comparing these consequences with each other and with H1. This allows one to filter out any hypothesis that leads to contradictory or absurd consequences. In addition, H1 is confirmed by identifying a further hypothesis H2 from which the truth of H1 can be derived. The process of confirming hypotheses by positing higher or prior hypotheses

---

[21] Benson (2016, 237–70). See also Benson (2010, 193).

continues until one reaches a first principle not in need of further support, the "something sufficient" mentioned at *Phaedo* 101d or the unhypothetical first principle mentioned in the image of the Divided Line. This is the confirmation-stage of the method.[22] Dianoia in *Republic* 6 and 7 is an incomplete use of this method of hypothesis. The mathematicians mentioned in the Divided Line at some point treat their hypotheses as known and evident to all, as not in need of further confirmation, when in fact knowing these hypotheses requires further use of the method of hypothesis. Dialectic is the complete use of the same method.[23] The dialectician gives a satisfactory account of the mathematician's hypotheses by applying the method of hypothesis until the unhypothetical first principle is reached and then deriving the supporting hypotheses H1, H2, etc., from that first principle.

Leaving aside the *Meno* and the *Phaedo*, I would argue that Benson's method of hypothesis, even if carried out completely, is not the same as dialectic in the *Republic*. The method of hypothesis as he describes it, namely the complete use of the same method used incompletely in dianoia, does not address the special task set for dialectic in giving an account of definitions. As we have seen, the hypotheses employed in dianoia include definitions. Practitioners of dianoia do not see the need to give an account of these hypotheses, while dialecticians succeed in giving an account of those hypotheses and know the essences of things. That is, dialecticians give an account of such definitional hypotheses as "The just person is the person whose soul contains three parts, reason, spirit, and appetite, each of which does its own task" and thus can claim to know the essence of justice. To give an account of this definition using Benson's method of hypothesis would involve deriving the truth of such a statement from one or more prior hypotheses. The full use of the method of hypothesis would involve confirming these hypotheses all the way up to an unhypothetical first principle. However, deriving the truth of a statement offered as a definition does not by itself suffice for knowing the essence that is referred to by the proposed definition. A proposition with the formal appearance of a definition can be true and yet fail to be a satisfactory definition, one that reveals the essence of a thing. As an example of this, consider the third candidate for a definition of piety discussed at *Euthyphro* 9d-11b. Socrates and Euthyphro consider as a hypothesis (*hypothemenos*, 9d9) an idea formulated by Socrates, namely that the pious is what all the gods love. This candidate definition is rejected not because the proposition "The pious is what all the gods love" is false but because it points to an affection (*pathos*, 11a8) of the pious and not its essence. It may well be true that all the

---

[22] Benson (2016, 244).

[23] Benson's view of the underlying similarity between dianoia and dialectic is similar to that of Richard Robinson; according to Robinson, "... Plato is regarding the mathematicians as not treating certain propositions as hypotheses when they ought to, as not using the hypothetical method when they ought to. He thinks they are wrong to take the propositions from which they begin, 'the odd and even and the figures and three kinds of angles and related matters', as evident and known to be true. They should take them as tentative hypotheses. His complaint is that mathematicians do not use the hypothetical method although they should"; Robinson (1953, 152). Like Benson, Taylor (1967, 197) treats the task of giving an account of a hypothesis as a matter of deriving the truth of the hypotheses from some prior proposition.

gods love what is pious, but being loved by all the gods is analogous to being carried or being seen: it is an affection of the pious distinct from that which is responsible for the gods' love. The gods love the pious because of what the pious is, and so the affection of being loved by all the gods is to be explained by what the pious is. The proposition "The pious is what is loved by all the gods" is true and perhaps necessarily true given the nature of the gods, but still it is unsuited to play the role of a definition of the pious. The definitions that the dialectician of the *Republic* examines, such as a definition of a triangle or the definition of justice, may also be shown to be true by Benson's hypothetical method but may still be unsatisfactory as definitions.

These considerations indicate that the dialectician does something qualitatively different from what the practitioner of dianoia does. The dialectician knows the essences indicated by the definitions provided by dianoia. In order to know the essence of justice, it is necessary to do more than prove the truth of the statement that the just person is one whose soul has three parts each of which does its own task. One must know why such a definition states the basic reality of justice and how this essence explains other facts about justice, such as the nature of justice in the city. This is a tall order, clearly, and I do not have a satisfactory account to give of how one comes to know the essence of justice or piety. However, it must involve more than deriving the truth of definitional statements from prior hypotheses. If the dialectician simply does what the practitioner of dianoia does but keeps on going until she reaches a first principle that is not in need of further support, then the result will not be knowledge of the essence of things. Our review of the definitions produced by the propaedeutic studies suggests that the dialectician examines partial definitions of commensurability and uses these to achieve a more general, synthetic account of commensurability. This will involve discerning the limitations of each partial definition and then defending a more general account of commensurability. This suggests that the distinctive trait of the dialectician, the ability to give an account of the hypotheses used in dianoia and thus to know things in their essence, requires elenctic examination of definitions in addition to the procedures used in dianoia.

10.4 Conclusion

The final three chapters of this work have been dedicated to an examination of the images of Sun, Divided Line, and Cave and to an examination of the propaedeutic studies described in *Republic* 7. Our goal was to consider the Form of the Good as an end of human action and knowledge. Here I wish to pull together some of the salient results of this investigation. Our actions of seeing, learning, and knowing are carried out in the best case for the sake of understanding the Form of the Good. With regard to the propaedeutic studies, mathematicians are driven by properly mathematical considerations even as they carry out their inquiries for the sake of knowledge of the Form of the Good. They concern themselves with properly mathematical problems, such as squaring rectilineal figures and proving the incommensurability of the side and diagonal of a square, and their solutions to these problems are judged by properly mathematical criteria of generality and rigor. Their attempts to meet these criteria for successful solutions help to generate the definitions of ratio and commensurability, which the dialectician uses to gain greater insight in the Form of the Good. Thanks to these definitions derived from mathematical study, the dialectician achieves an explicit awareness of the ethical significance of commensurability and other fundamental notions of arithmetic and geometry. In the hands of the dialectician these fundamental mathematical notions provide the basis for full insight into the Form of the Good. This description of the relationship between mathematics and ethics makes sense of the explicit statements in Book 7 that in the best system of education mathematics is studied for the sake of the Good. It preserves Burnyeat's insight that, in Plato's eyes, the fundamental principles of mathematics are simultaneously principles of goodness. Yet it also allows for the necessary distinction between mathematics and ethics with regards to methods of reasoning and explicit concerns.

These comments deal with the manner in which it is possible to study mathematics for the sake of understanding the Form of the Good. We may also claim some progress in understanding the content of the Good Itself. The account presented here of the intellectual ascent to the Form of the Good confirms one way of characterizing Plato's Good. Since Aristotle, students of Plato have proposed that the Form of the Good is oneness or unity (*to hen*).[24] The good for a human being or a city or tree is that which allows it to exist and function as a unified whole belonging to some particular type. The influence of this basic principle of unity can be seen in the order and harmony that obtains within virtuous souls, well-crafted ships and houses, and the orbits of the heavenly bodies. As Nicholas White has pointed out, goodness in the *Republic* is seen most clearly in the just city and the just soul or personality. Goodness is a structural feature of these complex wholes that exhibit unity, stability, and harmonious organization.[25] We may surmise that the Form of the Good, that which is responsible for the presence of goodness in things such as cities and souls, is the source of unity; to put the thought another way, the Good Itself is unity itself.

Like all attempts to say what the Form of the Good is, this description of the Good Itself must be offered as at best a likely conjecture. With this being said, though, the discussion of the ascent to the Form of the Good through mathematics provides confirmation of this way of understanding the Form. The dialectician reflects on the definitions of mathematical entities and searches for a general account of commensurability as a defining property of such entities as numbers, geometrical figures, and the true motions of the planets in the heavens. An understanding of commensurability will then emerge from a careful review of the definitions used in arithmetic, geometry, and

---

[24] See Aristotle, *Eudemian Ethics* 1218a20; *Metaphysics* 988a8–16, b10–15; Aristoxenus, *Elementa Harmonica*, II. 30-1; Gaiser (1980); Burnyeat (2000); Krämer (1997); and Genzler (2004).
[25] See White (1979, 15–16, 19) and White (2006, 360–1).

astronomy. This understanding of commensurability will require a prior understanding of the units, of whatever kind, which are to be compared to each other and put in relation to a common measure. It is beyond the scope of this work to attempt to specify this understanding of units and how they are compared by some common measure. However, it is clear that the nature of unity and oneness will play an essential role in this account of commensurability.

This approach to characterizing the Good Itself faces an immediate objection. According to Aristoxenus, Aristotle used to relate the story of Plato's lecture on the Good Itself. Those who attended the lecture were disappointed with its content:

Each came expecting to learn something about the things which are generally considered good for men, such as wealth, good health, physical strength, and altogether a kind of wonderful happiness. But when the mathematical demonstrations came, including numbers, geometrical figures, and astronomy, and finally the statement, Good is One, it all seemed to them, I imagine, utterly unexpected and strange; hence some belittled the matter, while others rejected it.[26]

The notion that the Good Itself is unity would have seemed unexpected and strange because for these listeners would see no immediate connection between unity and the goods we desire as making for a happy and flourishing life. Even if unity is a reliable indicator of these recognized goods, such as health or strength or knowledge, it will not be for that reason the Good Itself.

Plato's functional teleology of action provides one way to reply to this style of criticism. One commonly accepted aspect of goodness is that it is that for the sake of which we act. The commonly recognized goods of health, strength, honor, pleasure, and knowledge have the status of goods in part because they are among the ends for the sake of which we act. A rational and wise person accepts these as worthy of pursuit and ranks them higher as ends than those items that are good only as means to ends, such as wealth or medical treatment. Through the functional teleology of action, Plato can place the Form of the Good in the constellation of ends for the sake of which we act. Wisdom is required for us to attain a happy life by the correct use of such goods as health, pleasure, and honor, and the pursuit of wisdom in the philosophic life turns out to be a case of acting for the sake of the Good Itself. Even if the Good Itself turns out to be something remote from the ordinary objects of desire and intention, be it unity or commensurability or some other reality grasped by mathematical inquiry, it will still have one of the characteristic marks of goodness. It will be an end or purpose of human action.

---

[26] Aristoxenus, *Elementa harmonica*, II. 30-1, translation by Gaiser (1980, 5).

Bibliography

Adam, James. 1963. *The Republic of Plato*. New York: Cambridge University Press.

Allan, D. J. 1940. *Plato: Republic, Book I*. London: Methuen and Company.

Annas, Julia. 1978. "Plato and Common Morality." *The Classical Quarterly* 28: 437–51.

Annas, Julia. 1981. *An Introduction to Plato's Republic*. New York: Oxford University Press.

Annas, Julia. 1993. *The Morality of Happiness*. New York: Oxford University Press.

Anscombe, Elizabeth. 2000. *Intention*, 2nd edition. Cambridge, Massachusetts: Harvard University Press.

Ariew, André. 2002. "Platonic and Aristotelian Roots of Teleological Arguments," in *Functions: New Essays in the Philosophy of Psychology and Biology*, ed. A. Ariew, R. Cummins, and M. Perlman, 7–21. New York: Oxford University Press.

Artmann, Benno. 1985. "Über voreuklidische 'Elemente', deren Autor Proportionen vermied." *Archive for History of Exact Sciences* 33: 291–306.

Audi, Robert. 1973. "Intending." *Journal of Philosophy* 70: 387–403.

Baltzly, Dirk. 1996. "'To an Unhypothetical First Principle' in Plato's *Republic*." *History of Philosophy Quarterly* 13: 149–65.

Barnes, Jonathan. 2012. "Justice Writ Large." In *Oxford Studies in Ancient Philosophy: Supplementary Volume; Essays in Honor of Julia Annas*, ed. R. Kamtekar, 31–49. New York: Oxford University Press.

Barney, Rachel. 2006. "Socrates' Refutation of Thrasymachus." In *The Blackwell Guide to Plato's Republic*, ed. G. Santas, 44–62. Malden, Massachusetts: Blackwell Publishing.

Becker, Oskar. 1936. "Die Lehre vom Geraden und Ungeraden im Neunten Buch des Euklidischen Elemente." *Quellen und Studien zur Geschichte der Mathematik, Astronomie, und Physik* 3: 533–53.

Benson, Hugh. 1997. "Socratic Dynamic Theory: A Sketch." *Apeiron* 30: 79–93.

Benson, Hugh. 2010. "Dialectic in the *Republic*: The Divided Line 510b-511d." In *The Cambridge Critical Guide to the Republic*, ed. M. McPherran, 188–208. New York: Cambridge University Press.

Benson, Hugh. 2016. *Cleitophon's Challenge*. New York: Oxford University Press.

Blondell, Ruby. 2002. *The Play of Character in Plato's Dialogues*. New York: Cambridge University Press.

Blundell, Mary Whitlock. 1989. *Helping Friends and Harming Enemies*. New York: Cambridge University Press.

Bobonich, Christopher. 2002. *Plato's Utopia Recast*. New York: Oxford University Press.

Bratman, Michael. 1993. "Shared Intention." *Ethics* 104: 97–113.

Bratman, Michael. 1999. *Faces of Intention*. Cambridge: Cambridge University Press.

Brennan, Tad. 2012. "The Nature of the Spirited Part of the Soul and its Object." In *Plato and the Divided Self*, ed. R. Barney, T. Brennan, and C. Brittain, 102–27. New York: Cambridge University Press.

Brown, Eric. 2004. "Minding the Gap in Plato's *Republic*." *Philosophical Studies* 117: 275–302.

Brown, Eric. 2012. "The Unity of the Soul in Plato's *Republic.*" In *Plato and the Divided Self*, ed. R. Barney, T. Brennan, and C. Brittain, 53–73. New York: Cambridge University Press.

Burge, Evan. 1971. "The Ideas as *Aitiai* in the *Phaedo.*" *Phronesis* 16: 1–13.

Burnyeat, Myles. 2000. "Plato on Why Mathematics is Good for the Soul" In *Mathematics and Necessity*, ed. T. Smiley, 1–81. New York: Oxford University Press.

Cambiano, Giuseppe. 2005. "La Méthode par Hypothèse en *République* II." In *Études sur la République de Platon*, vol. 2, ed. M. Dixsaut, 9–24. Paris: Librairie Philosophique Vrin.

Carone, Gabriela Roxana. 2001. "Akrasia in the *Republic*: Does Plato Change His Mind?" *Oxford Studies in Ancient Philosophy* 20: 107–48.

Charles, David. 1991. "Teleological Causation in the *Physics.*" In *Aristotle's Physics: A Collection of Essays*, ed. L. Judson, 101–28. New York: Oxford University Press.

Cooper, John. 1977. "The Psychology of Justice in Plato." *American Philosophical Quarterly* 14: 151–7.

Cooper, John. 1984. "Plato's Theory of Human Motivation." *History of Philosophy Quarterly* 1: 3–21.

Cooper, John (ed.). 1997. *Plato: Complete Works*. Indianapolis, Indiana: Hackett Publishing.

Cooper, Neil. 1966. "The Importance of *DIANOIA* in Plato's Theory of Forms." *Classical Quarterly* 16: 65–9.

Cornford, Francis. 1937. *Plato's Cosmology*. London: Kegan Paul.

Cross, R. C. and Woozley, A. D. 1964. *Plato's Republic: A Philosophical Commentary*. London: Macmillan Press.

Dahl, Norman. 1991. "Plato's Defense of Justice." *Philosophy and Phenomenological Review* 51: 809–34.

Demos, Raphael. 1971. "A Fallacy in Plato's *Republic*?" In *Plato: A Collection of Critical Essays*, vol. 2, ed. G. Vlastos, 52–6. Garden City, New York: Anchor Books.

Dicks, D. R. 1970. *Early Greek Astronomy to Aristotle*. Ithaca, New York: Cornell University Press.

Dominick, Yancey. 2010. "Seeing Through Images: The Bottom of Plato's Divided Line." *Journal of the History of Philosophy* 48: 1–13.

Evans, James. 1998. *The History and Practice of Ancient Astronomy*. New York: Oxford University Press.

Everson, Stephen. 2011. "Justice and Just Action in Plato's *Republic.*" In *Episteme, etc.: Essays in Honour of Jonathan Barnes*, ed. B. Morison and K. Ierodiakonou, 249–76. New York: Oxford University Press.

Ferber, Rafael. 1989. *Platos Idee des Guten*, 2nd edition. Sankt Augustin: Akademia Verlag Richarz.

Ferguson, A. S. 1921. "Plato's Simile of Light. Part 1. The Similes of the Sun and the Line." *Classical Quarterly* 15: 131–52.

Ferrari, G. R. F. 2005. *City and Soul in Plato's Republic*. Chicago: University of Chicago Press.

Foley, Richard. 2008. "Plato's Undividable Line: Contradiction and Method in *Republic* VI." *Journal of the History of Philosophy* 46: 1–24.

Foster, M. B. 1937. "A Mistake of Plato's in the *Republic.*" *Mind* 46: 386–93.

Fowler, David. 1999. *The Mathematics of Plato's Academy*, 2nd edition. Oxford: Oxford University Press.

Friedländer, Paul. 1964. *Plato: The Dialogues*. Princeton: Princeton University Press.

Gaiser, Konrad. 1980. "Plato's Enigmatic Lecture 'On the Good'." *Phronesis* 25: 5–37.

Gallop, David. 1965. "Image and Reality in Plato's *Republic*." *Archiv für Geschichte der Philosophie* 47: 113–31.

Gallop, David. 1971. "Dreaming and Waking in Plato." In *Essays in Ancient Greek Philosophy*, ed. J. Anton, G. Kustas, and A. Preus, 187–201. Albany, New York: State University of New York Press.

Ganson, Todd. 2005. "The Platonic Approach to Sense-Perception." *History of Philosophy Quarterly* 22: 1–15.

Ganson, Todd. 2009. "The Rational/Non-rational Distinction in the *Republic*." *Oxford Studies in Ancient Philosophy* 36: 179–97.

Genzler, Jyl. 2004. "The Attractions and Delights of Goodness." *Philosophical Quarterly* 54: 353–67.

Gifford, Mark. 2001. "Dramatic Dialectic in *Republic* Book 1." *Oxford Studies in Ancient Philosophy* 20: 35–106.

Gilbert, Margaret. 1989. *Social Facts*. New York: Routledge.

Gilbert, Margaret. 1990. "Walking Together." *Midwest Studies in Philosophy* 15: 1–14.

Gotthelf, Allen. 1988. "The Place of the Good in Aristotle's Natural Teleology." *Proceedings of the Boston Area Colloquium in Ancient Philosophy* 4: 113–39.

Gutglueck, John. 1988. "From *Pleonexia* to *Polupragmosunē*: A Conflation of Possession and Action in Plato's *Republic*." *American Journal of Philology* 109: 20–39.

Hadgopoulos, Demetrius. 1973. "Thrasymachus and Legalism." *Phronesis* 18: 204–8.

Halfwassen, Jens. 1992. *Der Aufstieg zum Einen*. Stuttgart: B. G. Teubner Verlag.

Hamlyn, D. W. 1958. "Eikasia in Plato's *Republic*." *Philosophical Quarterly* 8: 14–23.

Hardcastle, Valerie Gray. 2002. "On the Normativity of Functions." In *Functions*, ed. A. Ariew, R. Cummins, and M. Perlman, 144–56. New York: Oxford University Press.

Hare, Richard. 1965. "Plato and the Mathematicians." In *New Essays on Plato and Aristotle*, ed. R. Brumbaugh, 21–38. New York: Routledge.

Heath, Thomas. 1956. *The Thirteen Books of Euclid's Elements*, 2nd edition. New York: Dover Publications.

Heinaman, Robert. 2003. "Plato's Division of Goods in the *Republic*." *Phronesis* 48: 309–35.

Hemmenway, Scott. 1999. "The *Techne*-Analogy in Socrates' Healthy City: Justice and the Craftsman in the *Republic*." *Ancient Philosophy* 19: 267–84.

Horn, Christoph and Rapp, Christof. 2005. "Intuition und Methode: Abschied von einem Dogma der Platon- und Aristoteles-Exegese." *Logical Analysis and History of Philosophy* 8: 11–45.

Hourani, G. F. 1962. "Thrasymachus' Definition of Justice in Plato's *Republic*." *Phronesis* 7: 110–20.

Huffman, Carl. 1993. *Philolaus of Croton: Pythagorean and Presocratic*. Cambridge: Cambridge University Press.

Huffman, Carl. 2005. *Archytas of Tarentum: Pythagorean, Philosopher and Mathematician King*. New York: Cambridge University Press.

Irwin, Terence. 1977. *Plato's Moral Theory*. New York: Oxford University Press.

Irwin, Terence. 1995. *Plato's Ethics*. New York: Oxford University Press.

Jeffrey, Andrew. 1979. "Polemarchus and Socrates on Justice and Harm." *Phronesis* 24: 54–69.

Johansen, Thomas. 2005. *Plato's Natural Philosophy*. New York: Cambridge University Press.

Joseph, H. W. B. 1935. *Essays in Ancient and Modern Philosophy*. Oxford: Clarendon Press.

Kahn, Charles. 1981. "Some Philosophical Uses of 'To Be' in Plato." *Phronesis* 26: 105–34.

Kahn, Charles. 1993. "Proleptic Composition in the *Republic*, or Why Book 1 Was Never a Separate Dialogue." *Classical Quarterly* 43: 131–42.

Kamtekar, Rachana. 2004. "What's the Good of Agreeing? *Homonoia* in Platonic Politics." *Oxford Studies in Ancient Philosophy* 26: 131–70.

Kamtekar, Rachana. 2008. "The Powers of Plato's Tripartite Psychology." *Proceedings of the Boston Area Colloquium in Ancient Philosophy* 24: 127–50.

Karasmanis, Vassilis. 1988. "Plato's *Republic*: The Line and the Cave." *Apeiron* 21: 147–71.

Kerferd, G. B. 1947. "The Doctrine of Thrasymachus in Plato's *Republic*." *Durham University Journal* 9: 19–27.

Kerferd, G. B. 1964. "Thrasymachus and Justice: A Reply." *Phronesis* 9: 12–16.

Kirwan, Christopher. 1965. "Glaucon's Challenge." *Phronesis* 10: 162–73.

Klosko, Gregory. 1981. "The Technical Conception of Virtue." *Journal of the History of Philosophy* 18: 98–106.

Knorr, Wilbur. 1975. *The Evolution of the Euclidean Elements*. Dordrecht: Reidel.

Krämer, Hans. 1997. "Die Idee des Guten, Sonnen- und Liniengleichnis." In *Politeia*, ed. O. Höffe, 179–203. Berlin: Akademia Verlag.

Kraut, Richard. 1973a. "Egoism, Love, and Political Office in Plato." *Philosophical Review* 82: 330–44.

Kraut, Richard. 1973b. "Reason and Justice in Plato's *Republic*." In *Exegesis and Argument: Studies in Greek Philosophy*, ed. E. Lee, A. Mourelatos, and R. Rorty, 207–24. Assen: Van Gorcum.

Kraut, Richard. 1989. *Aristotle on the Human Good*. Princeton: Princeton University Press.

Kraut, Richard. 1992. "The Defense of Justice in the *Republic*." In *The Cambridge Companion to Plato*, ed. R. Kraut, 311–37. New York: Cambridge University Press.

Kung, Joan. 1988. "Why the Receptacle is Not a Mirror." *Archiv für Geschichte der Philosophie* 70: 167–78.

Lear, Jonathan. 1992. "Inside and Outside the *Republic*." *Phronesis* 37: 184–215.

Lennox, James. 1985. "Plato's Unnatural Teleology." In *Platonic Investigations*, ed. D. O'Meara, 195–218. Washington, D.C.: Catholic University of America Press.

Lindberg, David. 1976. *Theories of Vision from Al-Kindi to Kepler*. Chicago: University of Chicago Press.

Long, A. A. 1970. "Thinking and Sense-Perception in Empedocles: Mysticism or Materialism?" *Classical Quarterly* 16: 256–76.

Lorenz, Hendrik. 2006. *The Brute Within: Appetitive Desire in Plato and Aristotle*. Oxford: Clarendon Press.

Lycos, Kymon. 1987. *Plato on Justice and Power*. Albany, New York: State University of New York Press.

Mabbott, J. D. 1937. "Is Plato's *Republic* Utilitarian?" *Mind* 46: 468–74.

MacIntyre, Alasdair. 1981. *After Virtue*. Notre Dame, Indiana: University of Notre Dame Press.

Malcolm, Norman. 1968. "The Possibility of Mechanism." *Philosophical Review* 77: 45–72.

Marrou, H. I. 1956. *A History of Education in Antiquity*, translated by George Lamb. Madison, Wisconsin: University of Wisconsin Press.

Matthews, Gareth and Blackson, Thomas. 1989. "Causes in the *Phaedo*." *Synthese* 79: 581–91.

Mendell, Henry. 2010. "Plato by the Numbers." In *Logos and Language: Essays in Honour of Julius Moravcsik*, ed. D. Føllesdal and J. Woods, 125–60. Stanford: CSLI Publications.

Menn, Stephen. 1998. "Collecting the Letters." *Phronesis* 43: 291–305.

Merker, Ann. 2003. *La Vision chez Platon et Aristote*. Sankt Augustin: Akademia Verlag.

Miller, Fred D., Jr. 1999. "Plato on the Parts of the Soul." In *Plato and Platonism*, ed. J. van Ophuijsen, 84–101. Washington, D.C.: Catholic University Press.

Mohr, Richard. 1981. "The Number Theory in Plato's *Republic* VII and *Philebus*." *Isis* 72: 620–7.

Moline, Jon. 1978. "Plato on the Complexity of the Psyche." *Archiv für Geschichte der Philosophie* 60: 1–26.

Moss, Jessica. 2008. "Appearances and Calculations: Plato's Division of the Soul." *Oxford Studies in Ancient Philosophy* 34: 35–68.

Mourelatos, Alexander. 1980. "Plato's 'Real Astronomy': *Republic* 527D–531D." In *Science and the Sciences in Plato*, ed. J. Anton, 33–73. Albany, New York: Eidos Press.

Mourelatos, Alexander. 1981. "Astronomy and Kinematics in Plato's Project of Rationalist Explanation." *Studies in History and Philosophy of Science* 12: 1–32.

Mueller, Ian. 1980. "Ascending to Problems: Astronomy and Harmonics in *Republic* VII." In *Science and the Sciences in Plato*, ed. J. Anton, 103–22. Albany, New York: Eidos Press.

Mueller, Ian. 1981. *Philosophy of Mathematics and Deductive Structure in Euclid's Elements*. Cambridge, Massachusetts: MIT Press.

Mueller, Ian. 1991. "On the Notion of a Mathematical Starting Point in Plato, Aristotle, and Euclid." In *Science and Philosophy in Classical Greece*, ed. A. Bowen, 59–97. New York: Garland Press.

Nails, Debra. 1998. "The Dramatic Date of Plato's *Republic*." *Classical Journal* 9: 383–96.

Netz, Reviel. 1999. *The Shaping of Deduction in Greek Mathematics*. New York: Cambridge University Press.

Netz, Reviel. 2003. "How Propositions Begin: Toward an Interpretation of *hypothesis* in Plato's *Divided Line*." *Hyperboreus* 9: 295–317.

Nicholson, P. 1974. "Unraveling Thrasymachus' Arguments in *The Republic*." *Phronesis* 19: 210–32.

Nussbaum, Martha. 1986. *The Fragility of Goodness*. New York: Cambridge University Press.

O'Brien, Denis. 1970. "The Effect of a Simile: Empedocles' Theories of Seeing and Breathing." *The Journal of Hellenic Studies* 90: 149–70.

O'Connor, David K. 1988. "Aristotelian Justice as a Personal Virtue." *Midwest Studies in Philosophy* 13: 417–27.

Pappas, Nickolas. 1995. *Plato and the Republic*. New York: Routledge.

Parry, Richard. 1996. *Plato's Craft of Justice*. Albany, New York: State University of New York Press.

Paton, H. J. 1922. "Plato's Theory of *EIKASIA*." *Proceedings of the Aristotelian Society* 22: 69–104.

Payne, Andrew. 2008. "The Teleology of the Ascent in Plato's *Symposium*." *Apeiron* 41: 123–45.

Payne, Andrew. 2011. "The Division of Goods and Praising Justice for Itself in *Republic* II." *Phronesis* 56: 58–78.

Penner, Terry. 1971. "Thought and Desire in Plato." In *Plato: A Collection of Critical Essays*, vol. 2, ed. G. Vlastos, 96–118. Garden City, New York: Anchor Books.

Penner, Terry. 1988. "Socrates on the Impossibility of Belief-Relative Sciences." *Proceedings of the Boston Area Colloquium in Ancient Philosophy* 3: 263–325.

Penner, Terry. 2011. "Socratic Ethics and the Socratic Psychology of Action: A Philosophical Framework." In *The Cambridge Companion to Socrates*, ed. D. Morrison, 260–92. New York: Cambridge University Press.

Price, Anthony. 1995. *Mental Conflict*. New York: Routledge.

Price, Anthony. 2009. "Are Plato's Soul-Parts Psychological Subjects?" *Ancient Philosophy* 29: 1–15.

Prichard, H. A. 2002. "Duty and Interest." In *Moral Writings*, ed. J. Macadam, 21–49. Oxford: Clarendon Press.

Proclus. 1970. *A Commentary on the First Book of Euclid's Elements*, translated by Glenn Morrow. Princeton: Princeton University Press.

Raven, J. E. 1953. "Sun, Divided Line, and Cave." *Classical Quarterly* 3: 22–32.

Reeve, C. D. C. 1988. *Philosopher-Kings*. Princeton: Princeton University Press.

Robinson, Richard. 1953. *Plato's Earlier Dialectic*. New York: Oxford University Press.

Roochnik, David. 1986. "Socrates' Use of the Techne-Analogy." *Journal of the History of Philosophy* 24: 295–310.

Rudolph, Kelli. 2016. "Sight and the Presocratics." In *Sight and the Ancient Senses*, ed. M. Squire, 36–53. New York: Routledge.

Sachs, David. 1963. "A Fallacy in Plato's *Republic*." *Philosophical Review* 72: 141–58.

Salkever, Stephen. 1993. "Plato on Practices: The *Technai* and the Socratic Question in *Republic* 1." *Proceedings of the Boston Area Colloquium in Ancient Philosophy* 8: 243–67.

Schiller, Jerome. 1968. "Just Men and Just Acts in Plato's *Republic*." *Journal of the History of Philosophy* 6: 1–14.

Sheffield, Frisbee. 2006. *Plato's Symposium: the Ethics of Desire*. New York: Oxford University Press.

Shields, Christopher. 2007. "Unified Agency and *Akrasia* in Plato's *Republic*." In *Akrasia in Greek Philosophy*, ed. C. Bobonich and P. Destrée, 61–86. Boston: Brill.

Sier, Kurt. 1997. *Die Rede der Diotima*. Stuttgart: Teubner.

Singpurwalla, Rachel. 2006. "Plato's Defense of Justice in the *Republic*." In *The Blackwell Guide to Plato's Republic*, ed. G. Santas, 263–82. Malden, Massachusetts: Blackwell.

Singpurwalla, Rachel. 2013. "Why Spirit is the Natural Ally of Reason: Spirit, Reason, and the Fine in Plato's *Republic*." *Oxford Studies in Ancient Philosophy* 44: 41–65.

Sinhababu, Neil. 2013. "The Desire-Belief Account of Intention Explains Everything." *Nous* 47: 680–96.

Slings, S. R. (ed.). 2003. *Plato Respublica*. Oxford Classical Texts. Oxford: Oxford University Press.

Smith, Nicholas D. 1996. "Plato's Divided Line." *Ancient Philosophy* 16: 25–46.

Smith, Nicholas D. 1999a. "How the Prisoners in Plato's Cave are 'Like Us.'" *Proceedings of the Boston Area Colloquium for Ancient Philosophy* 13: 187–204.

Smith, Nicholas D. 1999b. "Plato's Analogy of Soul and State." *Journal of Ethics* 3: 31–49.

Sorabji, Richard. 1964. "Function." *Philosophical Quarterly* 14: 289–302.

Sprague, Rosemary Kent. 1975. *Plato's Philosopher-King*. Columbia, South Carolina: University of South Carolina Press.

Stalley, R. F. 2007. "Persuasion and the Tripartite Soul in Plato's *Republic*." *Oxford Studies in Ancient Philosophy* 32: 63–89.

Szaif, Jan. 1996. *Platons Begriff der Wahrheit*. Freiburg: Verlag Karl Alber.

Tanner, R. G. 1970. "*DIANOIA* and Plato's Cave." *Classical Quarterly* 20: 81–91.

Tarán, Leonardo. 1985. "Platonism and Socratic Ignorance." In *Platonic Investigations*, ed. D. O'Meara, 85–109. Washington, D.C.: Catholic University of America Press.

Taylor, C. C. W. 1967. "Plato and the Mathematicians: An Examination of Professor Hare's Views." *Philosophical Quarterly* 17: 193–203.

Tiles, J. E. 1984. "Techne and Moral Expertise." *Philosophy* 59: 49–66.

van der Waerden, B. L. 1961. *Science Awakening*, translated by Arnold Dresden. New York: Oxford University Press.

Vlastos, Gregory. 1971. "Justice and Happiness in the *Republic*." In *Plato: A Collection of Critical Essays*, vol. 2, ed. G. Vlastos, 66–95. Garden City, New York: Anchor Books.

Vlastos, Gregory. 1991. *Socrates: Ironist and Moral Philosopher*. Ithaca, New York: Cornell University Press.

von Fritz, Kurt. 1953. "Democritus' Theory of Vision." In *Science, Medicine, and History: Essays on the Evolution of Scientific Thought and Medical Practice, Written in Honour of Charles Singer*, ed. E. Underwood, 83–99. New York: Oxford University Press.

Waterlow, Sarah. 1972. "The Good of Others in Plato's *Republic*." *Proceedings of the Aristotelian Society* 73: 19–36.

West, M. L. 1993. *Greek Lyric Poetry*. New York: Oxford University Press.

White, Nicholas. 1979. *A Companion to Plato's Republic*. Indianapolis, Indiana: Hackett Publishing.

White, Nicholas. 1984. "The Classification of Goods in Plato's *Republic*." *Journal for the History of Philosophy* 22: 393–421.

White, Nicholas. 2006. "Plato's Concept of Goodness." In *A Companion to Plato*, ed. H Benson, 356–72. Malden, Massachusetts: Blackwell.

Williams, Bernard. 1973. "The Analogy of City and Soul in Plato's *Republic*." In *Exegesis and Argument*, ed. E. Lee, A. Mourelatos, and R. Rorty, 196–206. Assen: Van Gorcum.

Wolfsdorf, David. 2008a. "The Method *ex hupotheseōs* at *Meno* 86e1-87d8." *Phronesis* 53: 35–64.

Wolfsdorf, David. 2008b. *Trials of Reason*. New York: Oxford University Press.

Woodfield, Andrew. 1976. *Teleology*. New York: Cambridge University Press.

Woodruff, Paul. 2012. "Justice as a Virtue of the Soul." In *Oxford Studies in Ancient Philosophy*: *Supplementary Volume; Essays in Honor of Julia Annas*, ed. R. Kamtekar, 89–101. New York: Oxford University Press.

Yang, Moon-Heum. 1999. "The 'Square Itself' and 'Diagonal Itself' in the *Republic*." *Ancient Philosophy* 19: 31–5.

Yang, Moon-Heum. 2005. "The Relationship between Hypotheses and Images in the Mathematical Subsection of the Divided Line of Plato's *Republic*." *Dialogue* 44: 285–312.

Young, Charles. 1974. "A Note on *Republic* 335C9-10 and 335C12." *Philosophical Review* 83: 97–106.

Index Locorum

Index